iry Tail: *Rhodonite* is a work of fiction. Names, characters, places, and incidents
e the products of the author's imagination or are used fictitiously. Any
semblance to actual events, locales, or persons, living or dead, is entirely
incidental.

Kodansha Comics Trade Paperback Original.

iblished in the United States by Kodansha Comics, an imprint of Kodansha
SA Publishing, LLC, New York.

iblication rights for this English edition arranged through Kodansha Ltd.,
kyo.

rst published in Japan in 2016 by Kodansha Ltd., Tokyo

BN 978-1-63236-524-8

inted in the United States of America.

ww.kodanshacomics.com

3 7 6 5 4 3 2 1

anslation: William Flanagan
ttering: AndWorld Design
liting: Ajani Oloye
dansha Comics edition cover design by Phil Balsman

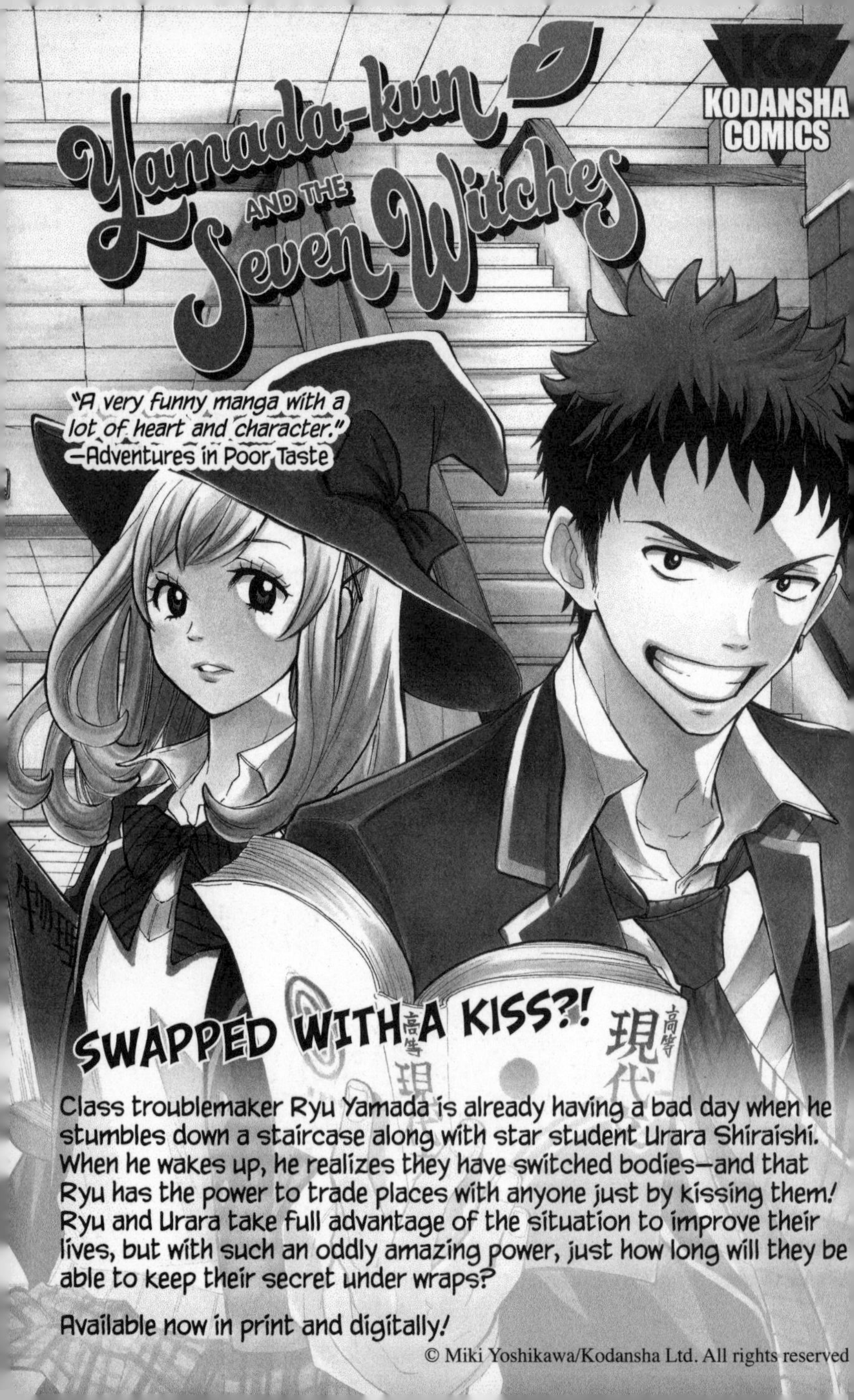
Yamada-kun AND THE Seven Witches
KODANSHA COMICS
"A very funny manga with a lot of heart and character."
—Adventures in Poor Taste
SWAPPED WITH A KISS?!
Class troublemaker Ryu Yamada is already having a bad day when he stumbles down a staircase along with star student Urara Shiraishi. When he wakes up, he realizes they have switched bodies—and that Ryu has the power to trade places with anyone just by kissing them! Ryu and Urara take full advantage of the situation to improve their lives, but with such an oddly amazing power, just how long will they be able to keep their secret under wraps?
Available now in print and digitally!
© Miki Yoshikawa/Kodansha Ltd. All rights reserved

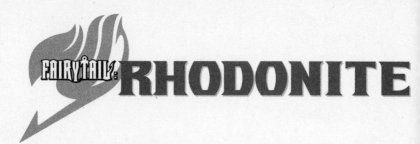

FAIRY TAIL: RHODONITE

2

MANGA BY
KYOUTA SHIBANO

BASED ON
A STORY BY
HIRO MASHIMA

CONTENTS

Chapter 1 ◆ Where is Gajeel 003

Chapter 2 ◆ My Town 021

Chapter 3 ◆ The Meeting in Denish 033

Chapter 4 ◆ Illegal Magic Drug 043

Chapter 5 ◆ The Road Knight 053

Chapter 6 ◆ The Gajeel I Never Knew 63

Chapter 7 ◆ Will You Just Shut Up 073

Chapter 8 ◆ His Fight 083

Chapter 9 ◆ Man Behind the Curtain 095

Chapter 10 ◆ Friend 105

Chapter 11 ◆ Rhodonite 115

Chapter 12 ◆ First Bout 127

Chapter 13 ◆ Slave Trade 137

Chapter 14 ◆ The Infallible Counter-plan ... 147

Chapter 15 ◆ Effective Use 157

Chapter 16 ◆ A Wish and a Prepared Soul ... 167

Final Chapter ◆ A Place to Go Home to 177

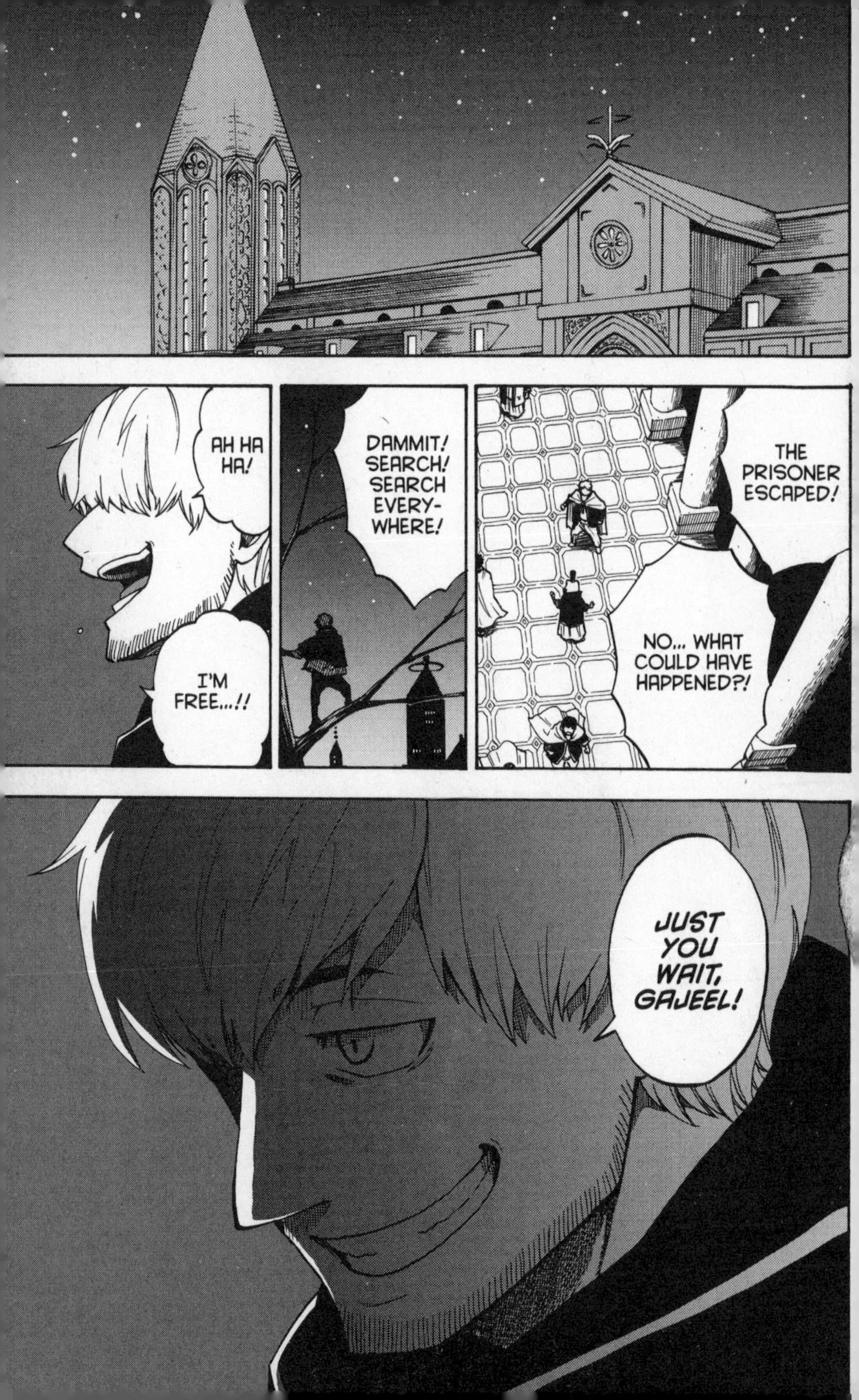
THE PRISONER ESCAPED!
NO... WHAT COULD HAVE HAPPENED?!
DAMMIT! SEARCH! SEARCH EVERY-WHERE!
AH HA HA!
I'M FREE...!!
JUST YOU WAIT, GAJEEL!

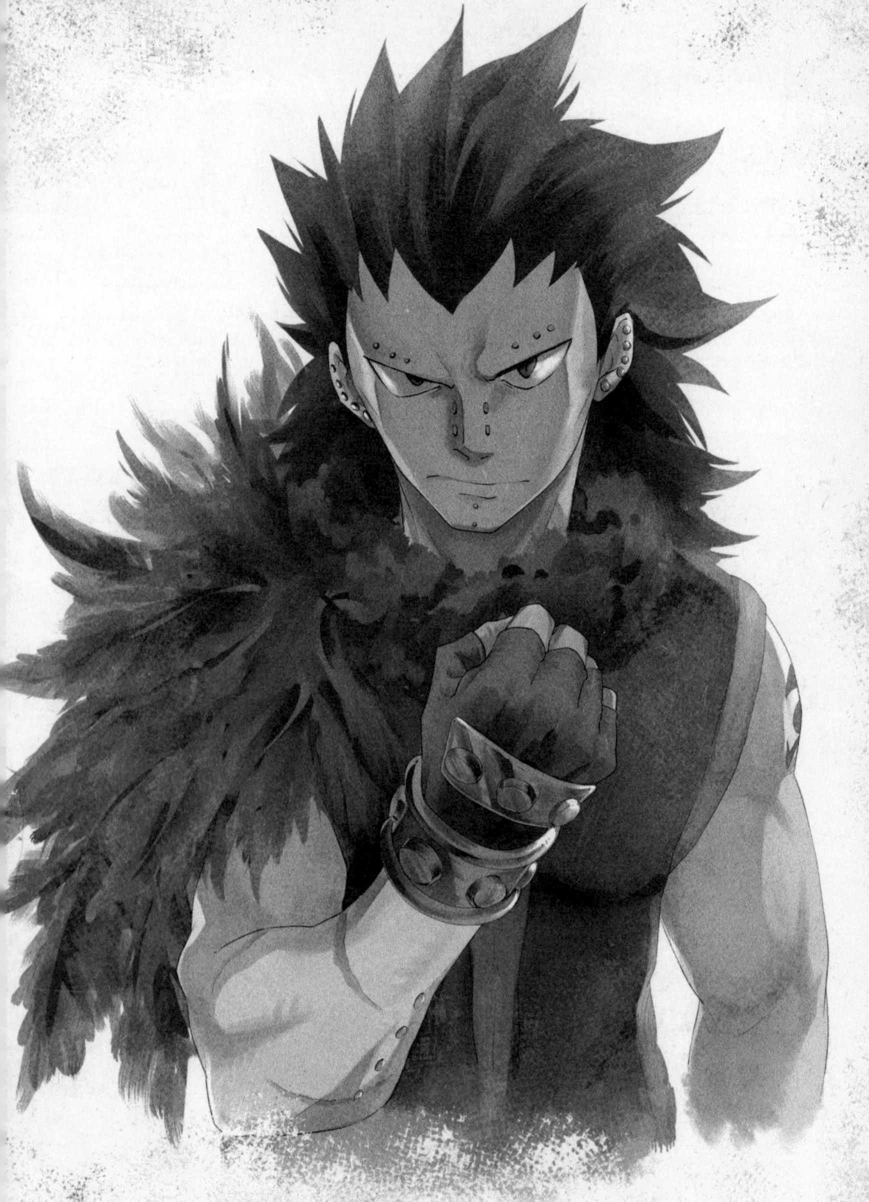

Chapter 1: Where is Gajeel?

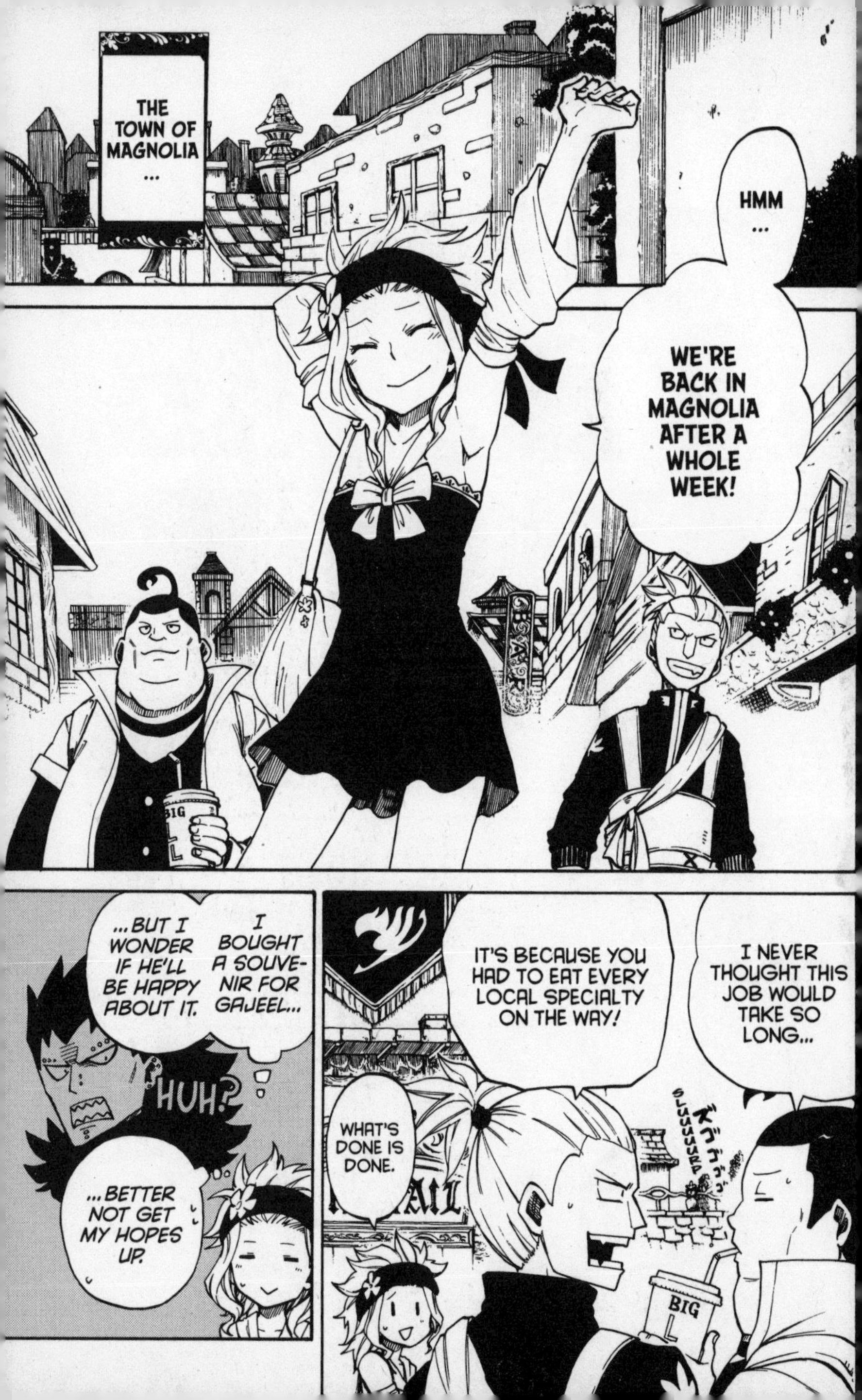
THE TOWN OF MAGNOLIA ...
HMM ...
WE'RE BACK IN MAGNOLIA AFTER A WHOLE WEEK!
I NEVER THOUGHT THIS JOB WOULD TAKE SO LONG...
IT'S BECAUSE YOU HAD TO EAT EVERY LOCAL SPECIALTY ON THE WAY!
SLUUUUURP
WHAT'S DONE IS DONE.
I BOUGHT A SOUVENIR FOR GAJEEL...
...BUT I WONDER IF HE'LL BE HAPPY ABOUT IT.
HUH?
...BETTER NOT GET MY HOPES UP.

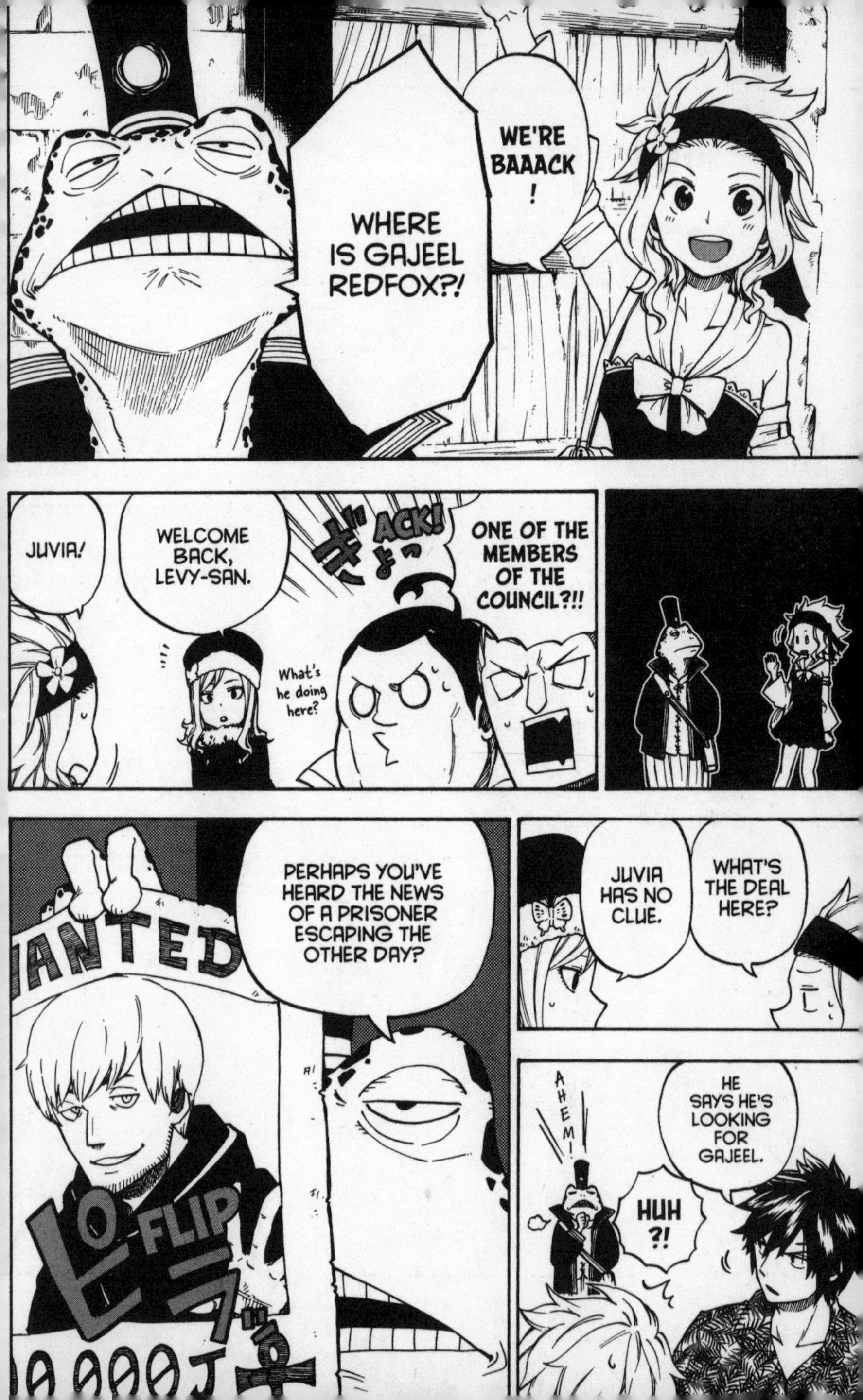
WE'RE BAAACK!
WHERE IS GAJEEL REDFOX?!
ONE OF THE MEMBERS OF THE COUNCIL?!!
ACK!
What's he doing here?
WELCOME BACK, LEVY-SAN.
JUVIA!
WHAT'S THE DEAL HERE?
JUVIA HAS NO CLUE.
HE SAYS HE'S LOOKING FOR GAJEEL.
HUH?!
AHEM!
PERHAPS YOU'VE HEARD THE NEWS OF A PRISONER ESCAPING THE OTHER DAY?
FLIP

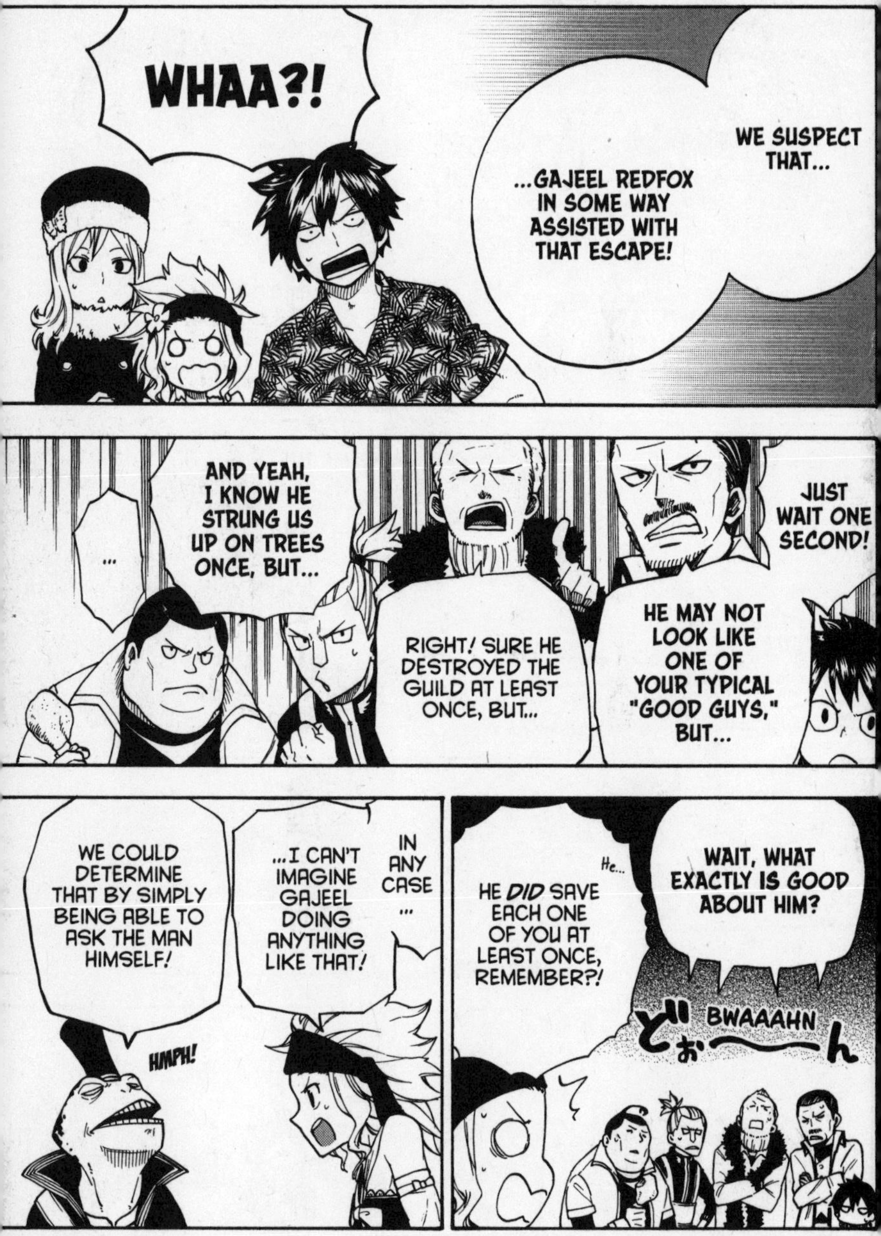
WE SUSPECT THAT...
...GAJEEL REDFOX IN SOME WAY ASSISTED WITH THAT ESCAPE!
WHAA?!
JUST WAIT ONE SECOND!
HE MAY NOT LOOK LIKE ONE OF YOUR TYPICAL "GOOD GUYS," BUT...
RIGHT! SURE HE DESTROYED THE GUILD AT LEAST ONCE, BUT...
AND YEAH, I KNOW HE STRUNG US UP ON TREES ONCE, BUT...
...
WAIT, WHAT EXACTLY IS GOOD ABOUT HIM?
BWAAAHN
どぉ——ん
He...
HE *DID* SAVE EACH ONE OF YOU AT LEAST ONCE, REMEMBER?!
IN ANY CASE...
...I CAN'T IMAGINE GAJEEL DOING ANYTHING LIKE THAT!
WE COULD DETERMINE THAT BY SIMPLY BEING ABLE TO ASK THE MAN HIMSELF!
HMPH!

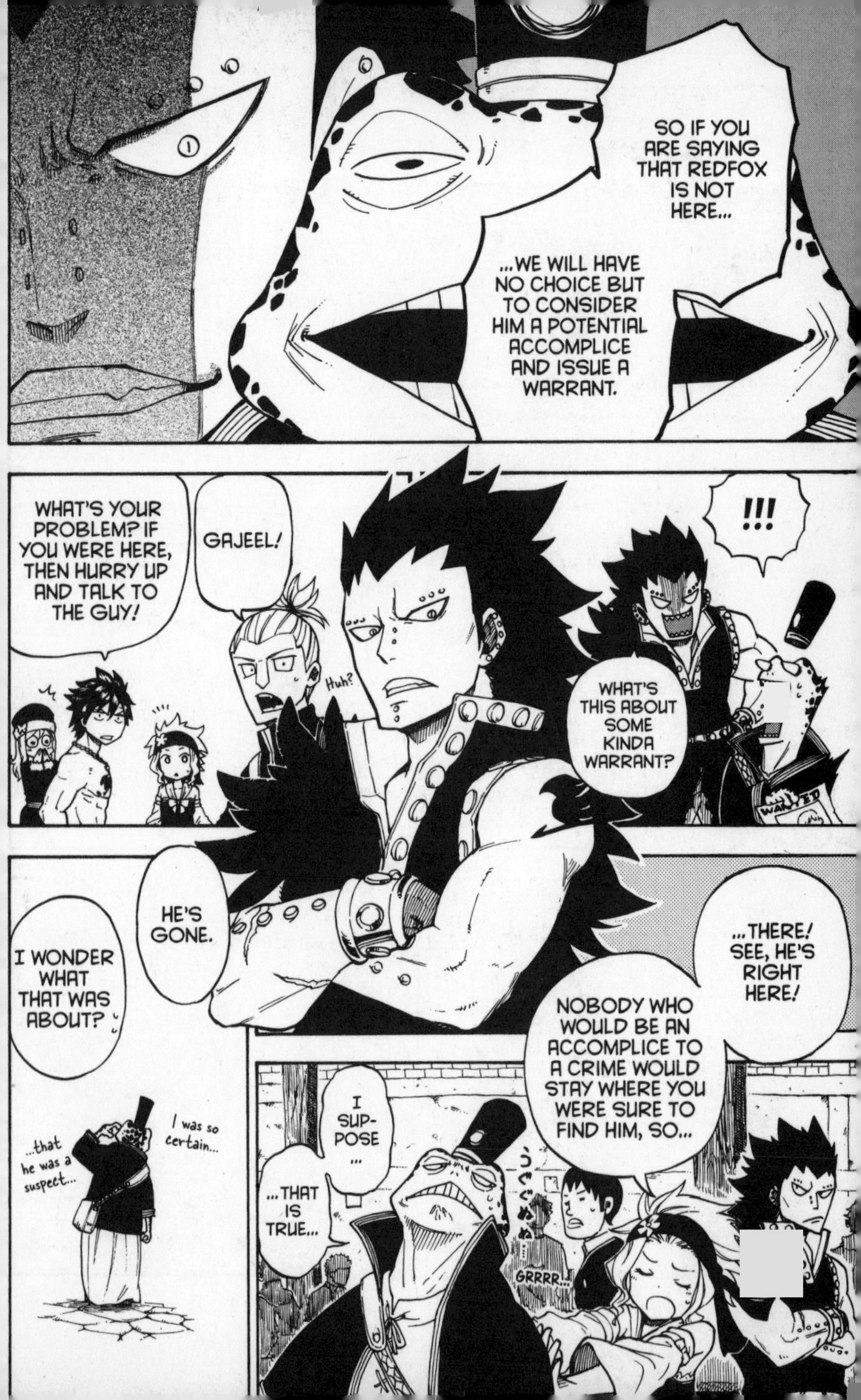
SO IF YOU ARE SAYING THAT REDFOX IS NOT HERE...
...WE WILL HAVE NO CHOICE BUT TO CONSIDER HIM A POTENTIAL ACCOMPLICE AND ISSUE A WARRANT.
!!!
WHAT'S THIS ABOUT SOME KINDA WARRANT?
GAJEEL!
WHAT'S YOUR PROBLEM? IF YOU WERE HERE, THEN HURRY UP AND TALK TO THE GUY!
Huh?
WANTED
...THERE! SEE, HE'S RIGHT HERE!
NOBODY WHO WOULD BE AN ACCOMPLICE TO A CRIME WOULD STAY WHERE YOU WERE SURE TO FIND HIM, SO...
I SUPPOSE...
...THAT IS TRUE...
うぐぐぬぬ…
GRRRR...
HE'S GONE.
I WONDER WHAT THAT WAS ABOUT?
I was so certain...
...that he was a suspect...

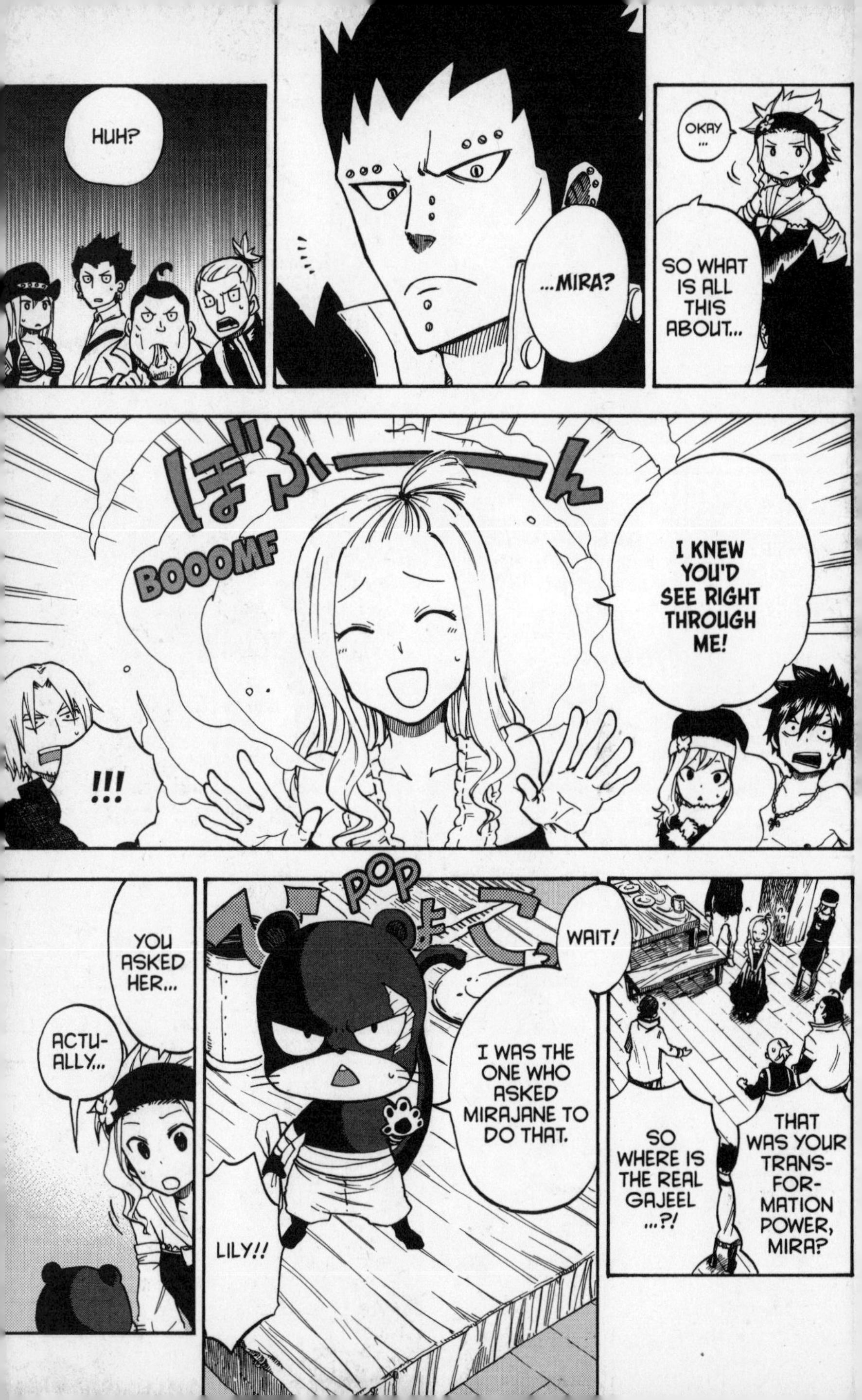
OKAY ...
SO WHAT IS ALL THIS ABOUT...
...MIRA?
HUH?
ぼふーーーん
BOOOMF
I KNEW YOU'D SEE RIGHT THROUGH ME!
!!!
THAT WAS YOUR TRANS-FORMATION POWER, MIRA?
SO WHERE IS THE REAL GAJEEL ...?!
POP
WAIT!
I WAS THE ONE WHO ASKED MIRAJANE TO DO THAT.
LILY!!
YOU ASKED HER...
ACTU-ALLY...

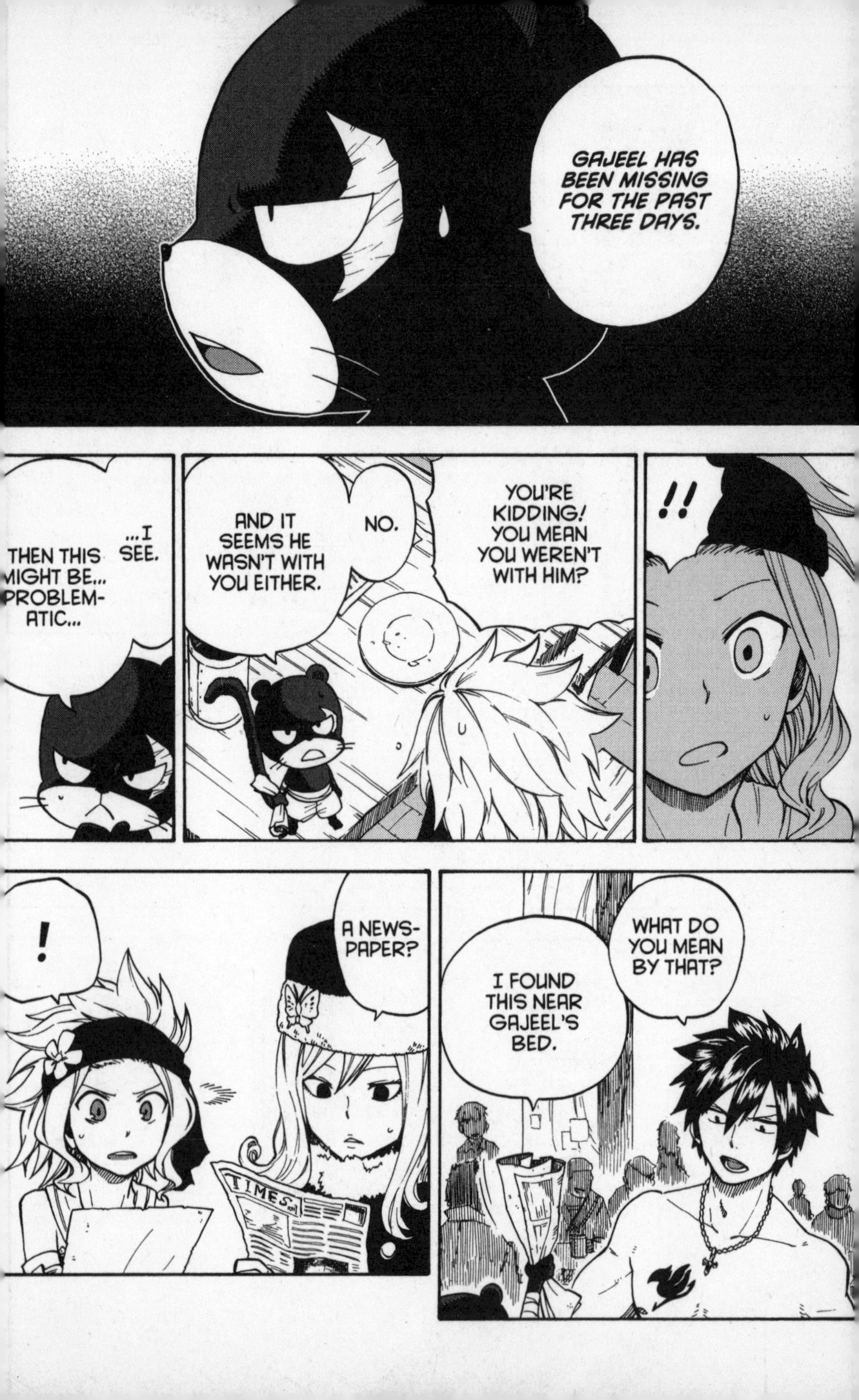
GAJEEL HAS BEEN MISSING FOR THE PAST THREE DAYS.
!!
YOU'RE KIDDING! YOU MEAN YOU WEREN'T WITH HIM?
NO.
AND IT SEEMS HE WASN'T WITH YOU EITHER.
...I SEE.
THEN THIS MIGHT BE... PROBLEMATIC...
WHAT DO YOU MEAN BY THAT?
I FOUND THIS NEAR GAJEEL'S BED.
A NEWSPAPER?
!
TIMES

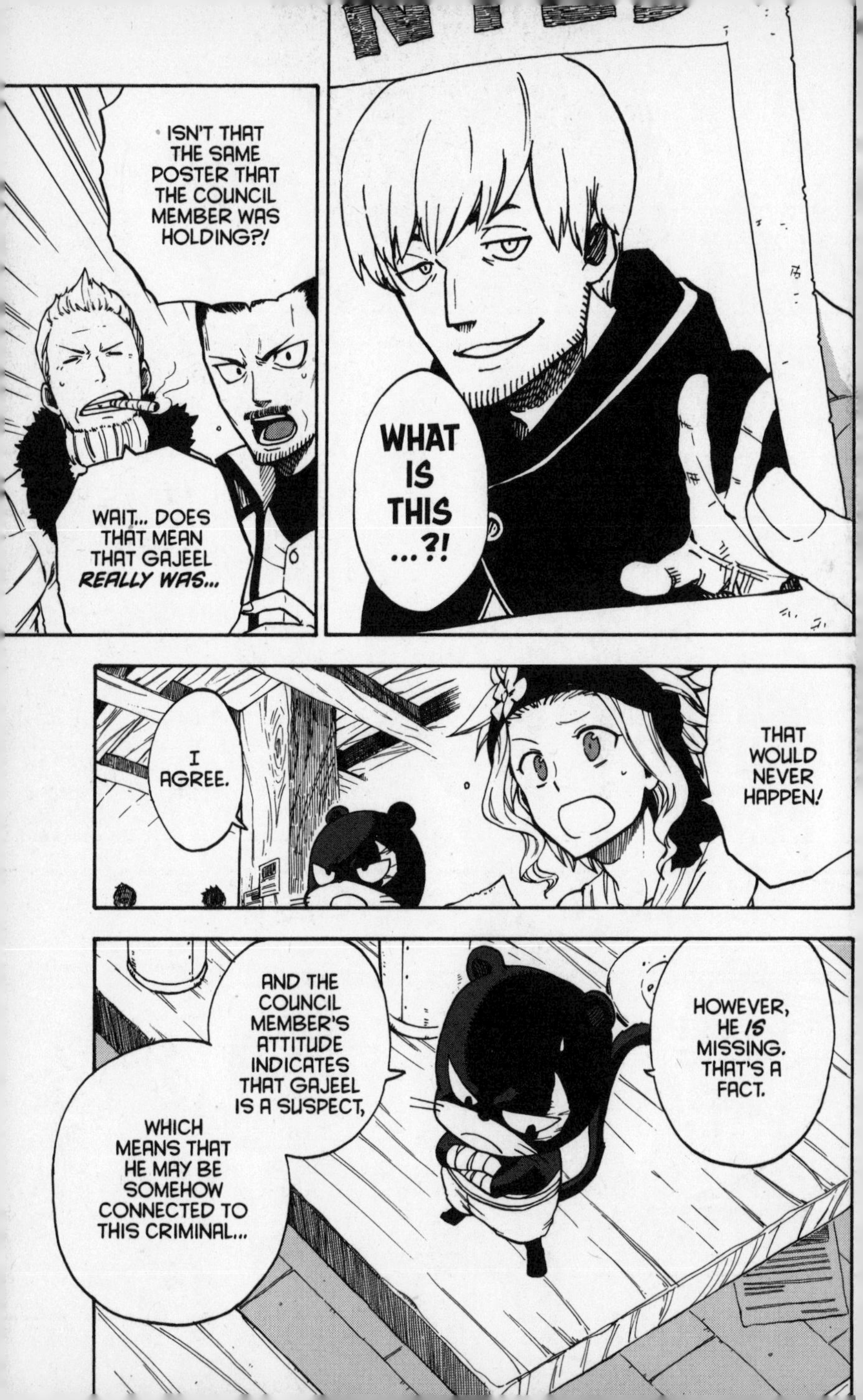
WHAT IS THIS ...?!
ISN'T THAT THE SAME POSTER THAT THE COUNCIL MEMBER WAS HOLDING?!
WAIT... DOES THAT MEAN THAT GAJEEL *REALLY WAS...*
THAT WOULD NEVER HAPPEN!
I AGREE.
HOWEVER, HE *IS* MISSING. THAT'S A FACT.
AND THE COUNCIL MEMBER'S ATTITUDE INDICATES THAT GAJEEL IS A SUSPECT,
WHICH MEANS THAT HE MAY BE SOMEHOW CONNECTED TO THIS CRIMINAL...

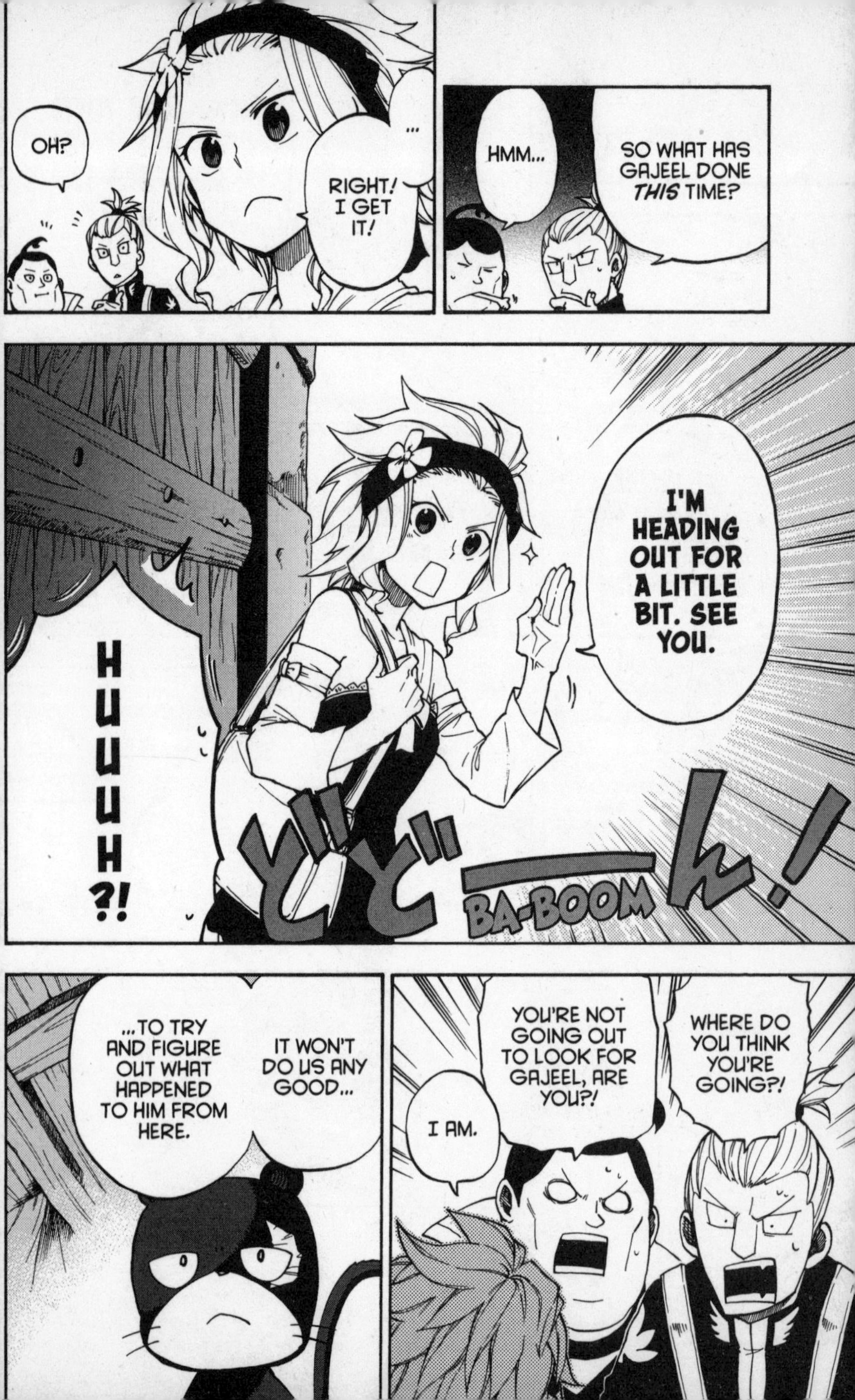
SO WHAT HAS GAJEEL DONE THIS TIME?
HMM...
...
RIGHT! I GET IT!
OH?
I'M HEADING OUT FOR A LITTLE BIT. SEE YOU.
BA-BOOM
HUUUUH?!
WHERE DO YOU THINK YOU'RE GOING?!
YOU'RE NOT GOING OUT TO LOOK FOR GAJEEL, ARE YOU?!
I AM.
IT WON'T DO US ANY GOOD...
...TO TRY AND FIGURE OUT WHAT HAPPENED TO HIM FROM HERE.

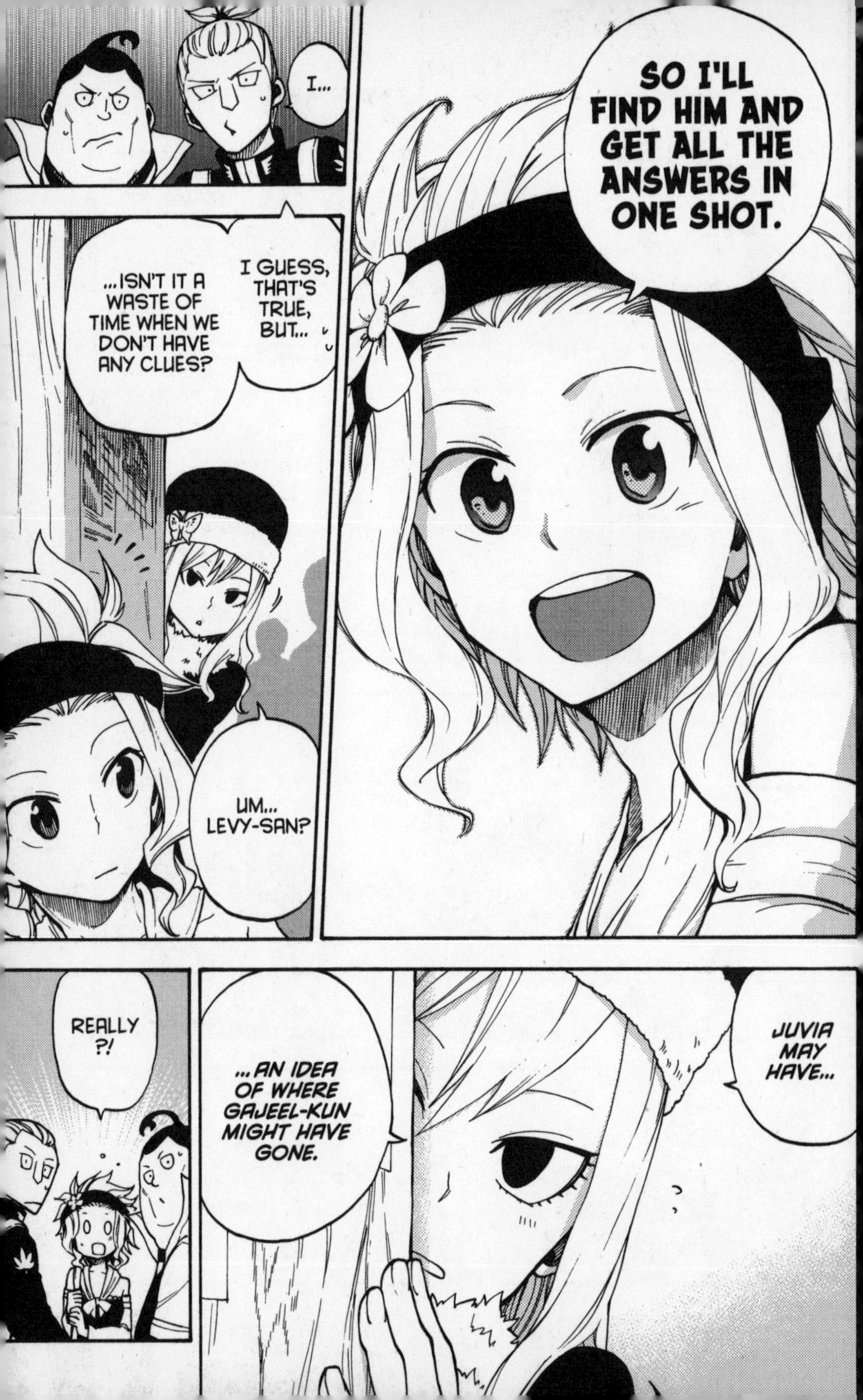
SO I'LL FIND HIM AND GET ALL THE ANSWERS IN ONE SHOT.
I...
I GUESS, THAT'S TRUE, BUT...
...ISN'T IT A WASTE OF TIME WHEN WE DON'T HAVE ANY CLUES?
UM... LEVY-SAN?
JUVIA MAY HAVE...
...AN IDEA OF WHERE GAJEEL-KUN MIGHT HAVE GONE.
REALLY ?!

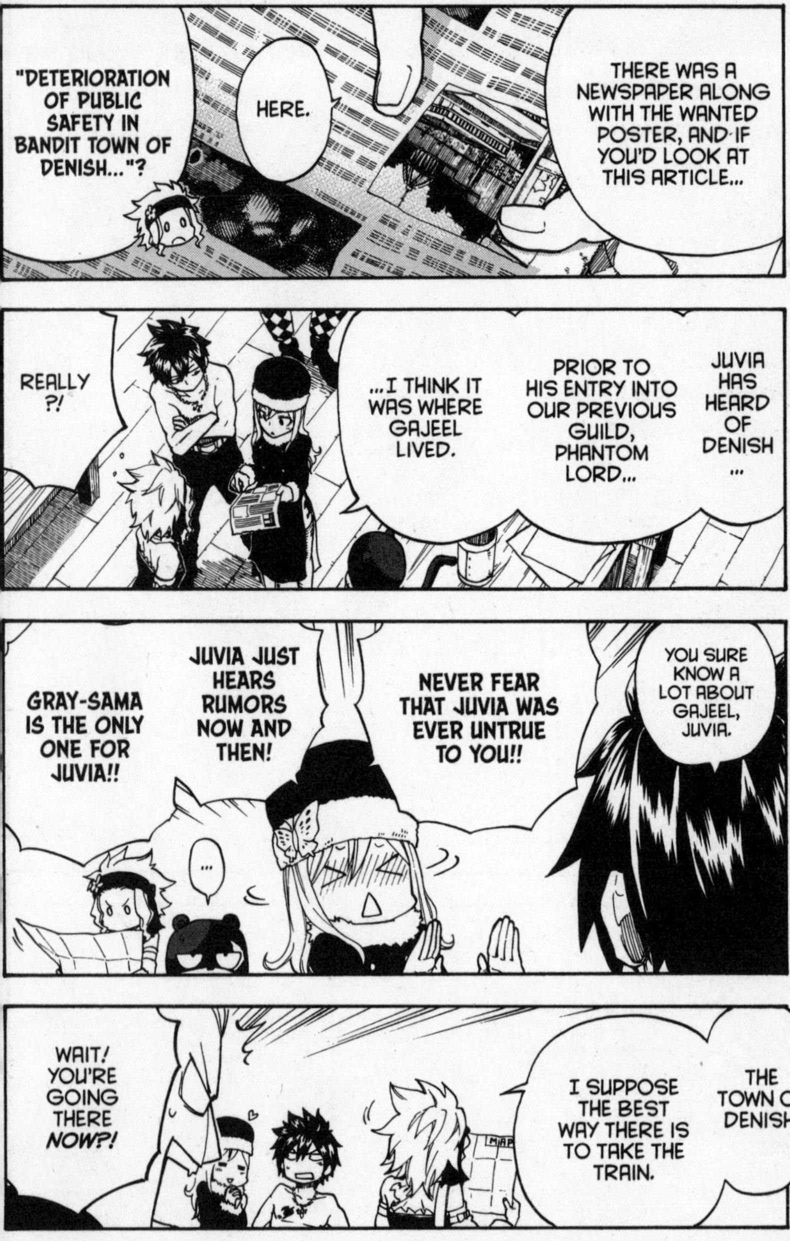
THERE WAS A NEWSPAPER ALONG WITH THE WANTED POSTER, AND IF YOU'D LOOK AT THIS ARTICLE...
HERE.
"DETERIORATION OF PUBLIC SAFETY IN BANDIT TOWN OF DENISH..."?
JUVIA HAS HEARD OF DENISH...
PRIOR TO HIS ENTRY INTO OUR PREVIOUS GUILD, PHANTOM LORD...
...I THINK IT WAS WHERE GAJEEL LIVED.
REALLY?!
YOU SURE KNOW A LOT ABOUT GAJEEL, JUVIA.
NEVER FEAR THAT JUVIA WAS EVER UNTRUE TO YOU!!
JUVIA JUST HEARS RUMORS NOW AND THEN!
GRAY-SAMA IS THE ONLY ONE FOR JUVIA!!
...
THE TOWN OF DENISH.
I SUPPOSE THE BEST WAY THERE IS TO TAKE THE TRAIN.
MAP
WAIT! YOU'RE GOING THERE *NOW?!*

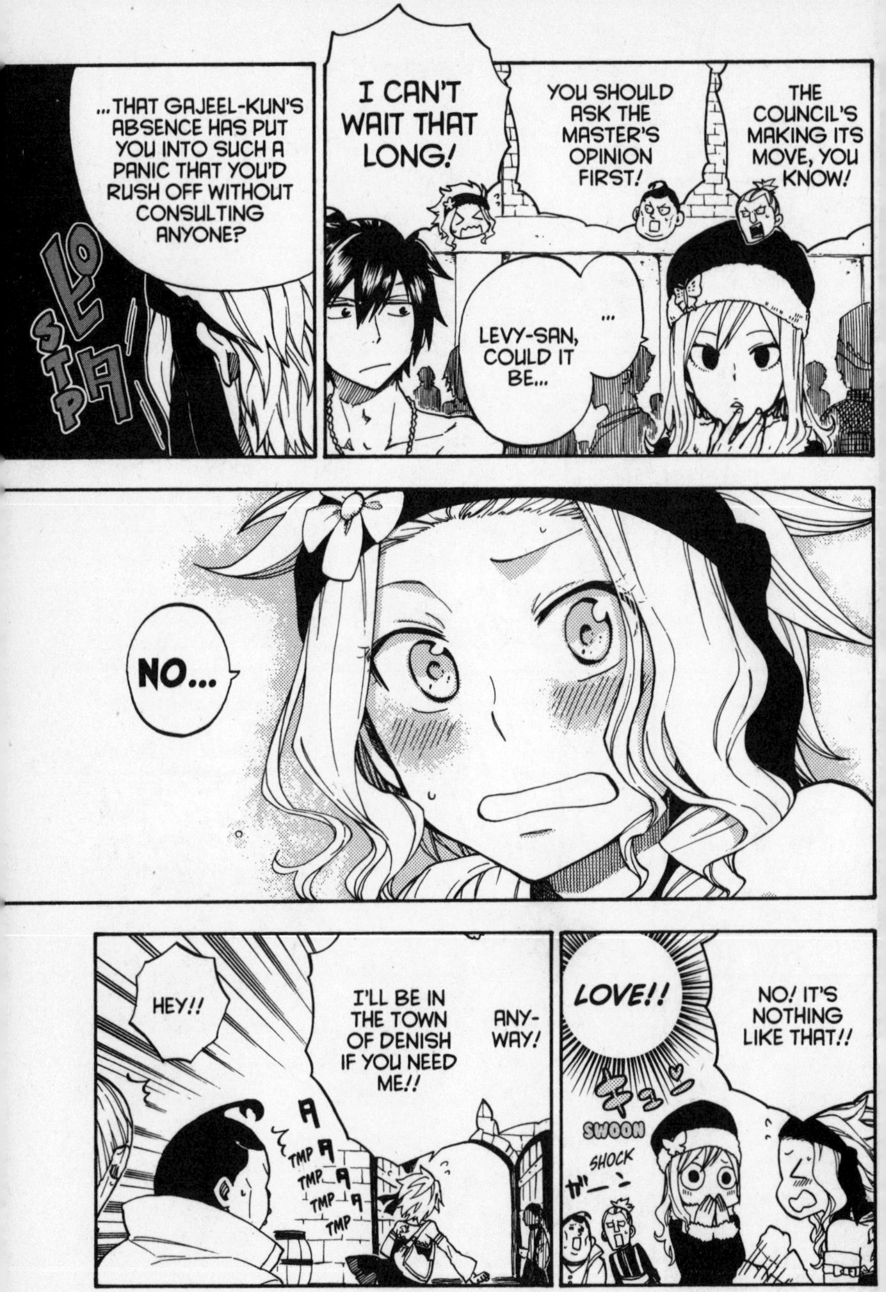
THE COUNCIL'S MAKING ITS MOVE, YOU KNOW!
YOU SHOULD ASK THE MASTER'S OPINION FIRST!
I CAN'T WAIT THAT LONG!
...
LEVY-SAN, COULD IT BE...
...THAT GAJEEL-KUN'S ABSENCE HAS PUT YOU INTO SUCH A PANIC THAT YOU'D RUSH OFF WITHOUT CONSULTING ANYONE?
STOP
NO...
NO! IT'S NOTHING LIKE THAT!!
LOVE!!
SWOON
SHOCK
ANY-WAY!
I'LL BE IN THE TOWN OF DENISH IF YOU NEED ME!!
HEY!!
TMP
TMP
TMP
TMP
TMP

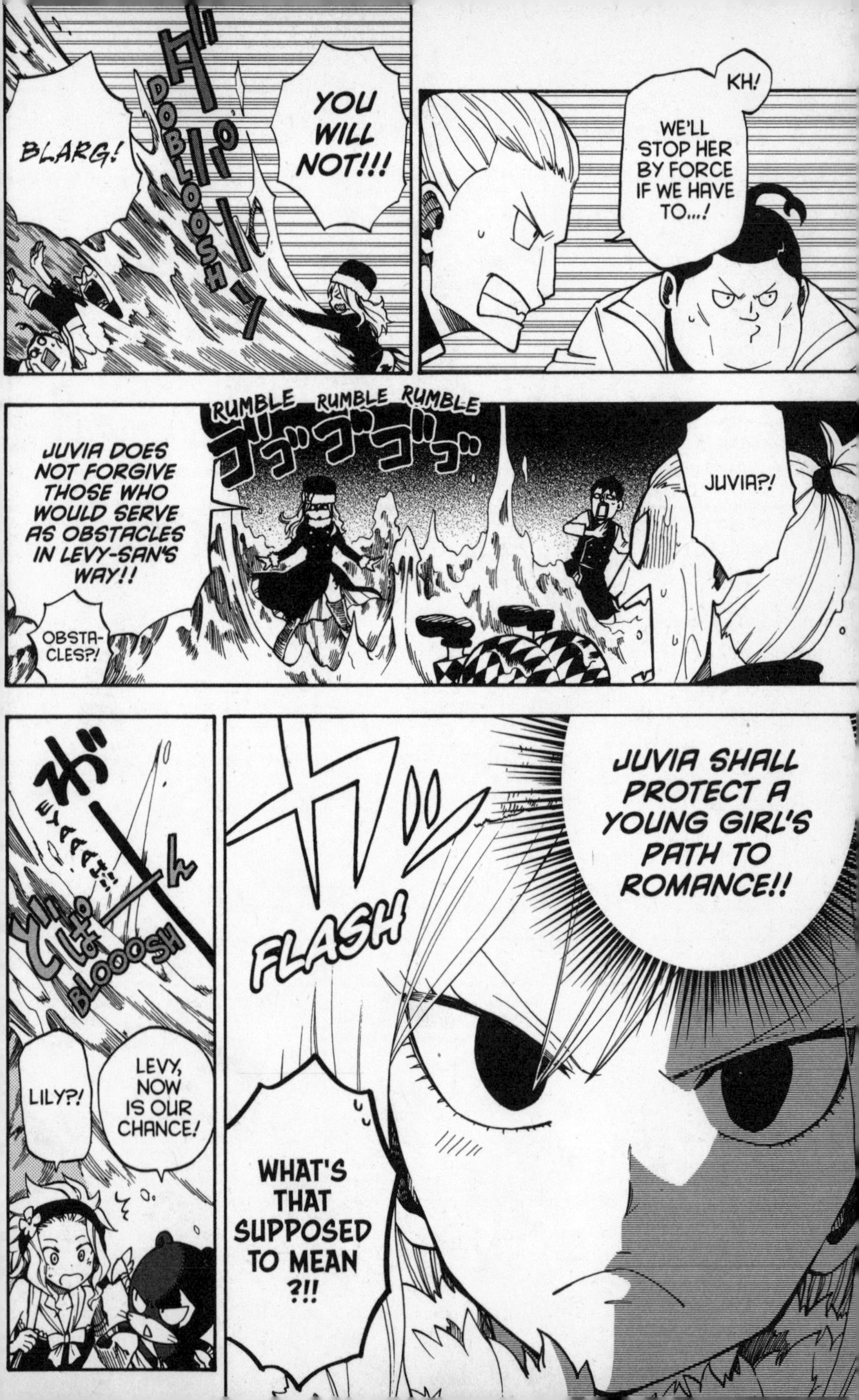
KH!
WE'LL STOP HER BY FORCE IF WE HAVE TO...!
YOU WILL NOT!!!
DOBLOOOSH
BLARG!
JUVIA?!
RUMBLE RUMBLE RUMBLE
JUVIA DOES NOT FORGIVE THOSE WHO WOULD SERVE AS OBSTACLES IN LEVY-SAN'S WAY!!
OBSTA-CLES?!
JUVIA SHALL PROTECT A YOUNG GIRL'S PATH TO ROMANCE!!
FLASH
WHAT'S THAT SUPPOSED TO MEAN?!!
EYAAAAH!!
BLOOOSH
LEVY, NOW IS OUR CHANCE!
LILY?!

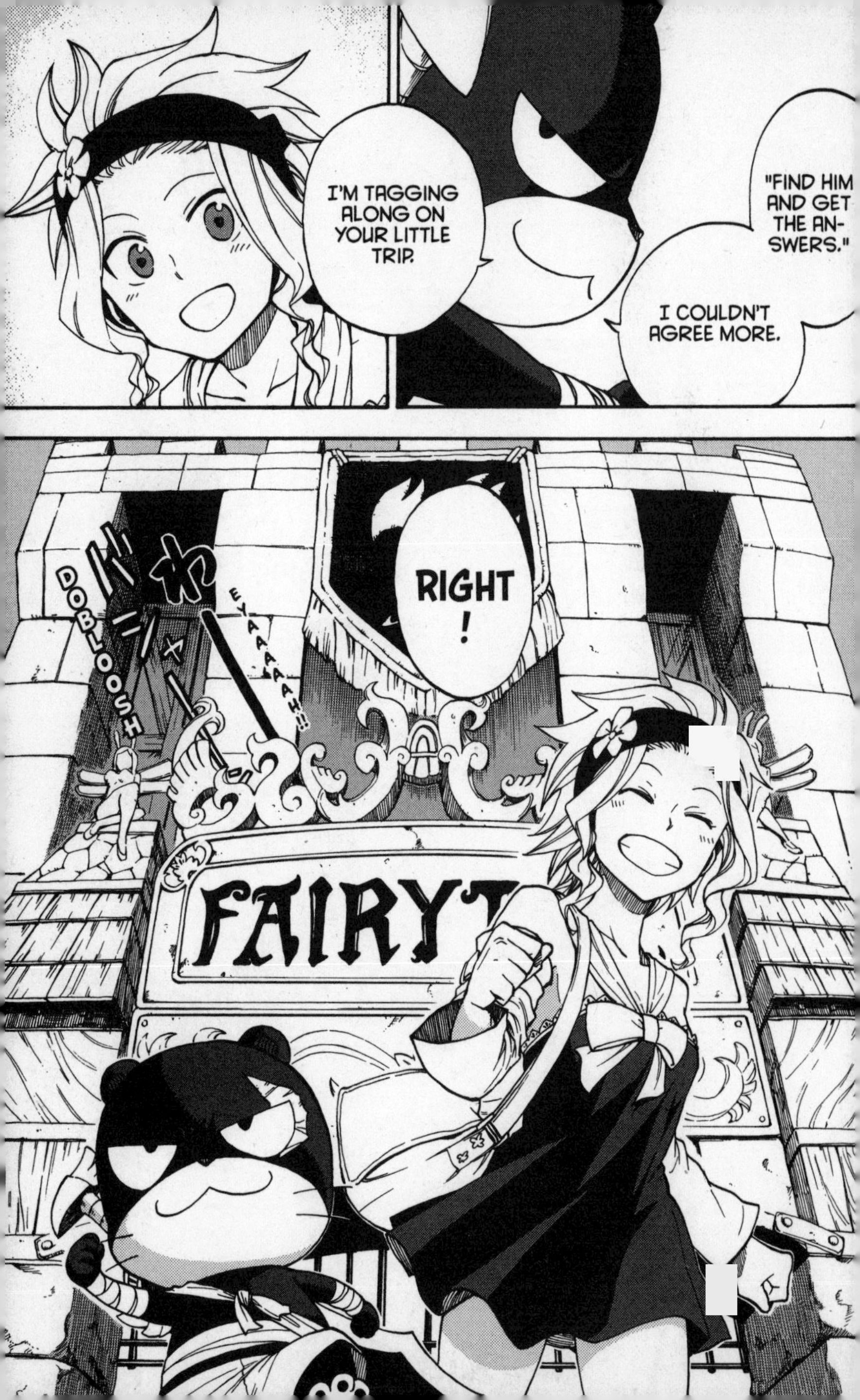
"FIND HIM AND GET THE AN-SWERS."
I COULDN'T AGREE MORE.
I'M TAGGING ALONG ON YOUR LITTLE TRIP.
RIGHT!
EYAAAAAAH!!
DOBLOOSH
FAIRY T

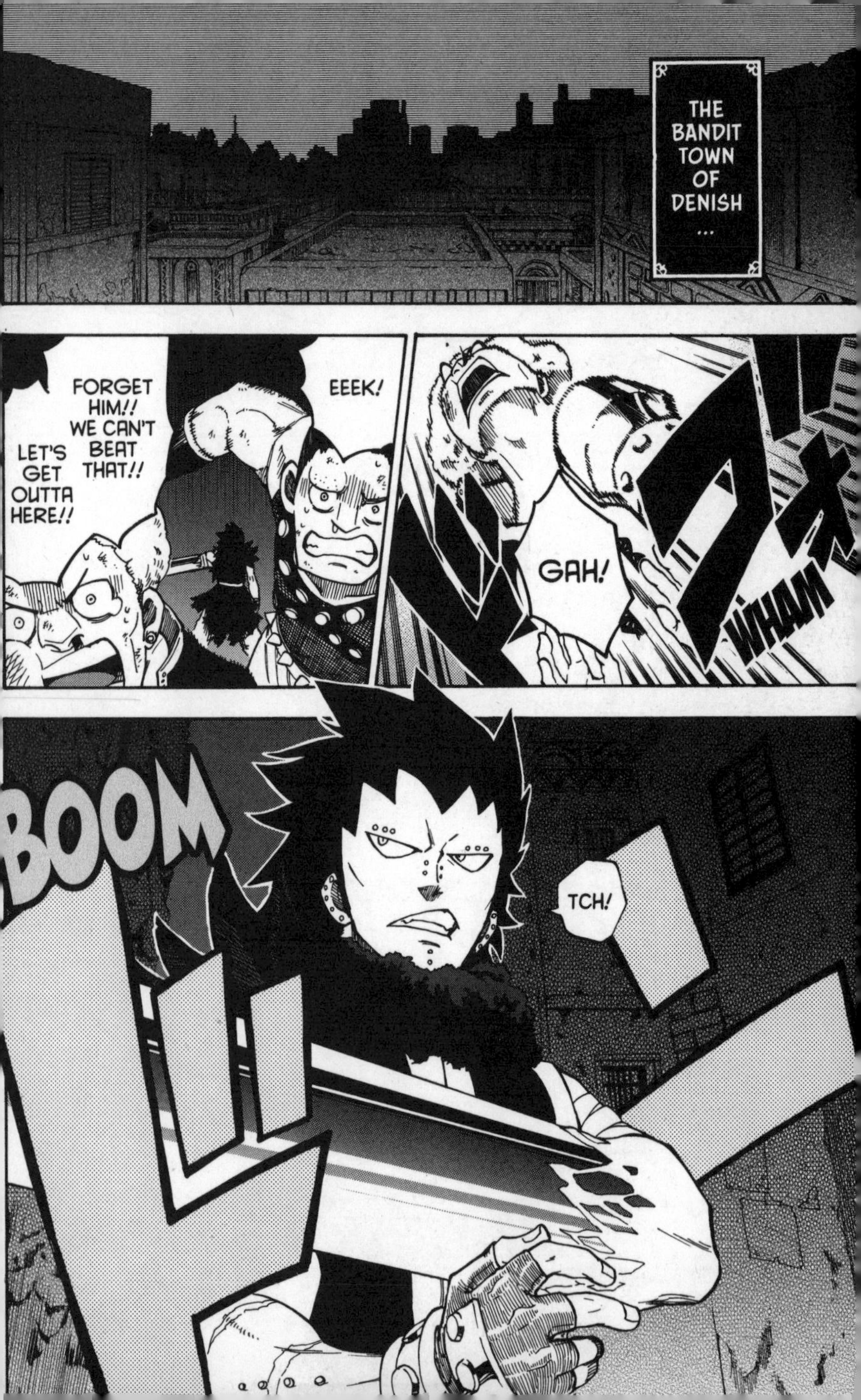
THE BANDIT TOWN OF DENISH ...
GAH!
WHAM
EEEK!
FORGET HIM!! WE CAN'T BEAT THAT!!
LET'S GET OUTTA HERE!!
TCH!
BOOM

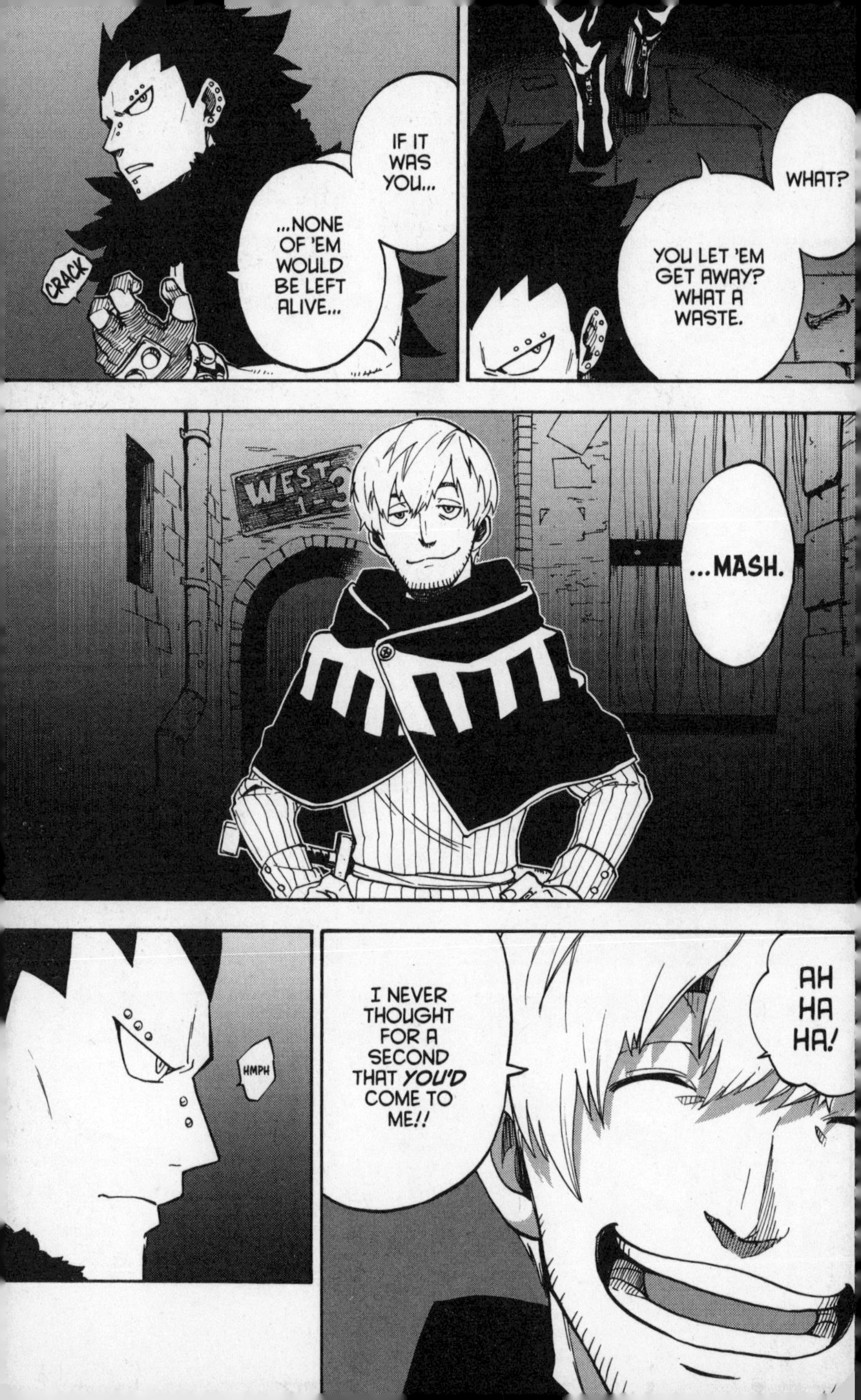
WHAT?
YOU LET 'EM GET AWAY? WHAT A WASTE.
IF IT WAS YOU...
...NONE OF 'EM WOULD BE LEFT ALIVE...
CRACK
...MASH.
AH HA HA!
I NEVER THOUGHT FOR A SECOND THAT *YOU'D* COME TO ME!!
HMPH

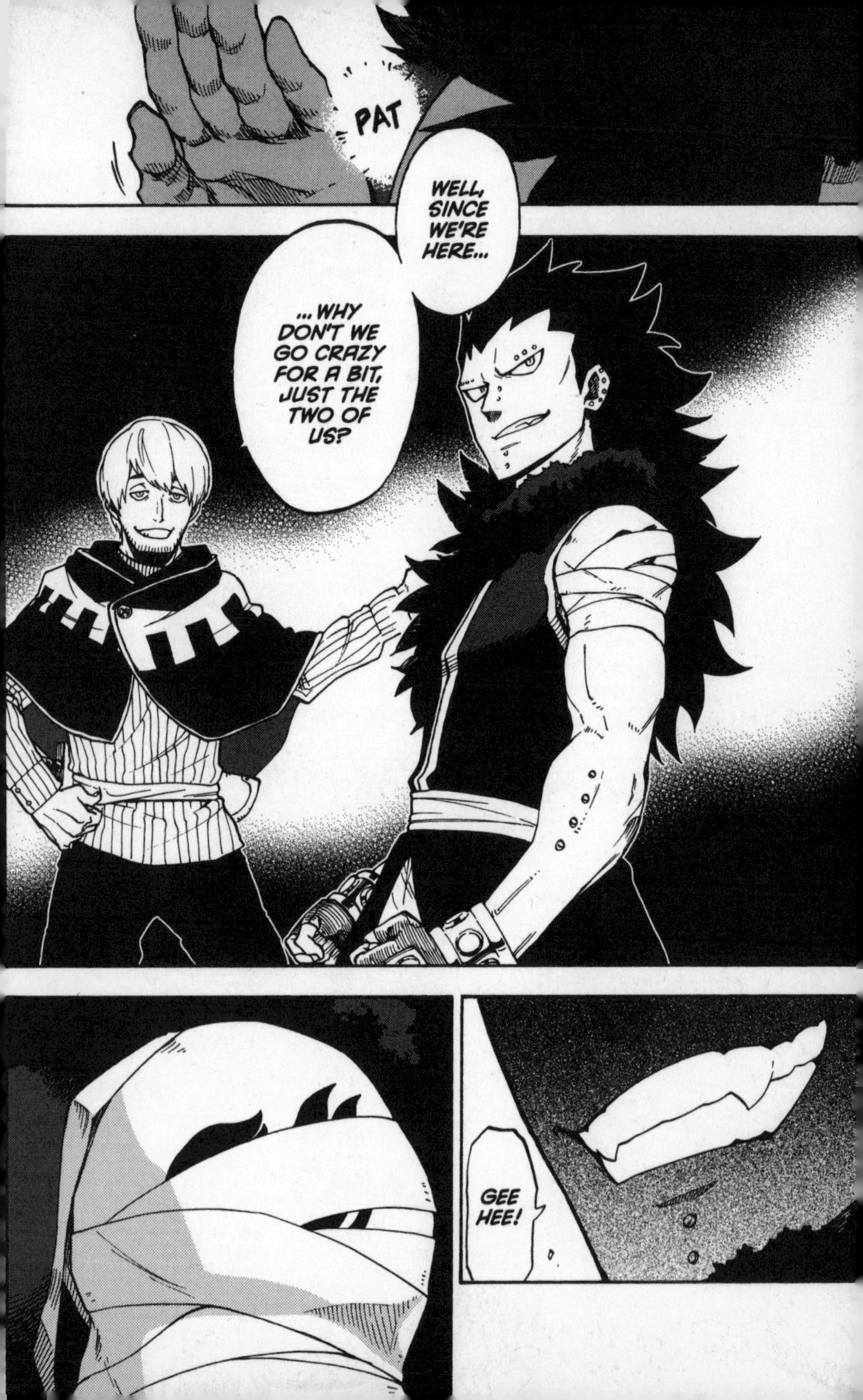
PAT
WELL, SINCE WE'RE HERE...
...WHY DON'T WE GO CRAZY FOR A BIT, JUST THE TWO OF US?
GEE HEE!

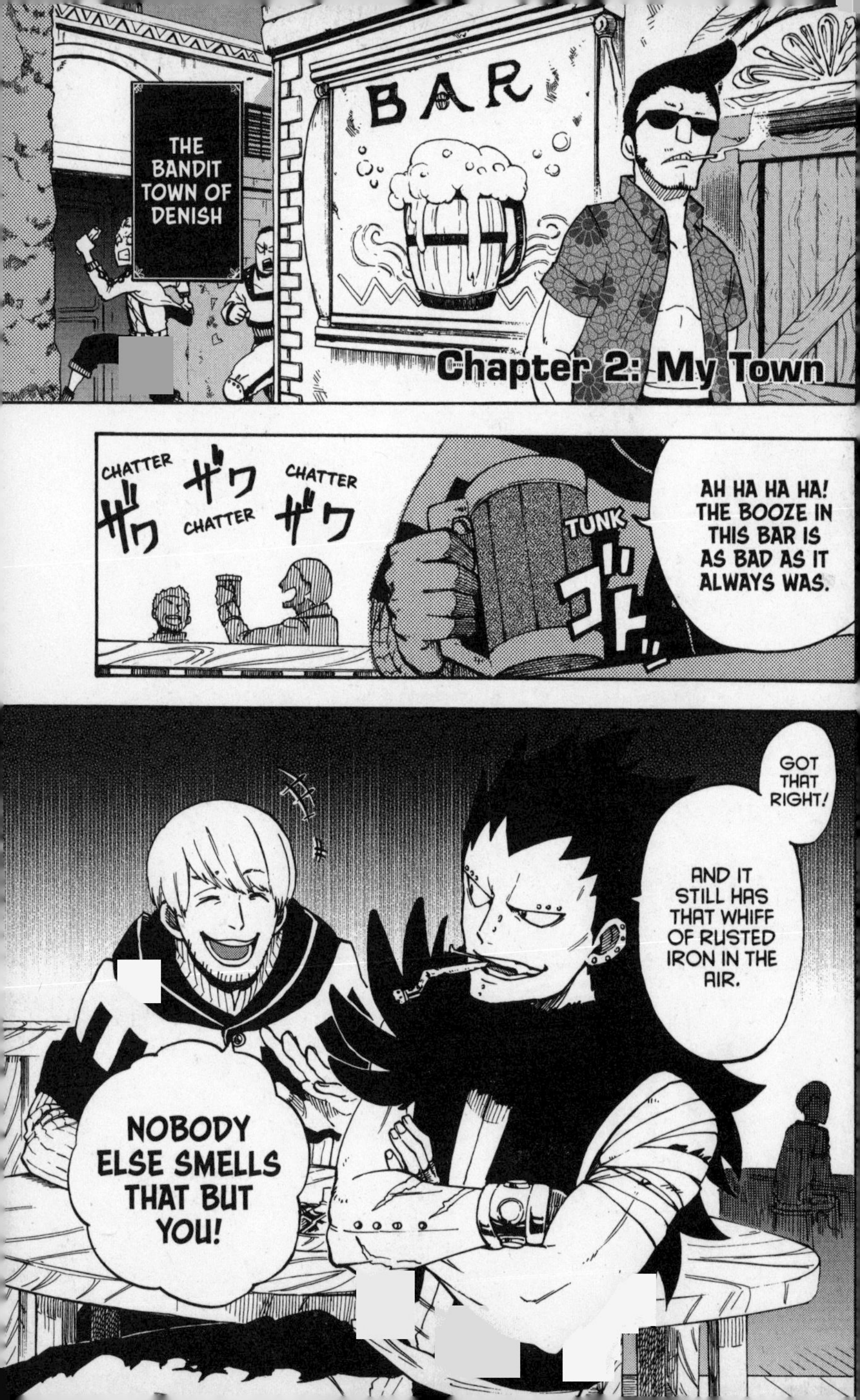
BAR
Chapter 2: My Town
THE BANDIT TOWN OF DENISH
AH HA HA HA! THE BOOZE IN THIS BAR IS AS BAD AS IT ALWAYS WAS.
TUNK
ゴトッ
CHATTER
ザワ
CHATTER
ザワ
CHATTER
ザワ
CHATTER
ザワ
GOT THAT RIGHT!
AND IT STILL HAS THAT WHIFF OF RUSTED IRON IN THE AIR.
NOBODY ELSE SMELLS THAT BUT YOU!

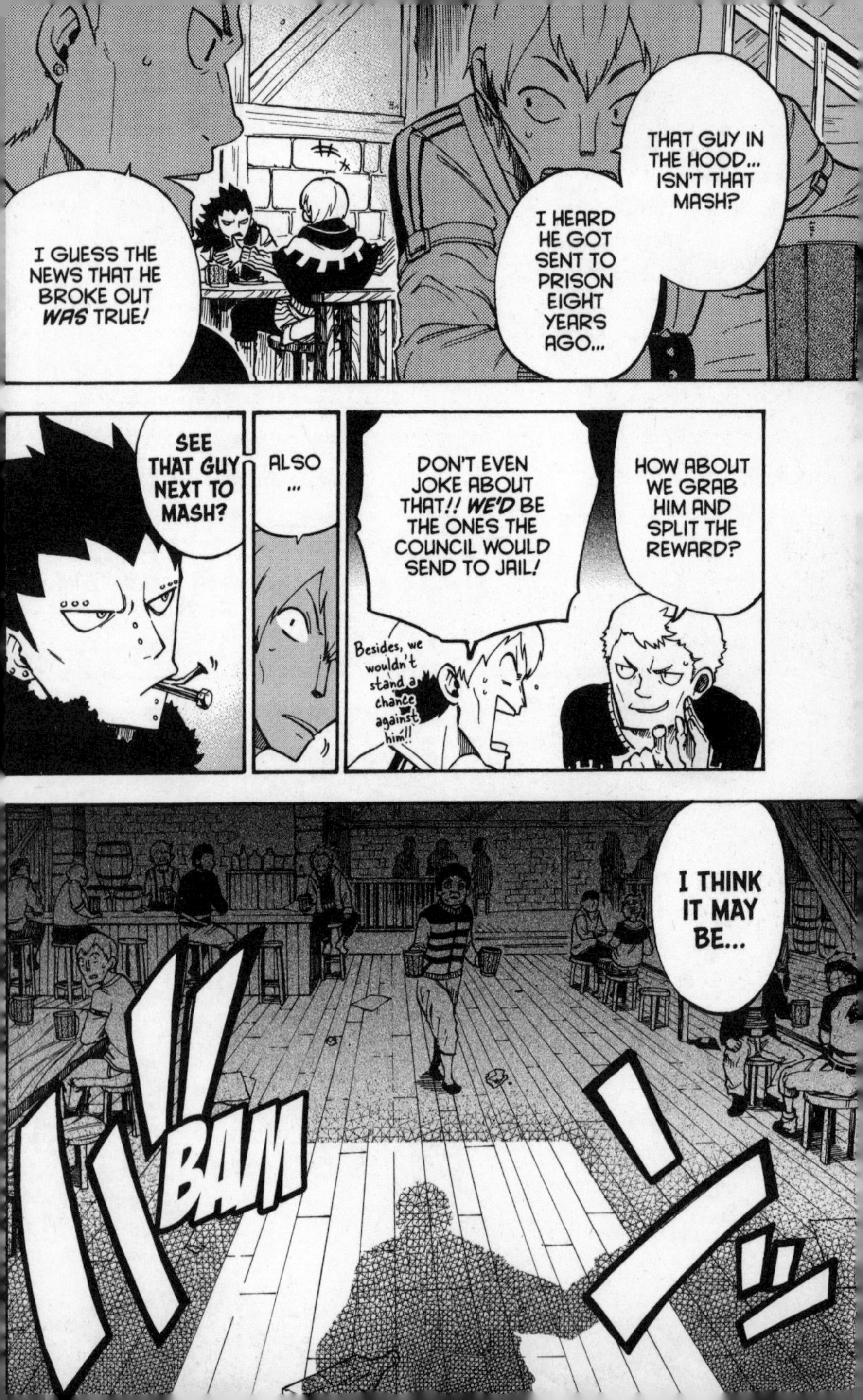
THAT GUY IN THE HOOD... ISN'T THAT MASH?
I HEARD HE GOT SENT TO PRISON EIGHT YEARS AGO...
I GUESS THE NEWS THAT HE BROKE OUT *WAS* TRUE!
HOW ABOUT WE GRAB HIM AND SPLIT THE REWARD?
DON'T EVEN JOKE ABOUT THAT!! *WE'D* BE THE ONES THE COUNCIL WOULD SEND TO JAIL!
Besides, we wouldn't stand a chance against him!!
ALSO ...
SEE THAT GUY NEXT TO MASH?
I THINK IT MAY BE...
BAM

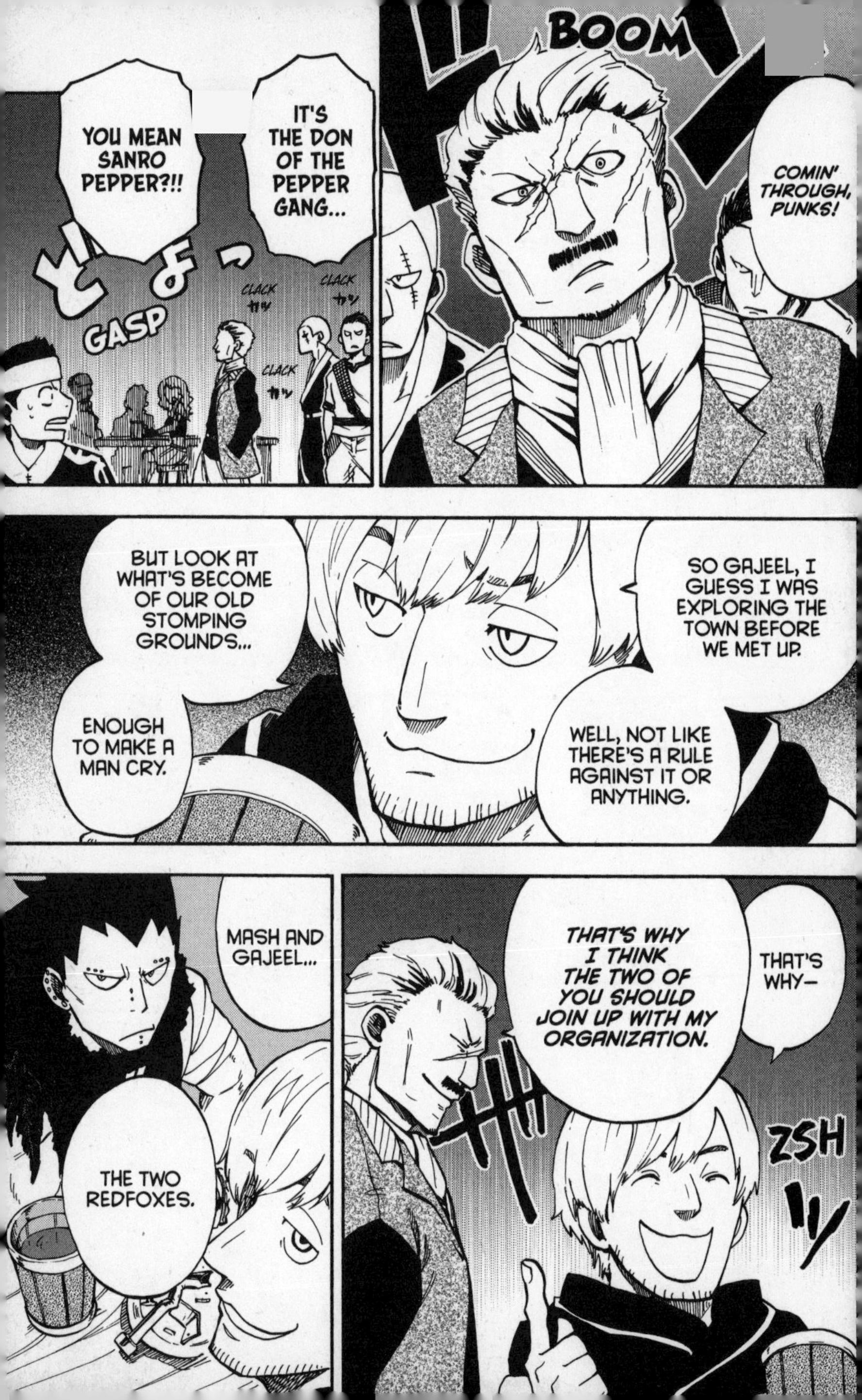
BOOM
COMIN' THROUGH, PUNKS!
IT'S THE DON OF THE PEPPER GANG...
YOU MEAN SANRO PEPPER?!!
どよっ
GASP
CLACK
CLACK
CLACK
SO GAJEEL, I GUESS I WAS EXPLORING THE TOWN BEFORE WE MET UP.
WELL, NOT LIKE THERE'S A RULE AGAINST IT OR ANYTHING.
BUT LOOK AT WHAT'S BECOME OF OUR OLD STOMPING GROUNDS...
ENOUGH TO MAKE A MAN CRY.
THAT'S WHY—
THAT'S WHY I THINK THE TWO OF YOU SHOULD JOIN UP WITH MY ORGANIZATION.
ZSH
MASH AND GAJEEL...
THE TWO REDFOXES.

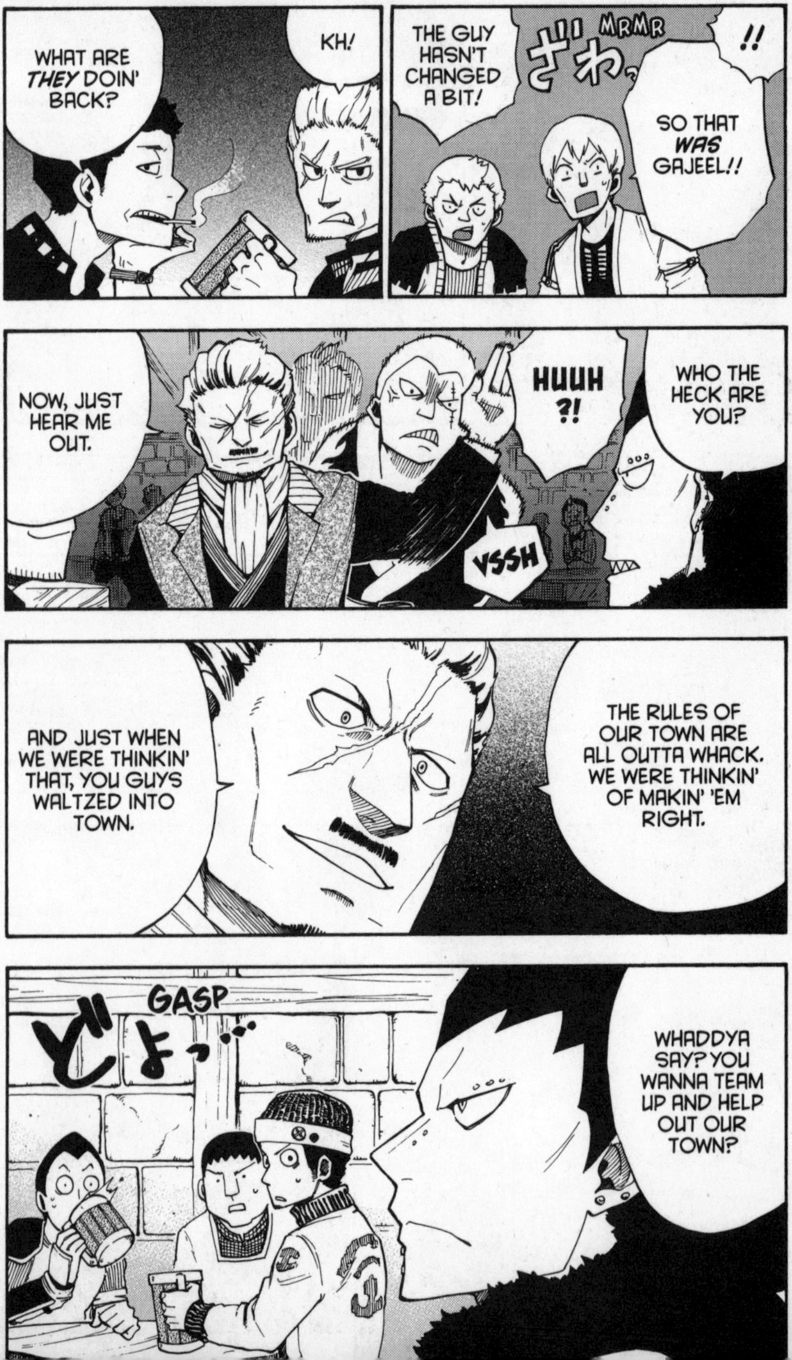
!!
ざわっ
MRMR
SO THAT WAS GAJEEL!!
THE GUY HASN'T CHANGED A BIT!
KH!
WHAT ARE THEY DOIN' BACK?
WHO THE HECK ARE YOU?
HUUH ?!
VSSH
NOW, JUST HEAR ME OUT.
THE RULES OF OUR TOWN ARE ALL OUTTA WHACK. WE WERE THINKIN' OF MAKIN' 'EM RIGHT.
AND JUST WHEN WE WERE THINKIN' THAT, YOU GUYS WALTZED INTO TOWN.
WHADDYA SAY? YOU WANNA TEAM UP AND HELP OUT OUR TOWN?
どよっ
GASP

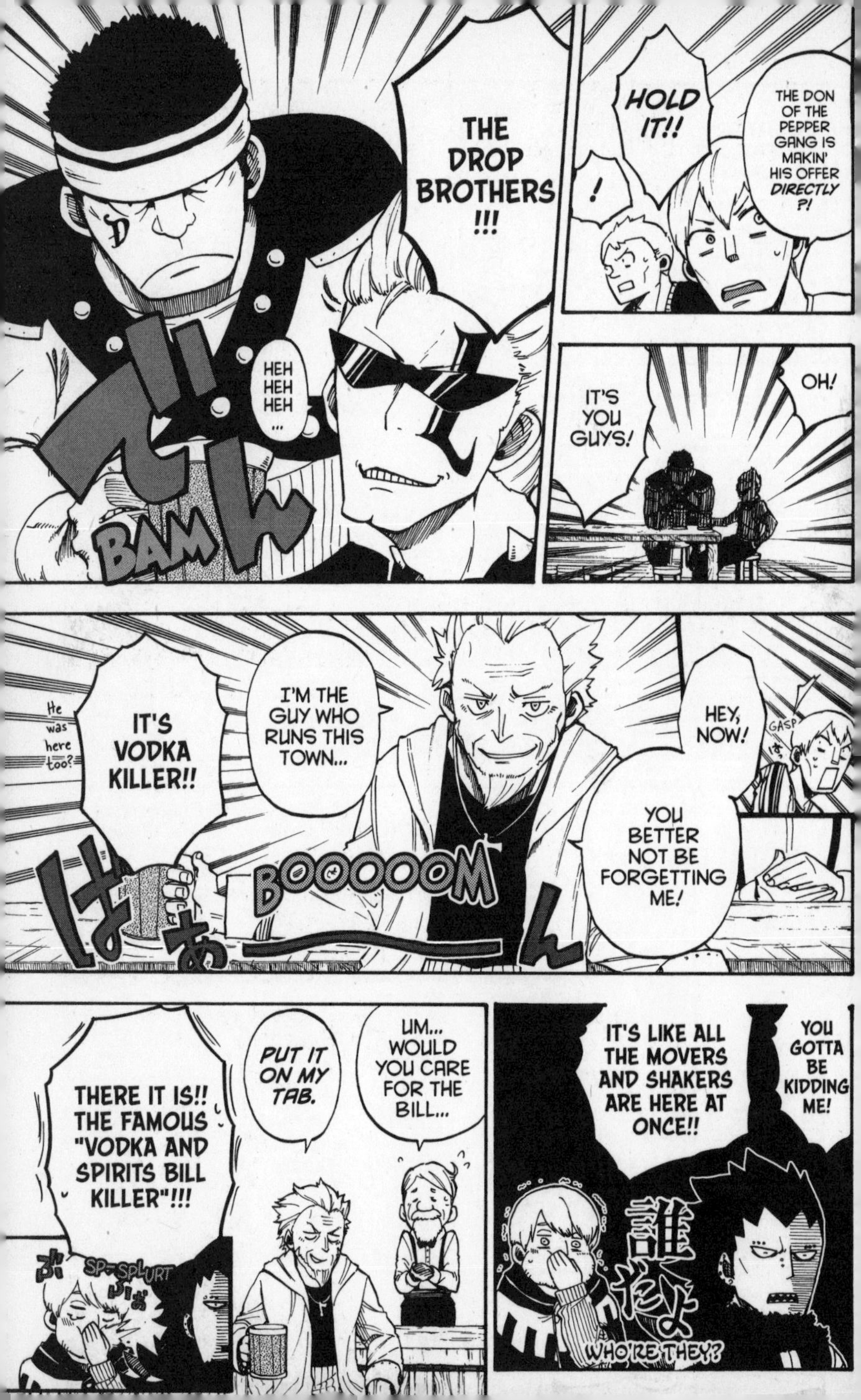
THE DON OF THE PEPPER GANG IS MAKIN' HIS OFFER DIRECTLY?!
HOLD IT!!
!
OH!
IT'S YOU GUYS!
THE DROP BROTHERS!!!
HEH HEH HEH...
BAM
HEY, NOW!
GASP
YOU BETTER NOT BE FORGETTING ME!
I'M THE GUY WHO RUNS THIS TOWN...
BOOOOOM
IT'S VODKA KILLER!!
He was here too?
YOU GOTTA BE KIDDING ME!
IT'S LIKE ALL THE MOVERS AND SHAKERS ARE HERE AT ONCE!!
WHO'RE THEY?
UM... WOULD YOU CARE FOR THE BILL...
PUT IT ON MY TAB.
THERE IT IS!! THE FAMOUS "VODKA AND SPIRITS BILL KILLER"!!!
SP-SPLURT

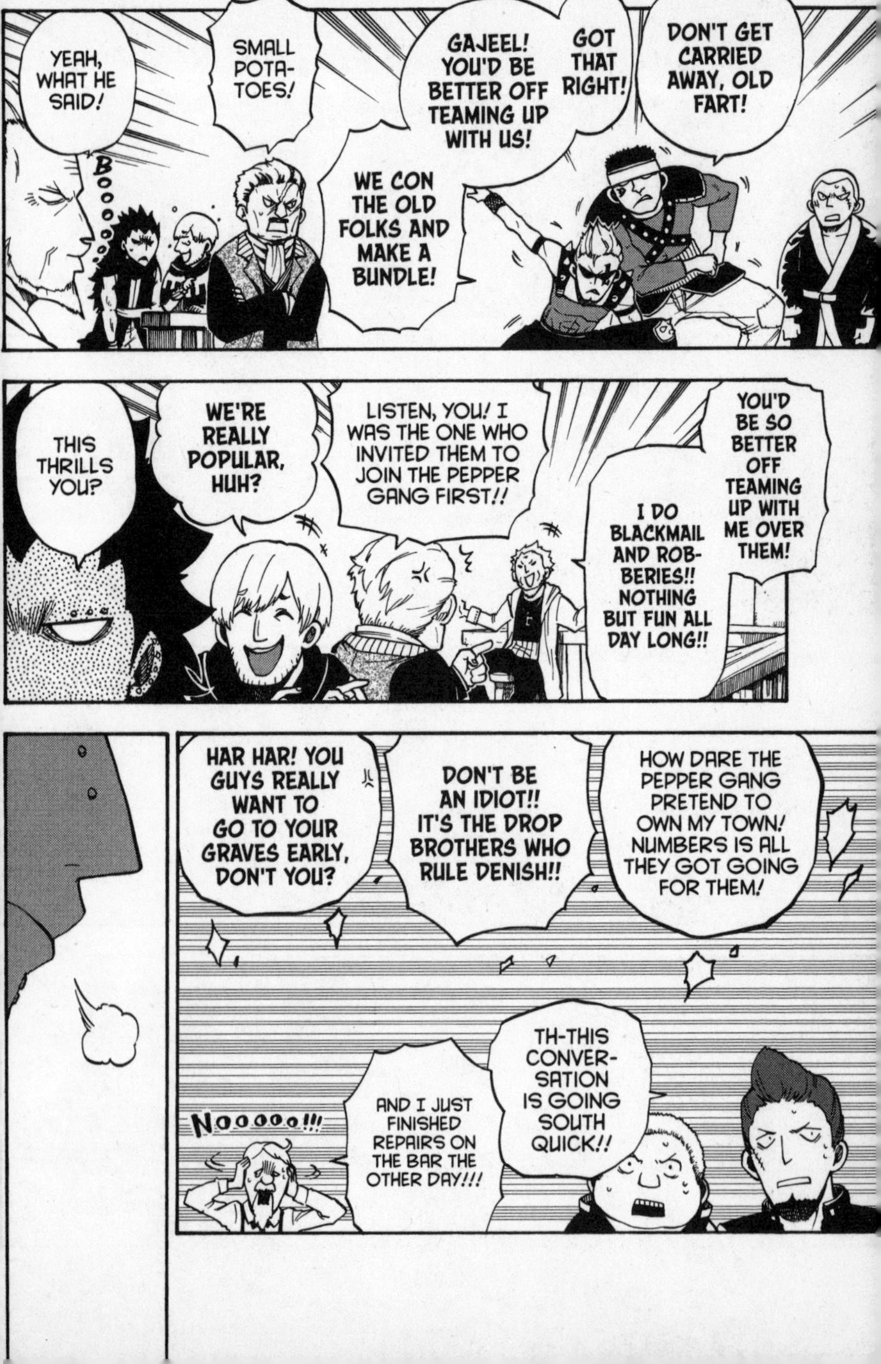
DON'T GET CARRIED AWAY, OLD FART!
GOT THAT RIGHT!
GAJEEL! YOU'D BE BETTER OFF TEAMING UP WITH US!
WE CON THE OLD FOLKS AND MAKE A BUNDLE!
SMALL POTA-TOES!
YEAH, WHAT HE SAID!
BOOOOO
YOU'D BE SO BETTER OFF TEAMING UP WITH ME OVER THEM!
I DO BLACKMAIL AND ROB-BERIES!! NOTHING BUT FUN ALL DAY LONG!!
LISTEN, YOU! I WAS THE ONE WHO INVITED THEM TO JOIN THE PEPPER GANG FIRST!!
WE'RE REALLY POPULAR, HUH?
THIS THRILLS YOU?
HOW DARE THE PEPPER GANG PRETEND TO OWN MY TOWN! NUMBERS IS ALL THEY GOT GOING FOR THEM!
DON'T BE AN IDIOT!! IT'S THE DROP BROTHERS WHO RULE DENISH!!
HAR HAR! YOU GUYS REALLY WANT TO GO TO YOUR GRAVES EARLY, DON'T YOU?
TH-THIS CONVER-SATION IS GOING SOUTH QUICK!!
AND I JUST FINISHED REPAIRS ON THE BAR THE OTHER DAY!!!
NOOOOO!!!

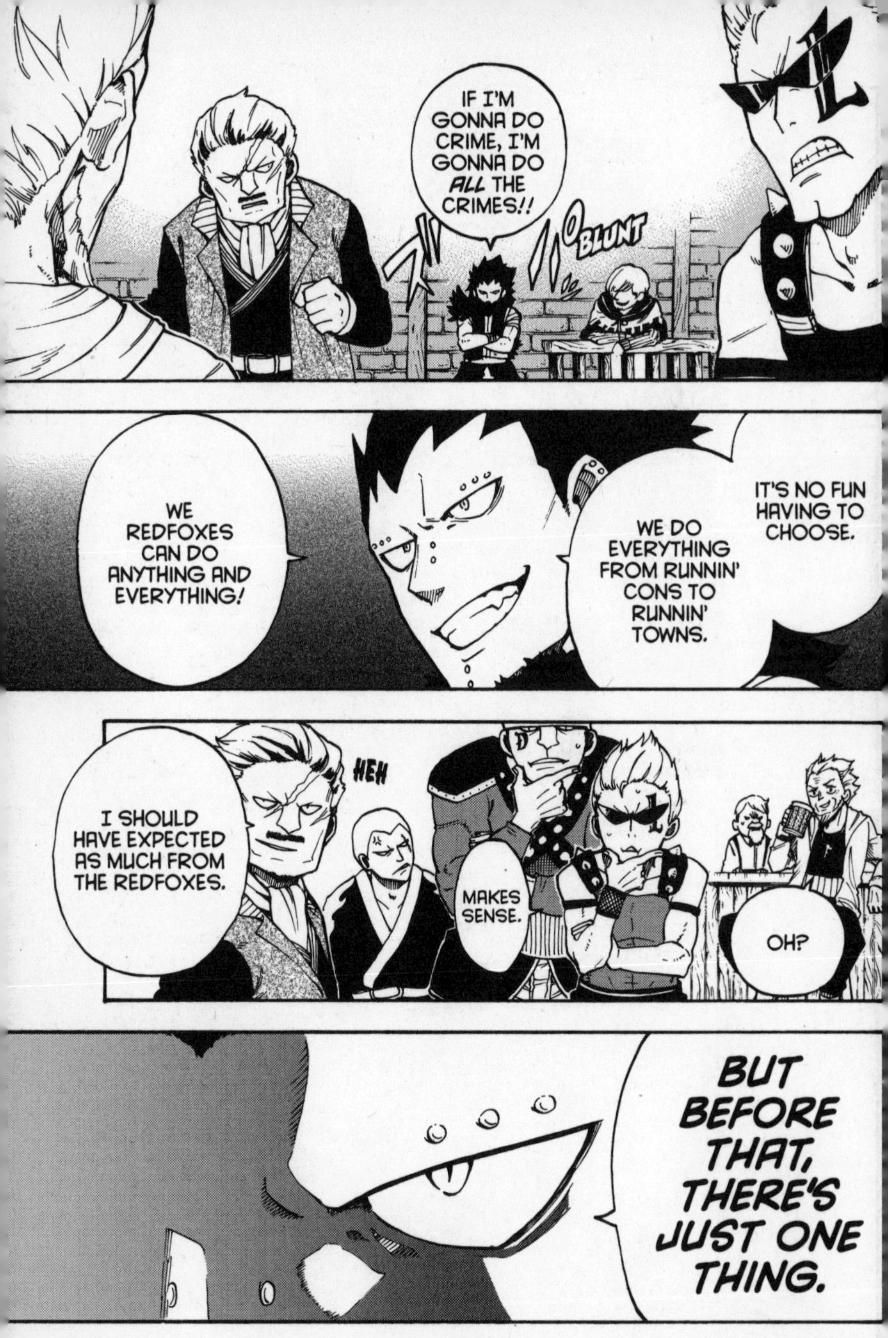
IF I'M GONNA DO CRIME, I'M GONNA DO ALL THE CRIMES!!
BLUNT
IT'S NO FUN HAVING TO CHOOSE.
WE DO EVERYTHING FROM RUNNIN' CONS TO RUNNIN' TOWNS.
WE REDFOXES CAN DO ANYTHING AND EVERYTHING!
OH?
MAKES SENSE.
HEH
I SHOULD HAVE EXPECTED AS MUCH FROM THE REDFOXES.
BUT BEFORE THAT, THERE'S JUST ONE THING.

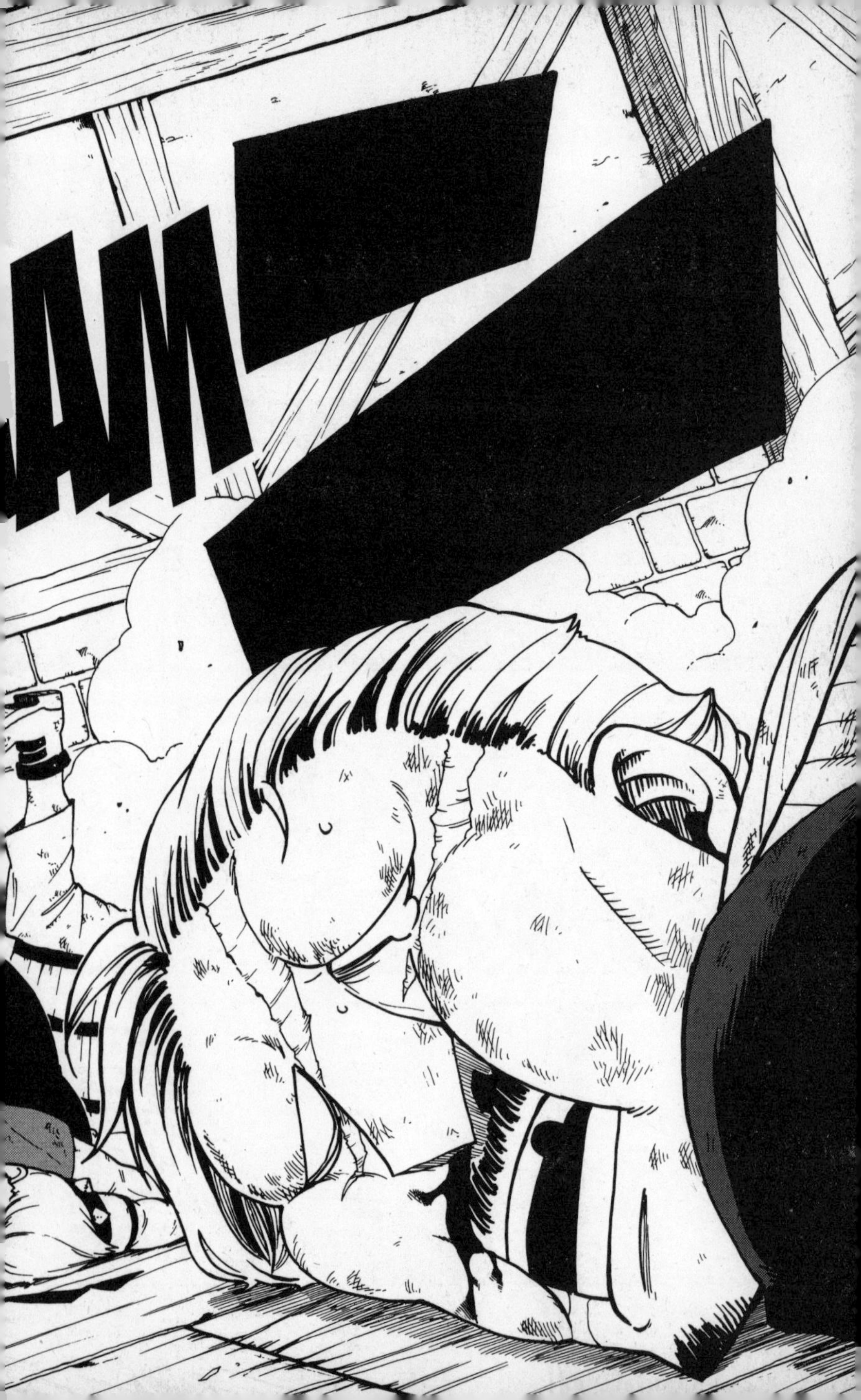
AM

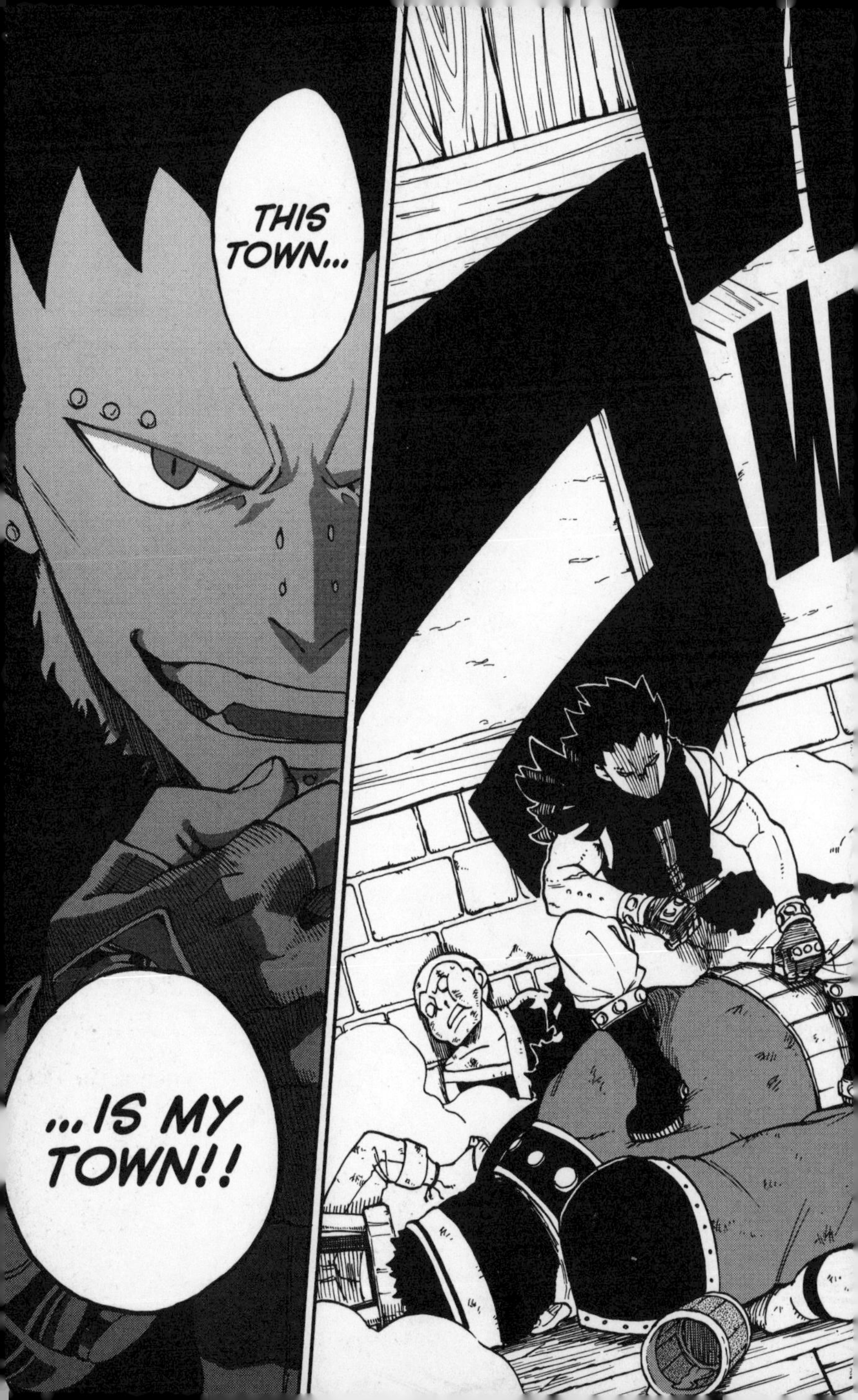
THIS TOWN...
...IS MY TOWN!!

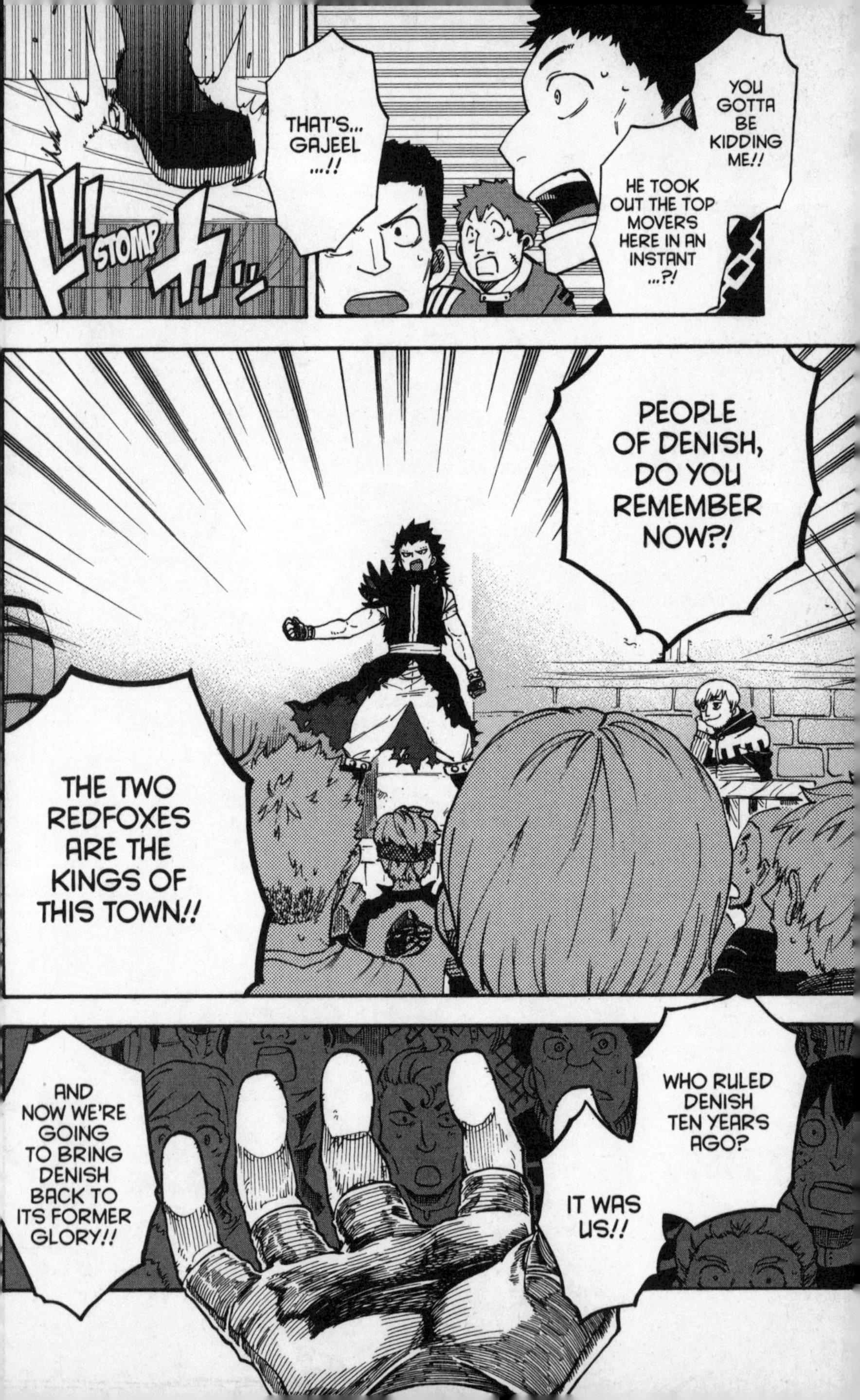
YOU GOTTA BE KIDDING ME!!
HE TOOK OUT THE TOP MOVERS HERE IN AN INSTANT ...?!
THAT'S... GAJEEL ...!!
STOMP
PEOPLE OF DENISH, DO YOU REMEMBER NOW?!
THE TWO REDFOXES ARE THE KINGS OF THIS TOWN!!
WHO RULED DENISH TEN YEARS AGO?
IT WAS US!!
AND NOW WE'RE GOING TO BRING DENISH BACK TO ITS FORMER GLORY!!

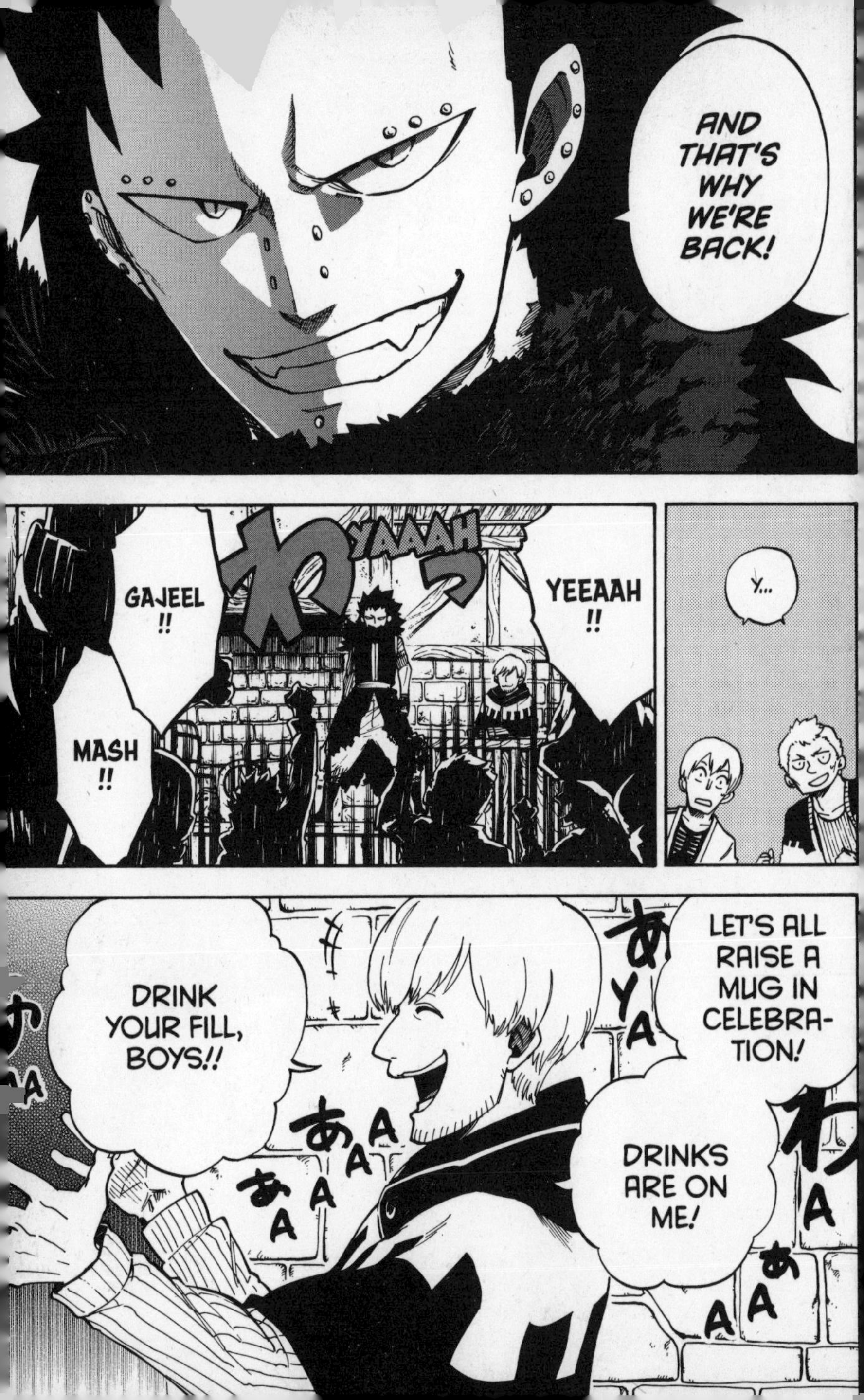
AND THAT'S WHY WE'RE BACK!
Y...
YAAAH
YEEAAH !!
GAJEEL !!
MASH !!
LET'S ALL RAISE A MUG IN CELEBRATION!
DRINK YOUR FILL, BOYS!!
DRINKS ARE ON ME!

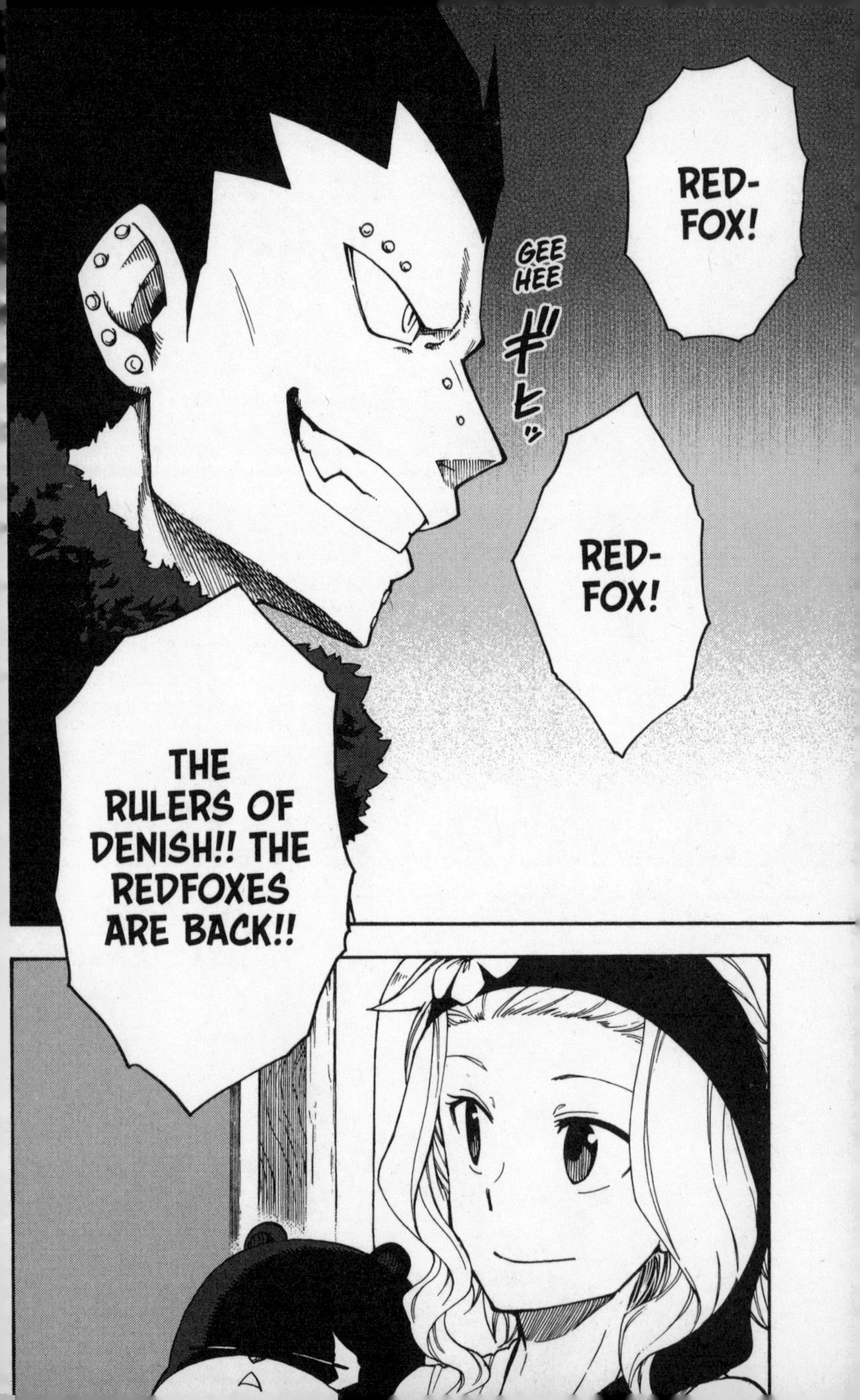
RED-FOX!
GEE HEE
ギヒッ
RED-FOX!
THE RULERS OF DENISH!! THE REDFOXES ARE BACK!!

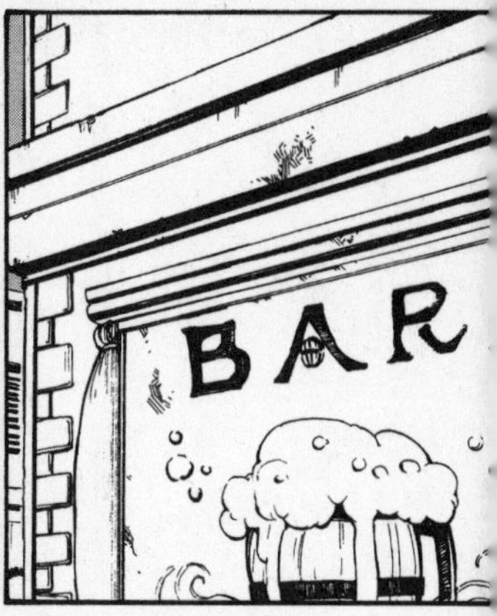
BAR

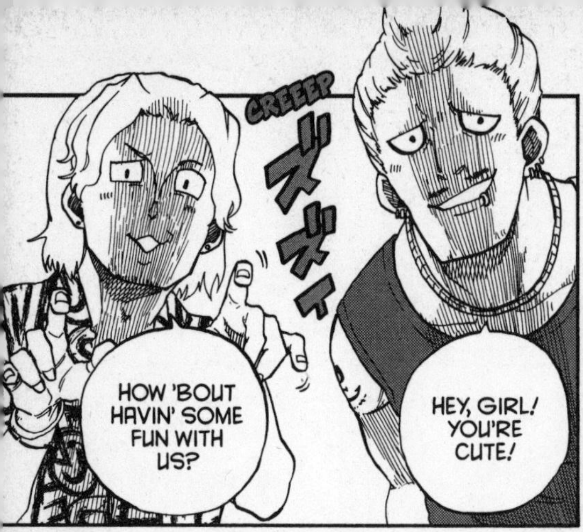
CREEEP
HEY, GIRL! YOU'RE CUTE!
HOW 'BOUT HAVIN' SOME FUN WITH US?

Chapter 3: A Meeting in Denish

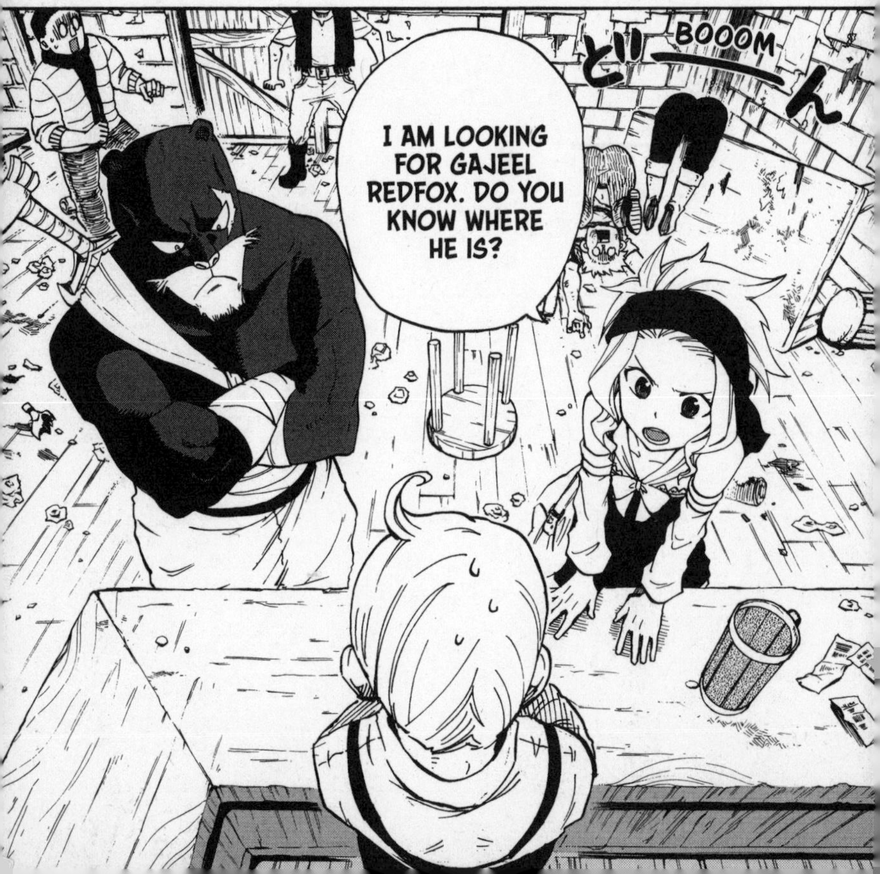
BOOOM
I AM LOOKING FOR GAJEEL REDFOX. DO YOU KNOW WHERE HE IS?

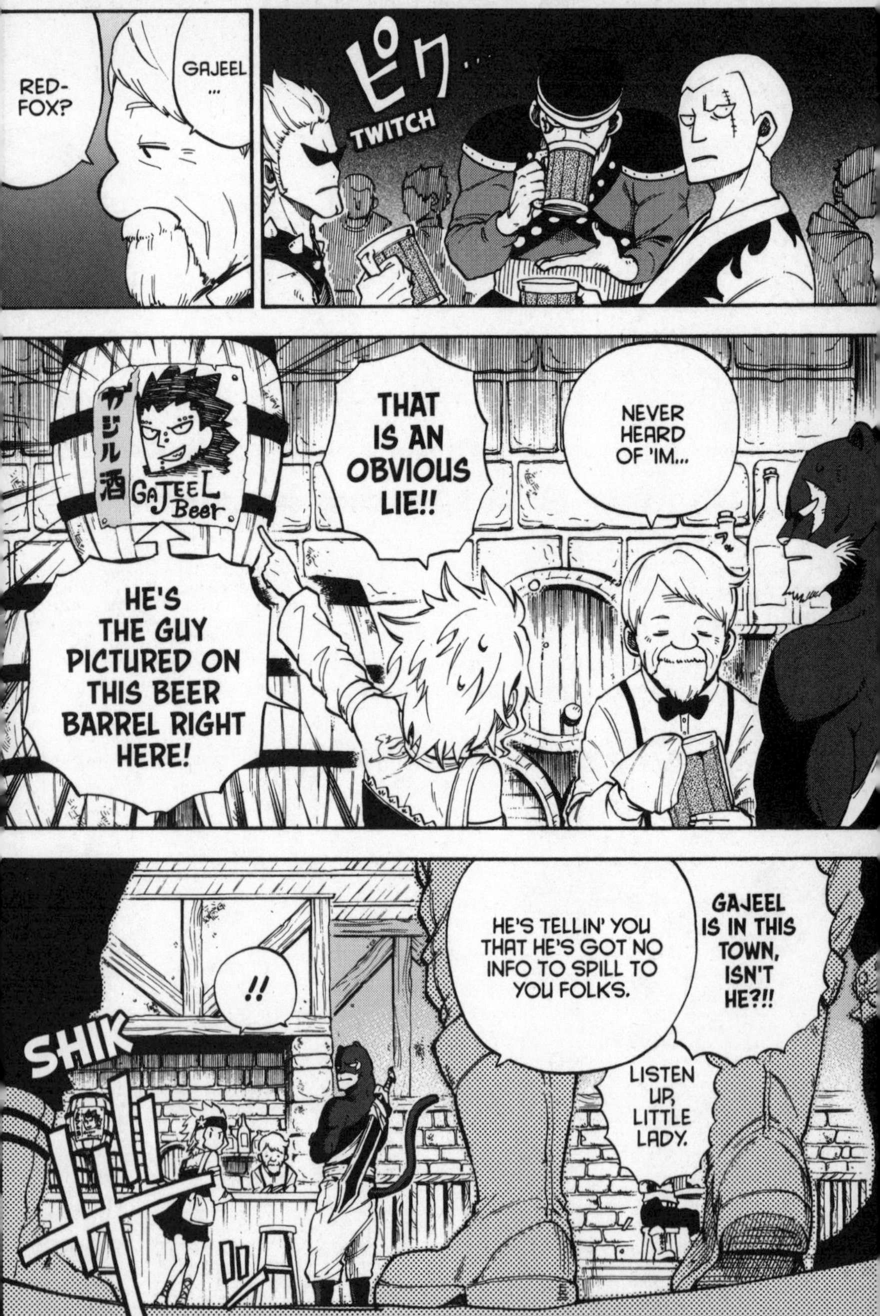
ピク
TWITCH
GAJEEL ...
RED-FOX?
NEVER HEARD OF 'IM...
THAT IS AN OBVIOUS LIE!!
ガジル酒
GAJEEL Beer
HE'S THE GUY PICTURED ON THIS BEER BARREL RIGHT HERE!
GAJEEL IS IN THIS TOWN, ISN'T HE?!!
HE'S TELLIN' YOU THAT HE'S GOT NO INFO TO SPILL TO YOU FOLKS.
LISTEN UP, LITTLE LADY.
!!
SHIK

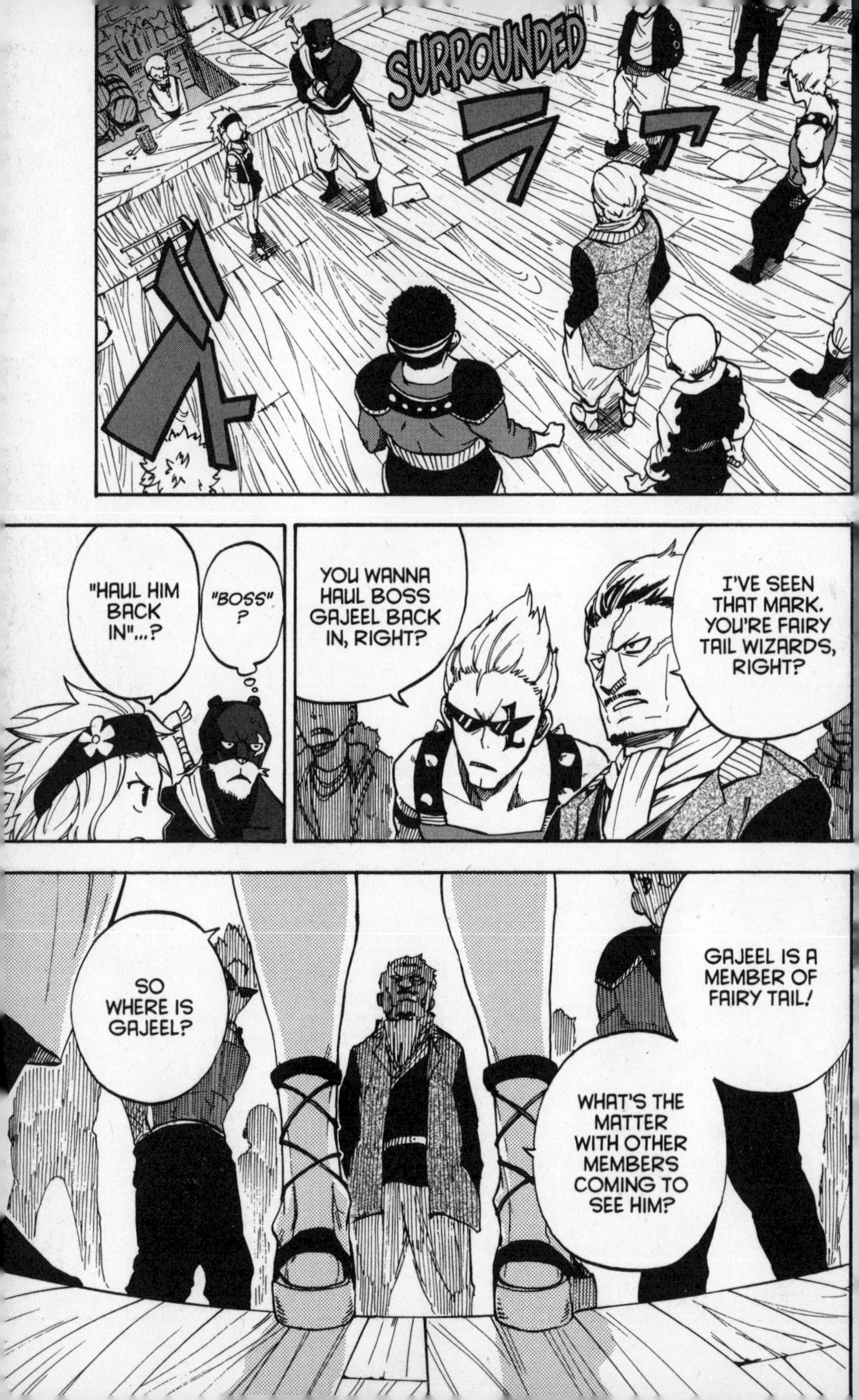
SURROUNDED
I'VE SEEN THAT MARK. YOU'RE FAIRY TAIL WIZARDS, RIGHT?
YOU WANNA HAUL BOSS GAJEEL BACK IN, RIGHT?
"BOSS" ?
"HAUL HIM BACK IN"...?
GAJEEL IS A MEMBER OF FAIRY TAIL!
WHAT'S THE MATTER WITH OTHER MEMBERS COMING TO SEE HIM?
SO WHERE IS GAJEEL?

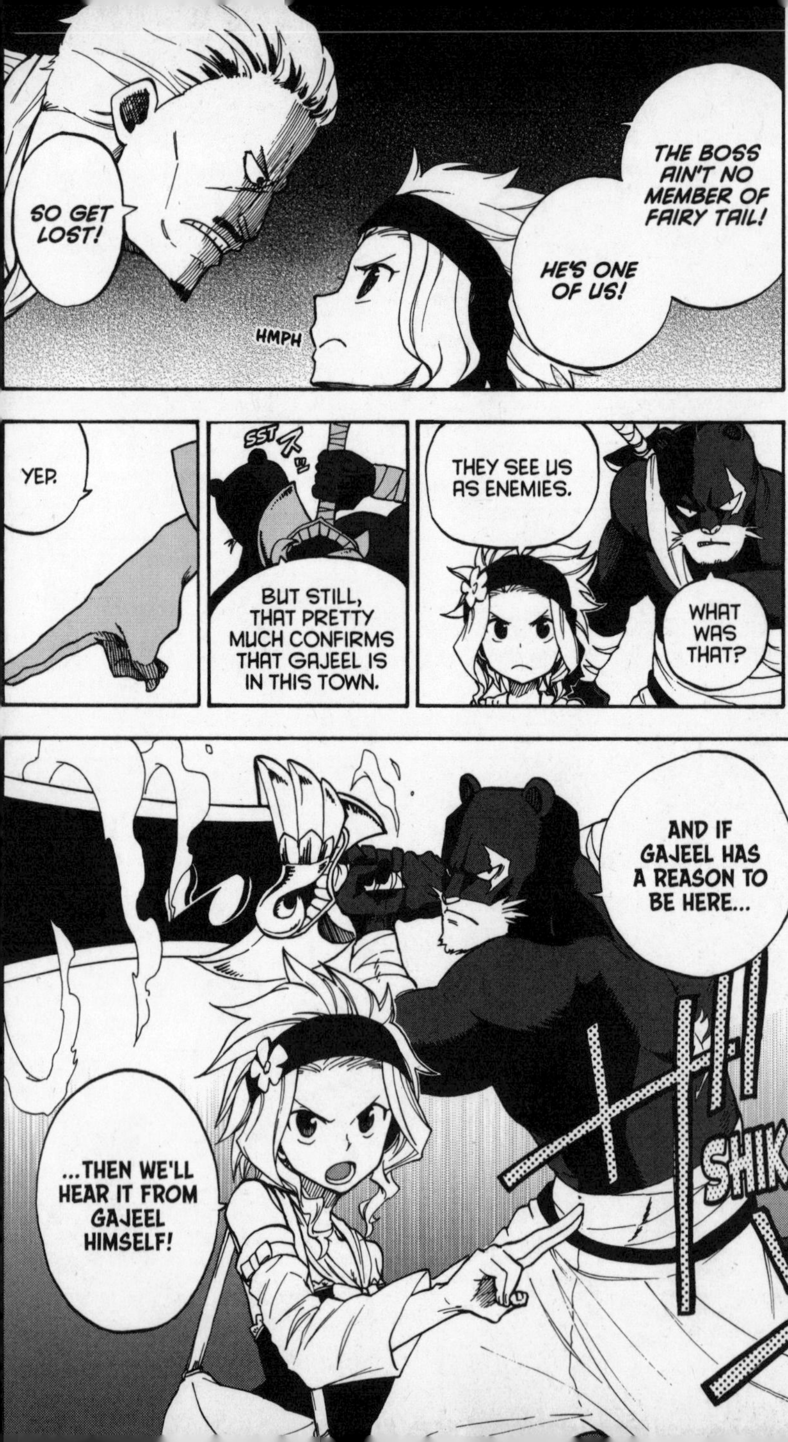
THE BOSS AIN'T NO MEMBER OF FAIRY TAIL!
HE'S ONE OF US!
SO GET LOST!
HMPH
THEY SEE US AS ENEMIES.
WHAT WAS THAT?
SST
BUT STILL, THAT PRETTY MUCH CONFIRMS THAT GAJEEL IS IN THIS TOWN.
YEP.
AND IF GAJEEL HAS A REASON TO BE HERE...
SHIK
...THEN WE'LL HEAR IT FROM GAJEEL HIMSELF!

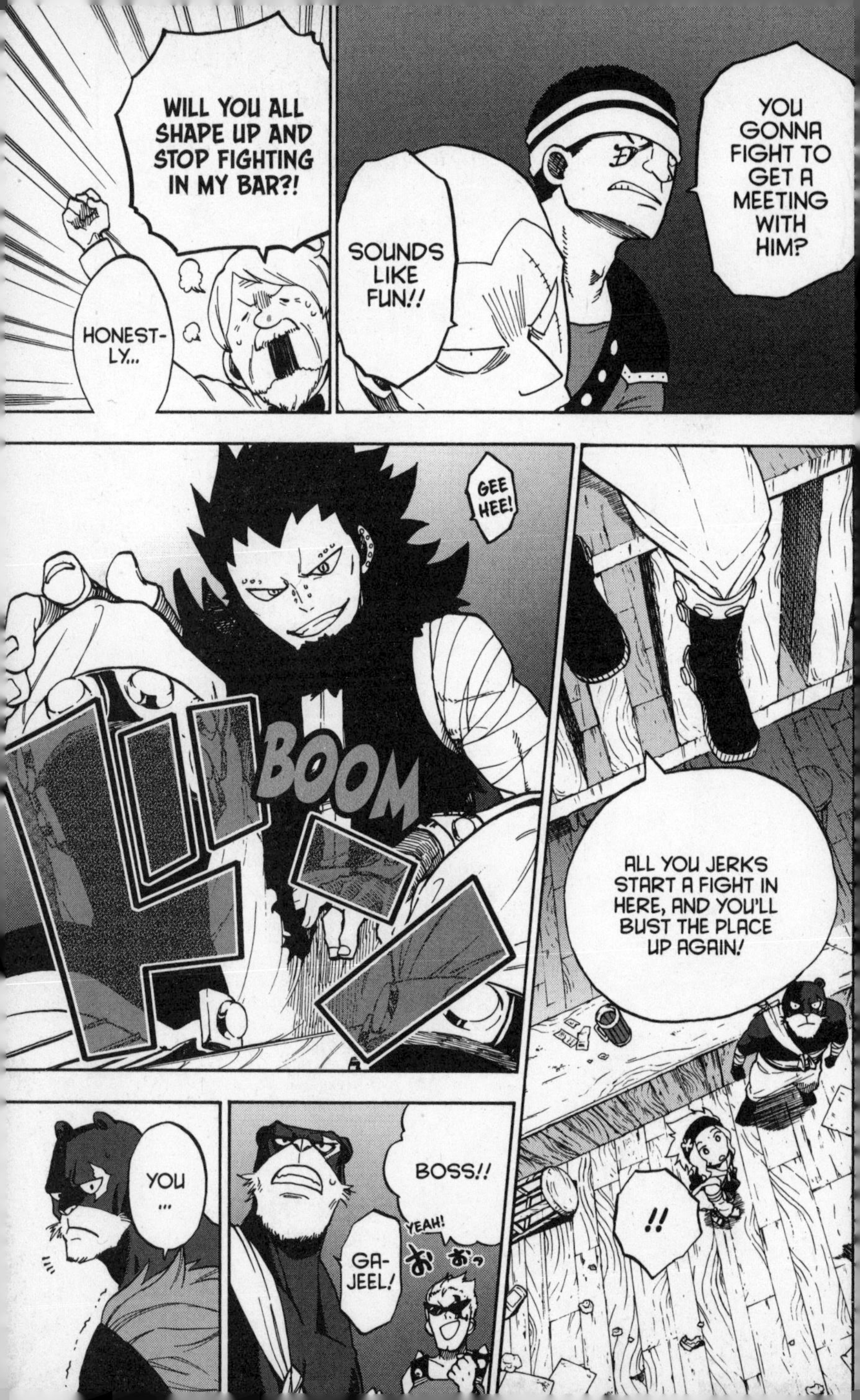
YOU GONNA FIGHT TO GET A MEETING WITH HIM?
SOUNDS LIKE FUN!!
WILL YOU ALL SHAPE UP AND STOP FIGHTING IN MY BAR?!
HONEST-LY...
ALL YOU JERKS START A FIGHT IN HERE, AND YOU'LL BUST THE PLACE UP AGAIN!
!!
GEE HEE!
BOOM
BOSS!!
YEAH!
お おっ
GA-JEEL!
YOU ...

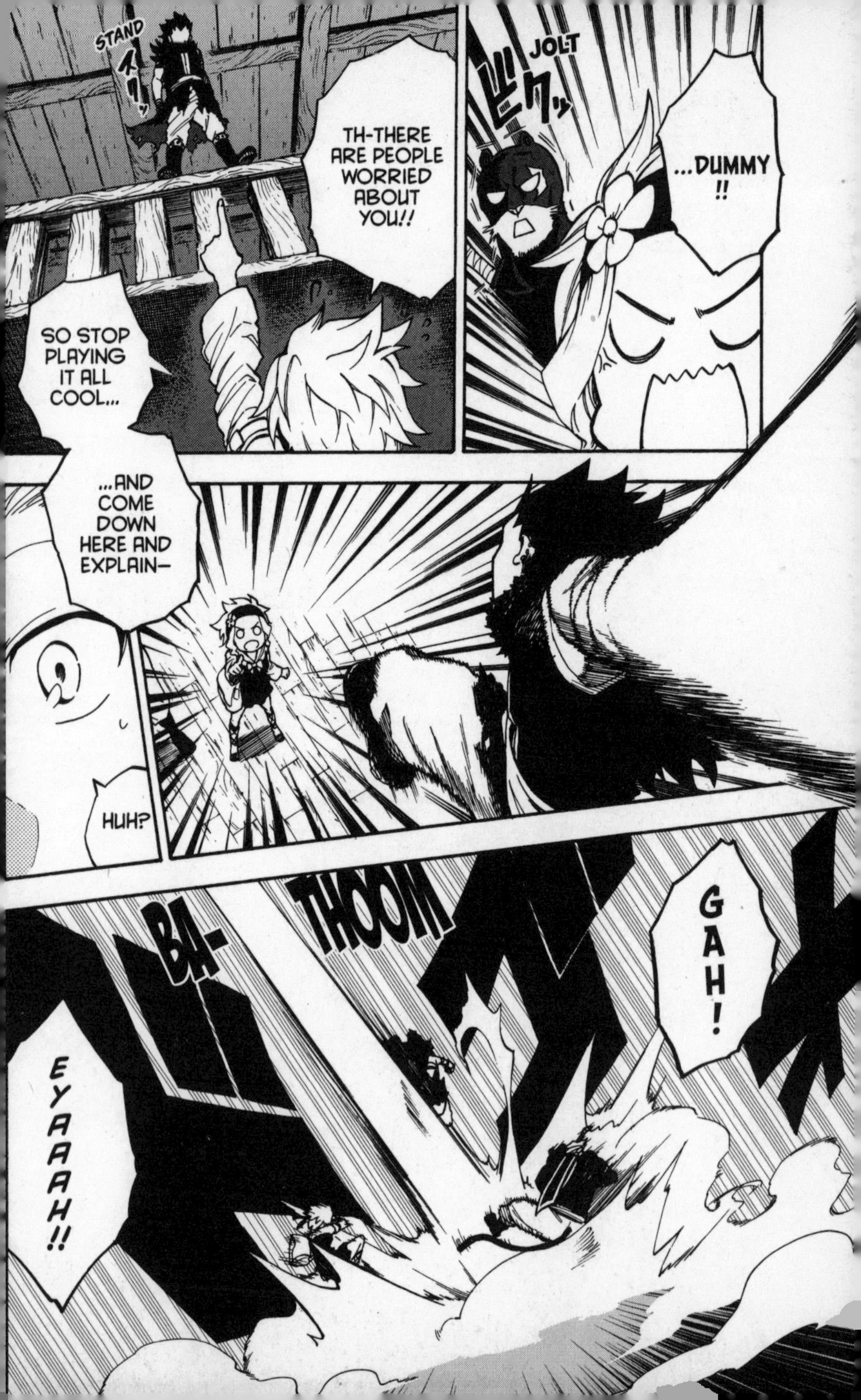
JOLT
...DUMMY!!
STAND
TH-THERE ARE PEOPLE WORRIED ABOUT YOU!!
SO STOP PLAYING IT ALL COOL...
...AND COME DOWN HERE AND EXPLAIN—
HUH?
GAH!
BA-
THOOM
EYAAAAH!!

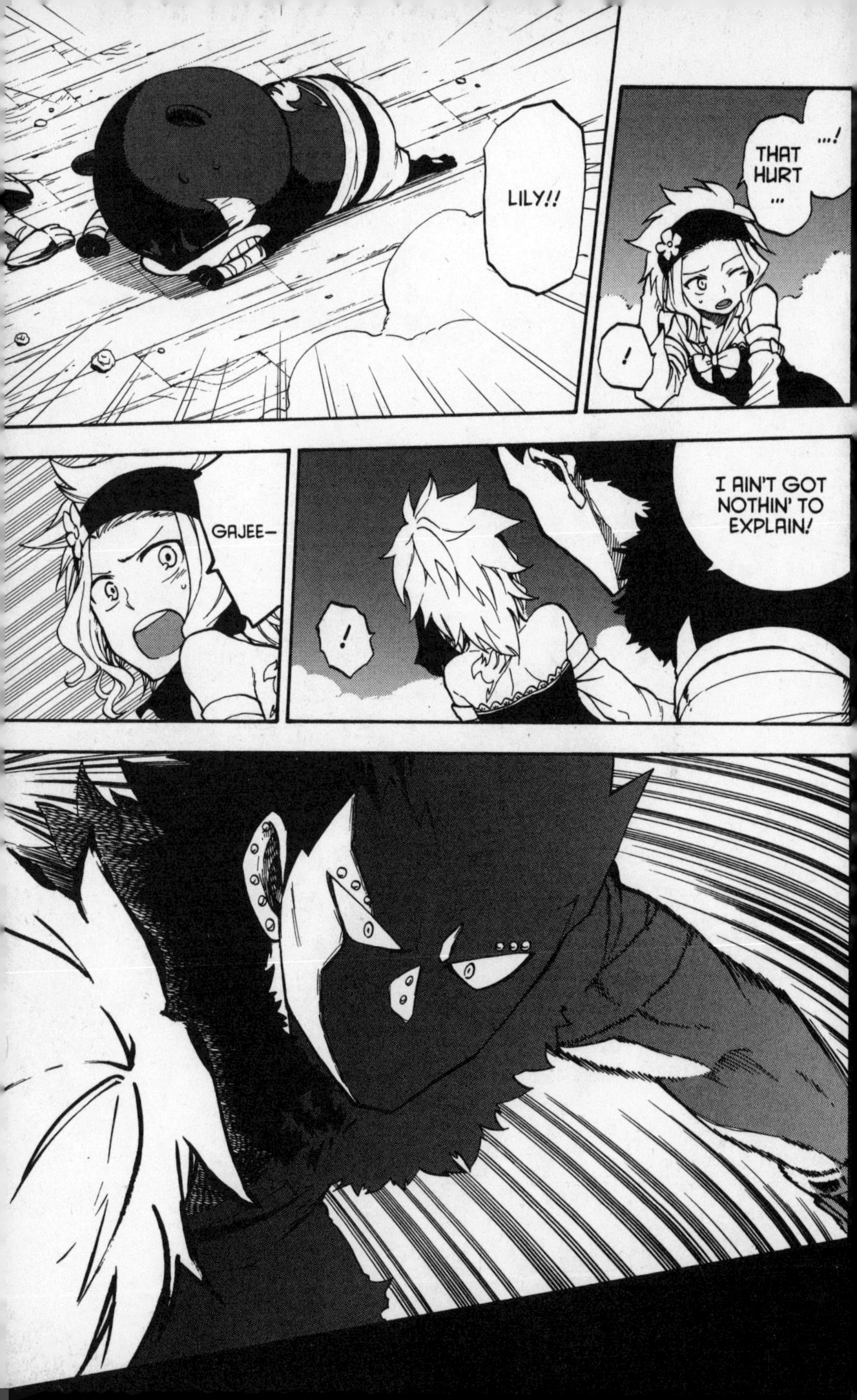
...!
THAT HURT ...
!
LILY!!
I AIN'T GOT NOTHIN' TO EXPLAIN!
!
GAJEE–

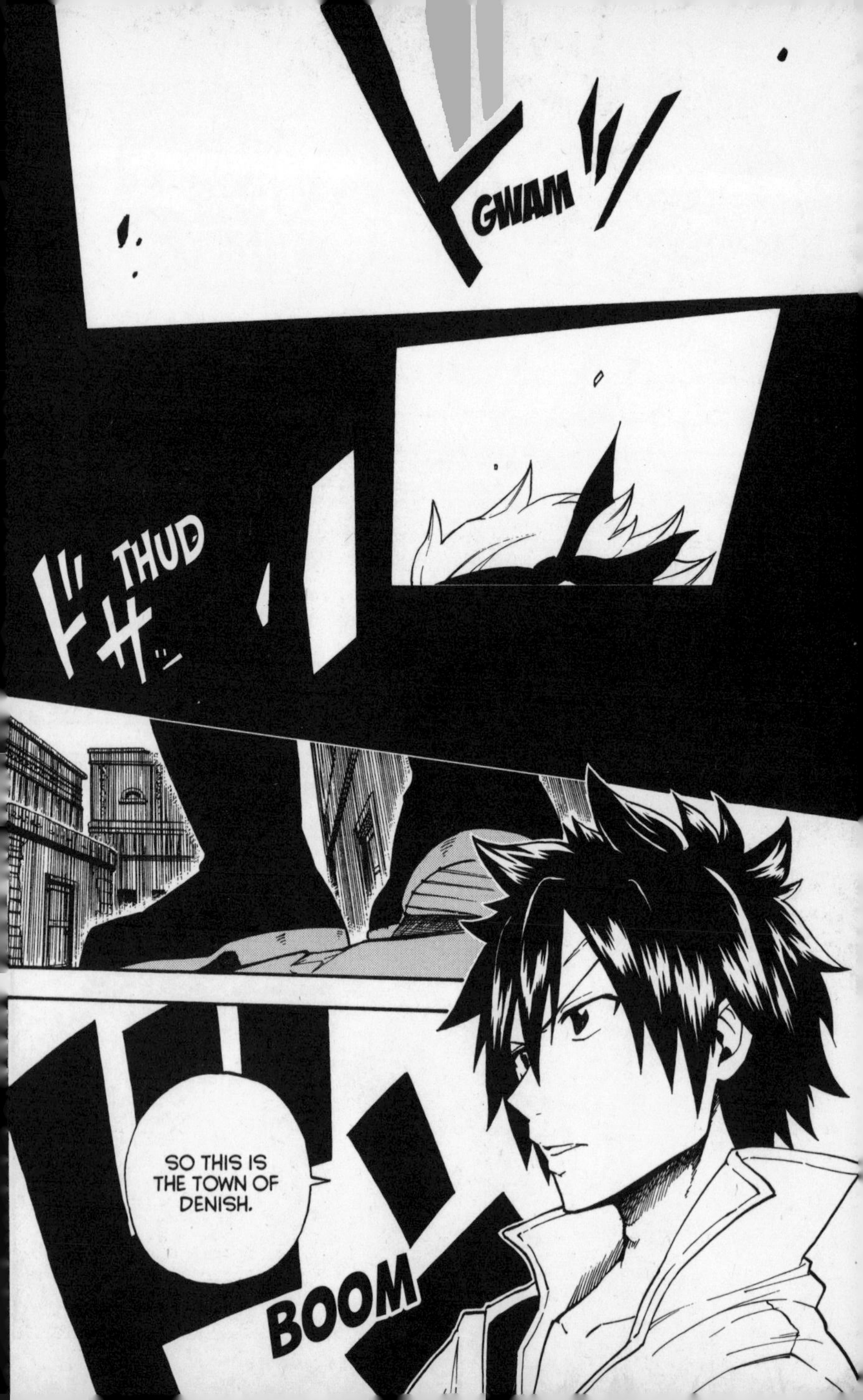
GWAM
THUD
SO THIS IS THE TOWN OF DENISH.
BOOM

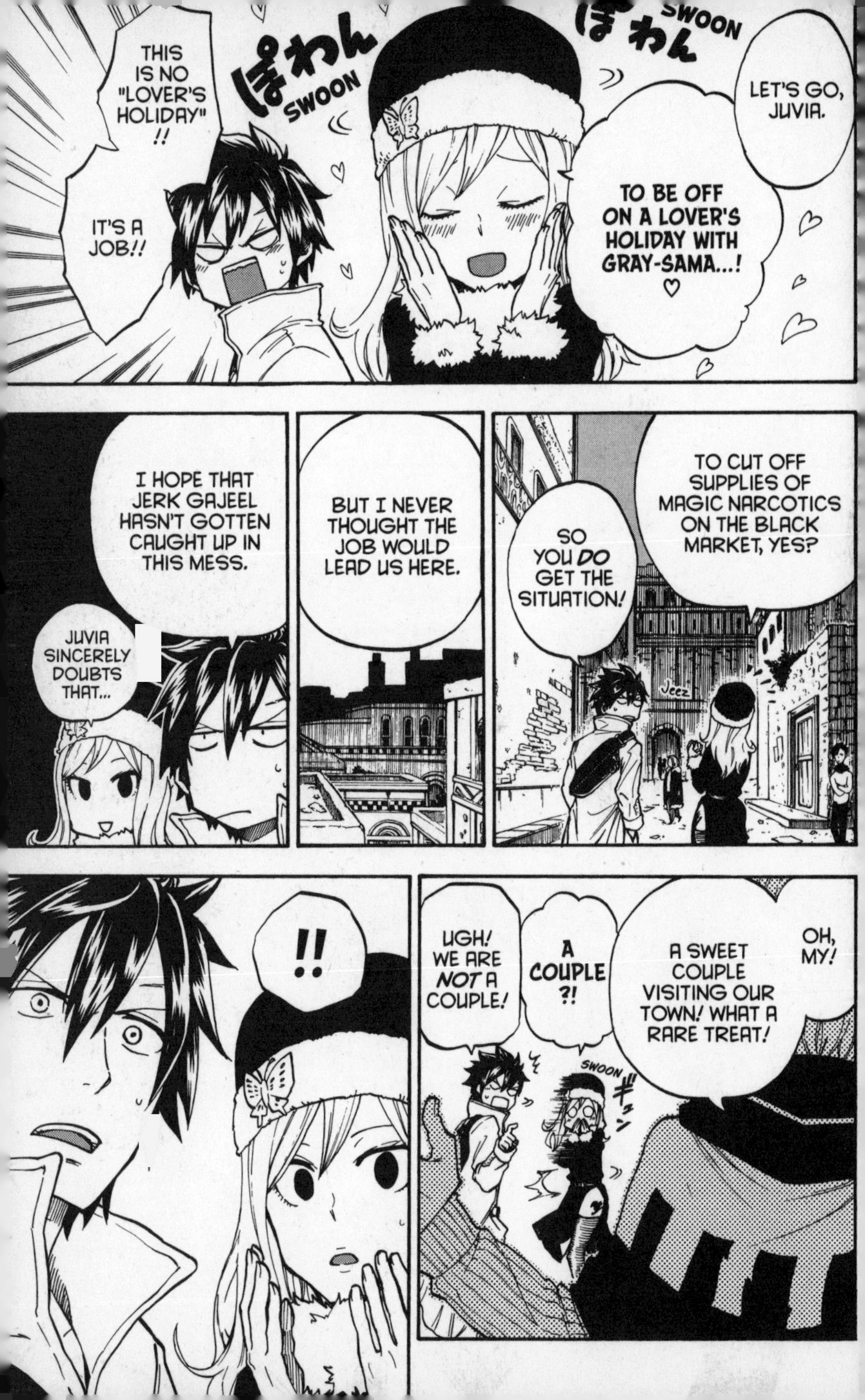
LET'S GO, JUVIA.
TO BE OFF ON A LOVER'S HOLIDAY WITH GRAY-SAMA...! ♡
ぽわん SWOON
ぽわん SWOON
THIS IS NO "LOVER'S HOLIDAY"!!
IT'S A JOB!!
TO CUT OFF SUPPLIES OF MAGIC NARCOTICS ON THE BLACK MARKET, YES?
SO YOU *DO* GET THE SITUATION!
Jeez
BUT I NEVER THOUGHT THE JOB WOULD LEAD US HERE.
I HOPE THAT JERK GAJEEL HASN'T GOTTEN CAUGHT UP IN THIS MESS.
JUVIA SINCERELY DOUBTS THAT...
OH, MY!
A SWEET COUPLE VISITING OUR TOWN! WHAT A RARE TREAT!
A COUPLE?!
UGH! WE ARE *NOT* A COUPLE!
SWOON
!!

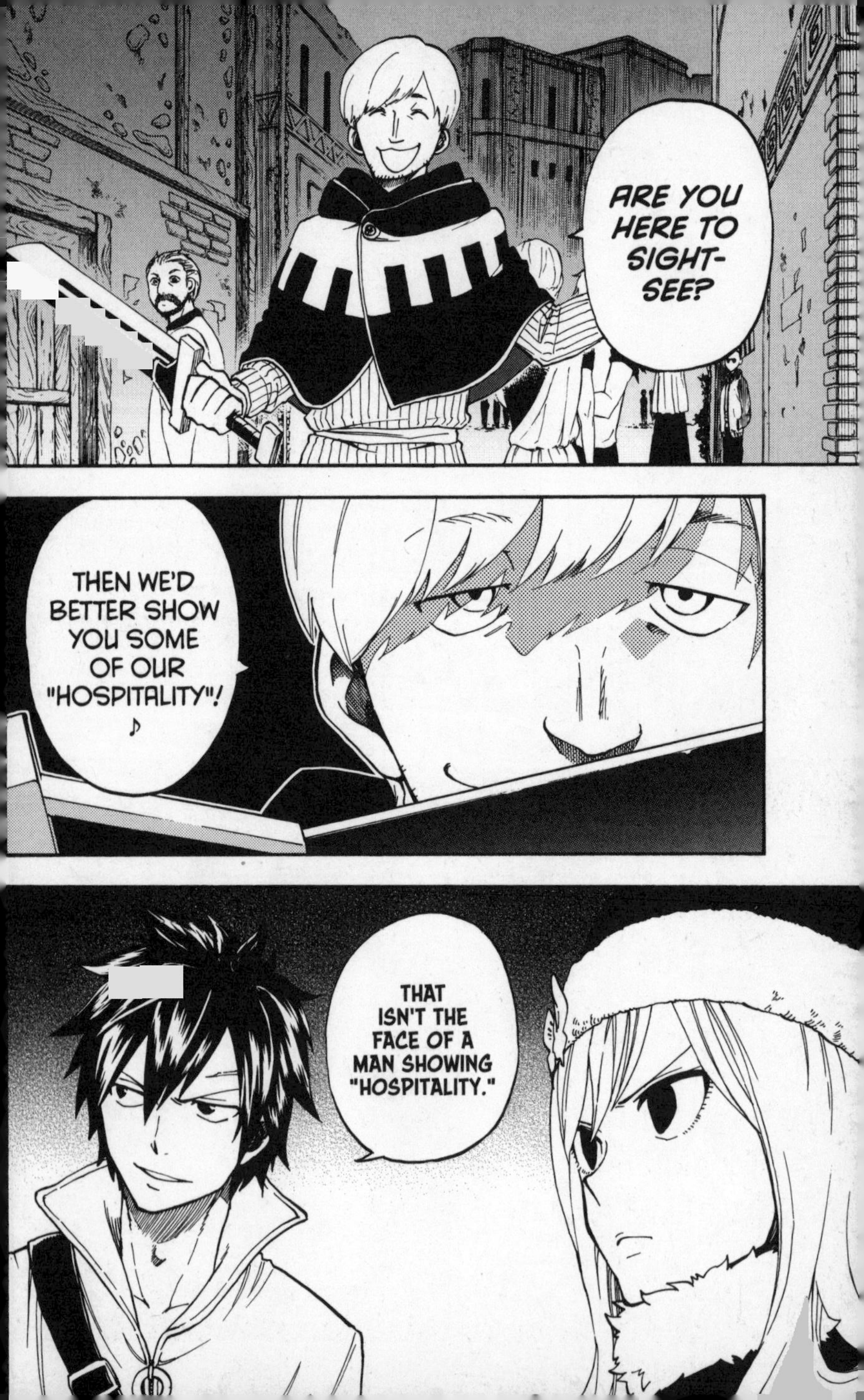
ARE YOU HERE TO SIGHT-SEE?
THEN WE'D BETTER SHOW YOU SOME OF OUR "HOSPITALITY"! ♪
THAT ISN'T THE FACE OF A MAN SHOWING "HOSPITALITY."

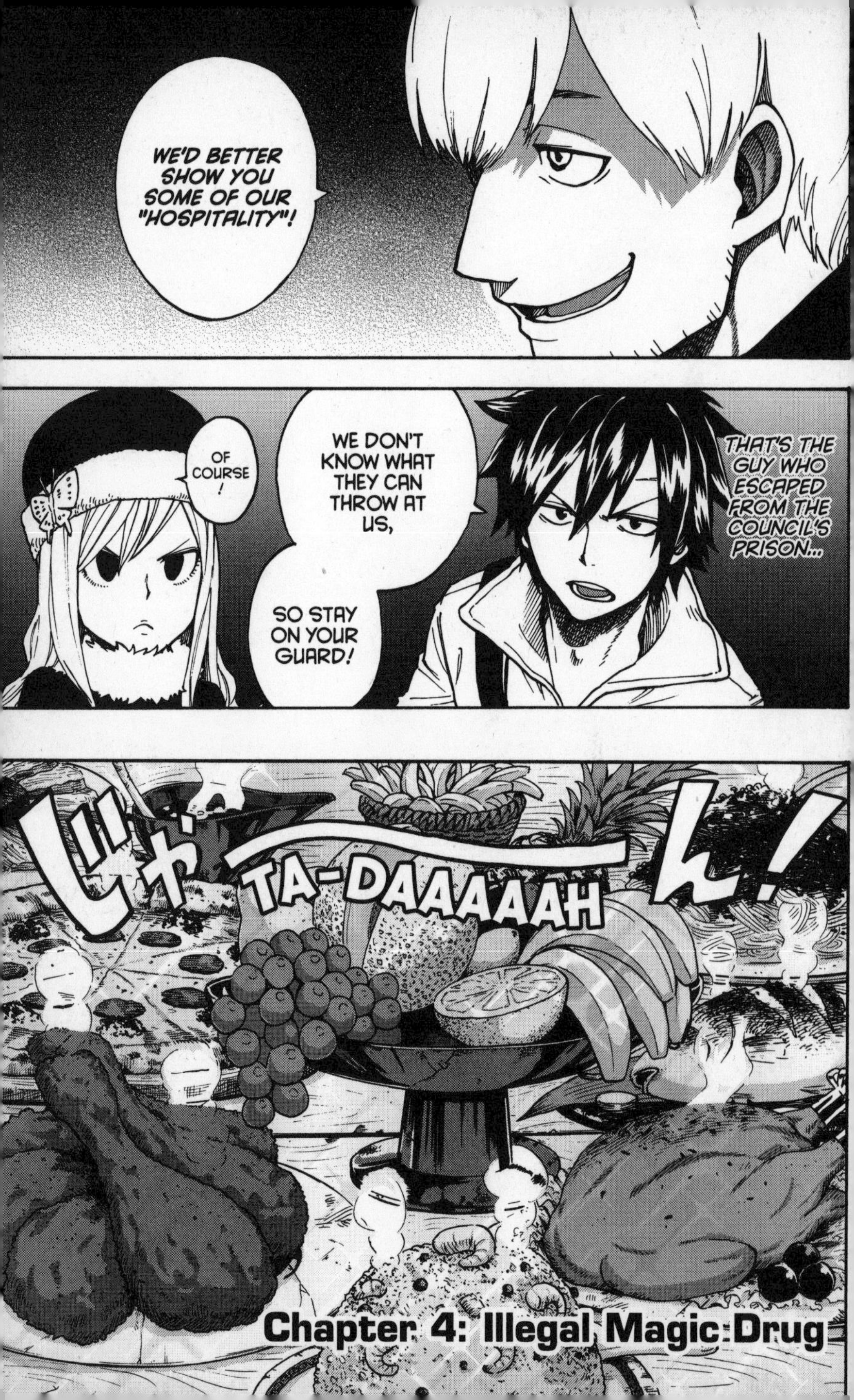
WE'D BETTER SHOW YOU SOME OF OUR "HOSPITALITY"!
THAT'S THE GUY WHO ESCAPED FROM THE COUNCIL'S PRISON...
WE DON'T KNOW WHAT THEY CAN THROW AT US,
SO STAY ON YOUR GUARD!
OF COURSE!
じゃーん!
TA-DAAAAAAH

Chapter 4: Illegal Magic Drug

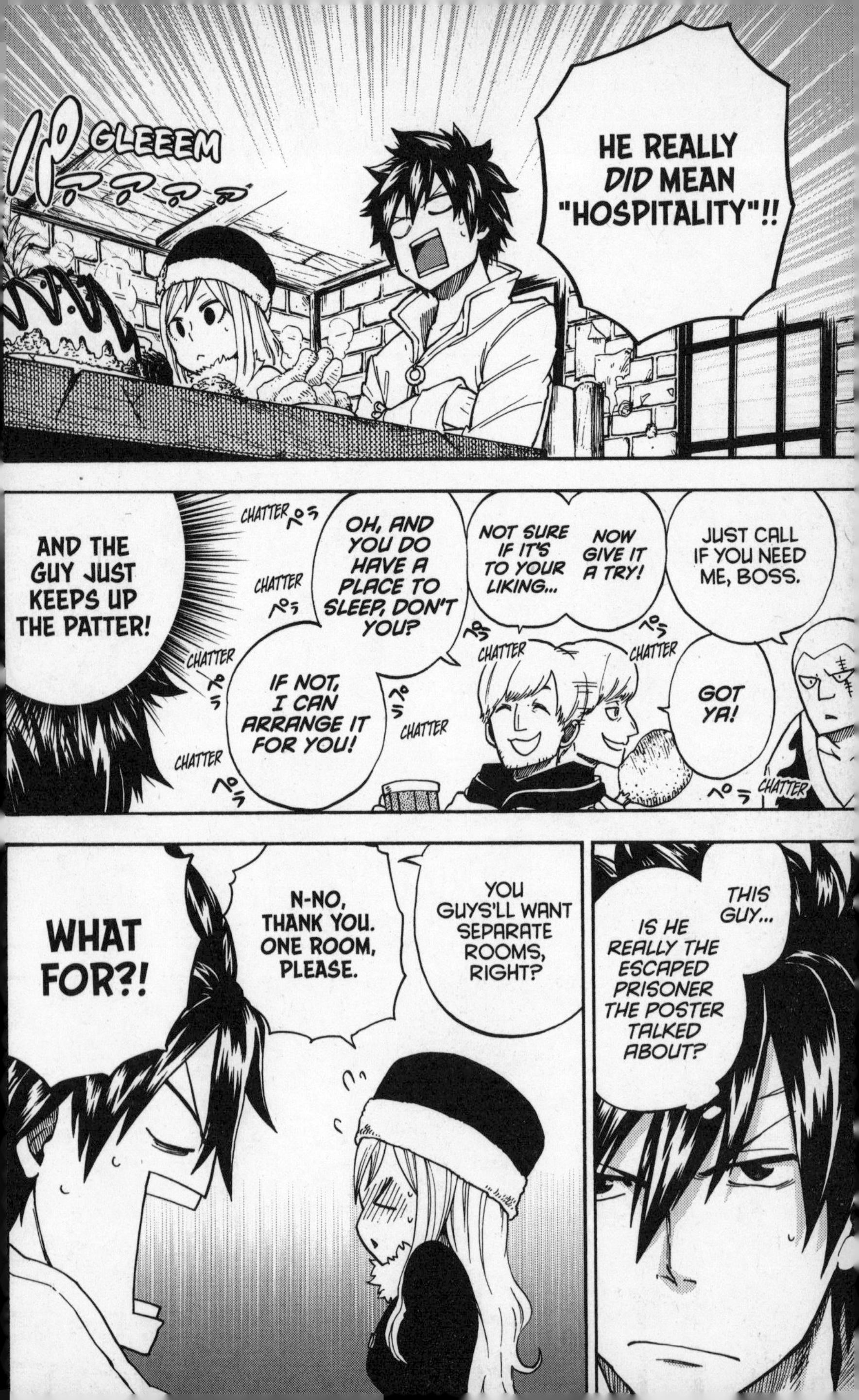
HE REALLY DID MEAN "HOSPITALITY"!!
GLEEEM
JUST CALL IF YOU NEED ME, BOSS.
CHATTER
GOT YA!
CHATTER
CHATTER
NOW GIVE IT A TRY!
NOT SURE IF IT'S TO YOUR LIKING...
CHATTER
CHATTER
OH, AND YOU DO HAVE A PLACE TO SLEEP, DON'T YOU?
CHATTER
IF NOT, I CAN ARRANGE IT FOR YOU!
CHATTER
CHATTER
CHATTER
AND THE GUY JUST KEEPS UP THE PATTER!
THIS GUY...
IS HE REALLY THE ESCAPED PRISONER THE POSTER TALKED ABOUT?
YOU GUYS'LL WANT SEPARATE ROOMS, RIGHT?
N-NO, THANK YOU. ONE ROOM, PLEASE.
WHAT FOR?!

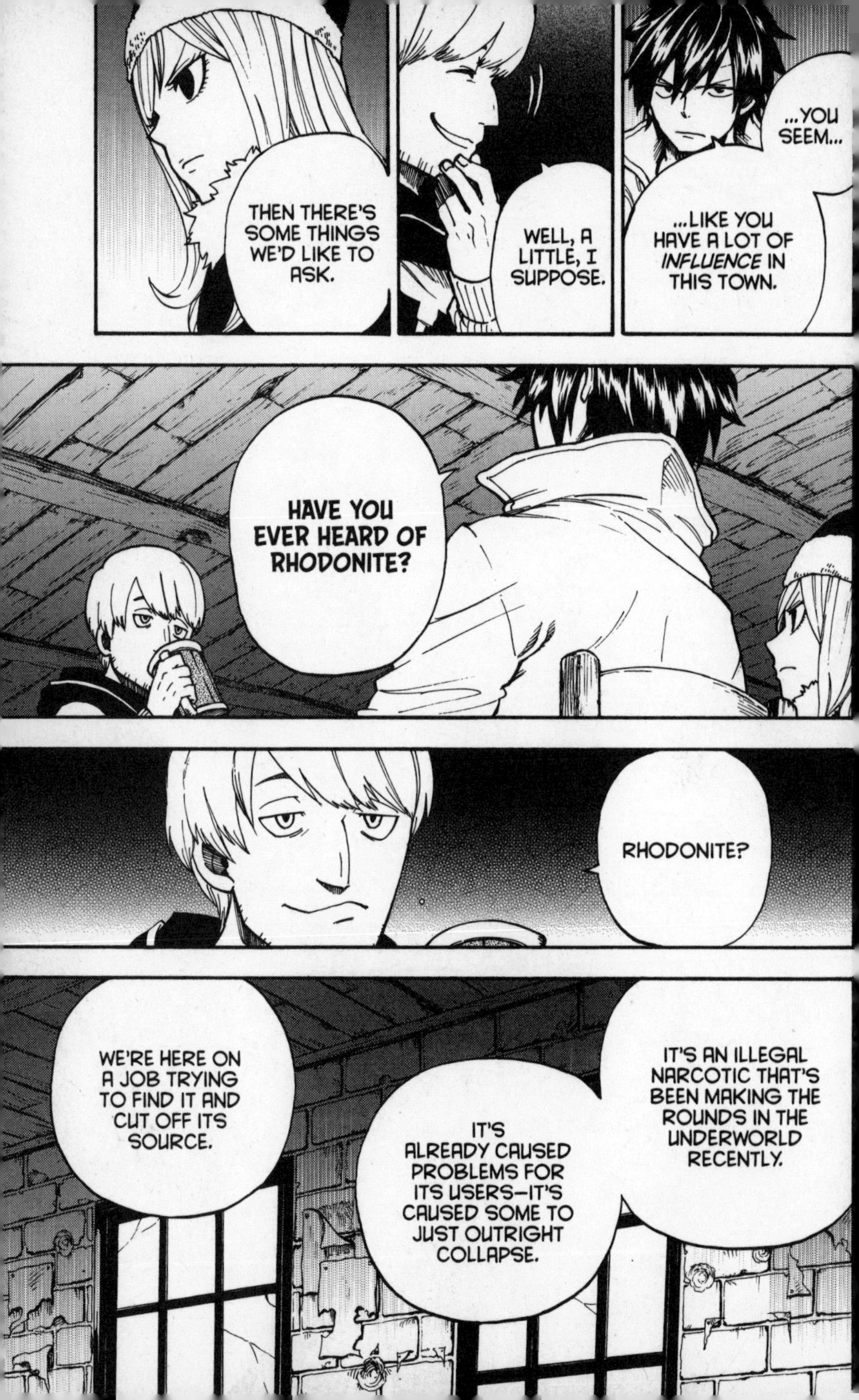
...YOU SEEM...
...LIKE YOU HAVE A LOT OF *INFLUENCE* IN THIS TOWN.
WELL, A LITTLE, I SUPPOSE.
THEN THERE'S SOME THINGS WE'D LIKE TO ASK.
HAVE YOU EVER HEARD OF RHODONITE?
RHODONITE?
IT'S AN ILLEGAL NARCOTIC THAT'S BEEN MAKING THE ROUNDS IN THE UNDERWORLD RECENTLY.
IT'S ALREADY CAUSED PROBLEMS FOR ITS USERS—IT'S CAUSED SOME TO JUST OUTRIGHT COLLAPSE.
WE'RE HERE ON A JOB TRYING TO FIND IT AND CUT OFF ITS SOURCE.

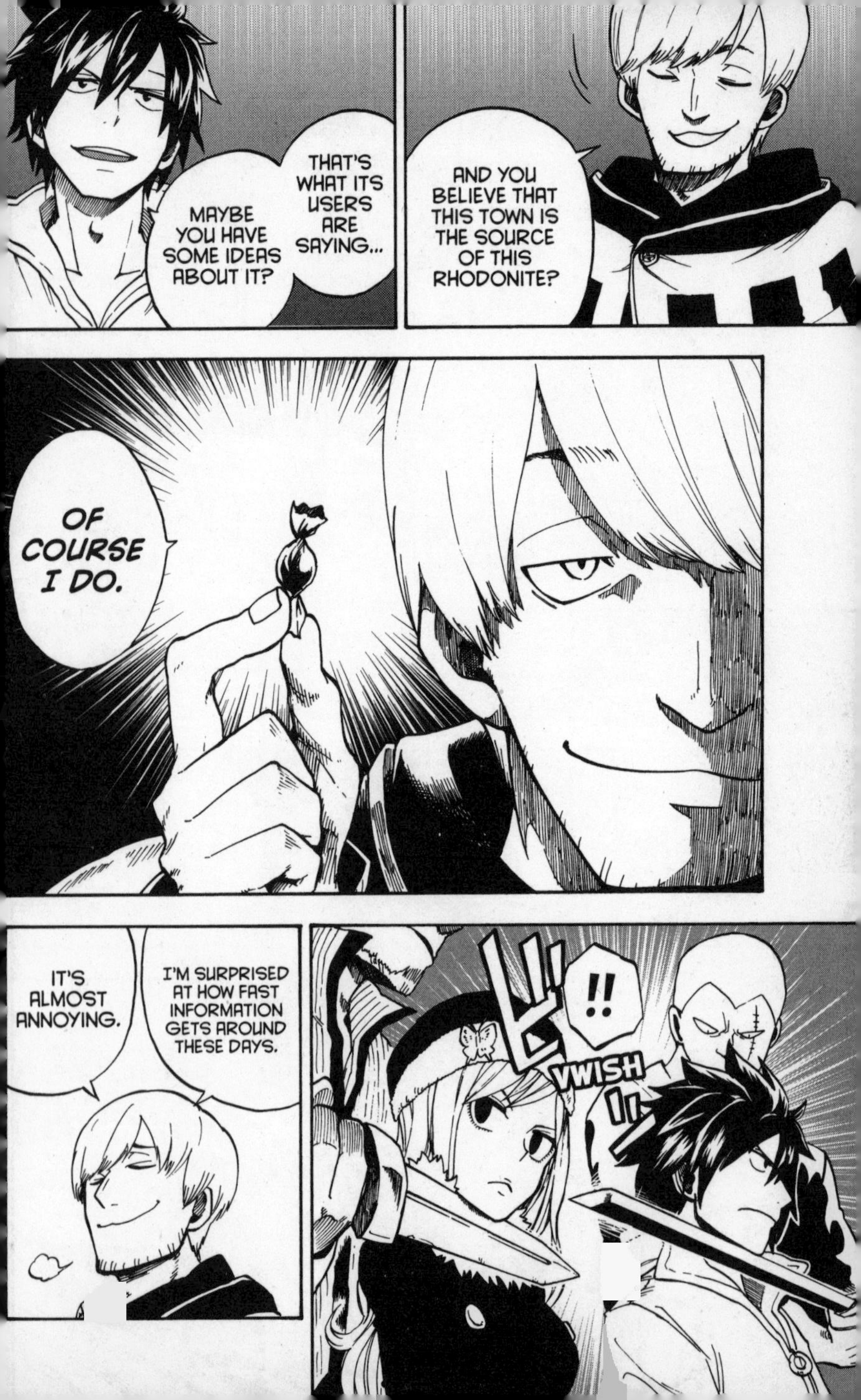
AND YOU BELIEVE THAT THIS TOWN IS THE SOURCE OF THIS RHODONITE?
THAT'S WHAT ITS USERS ARE SAYING...
MAYBE YOU HAVE SOME IDEAS ABOUT IT?
OF COURSE I DO.
!!
VWISH
I'M SURPRISED AT HOW FAST INFORMATION GETS AROUND THESE DAYS.
IT'S ALMOST ANNOYING.

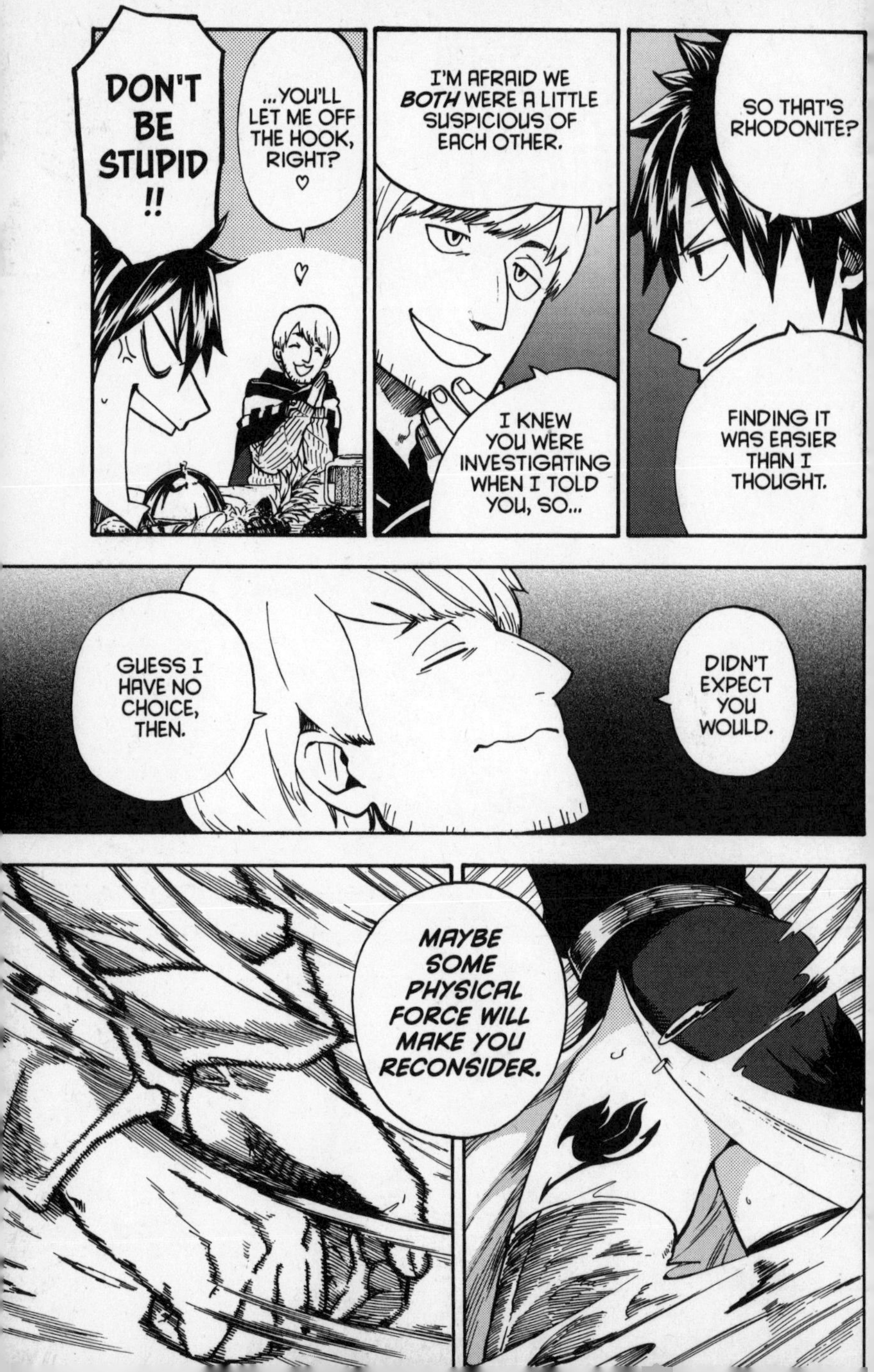
SO THAT'S RHODONITE?
FINDING IT WAS EASIER THAN I THOUGHT.
I'M AFRAID WE *BOTH* WERE A LITTLE SUSPICIOUS OF EACH OTHER.
I KNEW YOU WERE INVESTIGATING WHEN I TOLD YOU, SO...
...YOU'LL LET ME OFF THE HOOK, RIGHT? ♡
DON'T BE STUPID!!
DIDN'T EXPECT YOU WOULD.
GUESS I HAVE NO CHOICE, THEN.
MAYBE SOME PHYSICAL FORCE WILL MAKE YOU RECONSIDER.

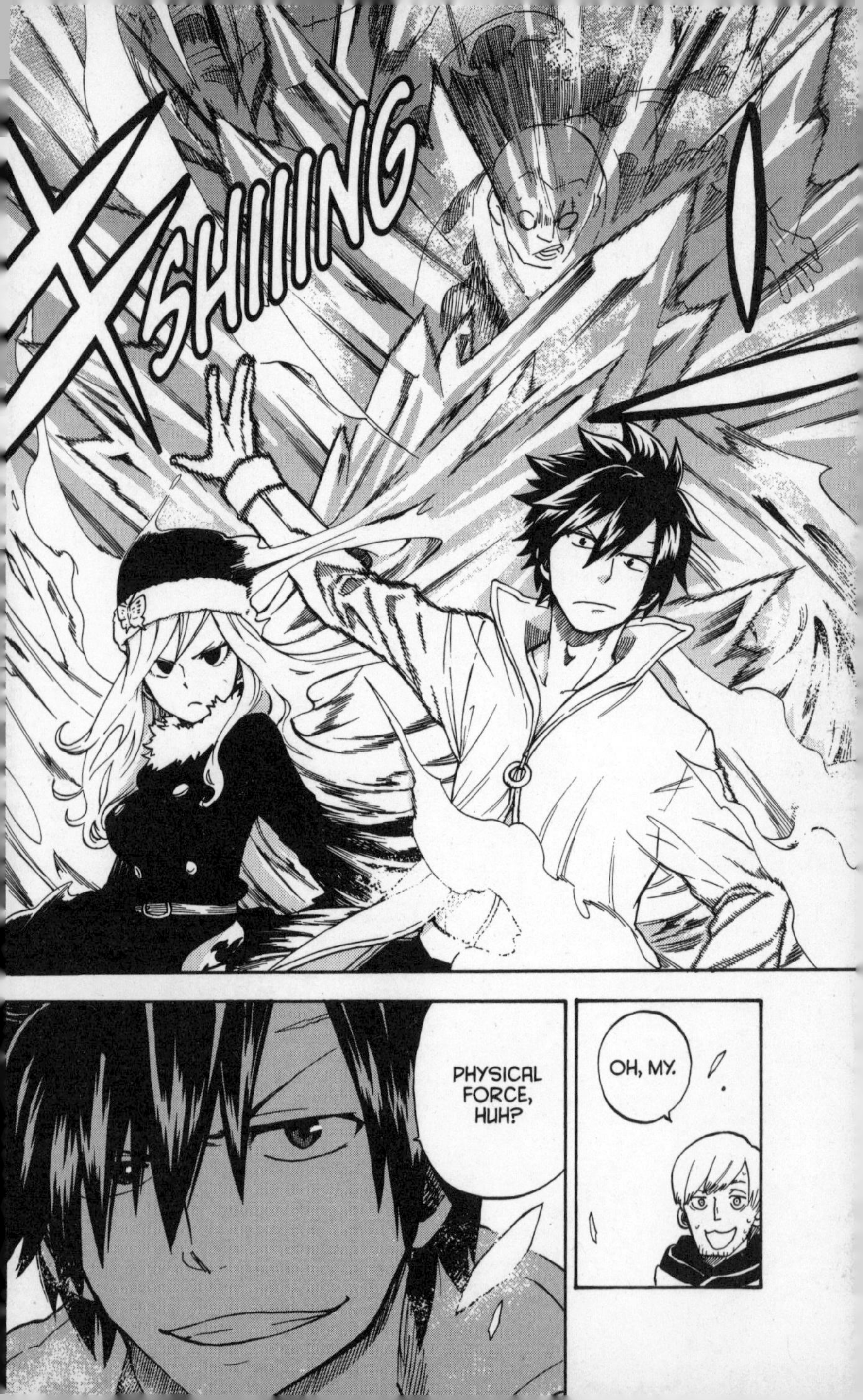
SHIIING
OH, MY.
PHYSICAL FORCE, HUH?

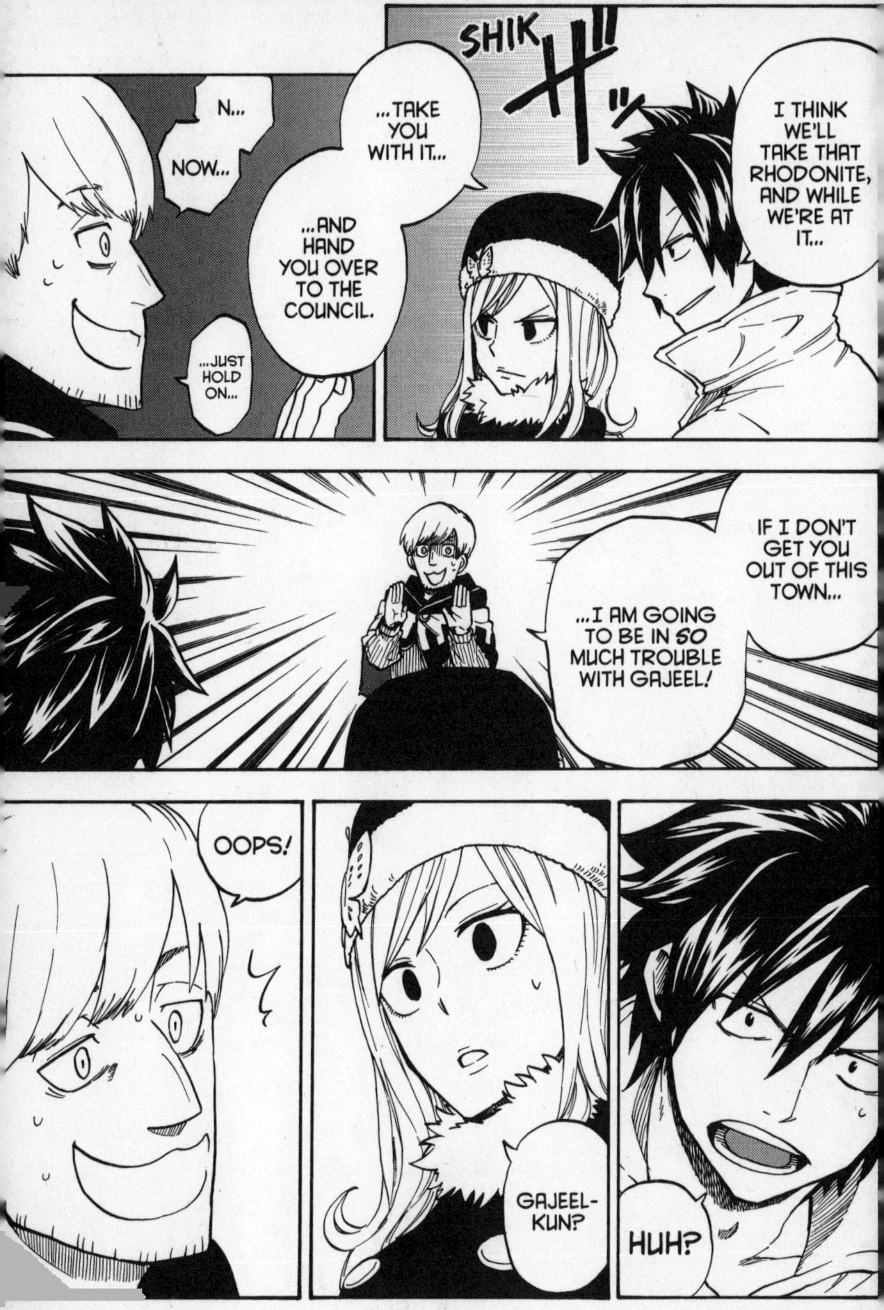
SHIKH!!
I THINK WE'LL TAKE THAT RHODONITE, AND WHILE WE'RE AT IT...
...TAKE YOU WITH IT...
...AND HAND YOU OVER TO THE COUNCIL.
N... NOW...
...JUST HOLD ON...
IF I DON'T GET YOU OUT OF THIS TOWN...
...I AM GOING TO BE IN SO MUCH TROUBLE WITH GAJEEL!
HUH?
GAJEEL-KUN?
OOPS!

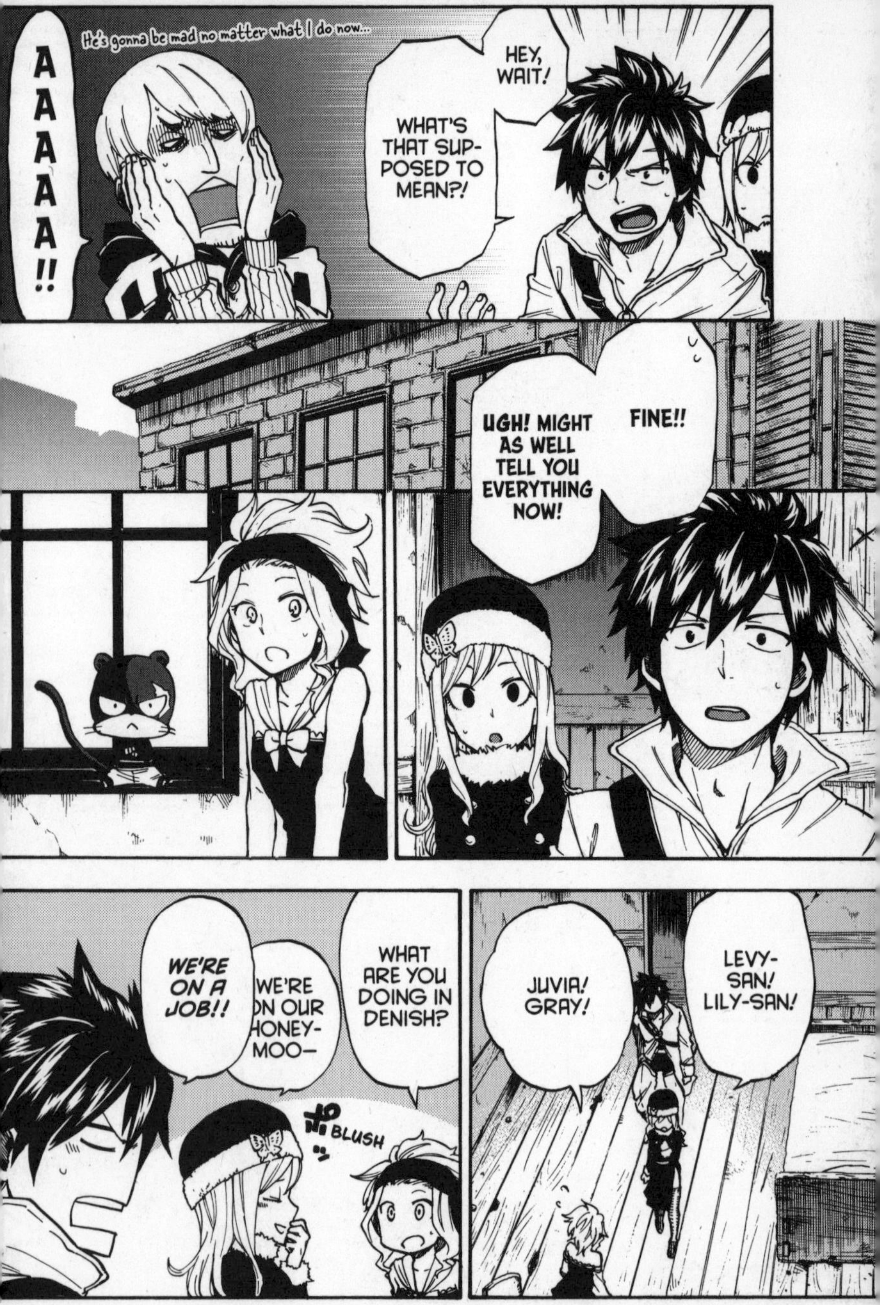
HEY, WAIT!
WHAT'S THAT SUP-POSED TO MEAN?!
He's gonna be mad no matter what I do now...
AAAAA!!
FINE!!
UGH! MIGHT AS WELL TELL YOU EVERYTHING NOW!
LEVY-SAN! LILY-SAN!
JUVIA! GRAY!
WHAT ARE YOU DOING IN DENISH?
WE'RE ON OUR HONEY-MOO—
WE'RE ON A JOB!!
BLUSH

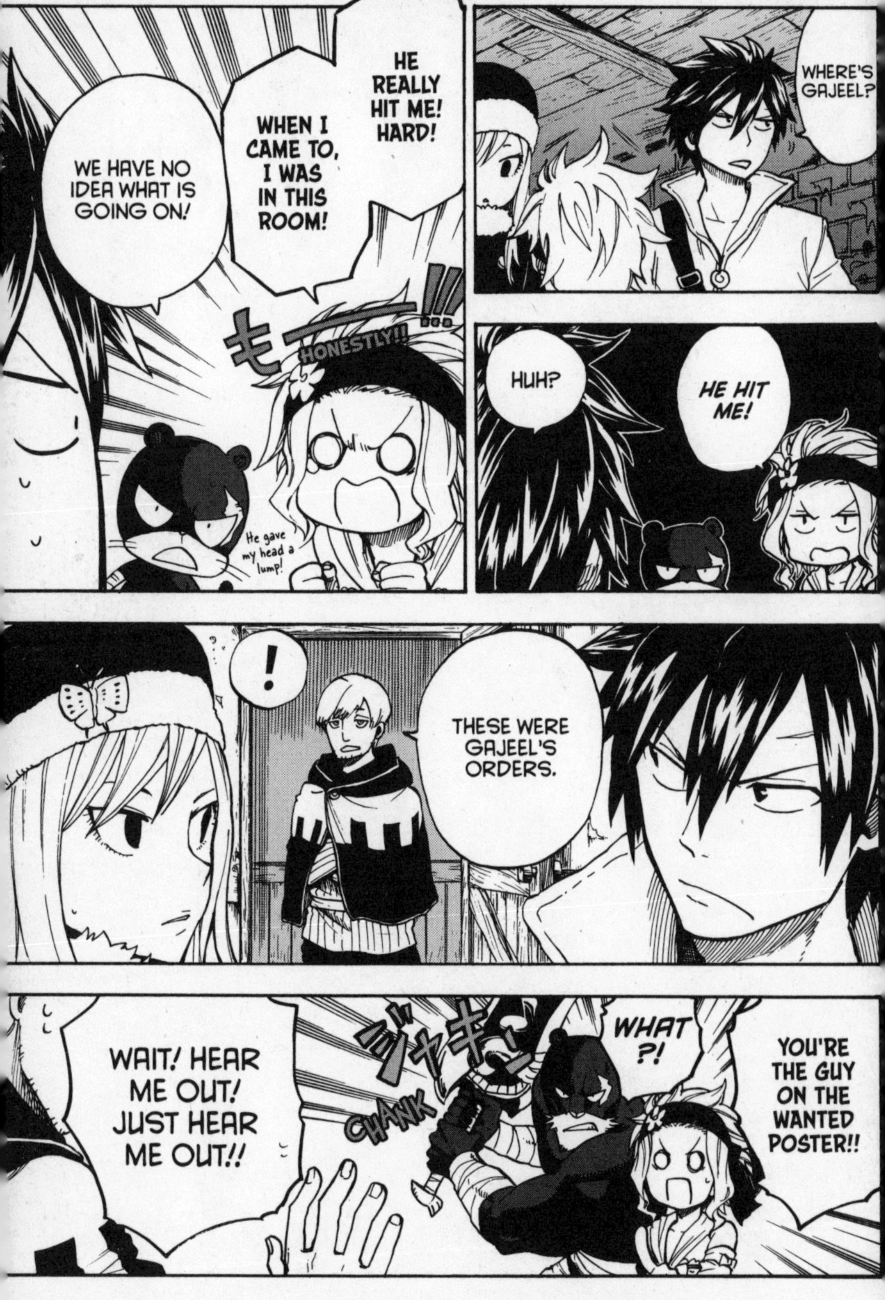
WHERE'S GAJEEL?
HE HIT ME!
HUH?
HE REALLY HIT ME! HARD!
WHEN I CAME TO, I WAS IN THIS ROOM!
WE HAVE NO IDEA WHAT IS GOING ON!
HONESTLY!!
He gave my head a lump!
THESE WERE GAJEEL'S ORDERS.
!
YOU'RE THE GUY ON THE WANTED POSTER!!
WHAT?!
CHANK
WAIT! HEAR ME OUT! JUST HEAR ME OUT!!

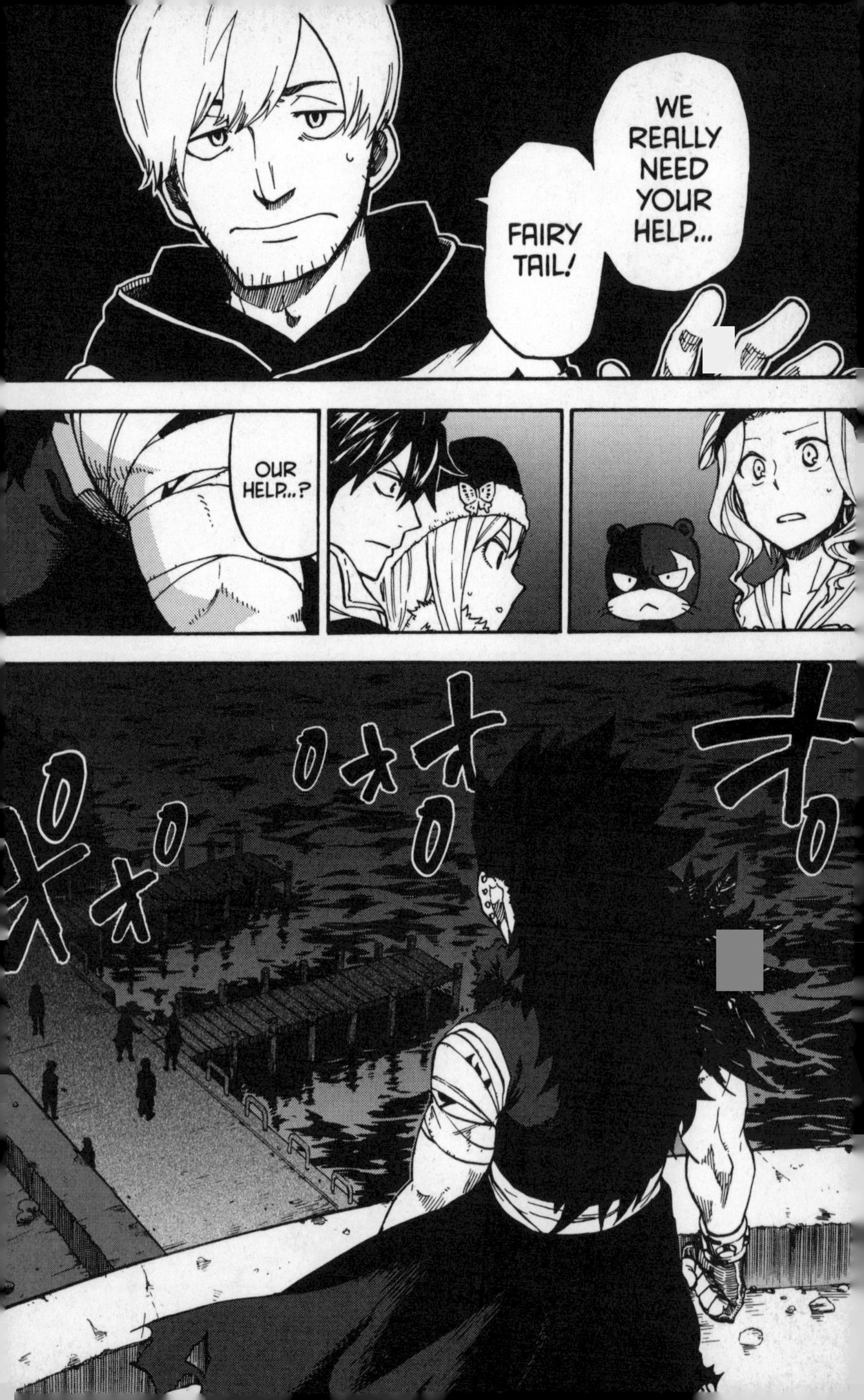
WE REALLY NEED YOUR HELP...
FAIRY TAIL!
OUR HELP...?

Chapter 5: Road Knight

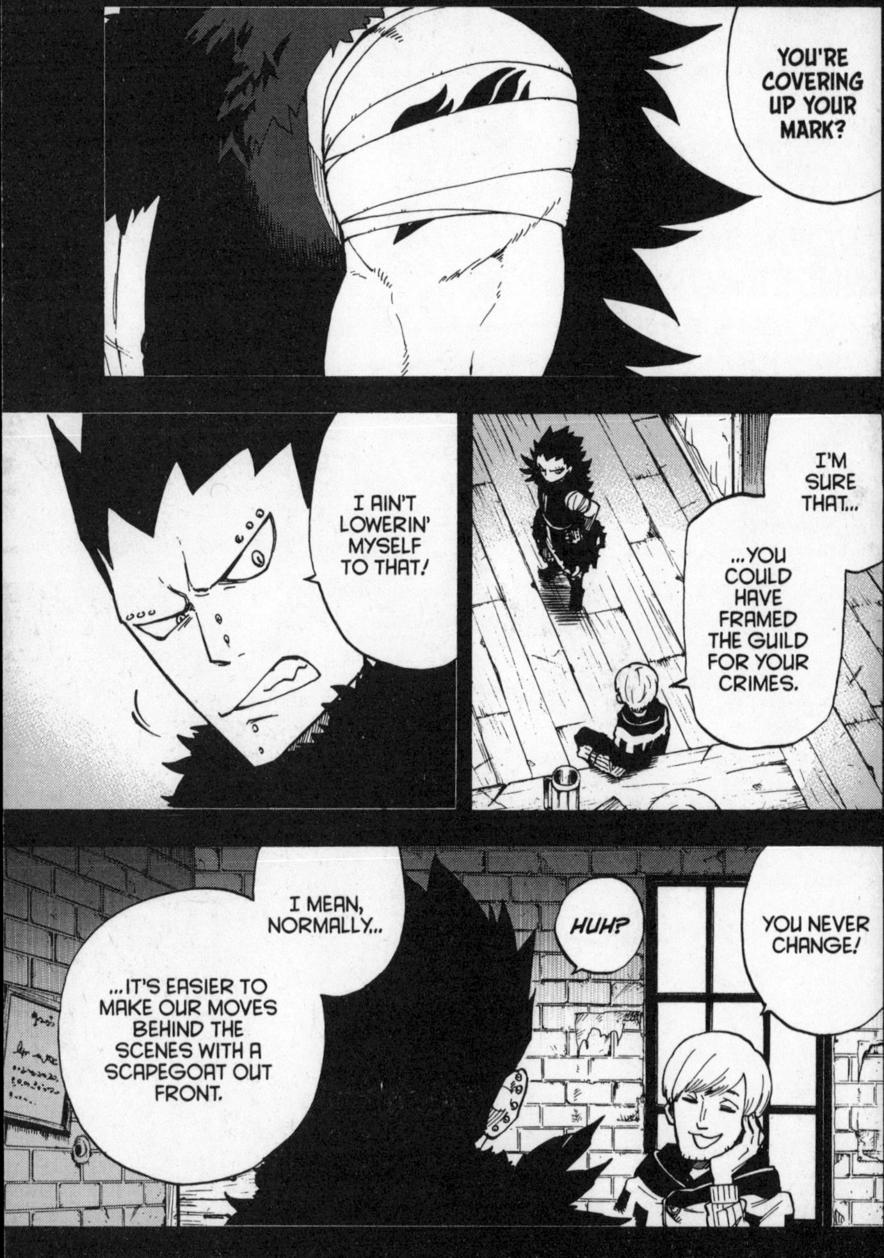
YOU'RE COVERING UP YOUR MARK?
I'M SURE THAT...
...YOU COULD HAVE FRAMED THE GUILD FOR YOUR CRIMES.
I AIN'T LOWERIN' MYSELF TO THAT!
YOU NEVER CHANGE!
HUH?
I MEAN, NORMALLY...
...IT'S EASIER TO MAKE OUR MOVES BEHIND THE SCENES WITH A SCAPEGOAT OUT FRONT.

BUT YOU ALWAYS CHARGE HEAD-ON...
...TRYING TO RUN DOWN THOSE UNDERWORLD ROADS ON YOUR OWN.
POW

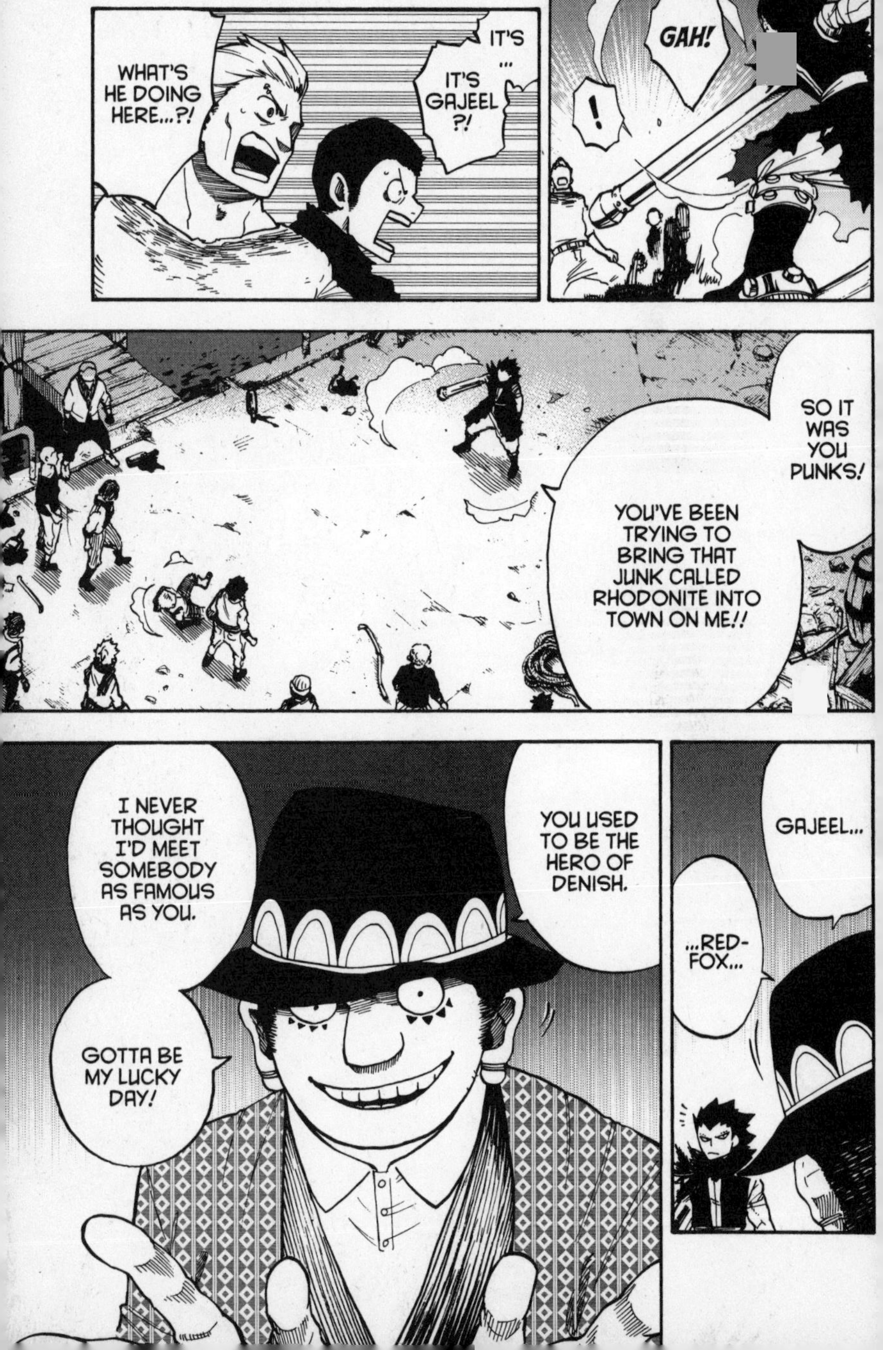
GAH!
!
IT'S ... IT'S GAJEEL ?!
WHAT'S HE DOING HERE...?!
SO IT WAS YOU PUNKS!
YOU'VE BEEN TRYING TO BRING THAT JUNK CALLED RHODONITE INTO TOWN ON ME!!
GAJEEL...
...RED-FOX...
YOU USED TO BE THE HERO OF DENISH.
I NEVER THOUGHT I'D MEET SOMEBODY AS FAMOUS AS YOU.
GOTTA BE MY LUCKY DAY!

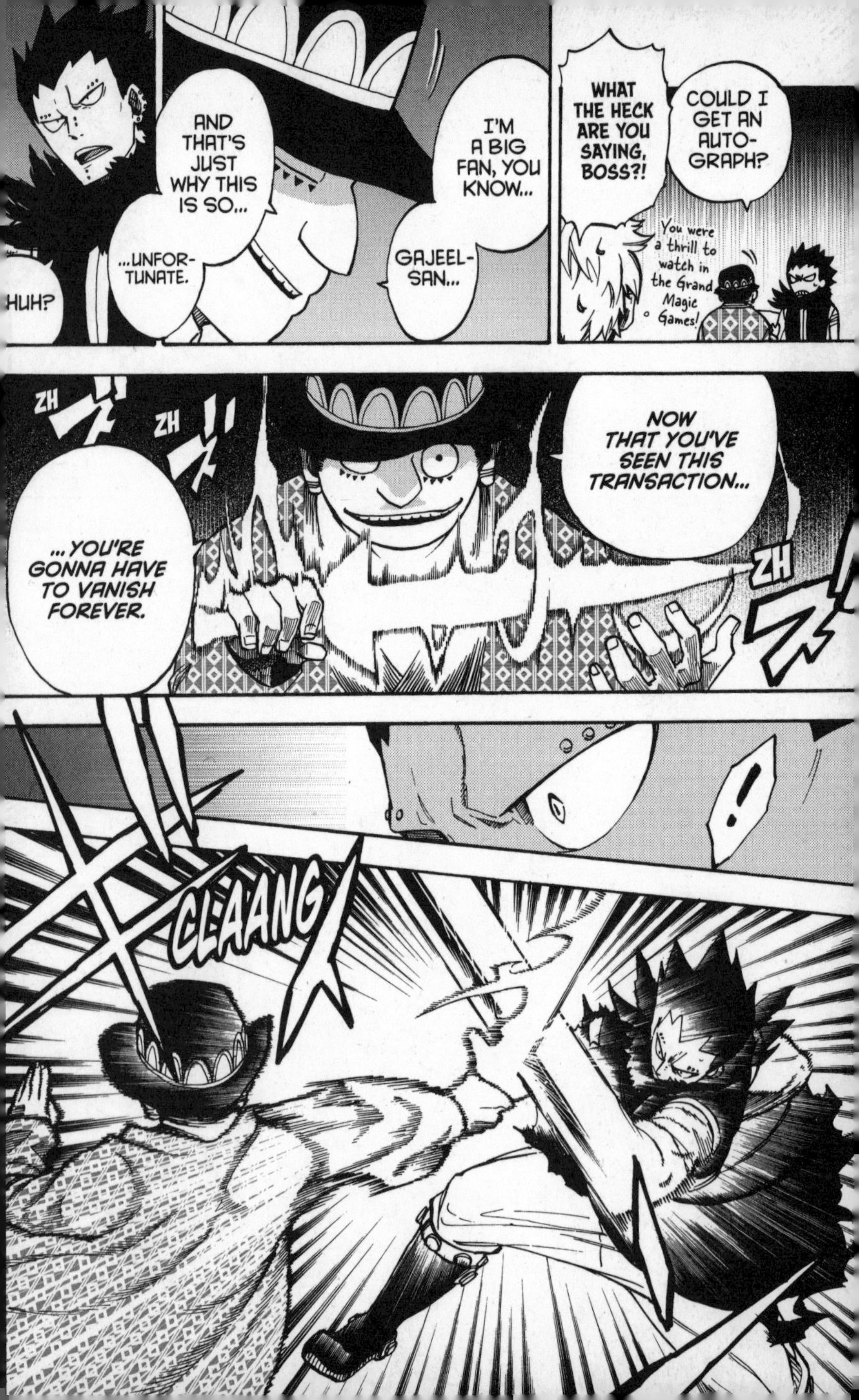
COULD I GET AN AUTO-GRAPH?
WHAT THE HECK ARE YOU SAYING, BOSS?!
You were a thrill to watch in the Grand Magic Games!
I'M A BIG FAN, YOU KNOW...
GAJEEL-SAN...
AND THAT'S JUST WHY THIS IS SO...
...UNFOR-TUNATE.
HUH?
NOW THAT YOU'VE SEEN THIS TRANSACTION...
ZH
ZH
ZH
...YOU'RE GONNA HAVE TO VANISH FOREVER.
!
CLAANG

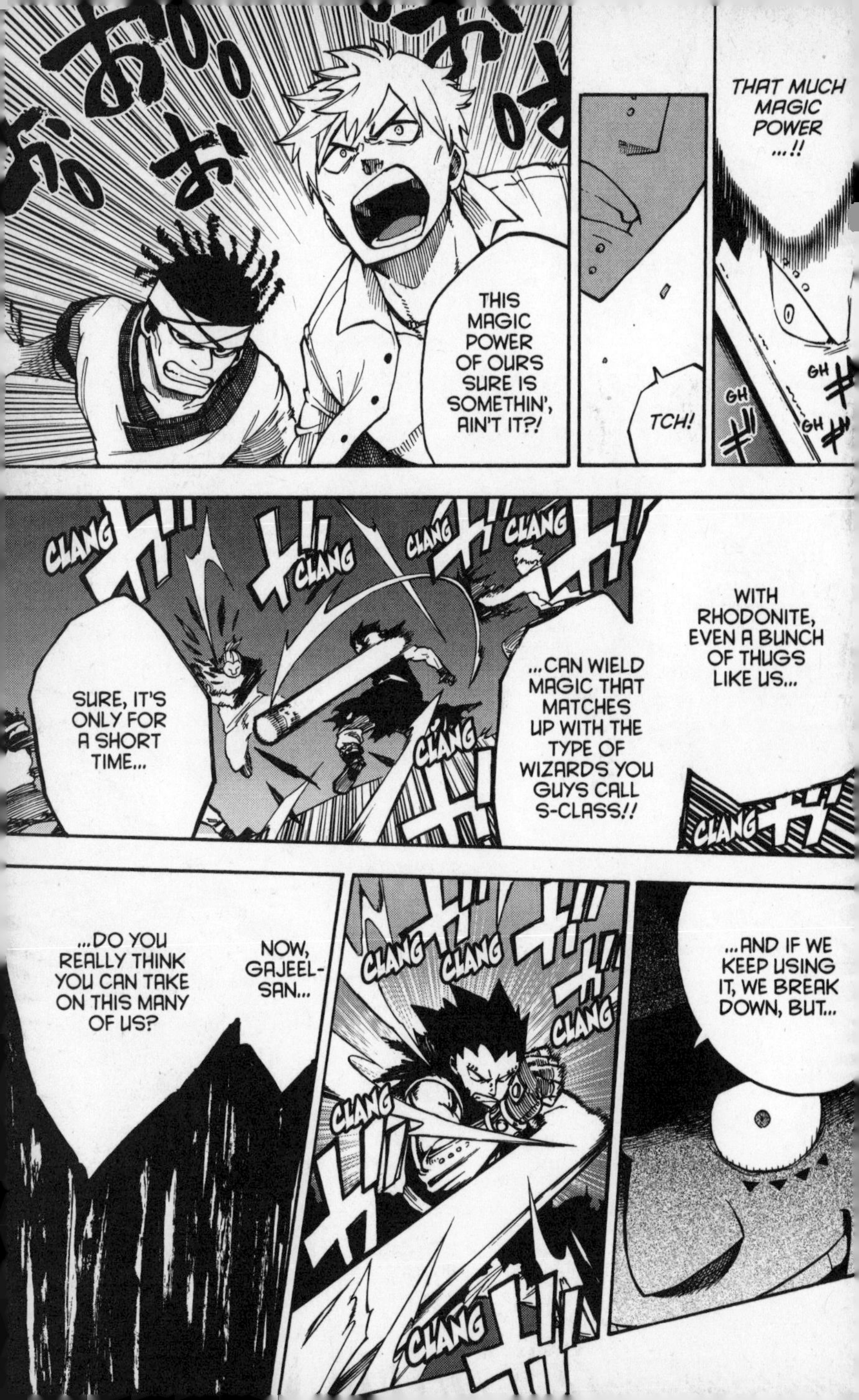
THAT MUCH MAGIC POWER ...!!
GH GH GH
TCH!
THIS MAGIC POWER OF OURS SURE IS SOMETHIN', AIN'T IT?!
WITH RHODONITE, EVEN A BUNCH OF THUGS LIKE US...
...CAN WIELD MAGIC THAT MATCHES UP WITH THE TYPE OF WIZARDS YOU GUYS CALL S-CLASS!!
SURE, IT'S ONLY FOR A SHORT TIME...
CLANG CLANG CLANG CLANG CLANG CLANG
...AND IF WE KEEP USING IT, WE BREAK DOWN, BUT...
CLANG CLANG CLANG CLANG CLANG
NOW, GAJEEL-SAN...
...DO YOU REALLY THINK YOU CAN TAKE ON THIS MANY OF US?

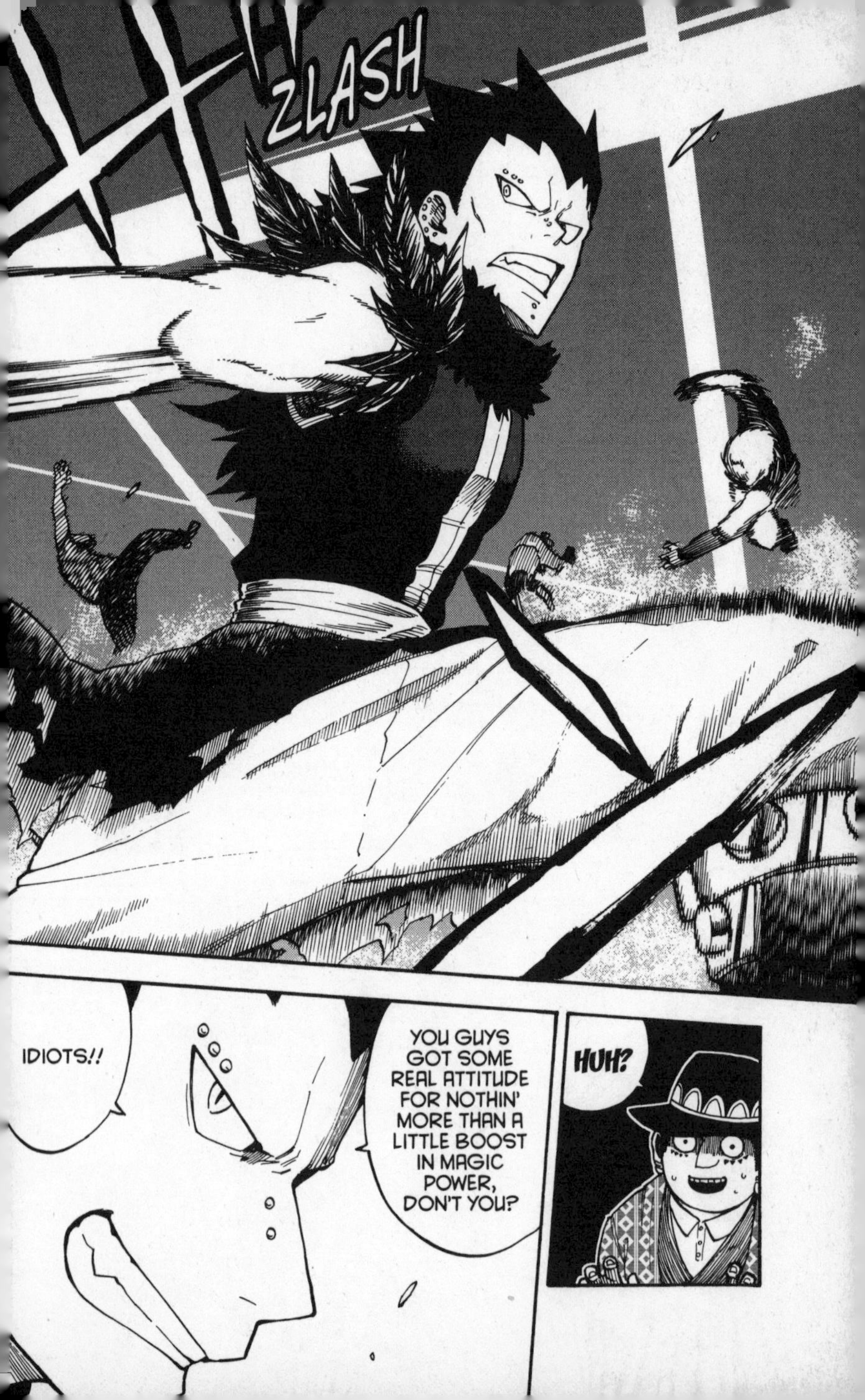
ZLASH
HUH?
YOU GUYS GOT SOME REAL ATTITUDE FOR NOTHIN' MORE THAN A LITTLE BOOST IN MAGIC POWER, DON'T YOU?
IDIOTS!!

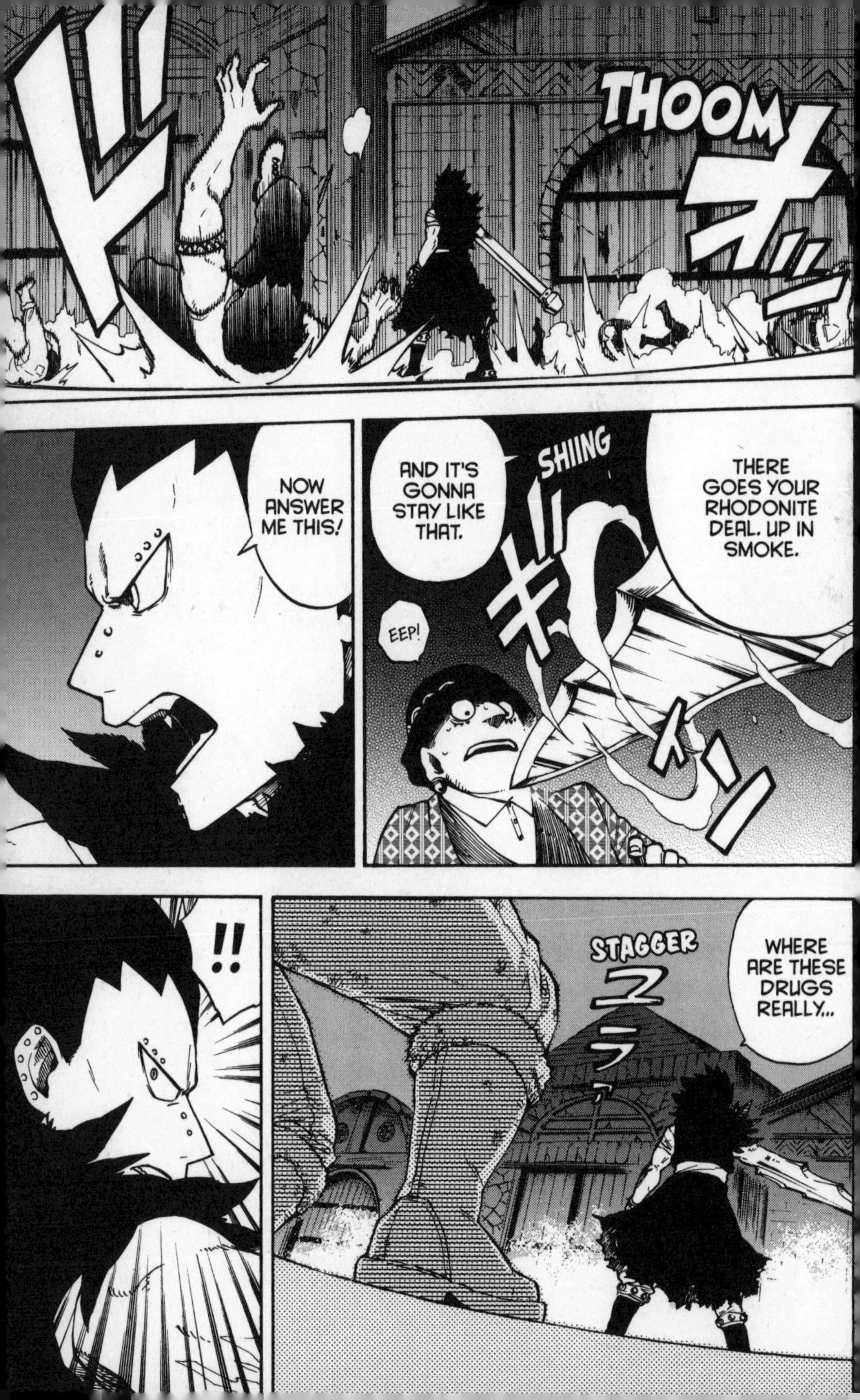
THOOM
THERE GOES YOUR RHODONITE DEAL. UP IN SMOKE.
SHIING
AND IT'S GONNA STAY LIKE THAT.
EEP!
NOW ANSWER ME THIS!
WHERE ARE THESE DRUGS REALLY...
STAGGER
!!

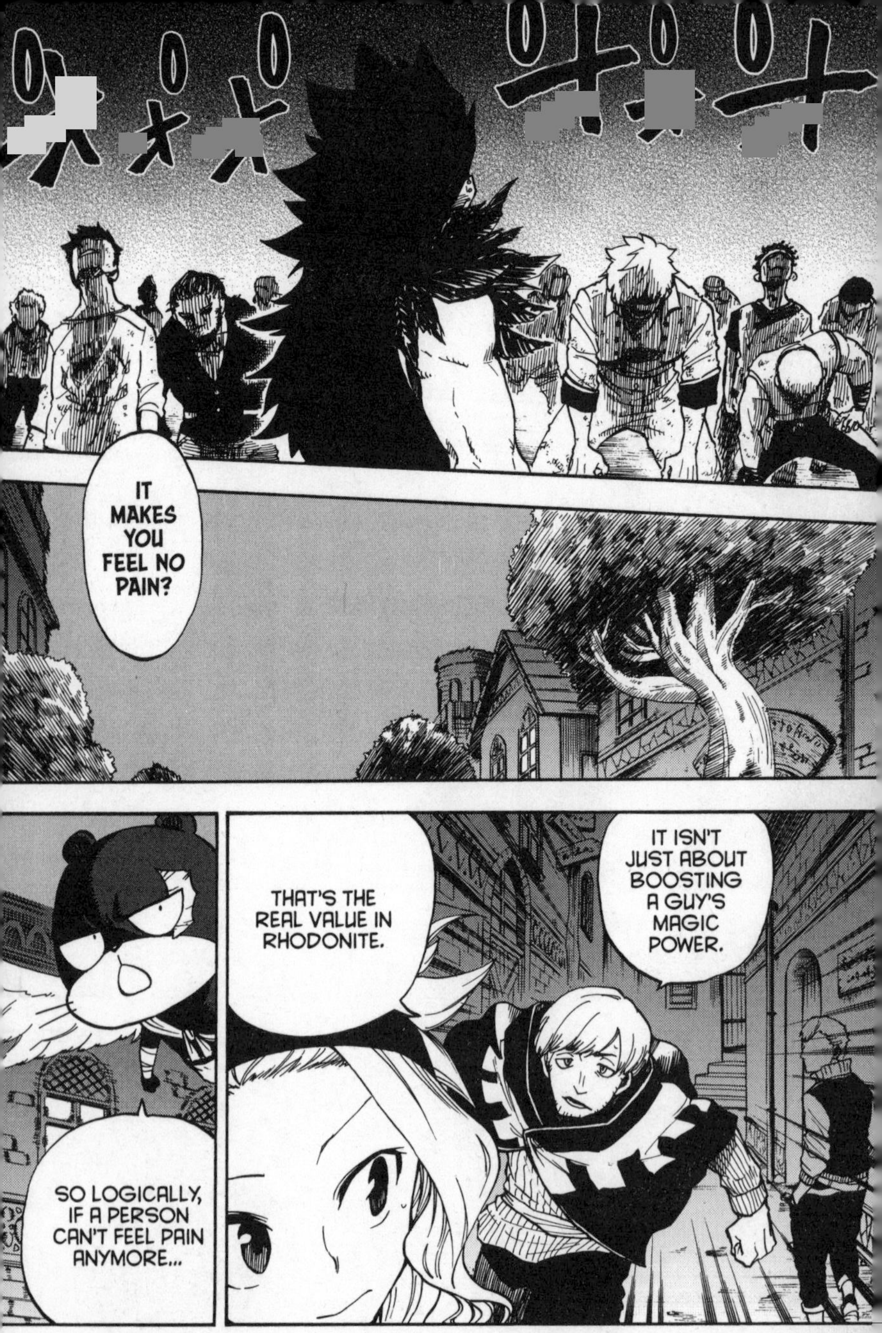
IT MAKES YOU FEEL NO PAIN?
IT ISN'T JUST ABOUT BOOSTING A GUY'S MAGIC POWER.
THAT'S THE REAL VALUE IN RHODONITE.
SO LOGICALLY, IF A PERSON CAN'T FEEL PAIN ANYMORE...

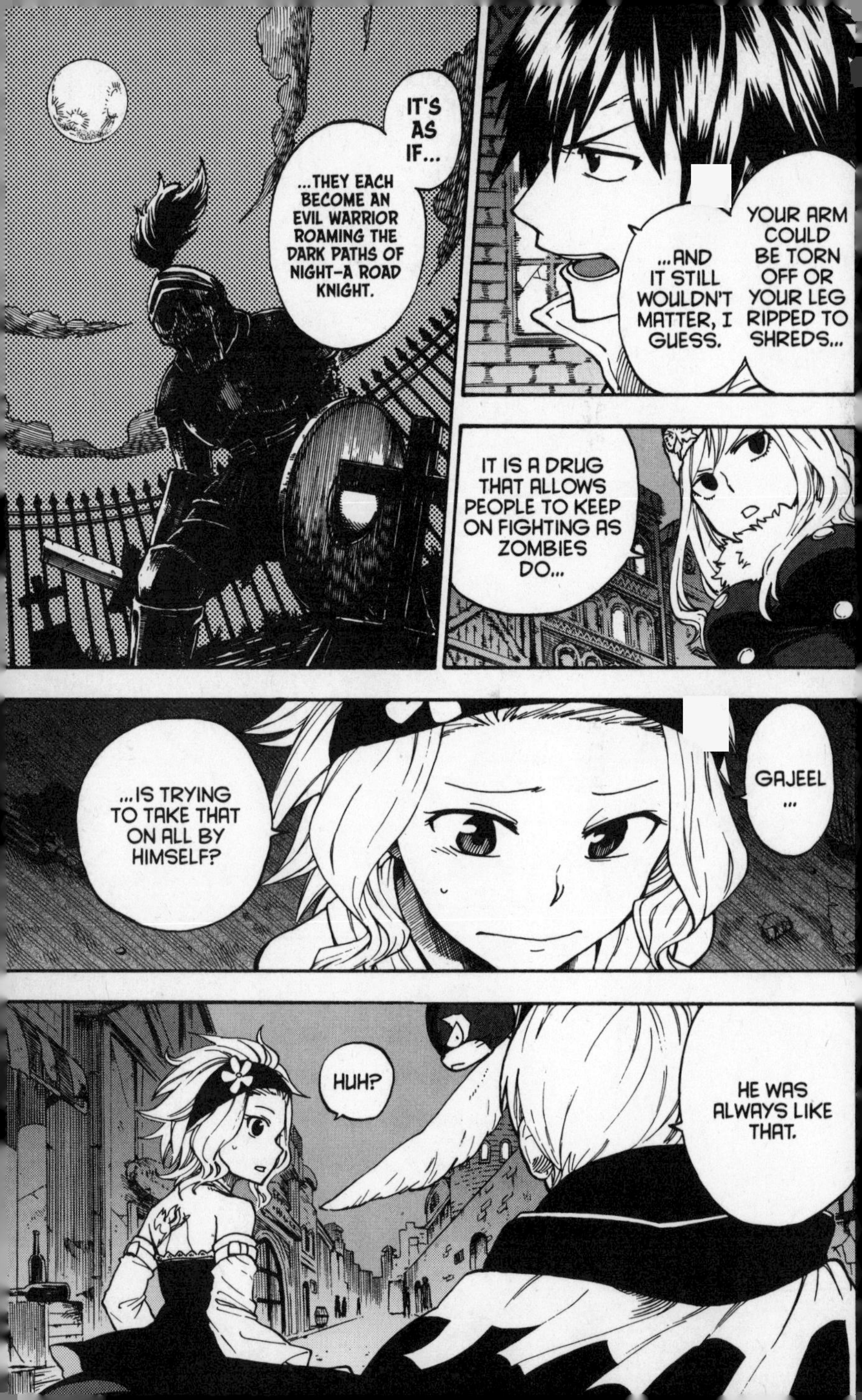
YOUR ARM COULD BE TORN OFF OR YOUR LEG RIPPED TO SHREDS...
...AND IT STILL WOULDN'T MATTER, I GUESS.
IT IS A DRUG THAT ALLOWS PEOPLE TO KEEP ON FIGHTING AS ZOMBIES DO...
IT'S AS IF...
...THEY EACH BECOME AN EVIL WARRIOR ROAMING THE DARK PATHS OF NIGHT—A ROAD KNIGHT.
GAJEEL ...
...IS TRYING TO TAKE THAT ON ALL BY HIMSELF?
HE WAS ALWAYS LIKE THAT.
HUH?

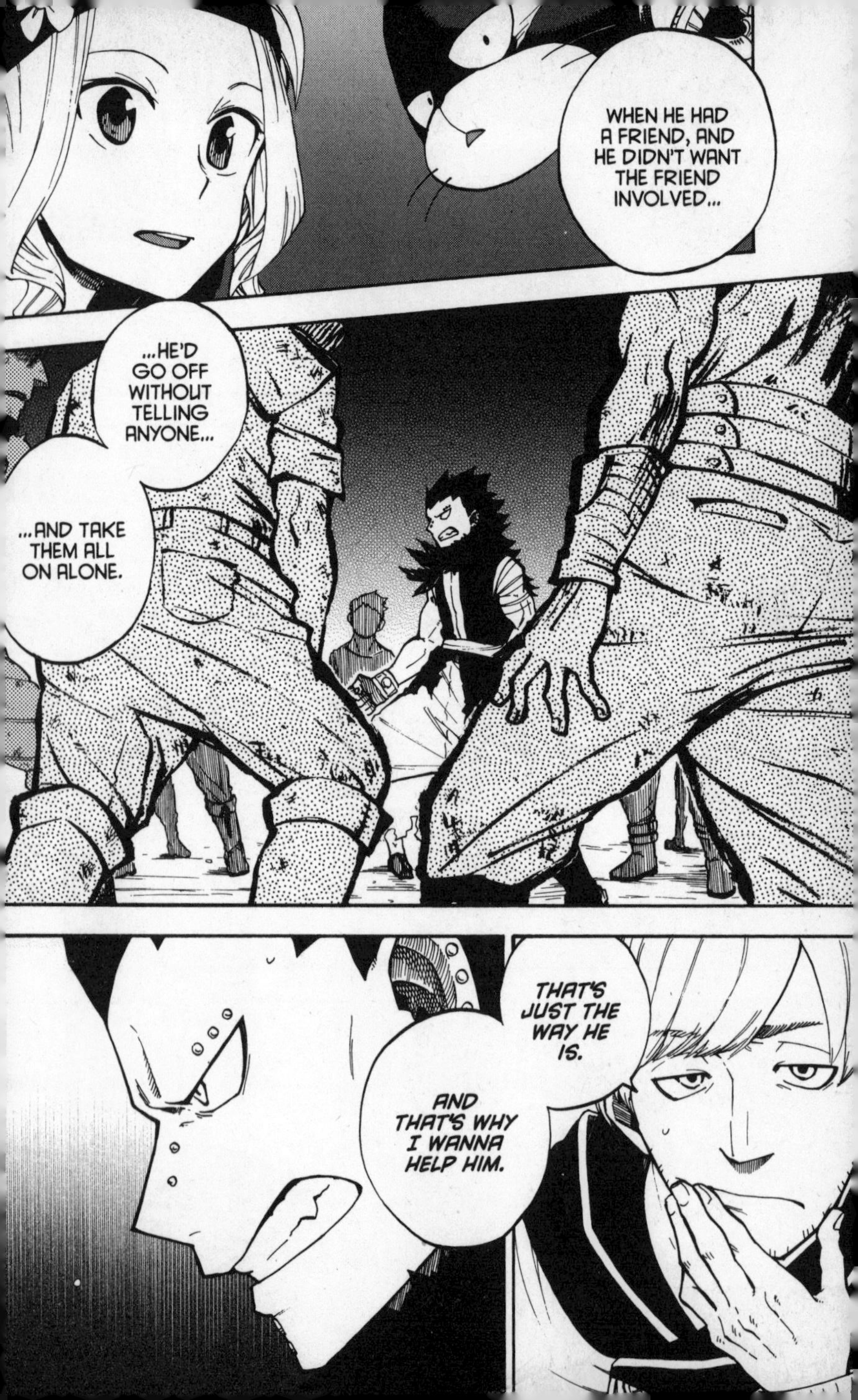
WHEN HE HAD A FRIEND, AND HE DIDN'T WANT THE FRIEND INVOLVED...
...HE'D GO OFF WITHOUT TELLING ANYONE...
...AND TAKE THEM ALL ON ALONE.
THAT'S JUST THE WAY HE IS.
AND THAT'S WHY I WANNA HELP HIM.

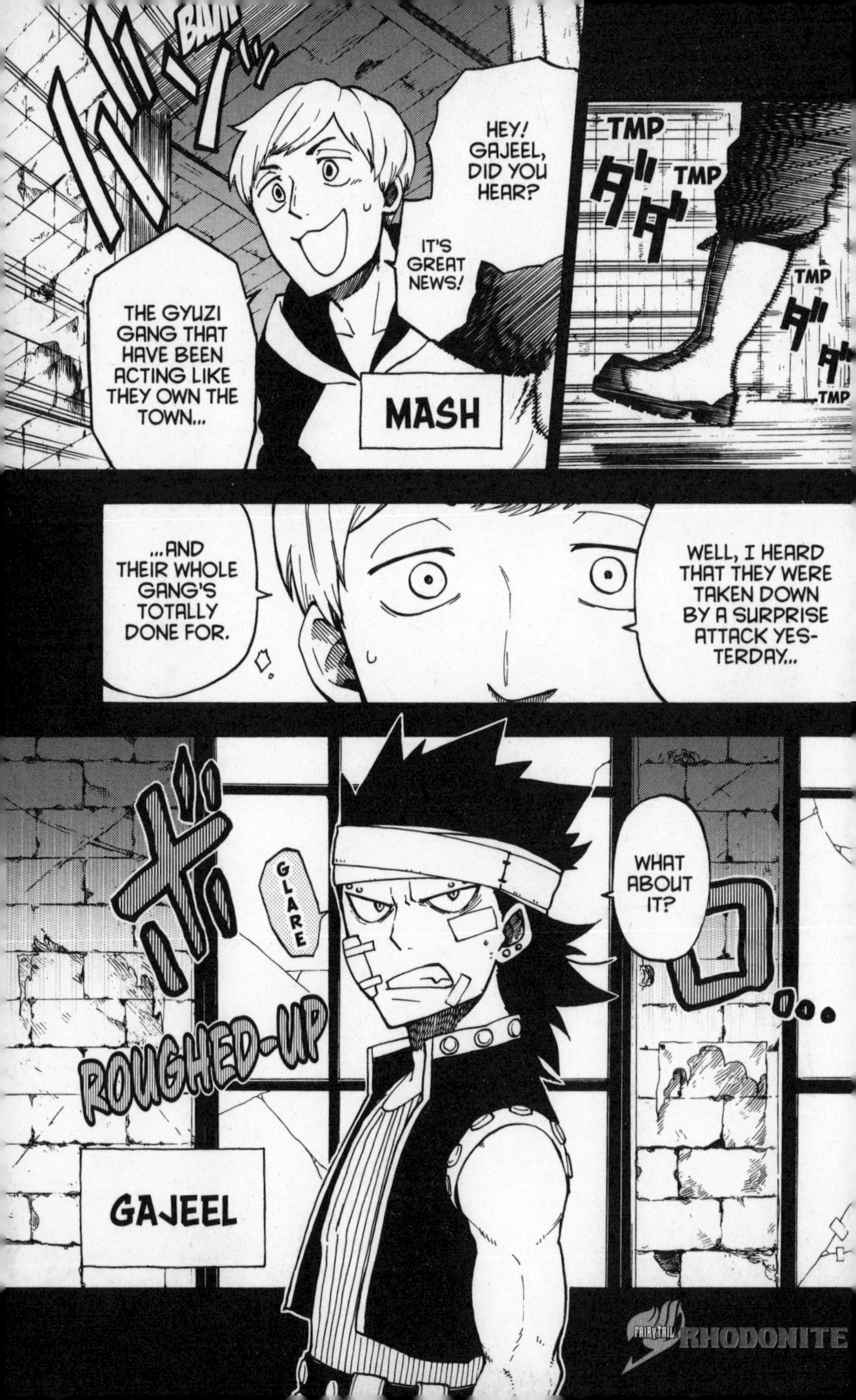
TMP
TMP
TMP
TMP
HEY! GAJEEL, DID YOU HEAR?
IT'S GREAT NEWS!
BAM
THE GYUZI GANG THAT HAVE BEEN ACTING LIKE THEY OWN THE TOWN...
MASH
WELL, I HEARD THAT THEY WERE TAKEN DOWN BY A SURPRISE ATTACK YES-TERDAY...
...AND THEIR WHOLE GANG'S TOTALLY DONE FOR.
WHAT ABOUT IT?
GLARE
ROUGHED-UP
GAJEEL

Chapter 6: The Gajeel I Never Knew

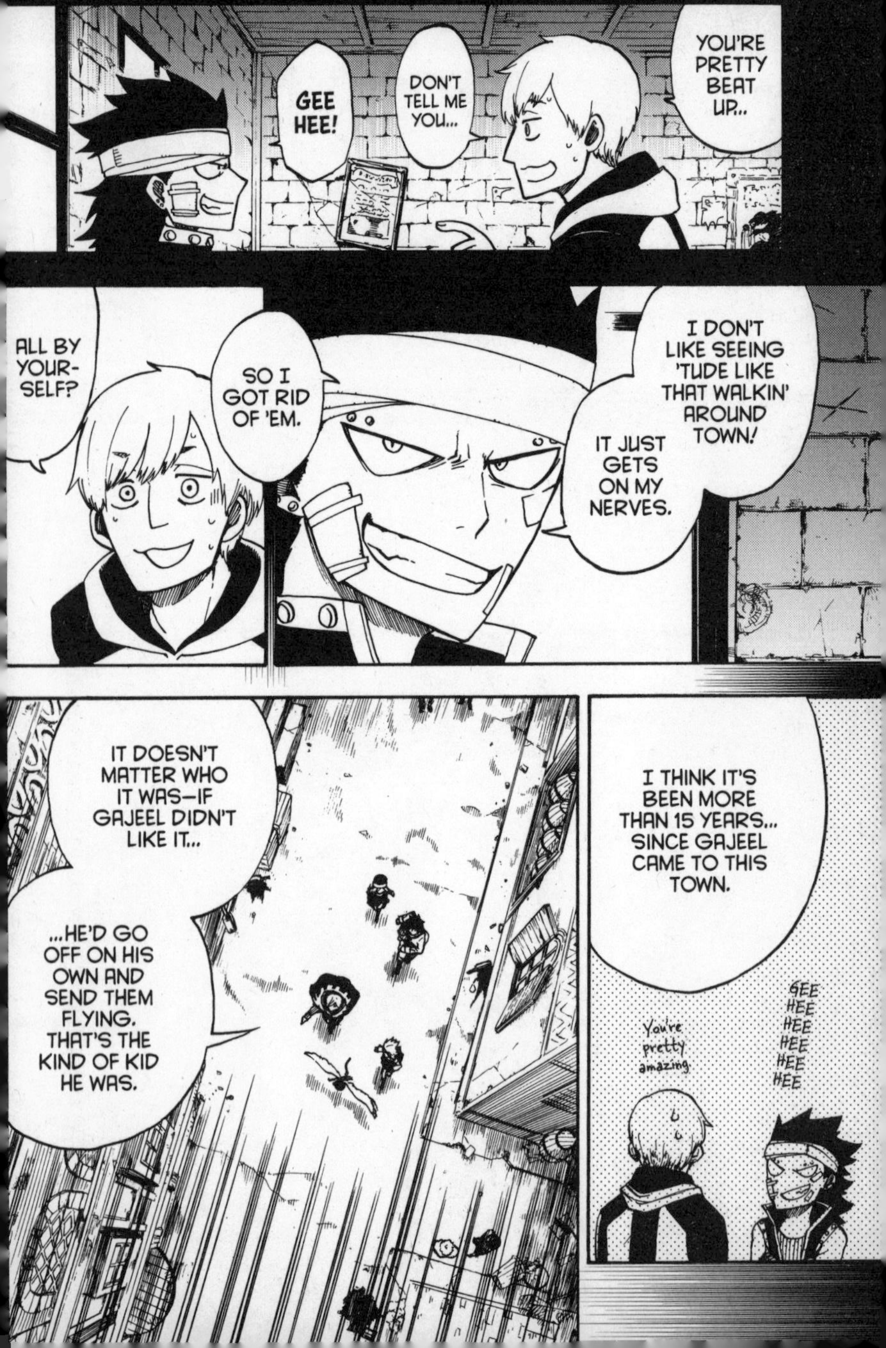

YOU'RE PRETTY BEAT UP...
DON'T TELL ME YOU...
GEE HEE!
I DON'T LIKE SEEING 'TUDE LIKE THAT WALKIN' AROUND TOWN!
IT JUST GETS ON MY NERVES.
SO I GOT RID OF 'EM.
ALL BY YOURSELF?
I THINK IT'S BEEN MORE THAN 15 YEARS... SINCE GAJEEL CAME TO THIS TOWN.
GEE HEE HEE HEE HEE HEE
You're pretty amazing
IT DOESN'T MATTER WHO IT WAS—IF GAJEEL DIDN'T LIKE IT...
...HE'D GO OFF ON HIS OWN AND SEND THEM FLYING. THAT'S THE KIND OF KID HE WAS.

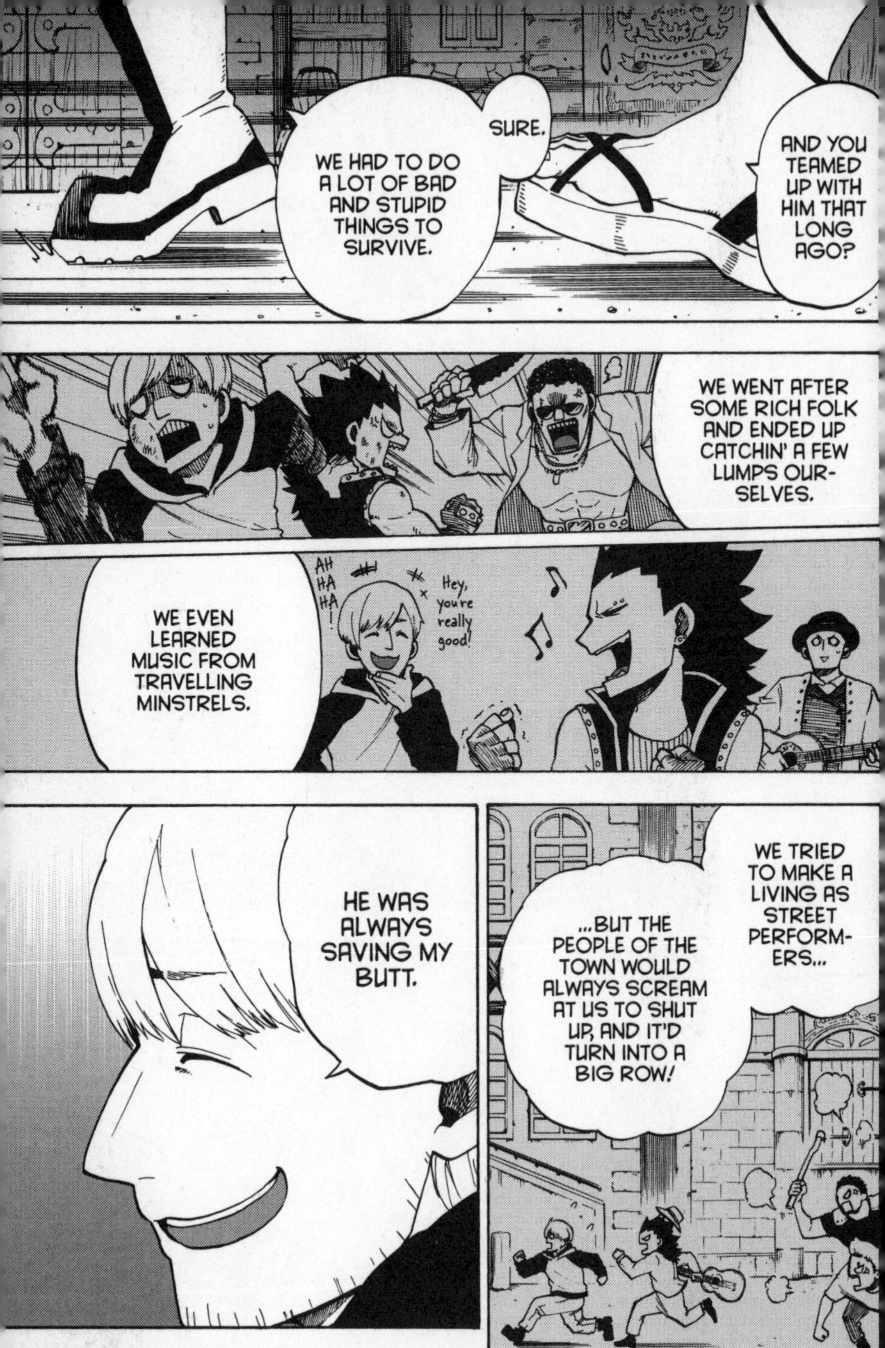
AND YOU TEAMED UP WITH HIM THAT LONG AGO?
SURE.
WE HAD TO DO A LOT OF BAD AND STUPID THINGS TO SURVIVE.
WE WENT AFTER SOME RICH FOLK AND ENDED UP CATCHIN' A FEW LUMPS OUR-SELVES.
Hey, you're really good!
AH HA HA!
WE EVEN LEARNED MUSIC FROM TRAVELLING MINSTRELS.
WE TRIED TO MAKE A LIVING AS STREET PERFORM-ERS...
...BUT THE PEOPLE OF THE TOWN WOULD ALWAYS SCREAM AT US TO SHUT UP, AND IT'D TURN INTO A BIG ROW!
HE WAS ALWAYS SAVING MY BUTT.

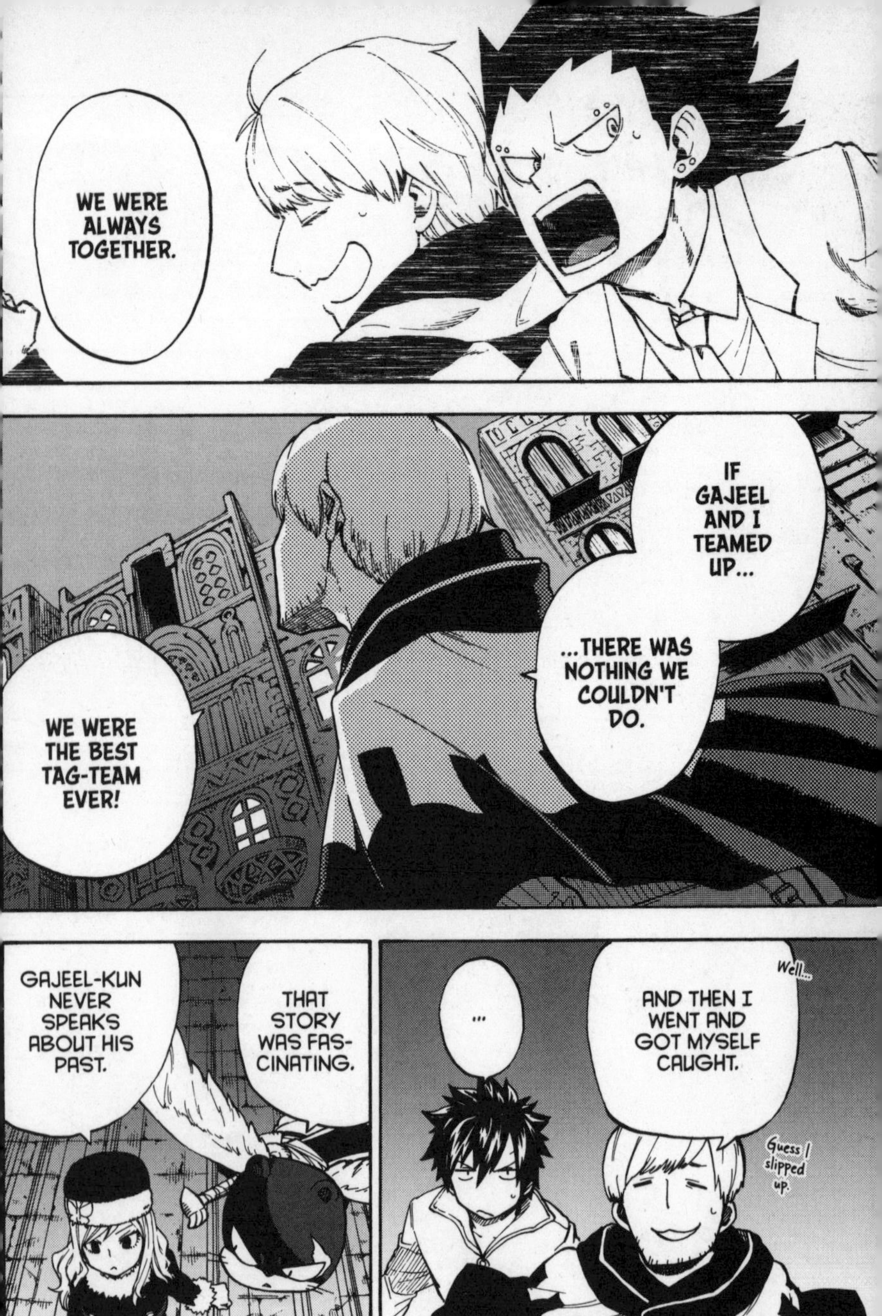
WE WERE ALWAYS TOGETHER.
IF GAJEEL AND I TEAMED UP...
...THERE WAS NOTHING WE COULDN'T DO.
WE WERE THE BEST TAG-TEAM EVER!
Well...
AND THEN I WENT AND GOT MYSELF CAUGHT.
...
Guess I slipped up.
THAT STORY WAS FAS-CINATING.
GAJEEL-KUN NEVER SPEAKS ABOUT HIS PAST.

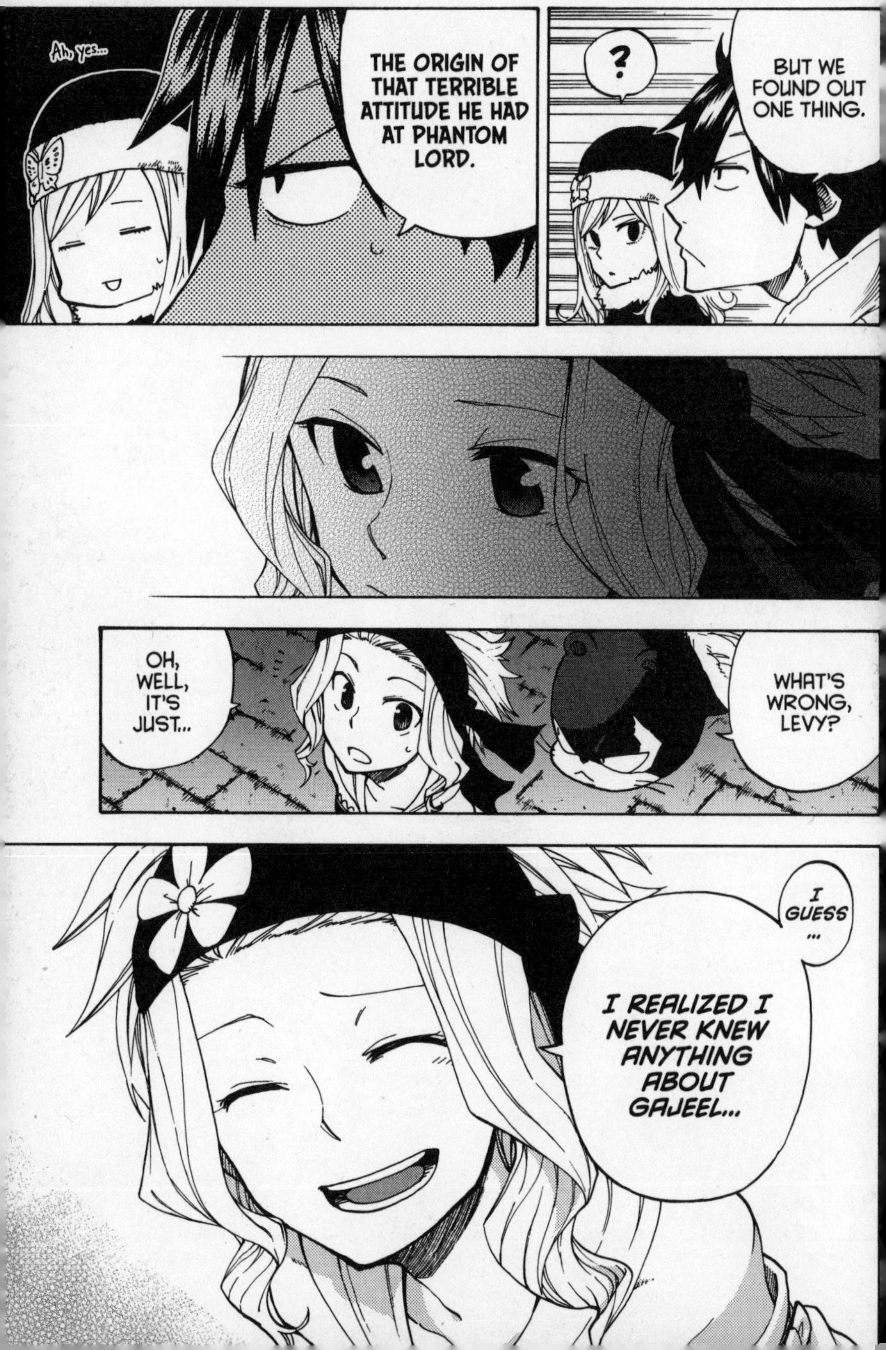
BUT WE FOUND OUT ONE THING.
?
THE ORIGIN OF THAT TERRIBLE ATTITUDE HE HAD AT PHANTOM LORD.
Ah, yes...
WHAT'S WRONG, LEVY?
OH, WELL, IT'S JUST...
I GUESS...
I REALIZED I NEVER KNEW ANYTHING ABOUT GAJEEL...

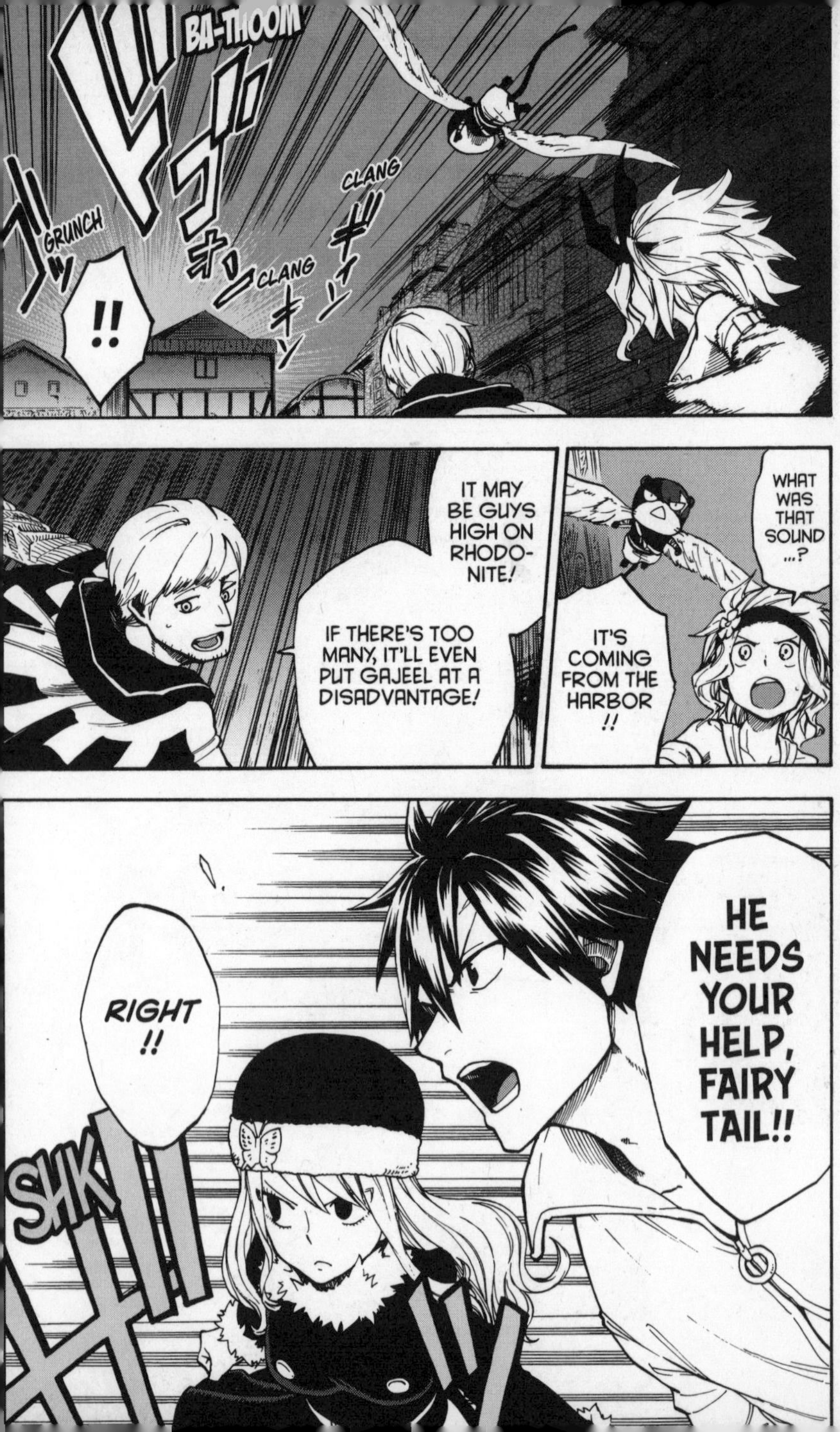
BA-THOOM
CLANG
CLANG
GRUNCH
!!
WHAT WAS THAT SOUND ...?
IT'S COMING FROM THE HARBOR !!
IT MAY BE GUYS HIGH ON RHODO-NITE!
IF THERE'S TOO MANY, IT'LL EVEN PUT GAJEEL AT A DISADVANTAGE!
HE NEEDS YOUR HELP, FAIRY TAIL!!
RIGHT !!
SHK

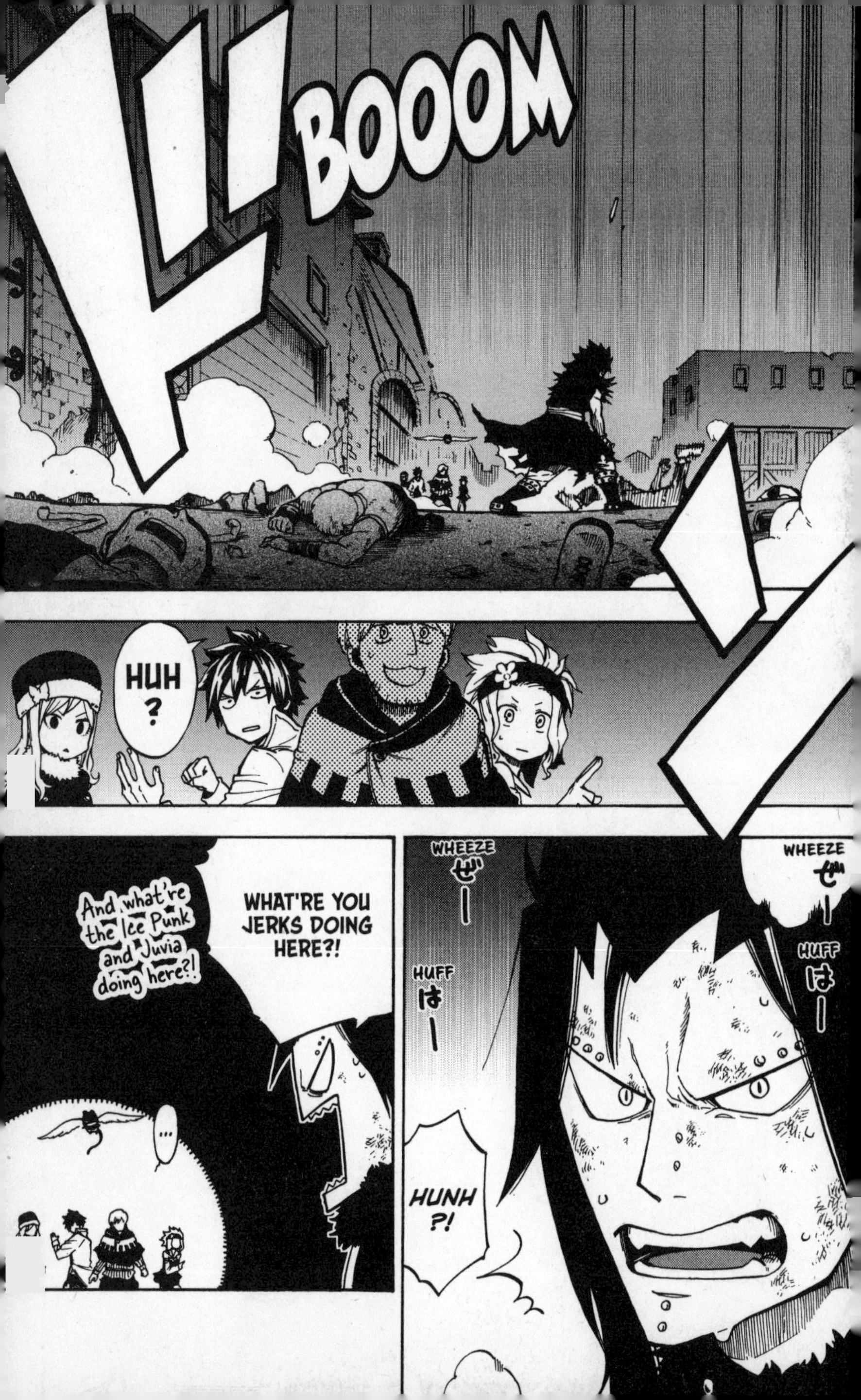
BOOOM
HUH?
WHEEZE ゼー
HUFF はー
WHEEZE ゼー
HUFF はー
HUNH?!
WHAT'RE YOU JERKS DOING HERE?!
And what're the Ice Punk and Juvia doing here?!
...

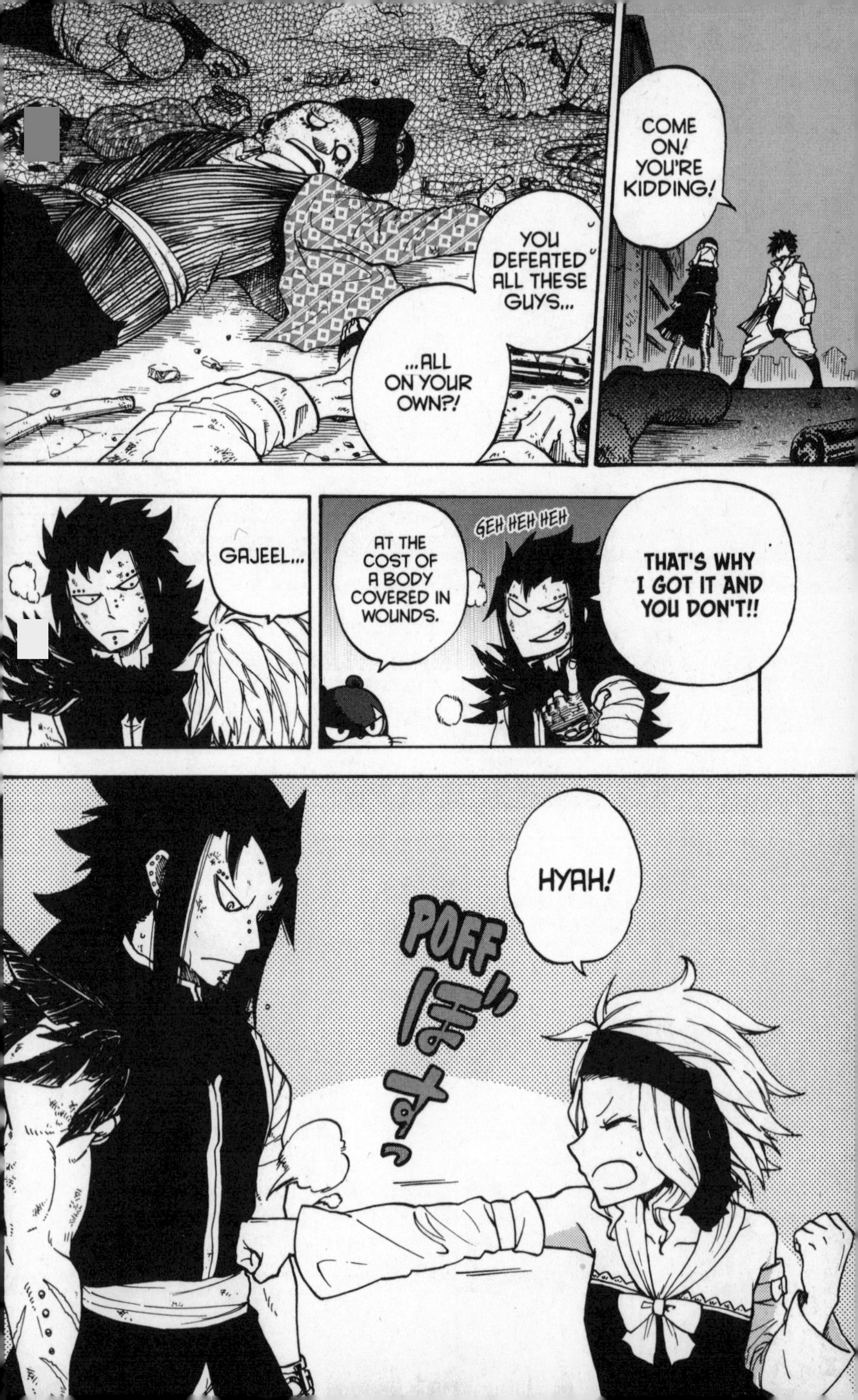
COME ON! YOU'RE KIDDING!
YOU DEFEATED ALL THESE GUYS...
...ALL ON YOUR OWN?!
THAT'S WHY I GOT IT AND YOU DON'T!!
GEH HEH HEH
AT THE COST OF A BODY COVERED IN WOUNDS.
GAJEEL...
HYAH!
POFF
ぼすっ

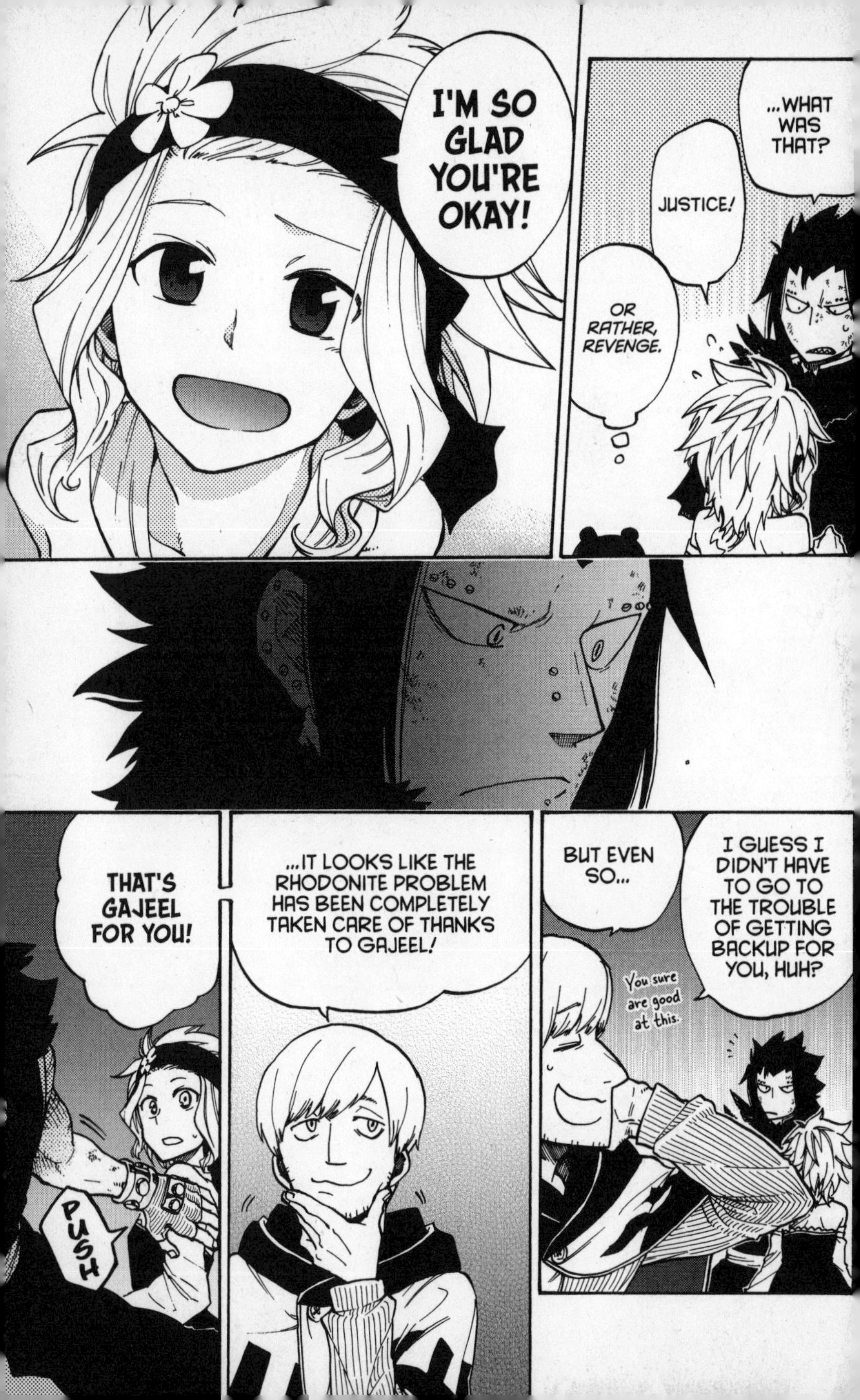
...WHAT WAS THAT?
JUSTICE!
OR RATHER, REVENGE.
I'M SO GLAD YOU'RE OKAY!
I GUESS I DIDN'T HAVE TO GO TO THE TROUBLE OF GETTING BACKUP FOR YOU, HUH?
BUT EVEN SO...
You sure are good at this.
...IT LOOKS LIKE THE RHODONITE PROBLEM HAS BEEN COMPLETELY TAKEN CARE OF THANKS TO GAJEEL!
THAT'S GAJEEL FOR YOU!
PUSH

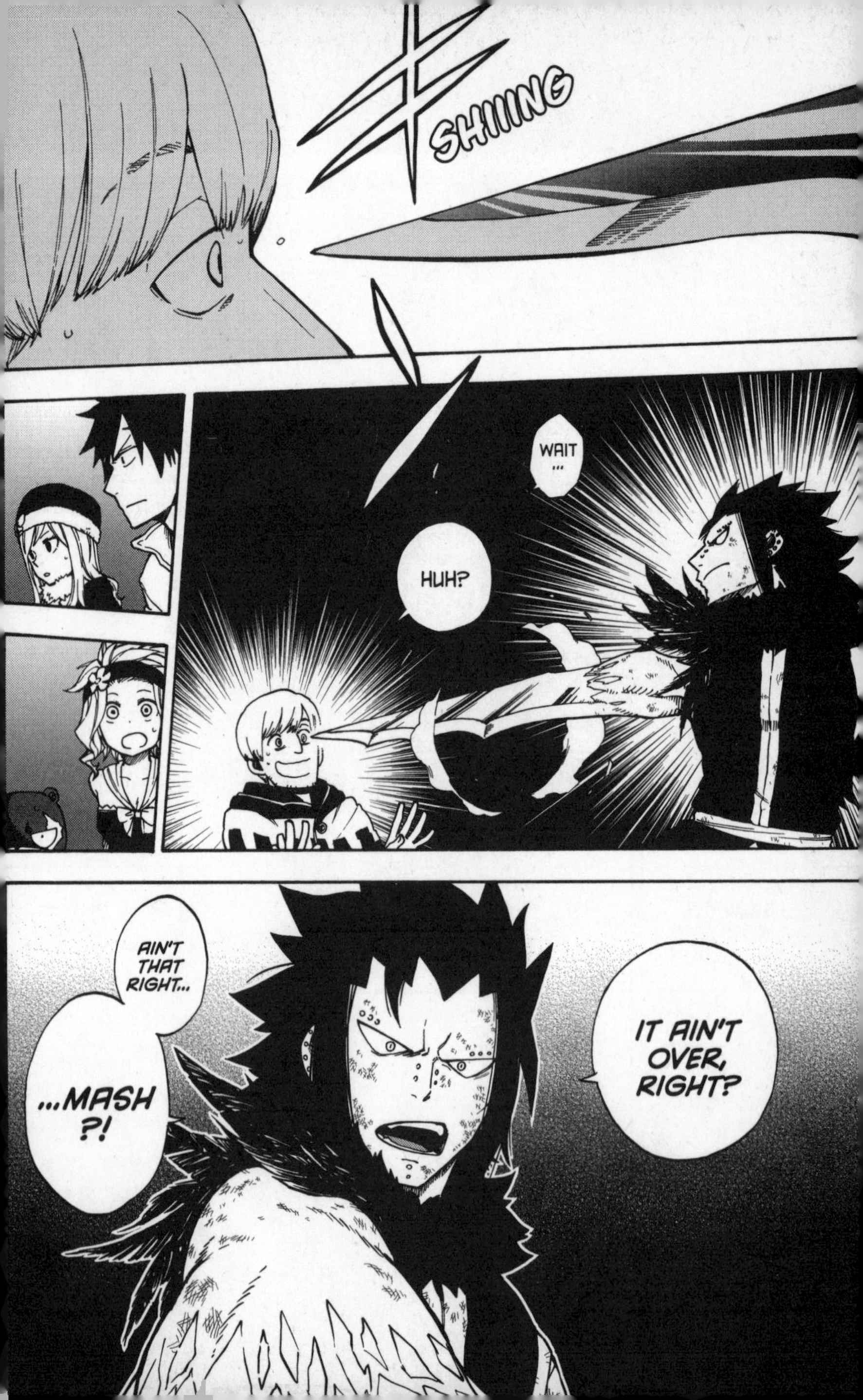
SHIIING
WAIT ...
HUH?
IT AIN'T OVER, RIGHT?
AIN'T THAT RIGHT...
...MASH ?!

Chapter 7: Will You Just Shut Up

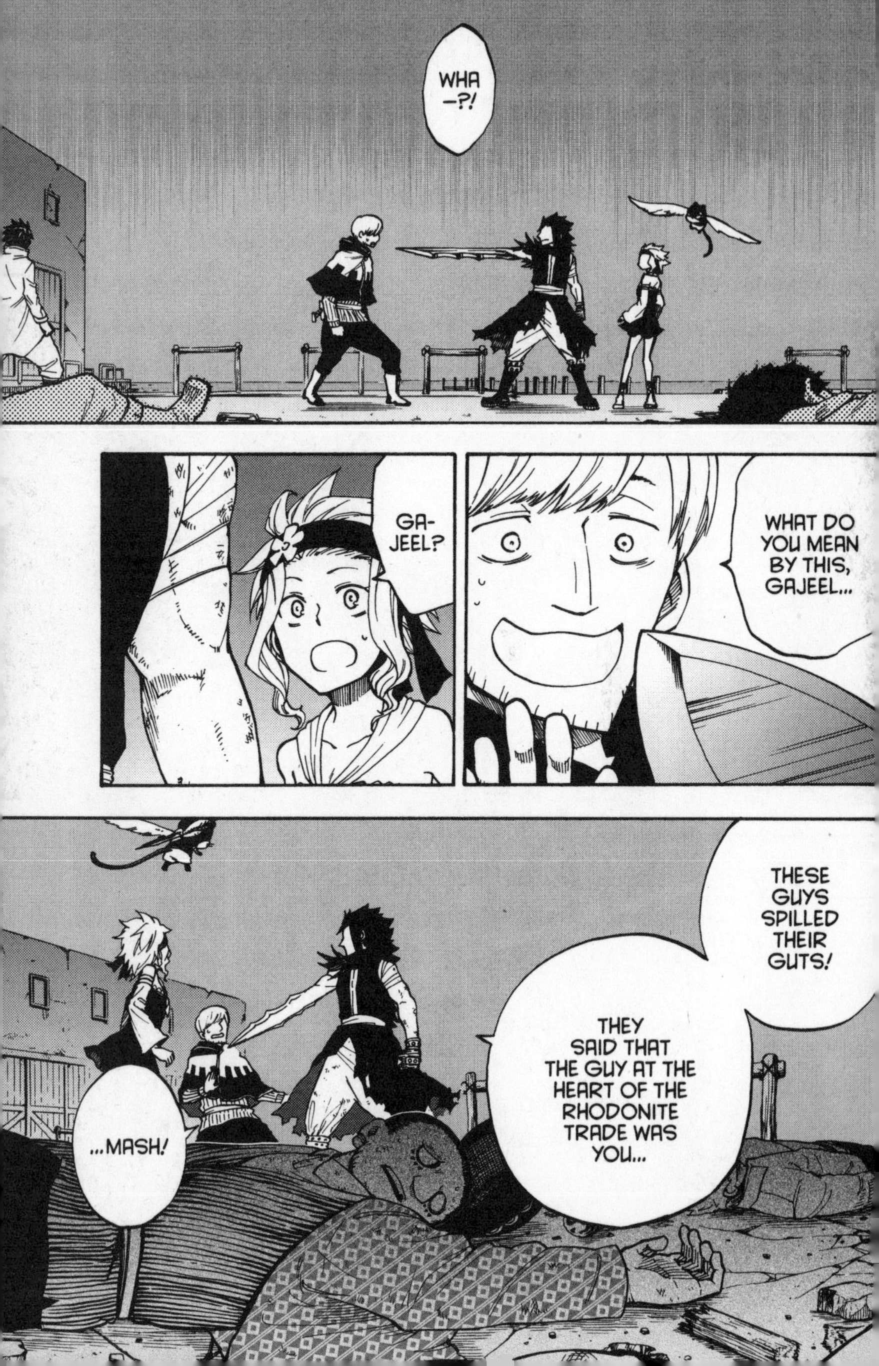
WHA
—?!
WHAT DO YOU MEAN BY THIS, GAJEEL...
GA-JEEL?
THESE GUYS SPILLED THEIR GUTS!
THEY SAID THAT THE GUY AT THE HEART OF THE RHODONITE TRADE WAS YOU...
...MASH!

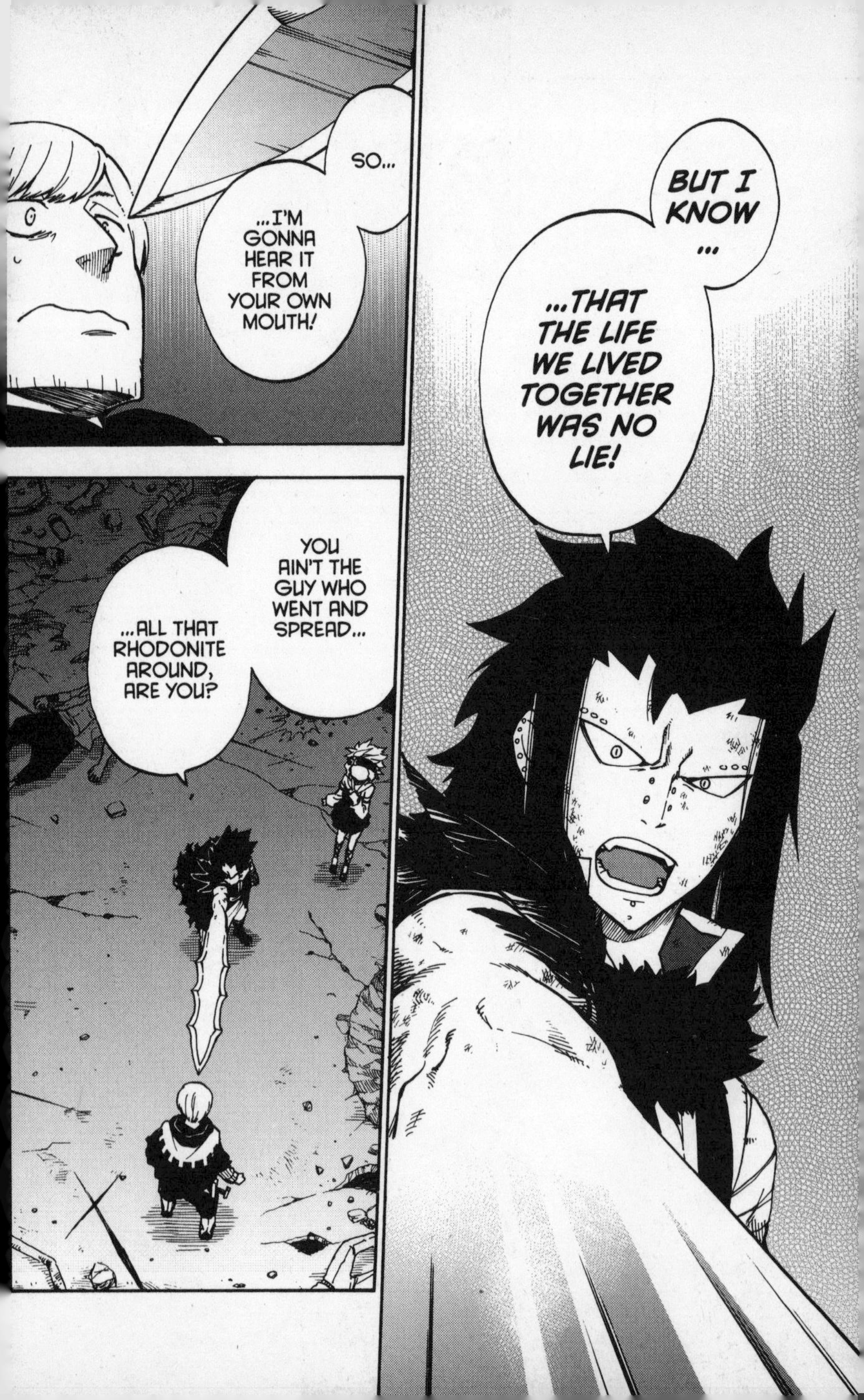
BUT I KNOW ...
...THAT THE LIFE WE LIVED TOGETHER WAS NO LIE!
SO...
...I'M GONNA HEAR IT FROM YOUR OWN MOUTH!
YOU AIN'T THE GUY WHO WENT AND SPREAD...
...ALL THAT RHODONITE AROUND, ARE YOU?

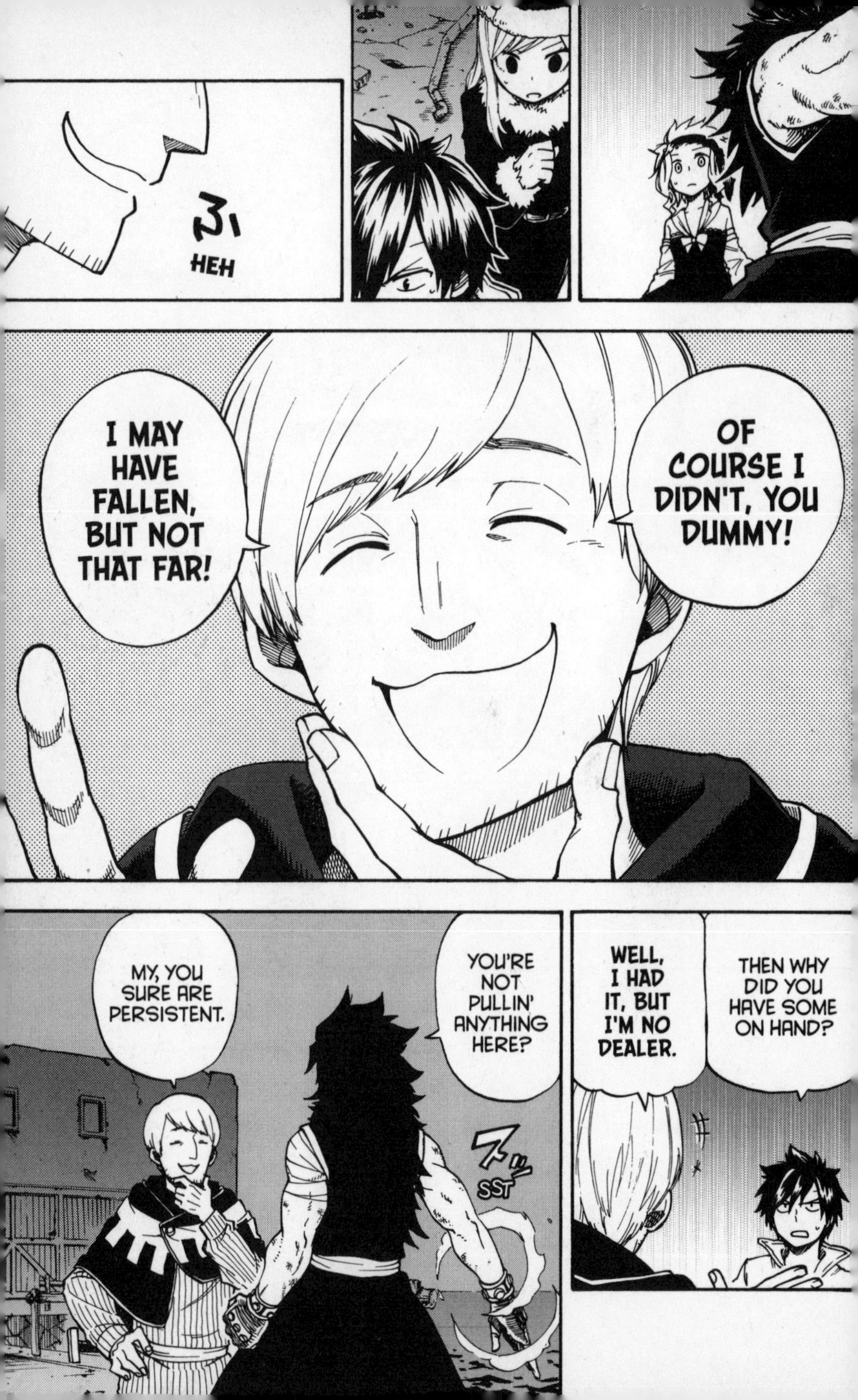
HEH
OF COURSE I DIDN'T, YOU DUMMY!
I MAY HAVE FALLEN, BUT NOT THAT FAR!
THEN WHY DID YOU HAVE SOME ON HAND?
WELL, I HAD IT, BUT I'M NO DEALER.
YOU'RE NOT PULLIN' ANYTHING HERE?
SST
MY, YOU SURE ARE PERSISTENT.

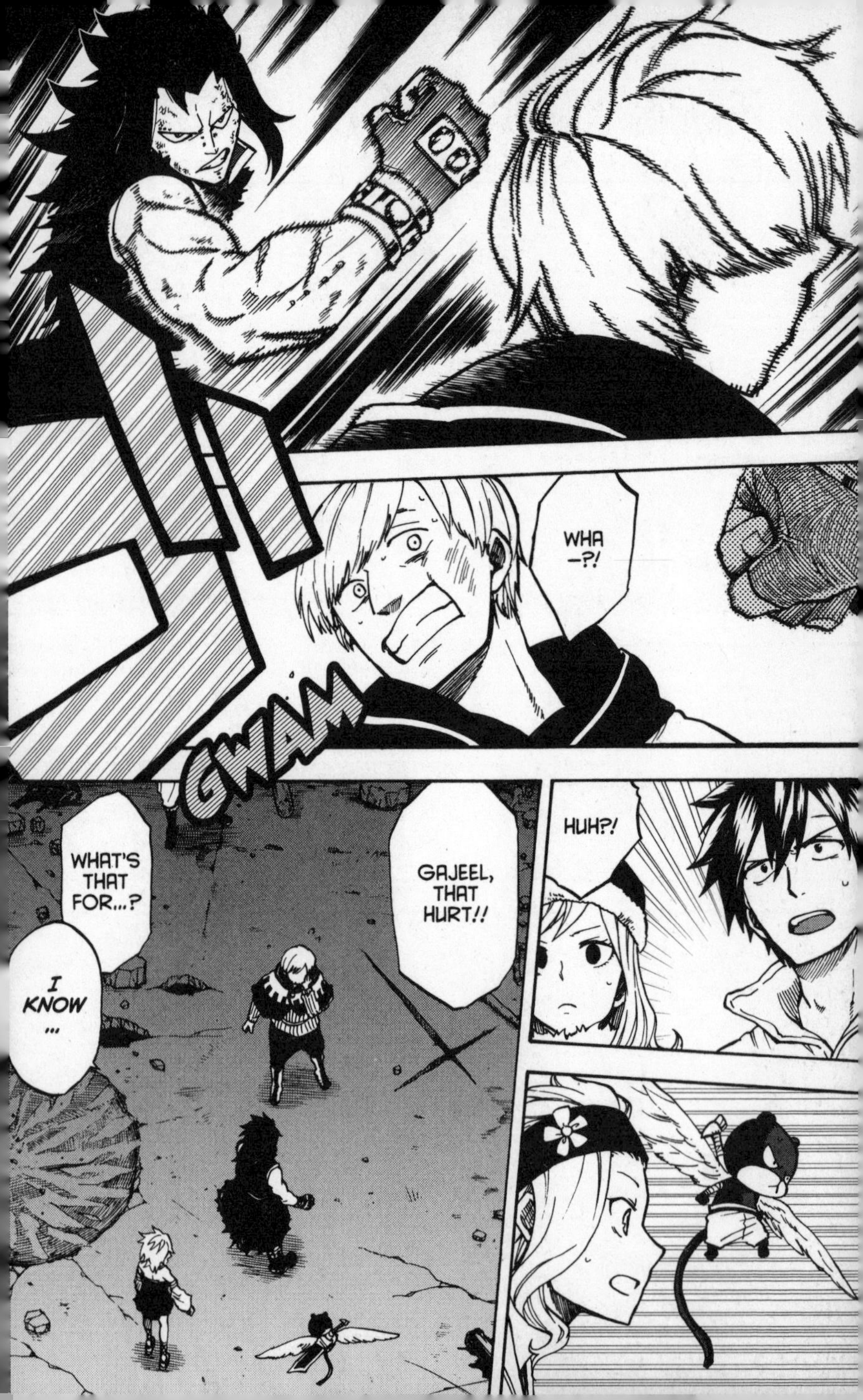
WHA—?!
GWAM
HUH?!
GAJEEL, THAT HURT!!
WHAT'S THAT FOR...?
I KNOW...

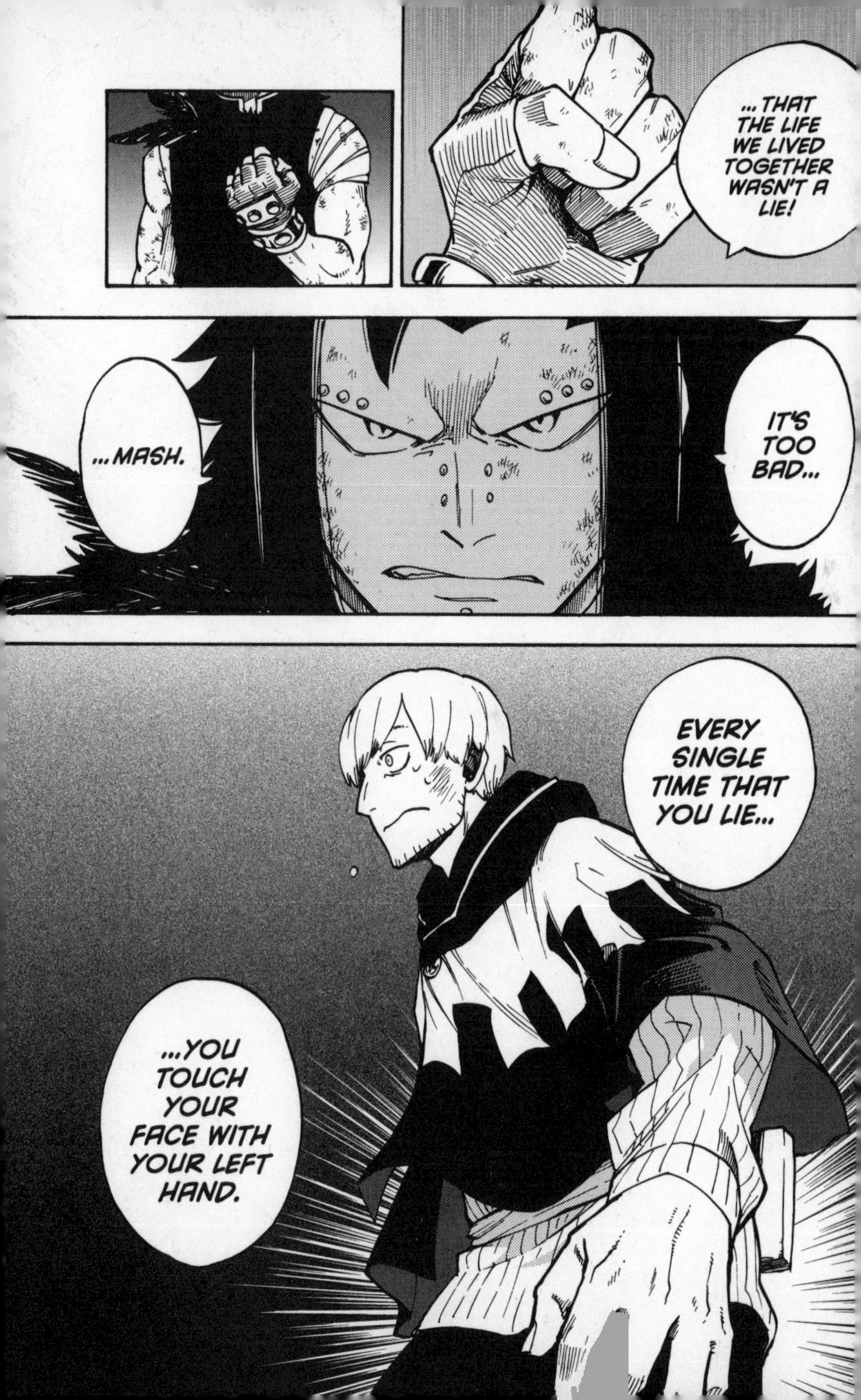
...THAT THE LIFE WE LIVED TOGETHER WASN'T A LIE!
IT'S TOO BAD...
...MASH.
EVERY SINGLE TIME THAT YOU LIE...
...YOU TOUCH YOUR FACE WITH YOUR LEFT HAND.

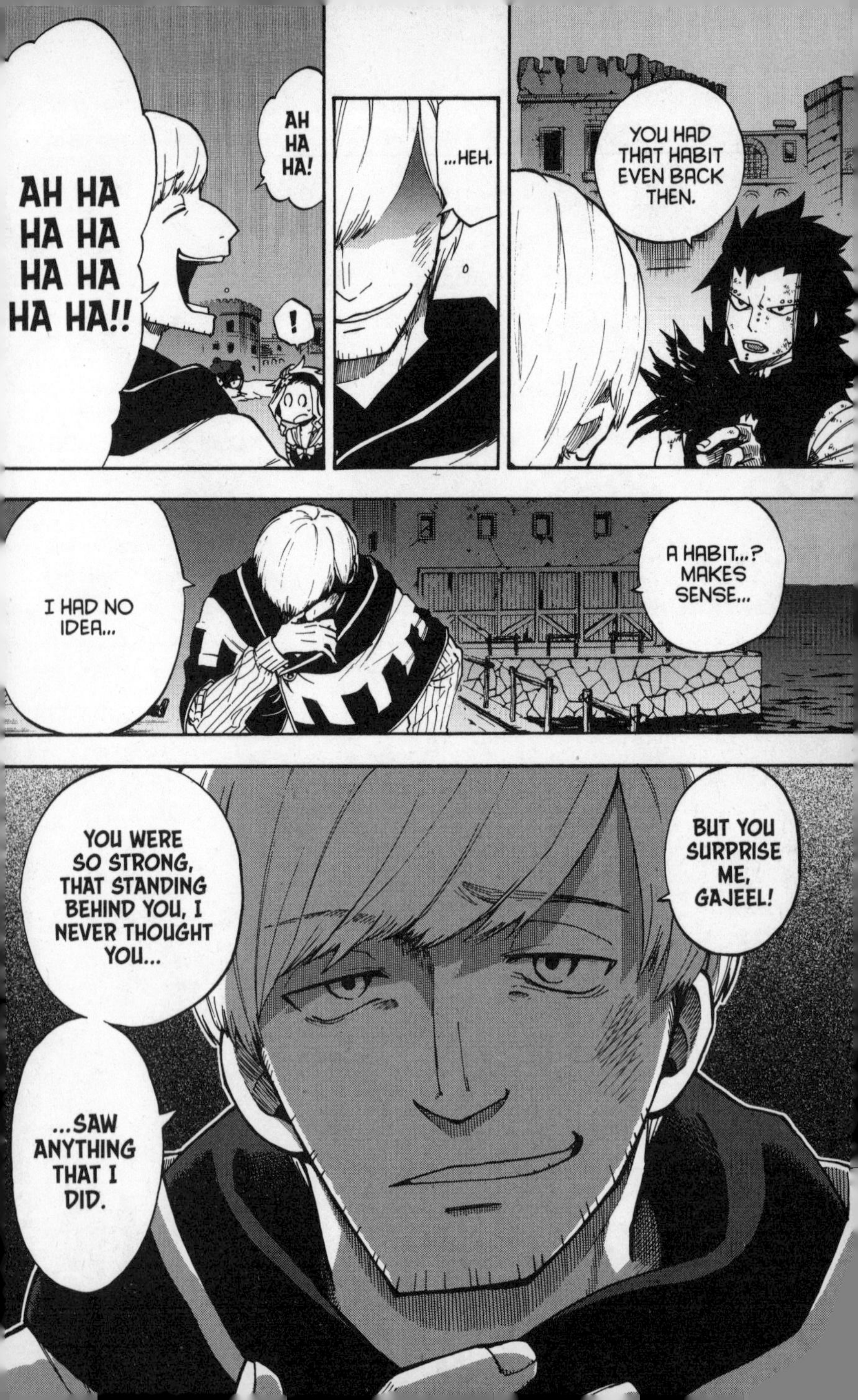
YOU HAD THAT HABIT EVEN BACK THEN.
...HEH.
AH HA HA!
AH HA HA HA HA HA HA HA!!
!
A HABIT...? MAKES SENSE...
I HAD NO IDEA...
BUT YOU SURPRISE ME, GAJEEL!
YOU WERE SO STRONG, THAT STANDING BEHIND YOU, I NEVER THOUGHT YOU...
...SAW ANYTHING THAT I DID.

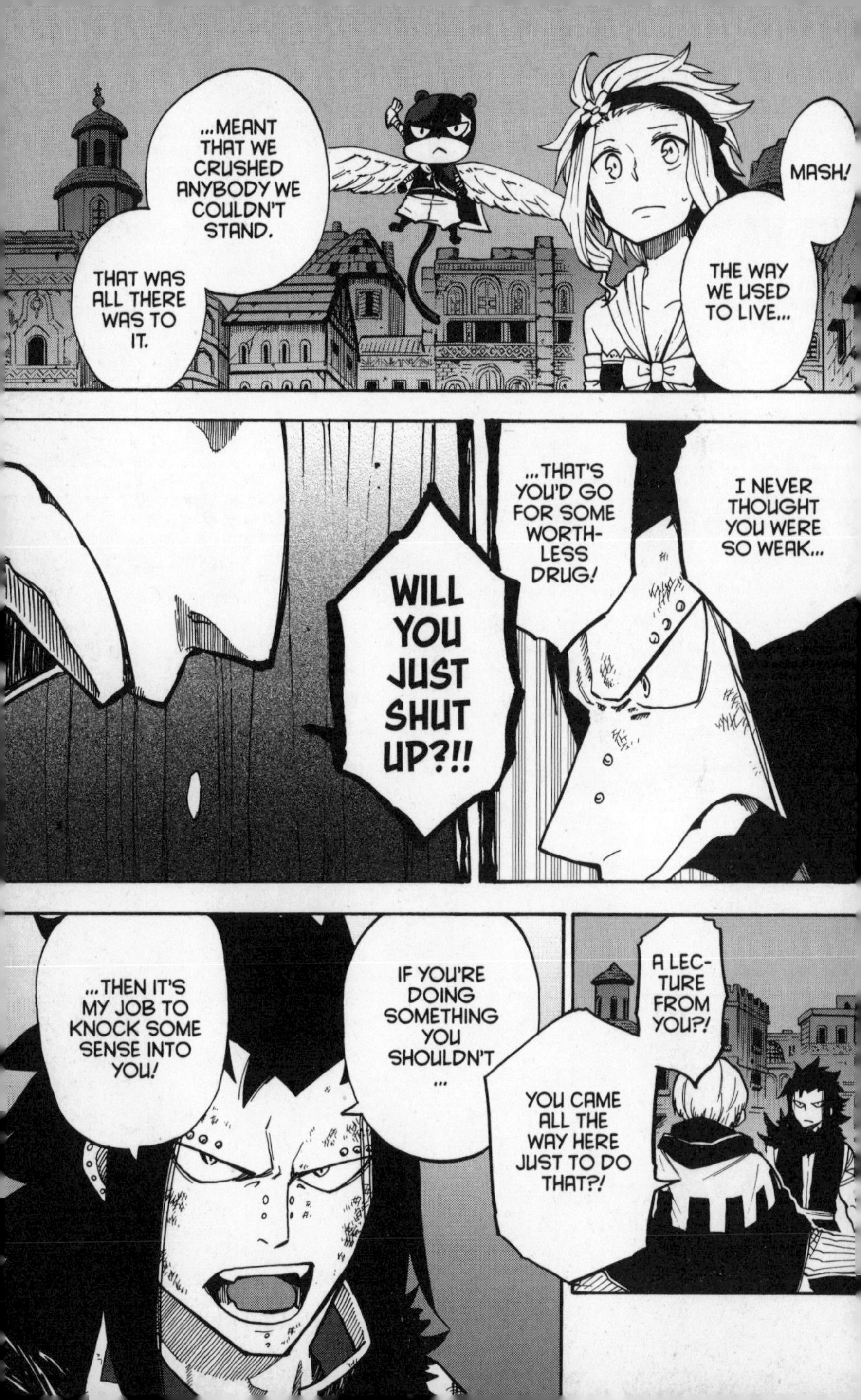
MASH!
THE WAY WE USED TO LIVE...
...MEANT THAT WE CRUSHED ANYBODY WE COULDN'T STAND.
THAT WAS ALL THERE WAS TO IT.
I NEVER THOUGHT YOU WERE SO WEAK...
...THAT'S YOU'D GO FOR SOME WORTHLESS DRUG!
WILL YOU JUST SHUT UP?!!
A LECTURE FROM YOU?!
YOU CAME ALL THE WAY HERE JUST TO DO THAT?!
IF YOU'RE DOING SOMETHING YOU SHOULDN'T ...
...THEN IT'S MY JOB TO KNOCK SOME SENSE INTO YOU!

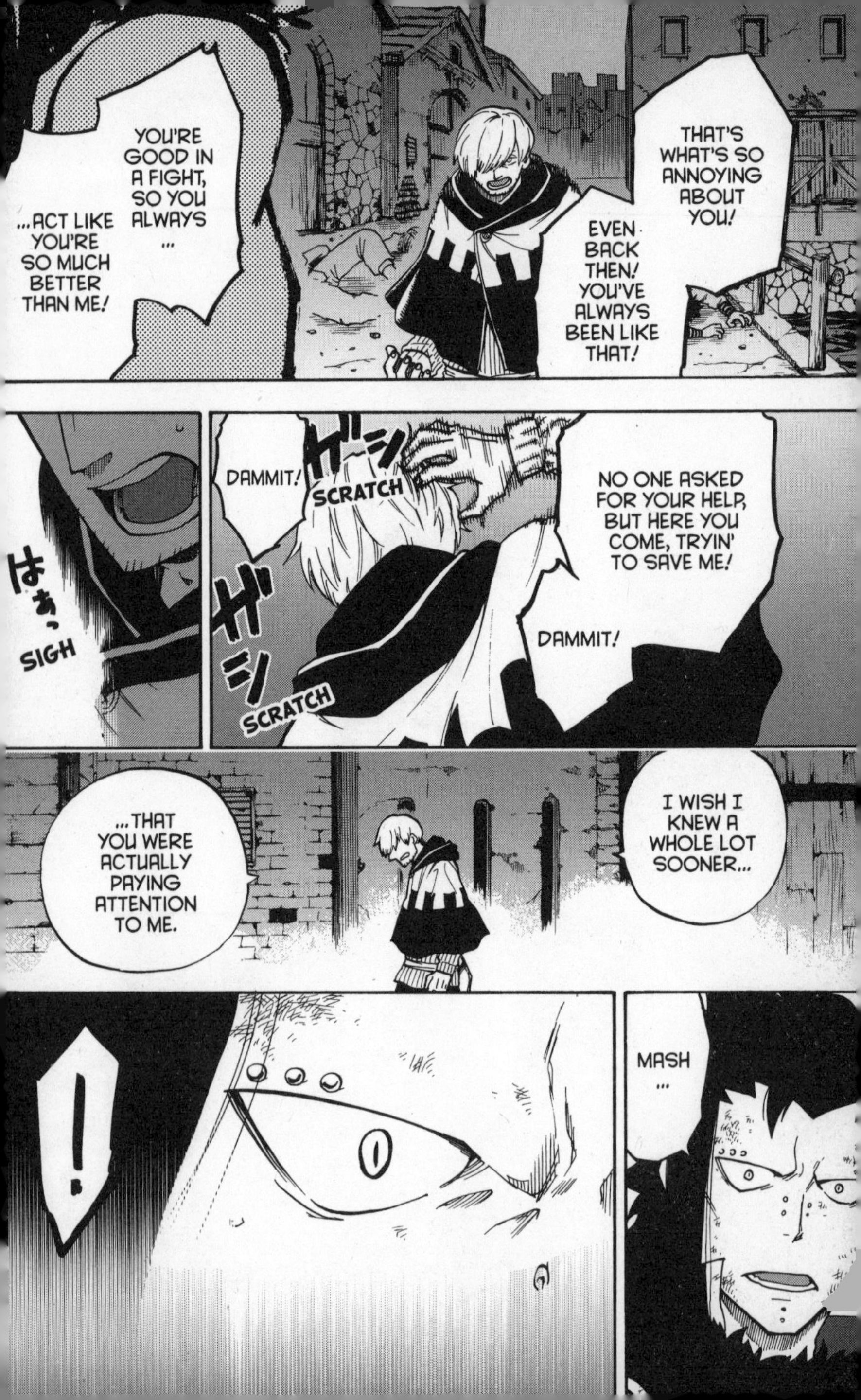
THAT'S WHAT'S SO ANNOYING ABOUT YOU!
EVEN BACK THEN! YOU'VE ALWAYS BEEN LIKE THAT!
YOU'RE GOOD IN A FIGHT, SO YOU ALWAYS ...
...ACT LIKE YOU'RE SO MUCH BETTER THAN ME!
NO ONE ASKED FOR YOUR HELP, BUT HERE YOU COME, TRYIN' TO SAVE ME!
DAMMIT!
SCRATCH
DAMMIT!
SCRATCH
はぁっ
SIGH
I WISH I KNEW A WHOLE LOT SOONER...
...THAT YOU WERE ACTUALLY PAYING ATTENTION TO ME.
MASH ...
!

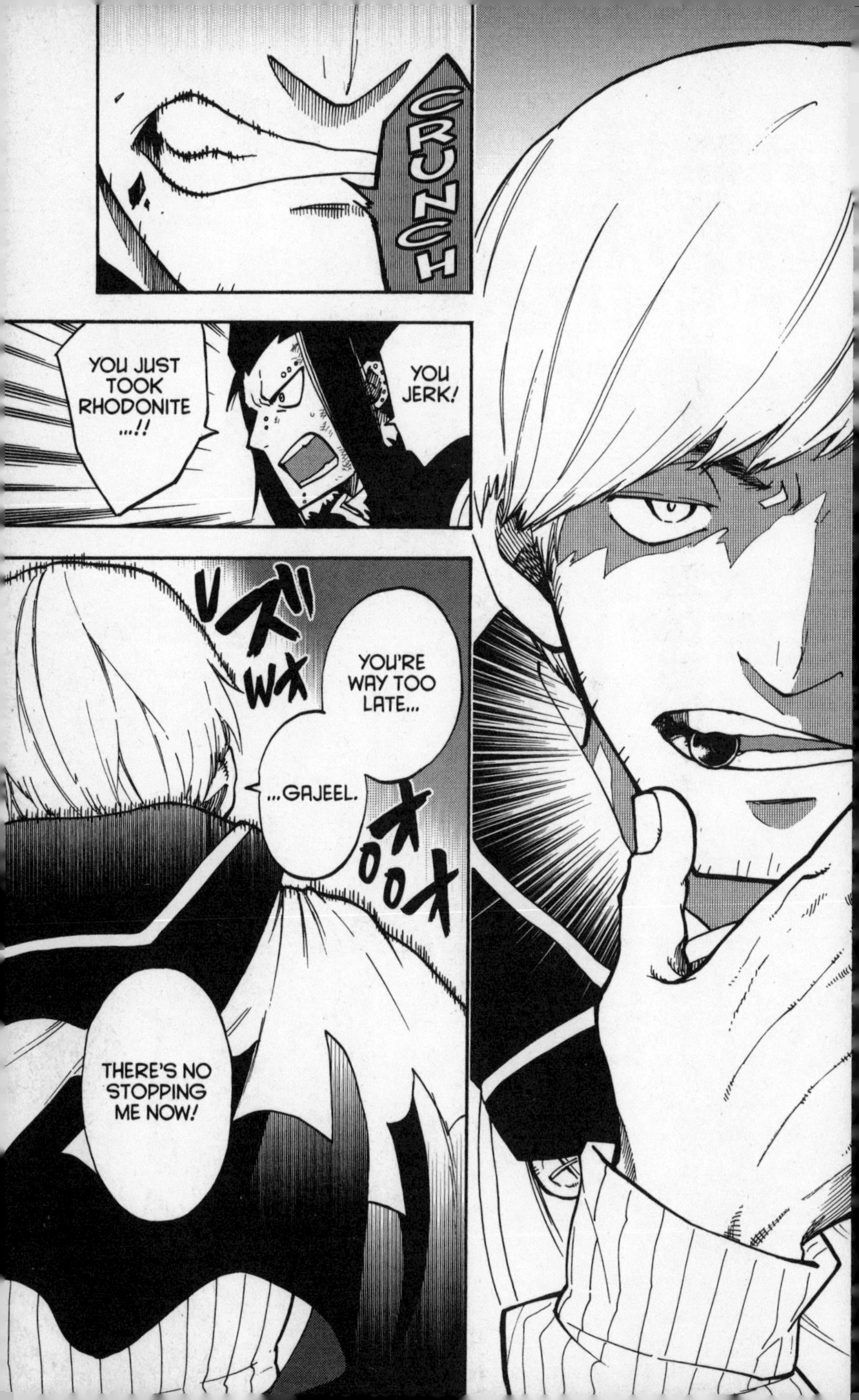
CRUNCH
YOU JERK!
YOU JUST TOOK RHODONITE ...!!
YOU'RE WAY TOO LATE...
...GAJEEL.
THERE'S NO STOPPING ME NOW!

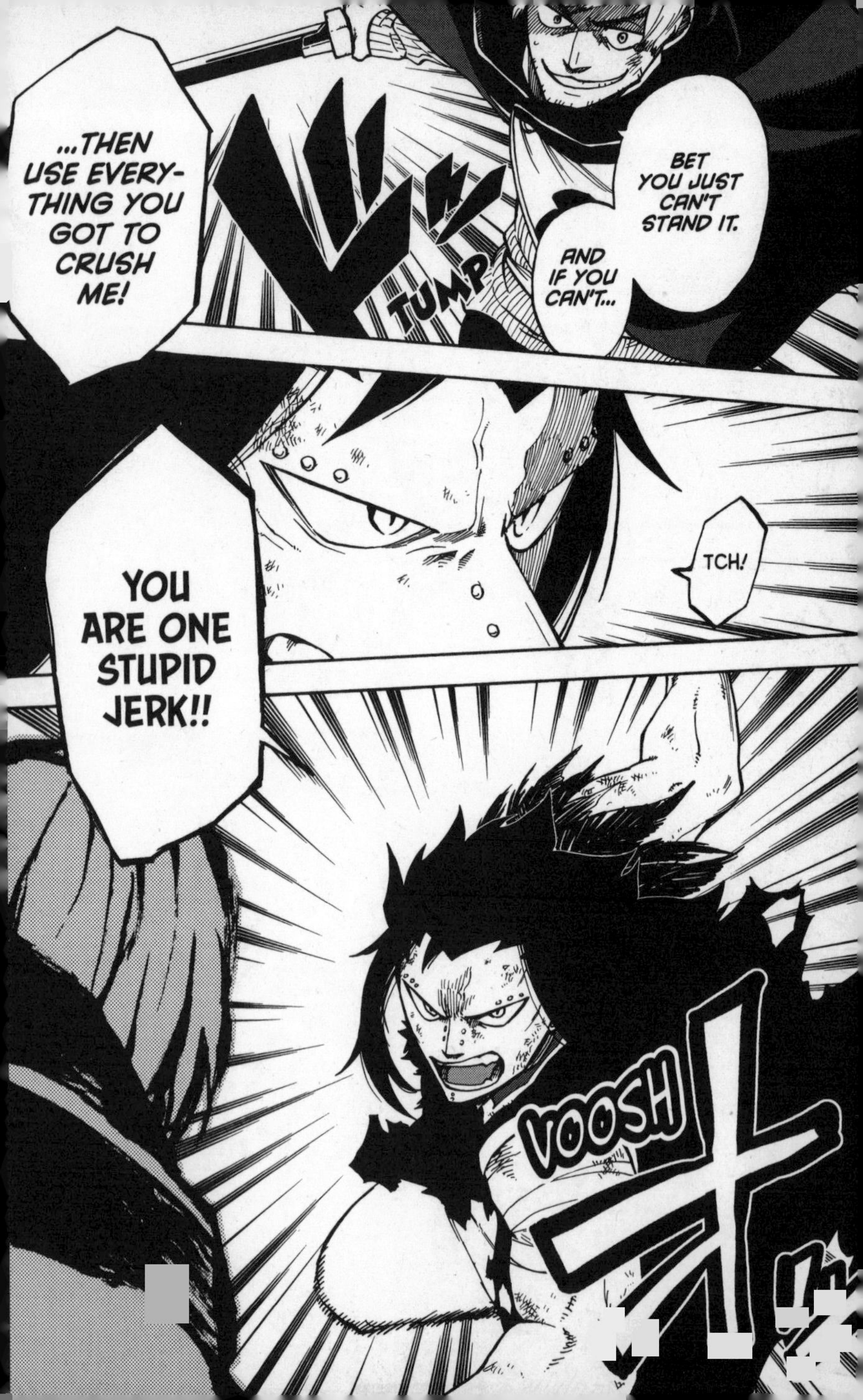
BET YOU JUST CAN'T STAND IT.
AND IF YOU CAN'T...
TUMP
...THEN USE EVERY-THING YOU GOT TO CRUSH ME!
TCH!
YOU ARE ONE STUPID JERK!!
VOOSH

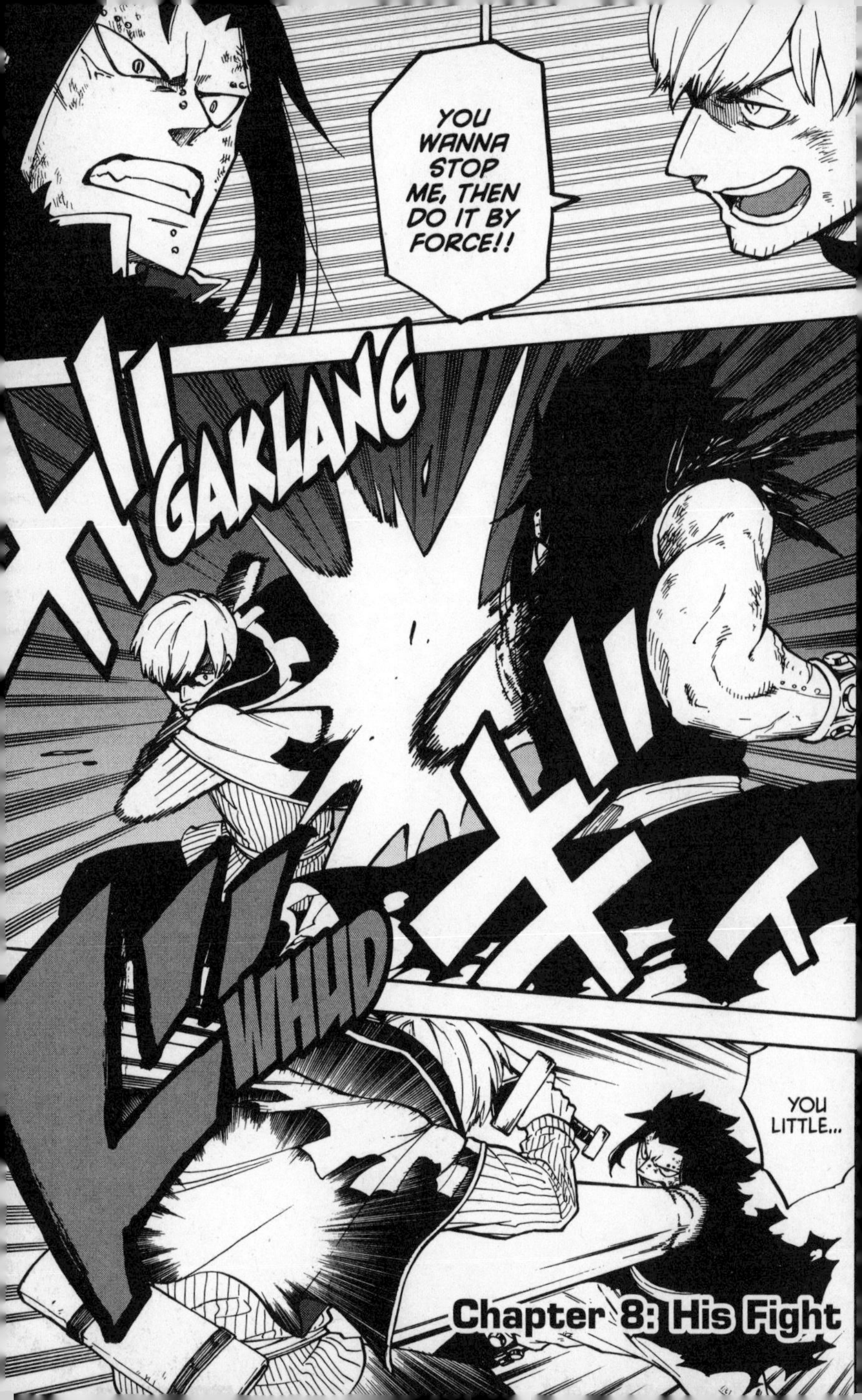
YOU WANNA STOP ME, THEN DO IT BY FORCE!!
GAKLANG
WHUD
YOU LITTLE...

Chapter 8: His Fight

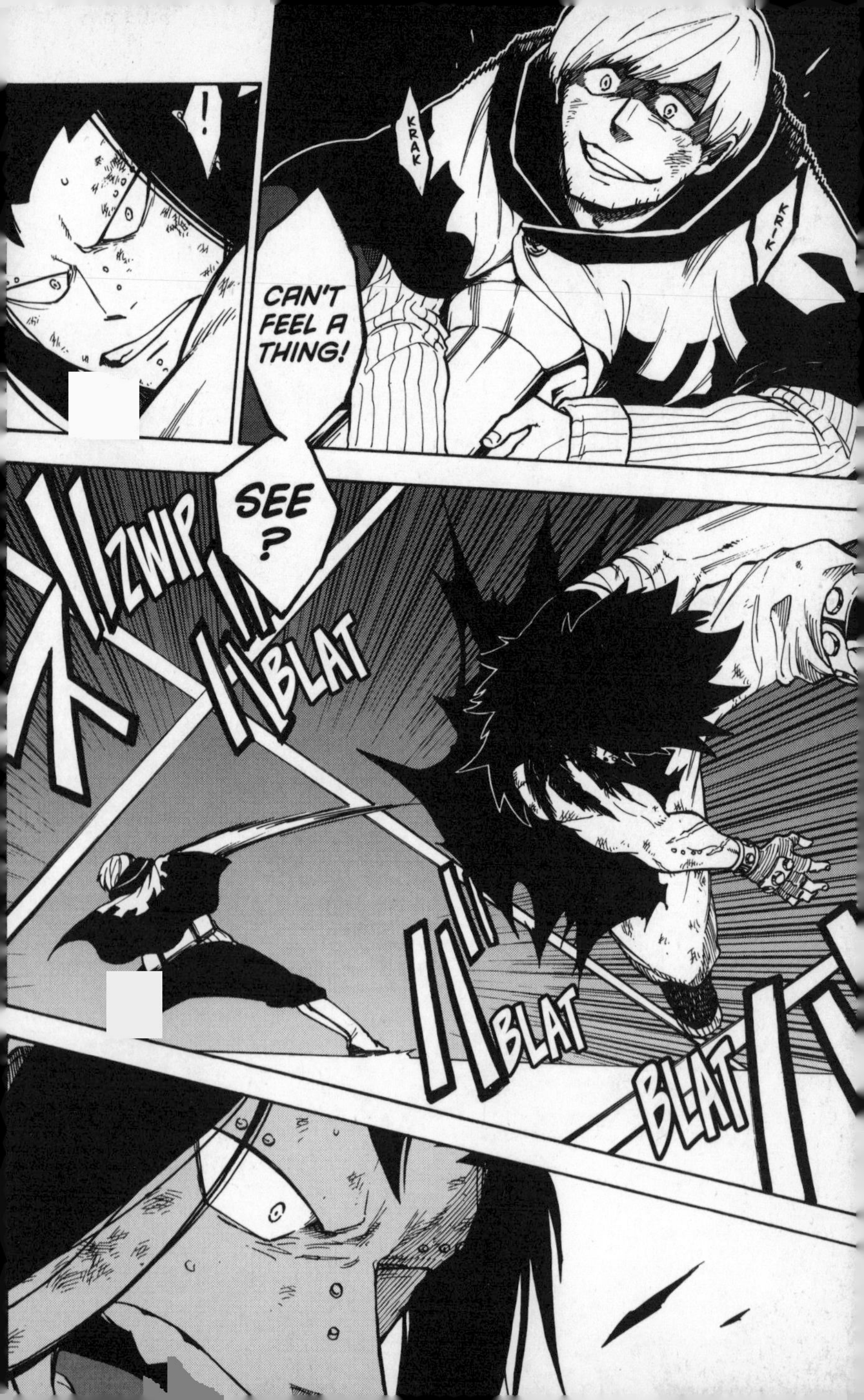
KRAK
KRIK
CAN'T FEEL A THING!
!
SEE ?
ZWIP
BLAT
BLAT
BLAT

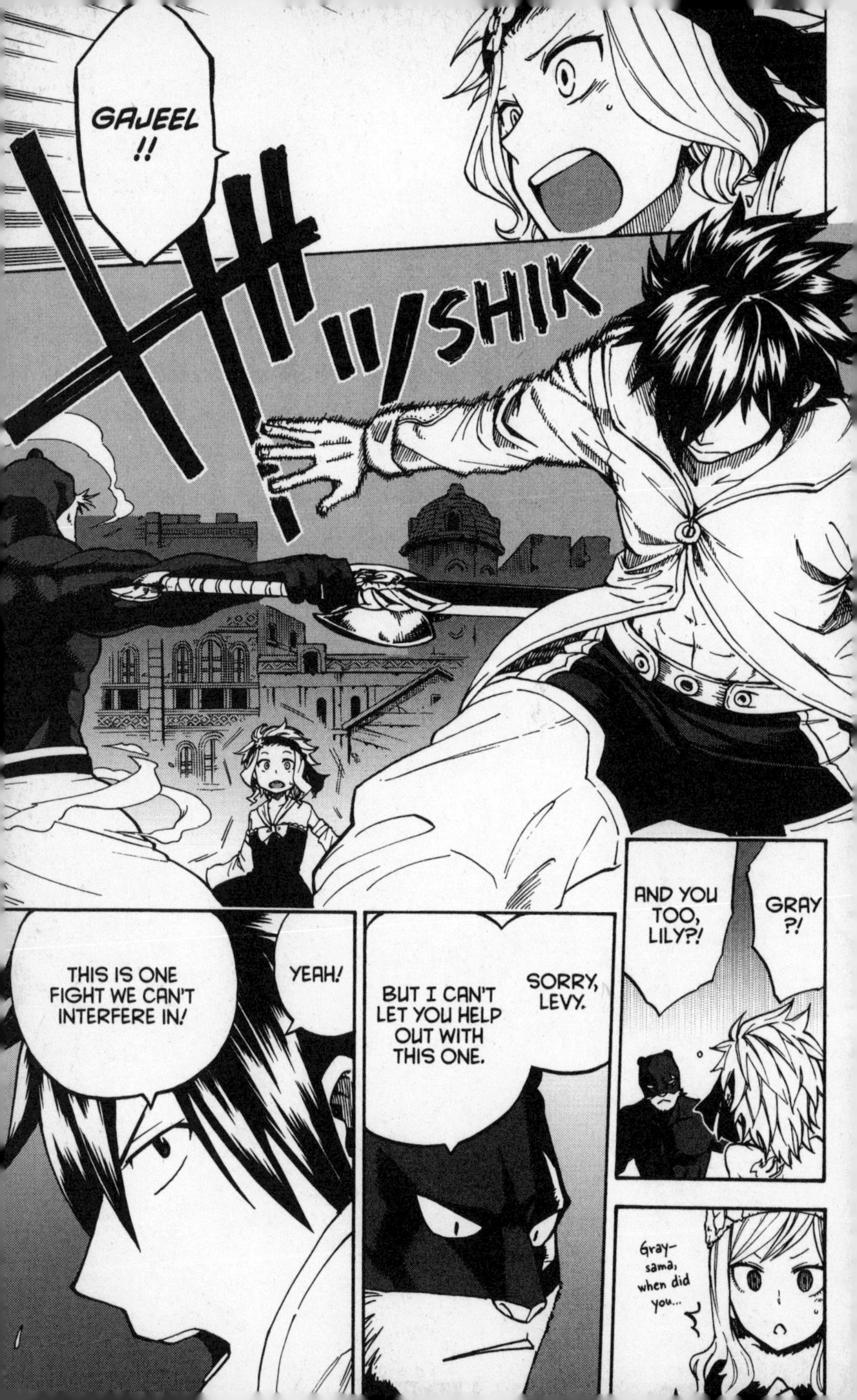
GAJEEL !!
SHIK
GRAY ?!
AND YOU TOO, LILY?!
Gray-sama, when did you...
SORRY, LEVY.
BUT I CAN'T LET YOU HELP OUT WITH THIS ONE.
YEAH!
THIS IS ONE FIGHT WE CAN'T INTERFERE IN!

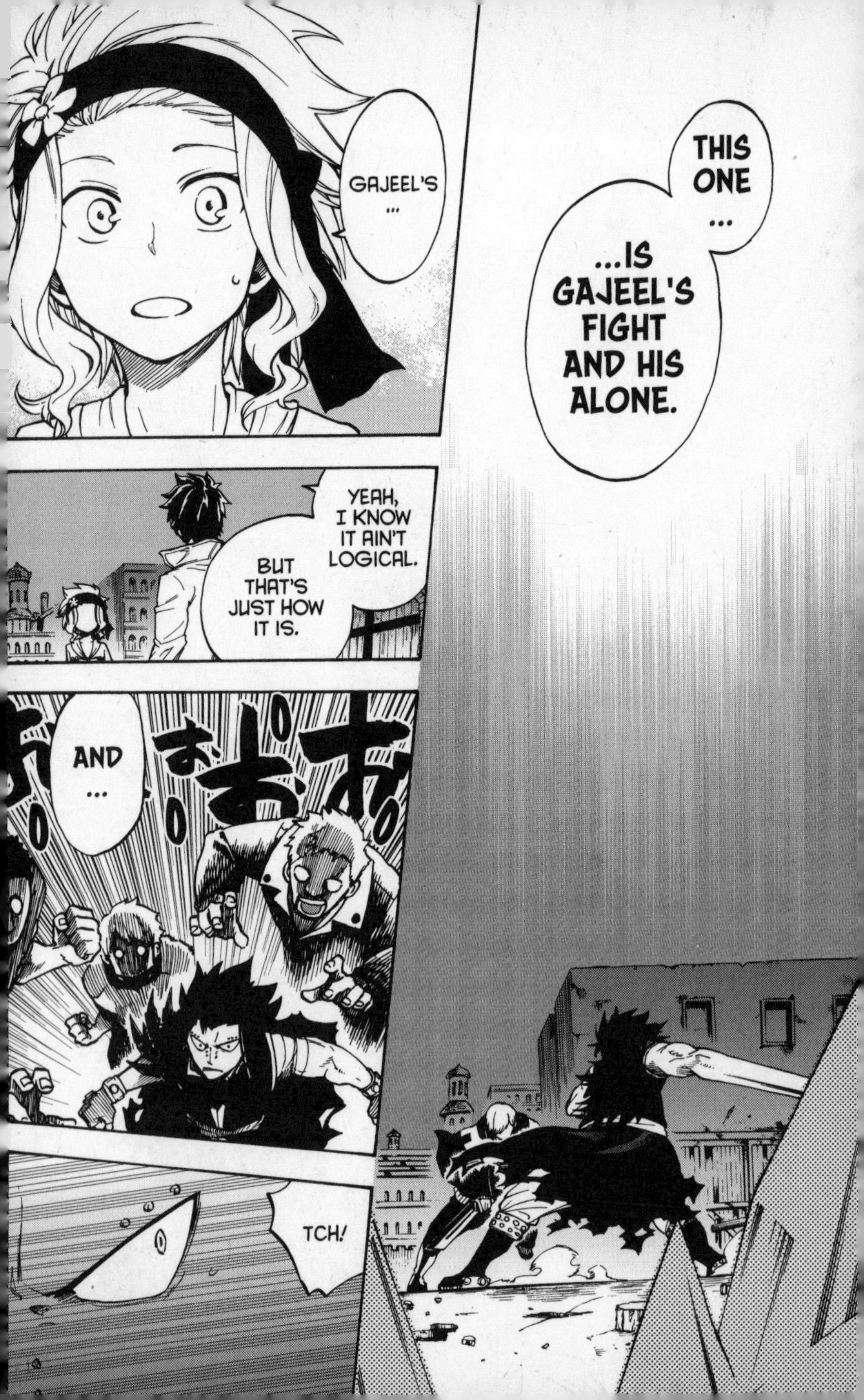
THIS ONE ...
...IS GAJEEL'S FIGHT AND HIS ALONE.
GAJEEL'S ...
YEAH, I KNOW IT AIN'T LOGICAL.
BUT THAT'S JUST HOW IT IS.
AND ...
TCH!

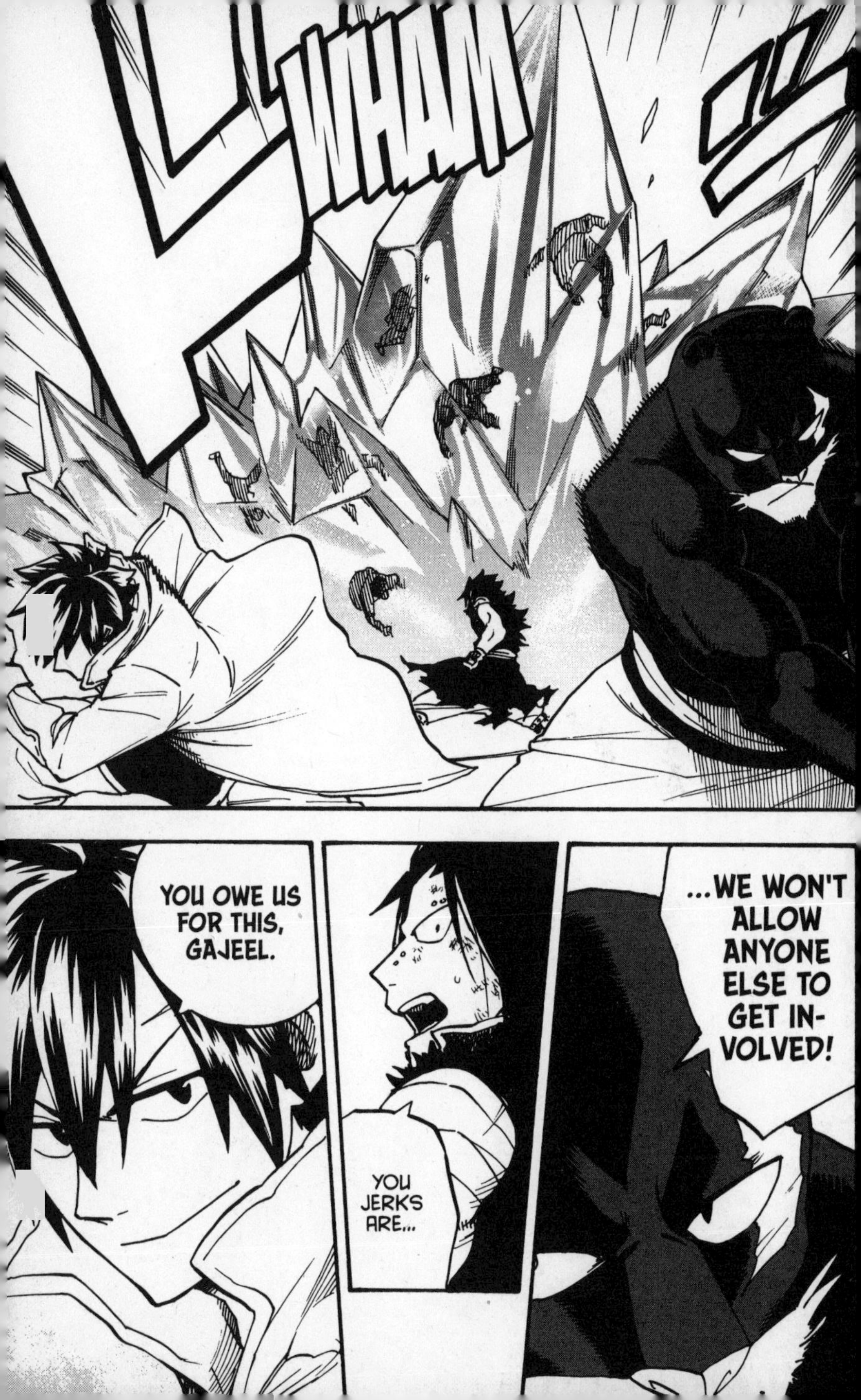
WHAM
...WE WON'T ALLOW ANYONE ELSE TO GET IN-VOLVED!
YOU JERKS ARE...
YOU OWE US FOR THIS, GAJEEL.

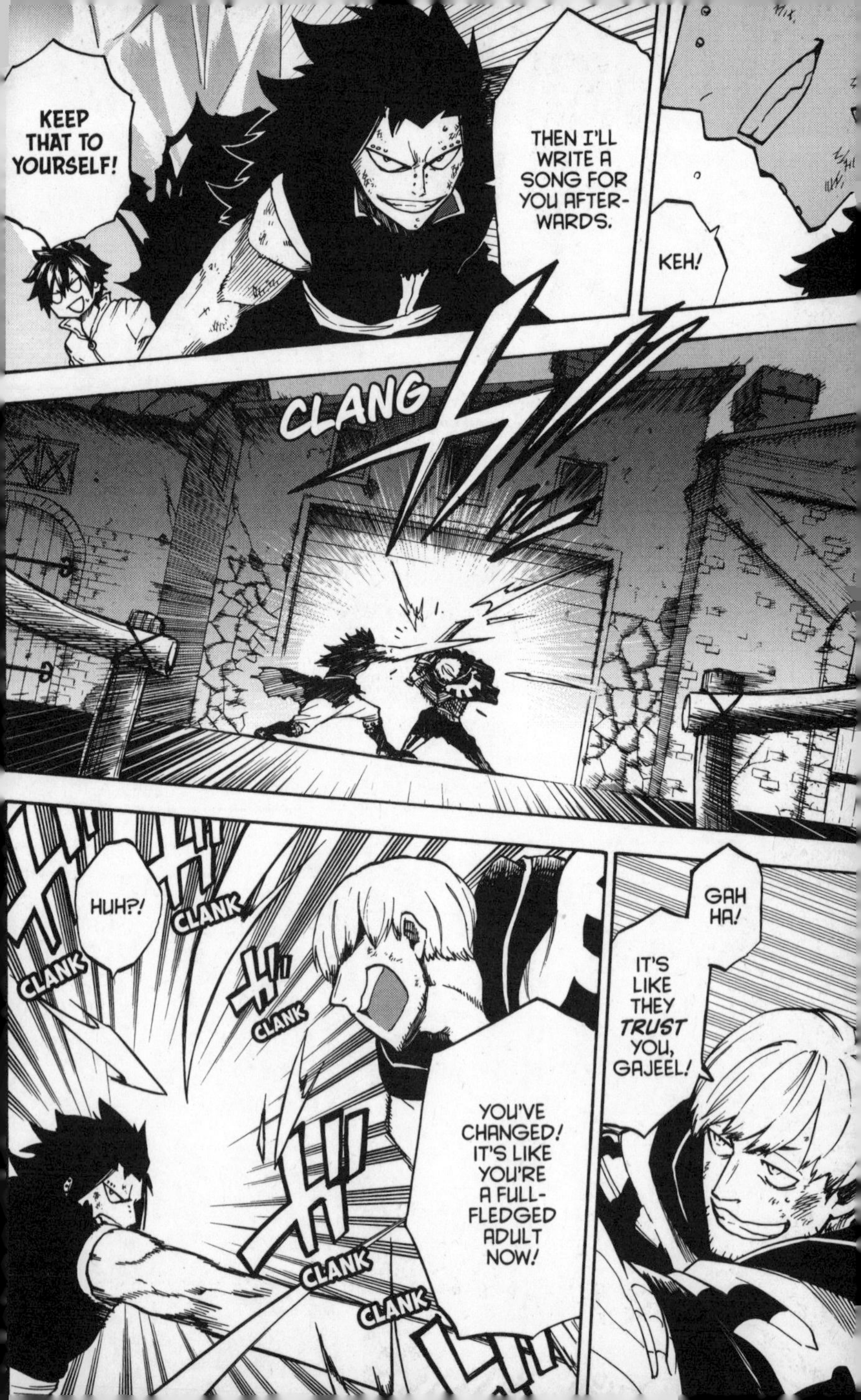
KEH!
THEN I'LL WRITE A SONG FOR YOU AFTER-WARDS.
KEEP THAT TO YOURSELF!
CLANG
GAH HA!
IT'S LIKE THEY *TRUST* YOU, GAJEEL!
YOU'VE CHANGED! IT'S LIKE YOU'RE A FULL-FLEDGED ADULT NOW!
CLANK
HUH?!
CLANK
CLANK
CLANK
CLANK

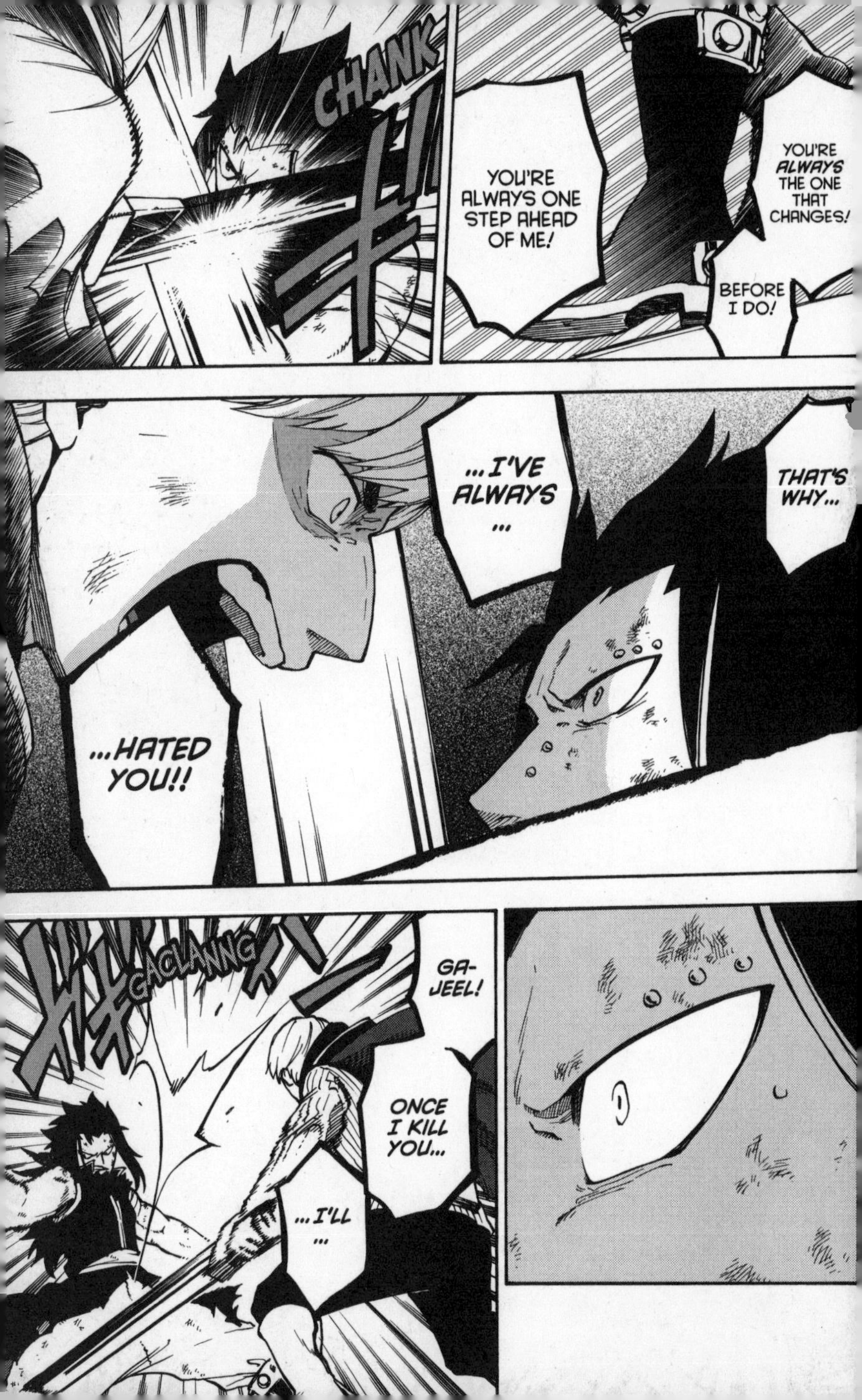
YOU'RE ALWAYS THE ONE THAT CHANGES!
YOU'RE ALWAYS ONE STEP AHEAD OF ME!
BEFORE I DO!
CHANK
THAT'S WHY...
...I'VE ALWAYS...
...HATED YOU!!
GA-JEEL!
CACLANNG
ONCE I KILL YOU...
...I'LL...

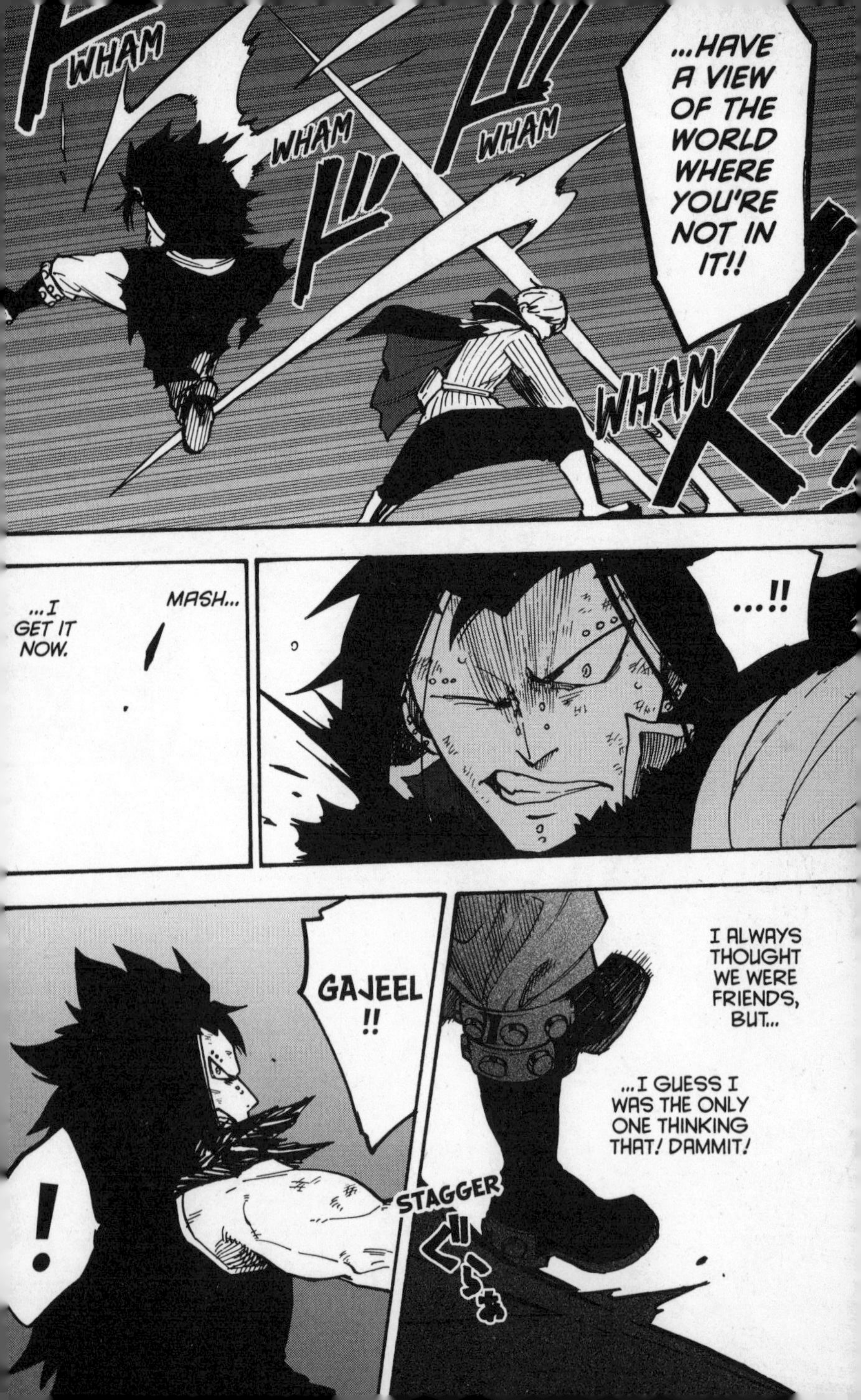
...HAVE A VIEW OF THE WORLD WHERE YOU'RE NOT IN IT!!
WHAM
WHAM
WHAM
WHAM
...!!
MASH...
...I GET IT NOW.
I ALWAYS THOUGHT WE WERE FRIENDS, BUT...
...I GUESS I WAS THE ONLY ONE THINKING THAT! DAMMIT!
STAGGER
GAJEEL!!
!

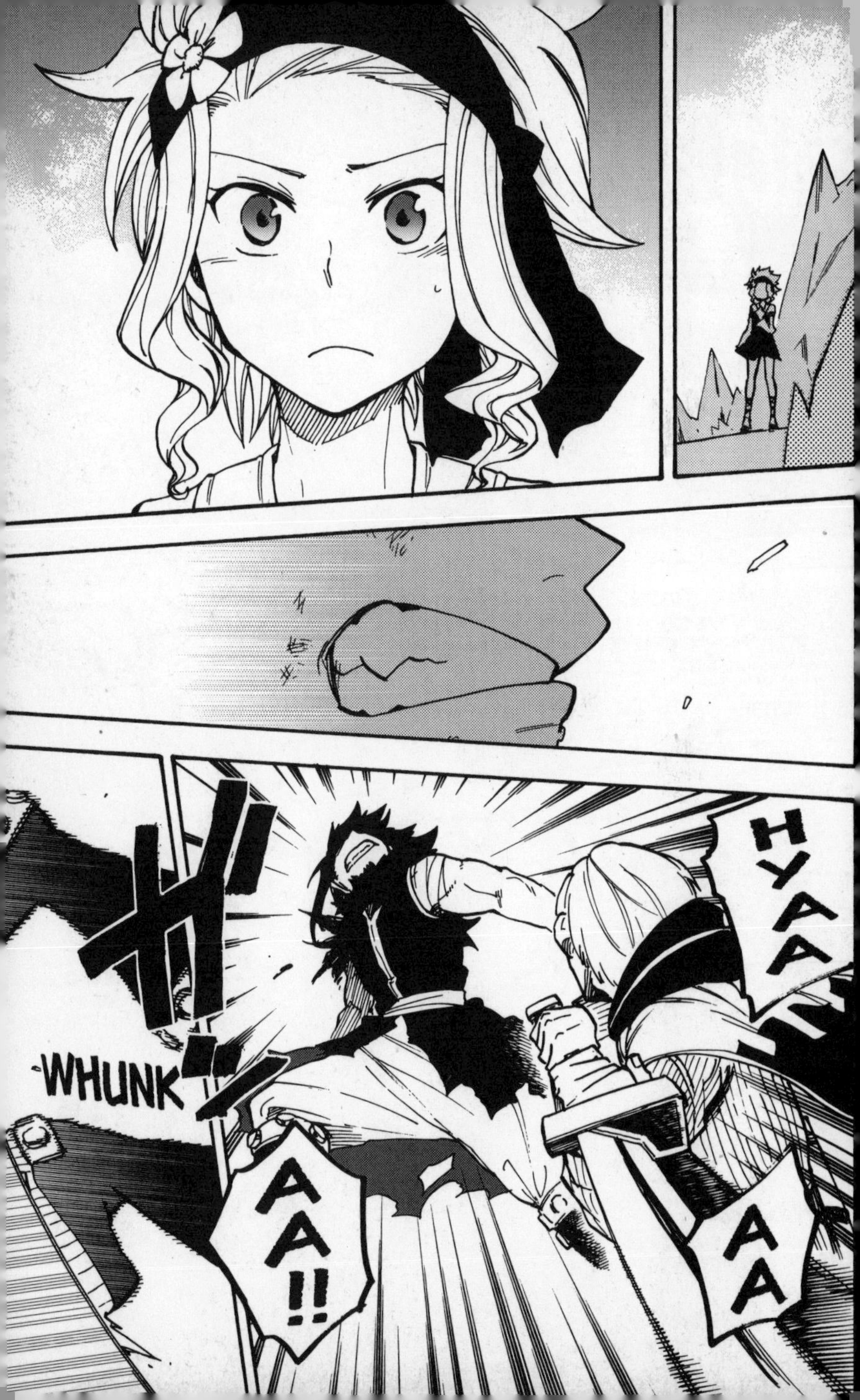
HYAAA
AA
AA!!
WHUNK

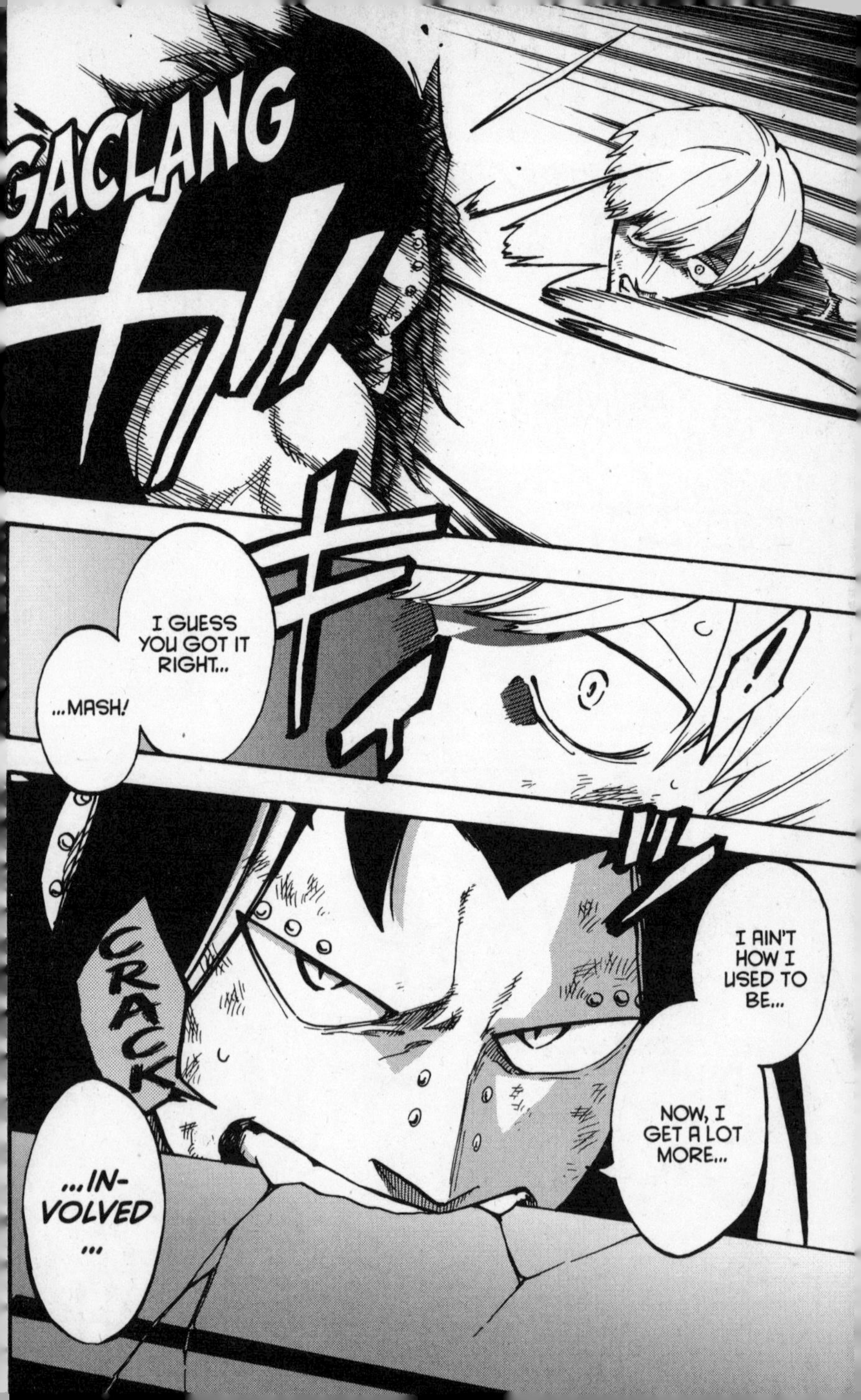
GACLANG
I GUESS YOU GOT IT RIGHT...
...MASH!
I AIN'T HOW I USED TO BE...
NOW, I GET A LOT MORE...
CRACK
...IN-VOLVED ...

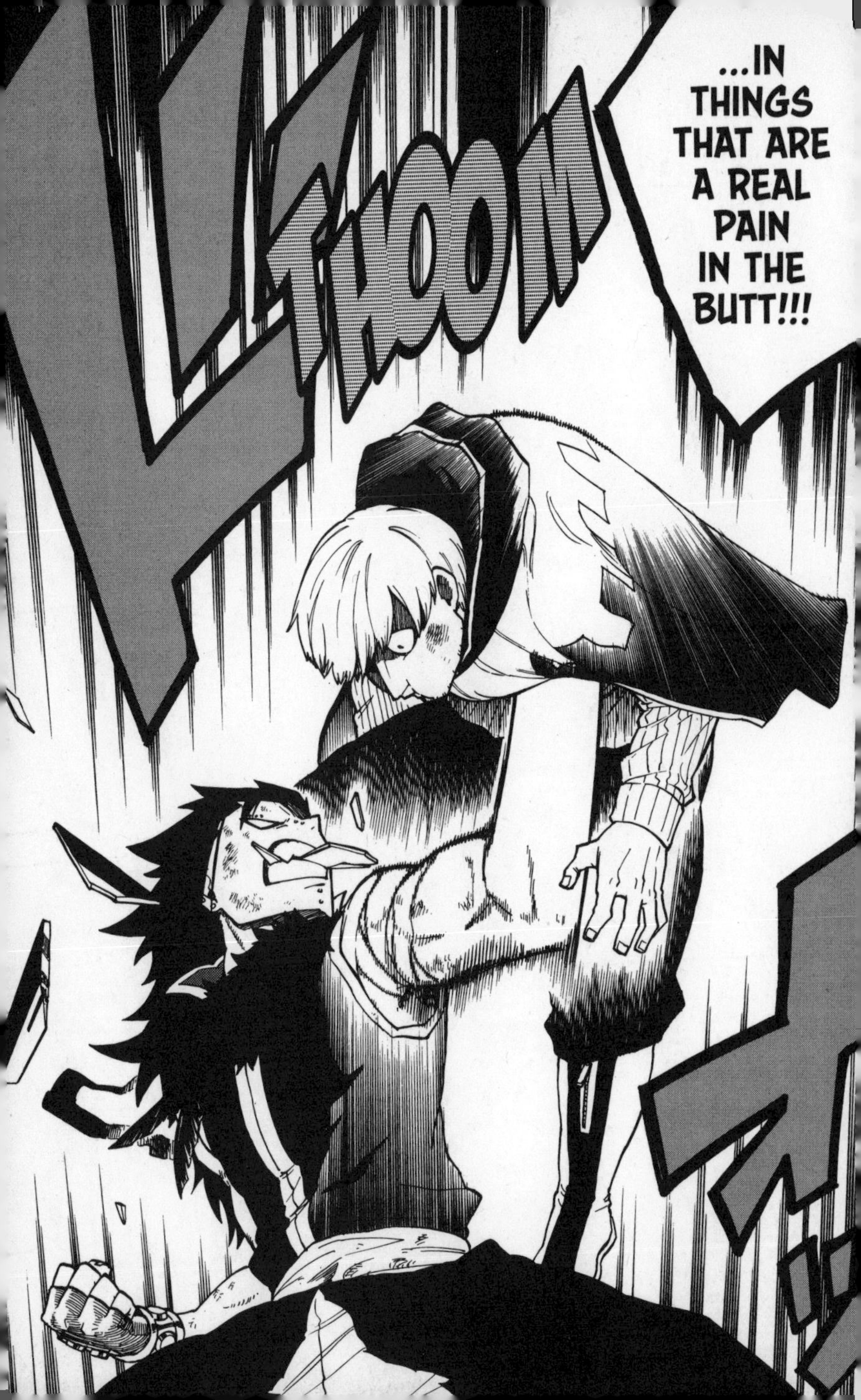
...IN THINGS THAT ARE A REAL PAIN IN THE BUTT!!!
THOOM

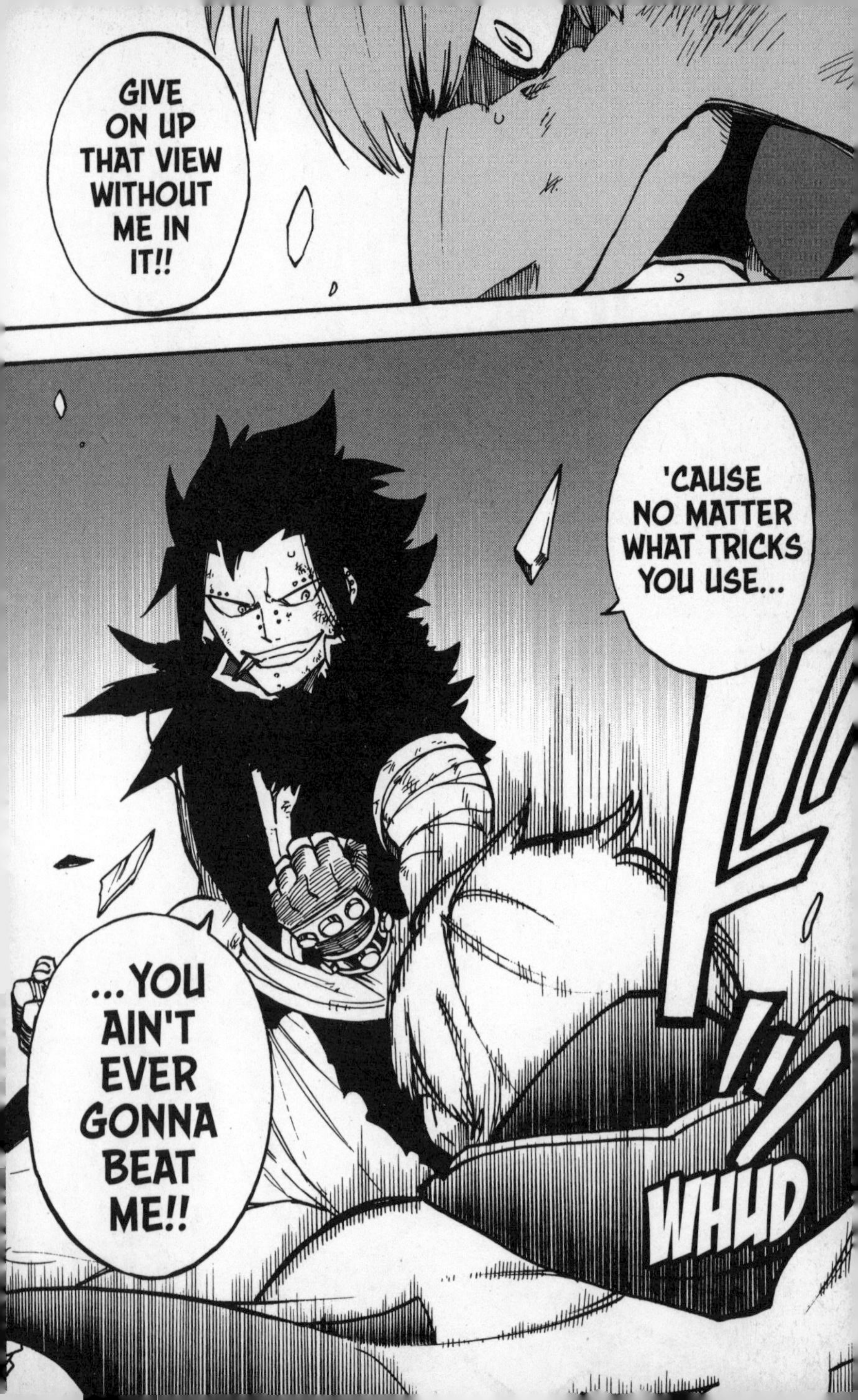
GIVE ON UP THAT VIEW WITHOUT ME IN IT!!
'CAUSE NO MATTER WHAT TRICKS YOU USE...
...YOU AIN'T EVER GONNA BEAT ME!!
WHUD

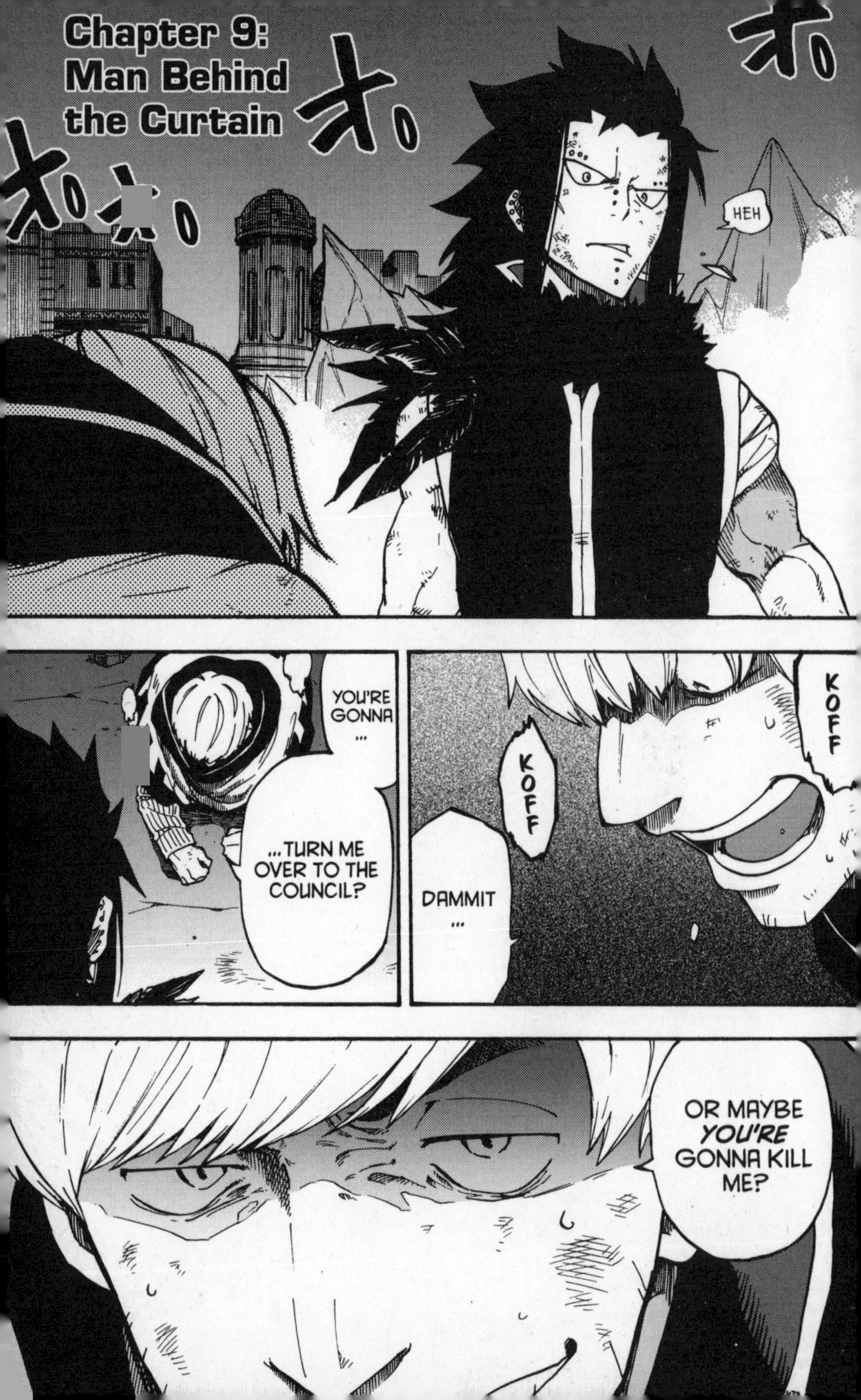
Chapter 9: Man Behind the Curtain
HEH
KOFF KOFF
KOFF
DAMMIT ...
YOU'RE GONNA ...
...TURN ME OVER TO THE COUNCIL?
OR MAYBE *YOU'RE* GONNA KILL ME?

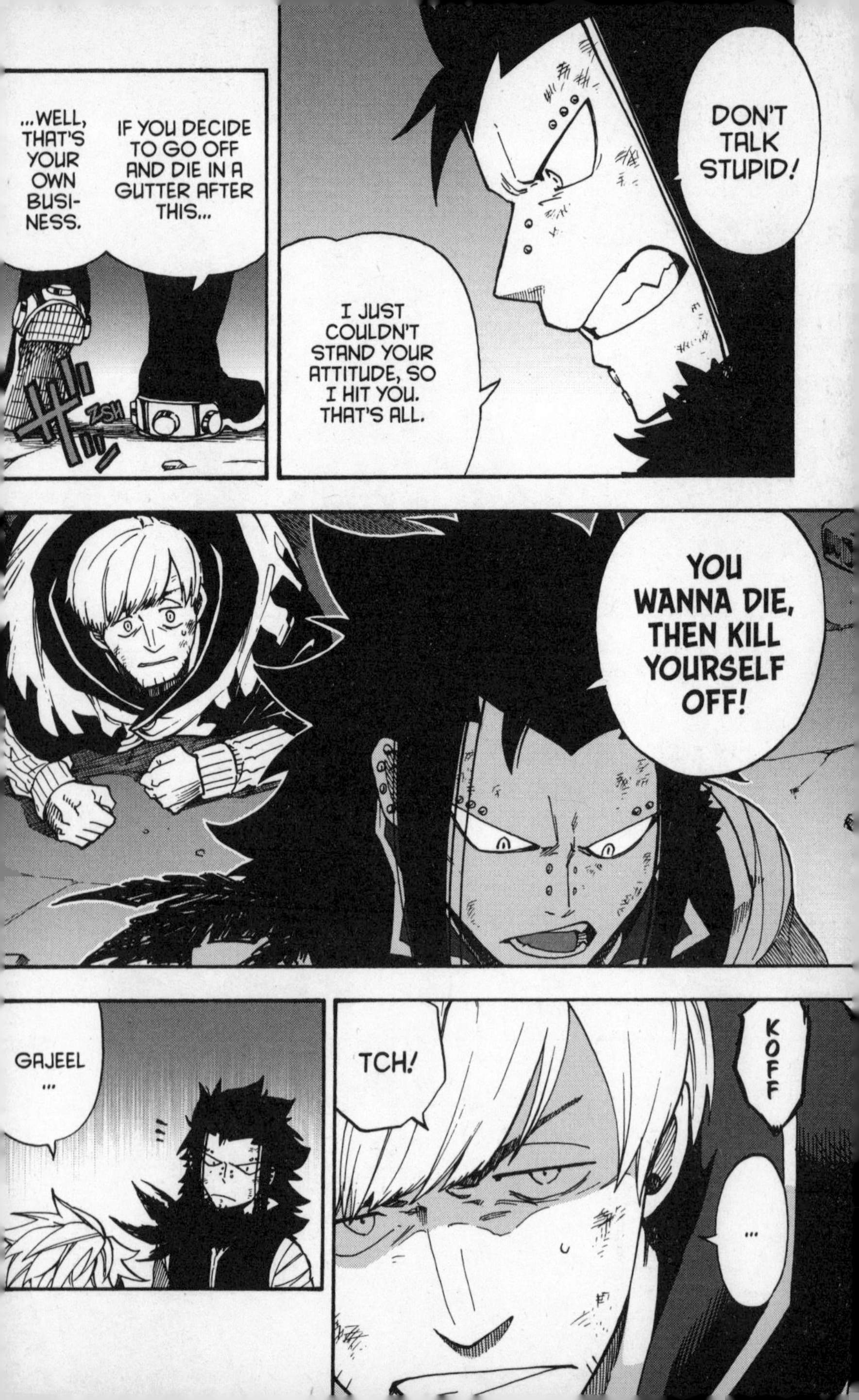
DON'T TALK STUPID!
I JUST COULDN'T STAND YOUR ATTITUDE, SO I HIT YOU. THAT'S ALL.
IF YOU DECIDE TO GO OFF AND DIE IN A GUTTER AFTER THIS...
...WELL, THAT'S YOUR OWN BUSINESS.
ZSH
YOU WANNA DIE, THEN KILL YOURSELF OFF!
KOFF
...
TCH!
GAJEEL ...

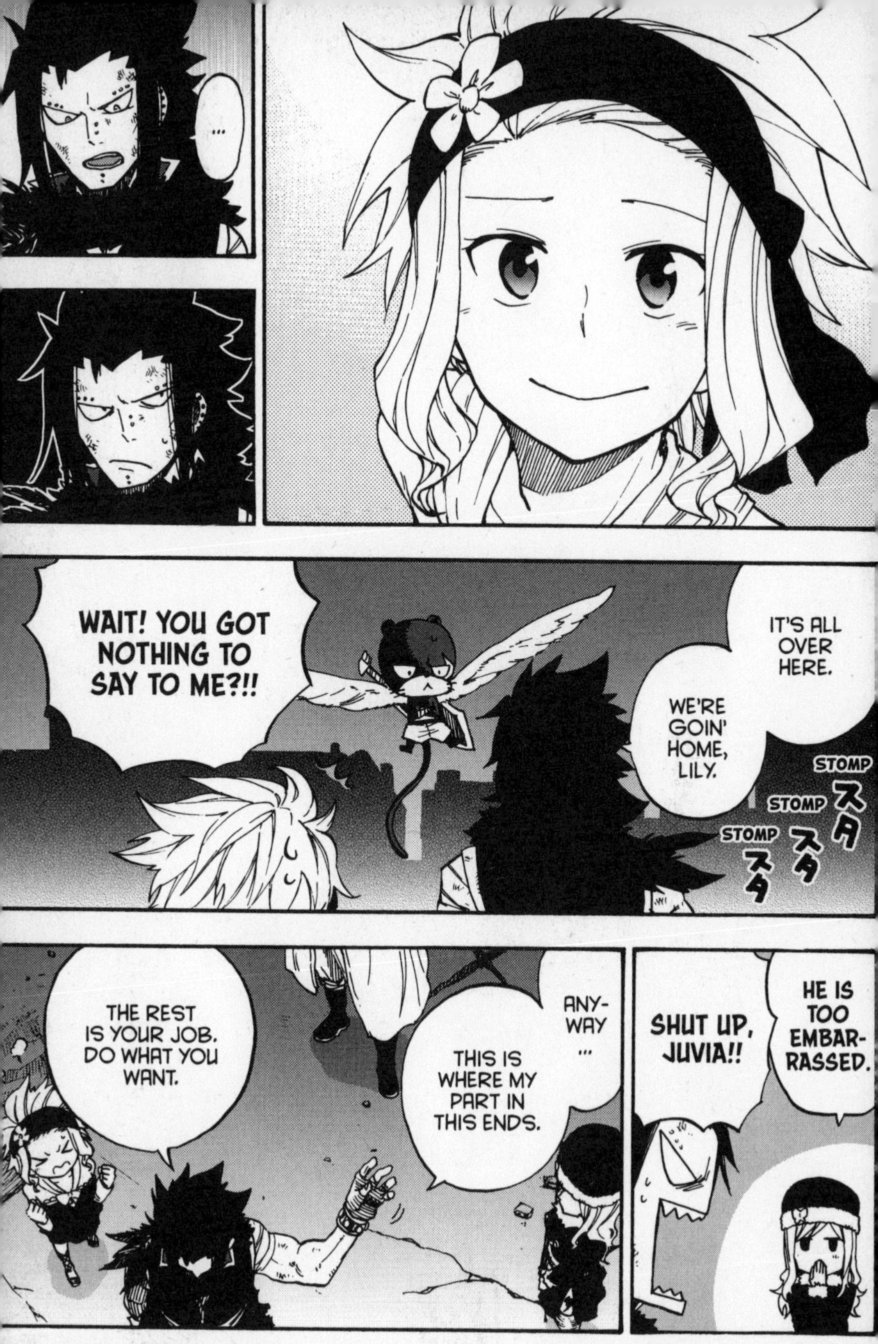
...
IT'S ALL OVER HERE.
WE'RE GOIN' HOME, LILY.
STOMP スタ
STOMP スタ
STOMP スタ
WAIT! YOU GOT NOTHING TO SAY TO ME?!!
HE IS TOO EMBARRASSED.
SHUT UP, JUVIA!!
ANYWAY ...
THIS IS WHERE MY PART IN THIS ENDS.
THE REST IS YOUR JOB. DO WHAT YOU WANT.

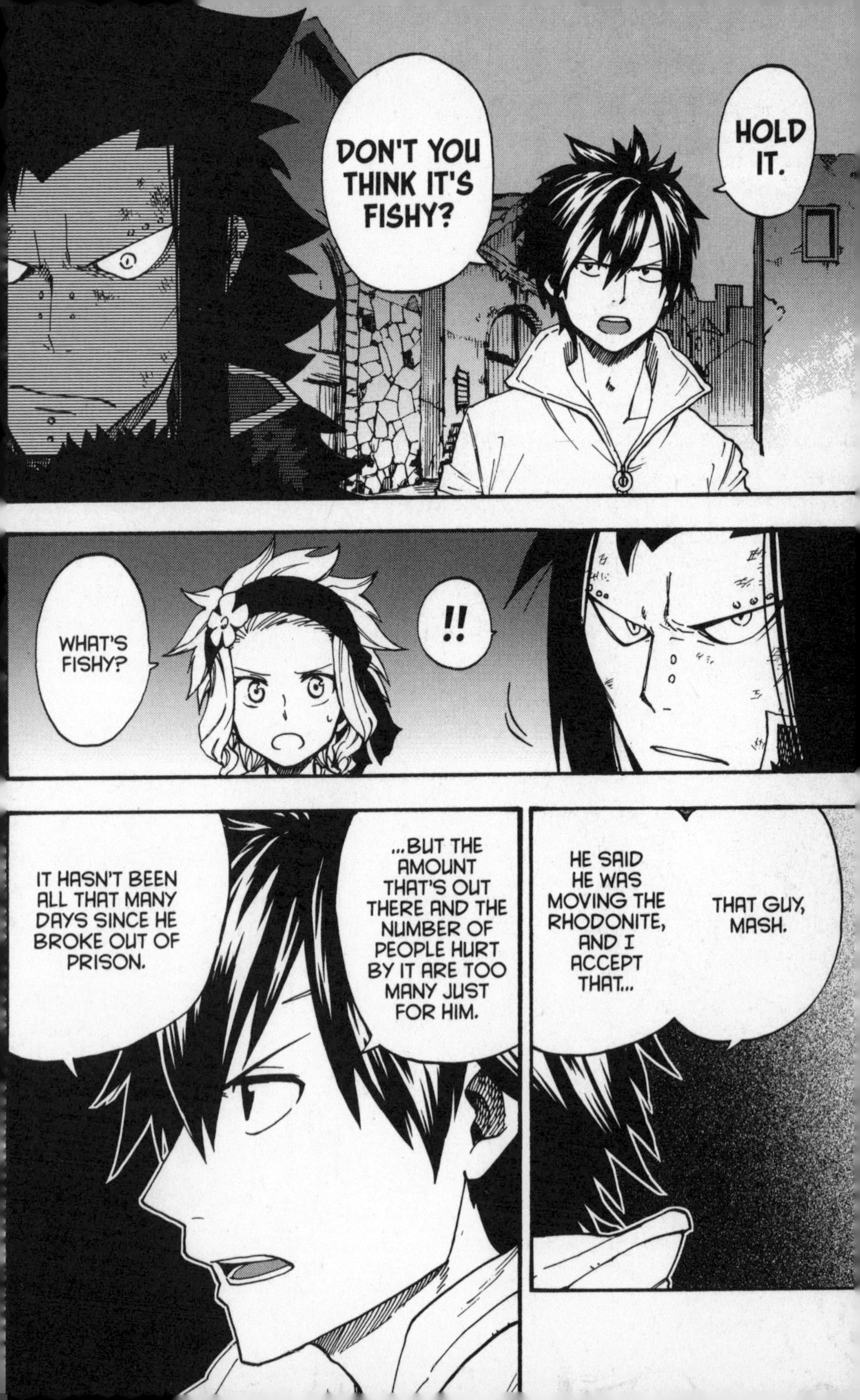
HOLD IT.
DON'T YOU THINK IT'S FISHY?
!!
WHAT'S FISHY?
THAT GUY, MASH.
HE SAID HE WAS MOVING THE RHODONITE, AND I ACCEPT THAT...
...BUT THE AMOUNT THAT'S OUT THERE AND THE NUMBER OF PEOPLE HURT BY IT ARE TOO MANY JUST FOR HIM.
IT HASN'T BEEN ALL THAT MANY DAYS SINCE HE BROKE OUT OF PRISON.

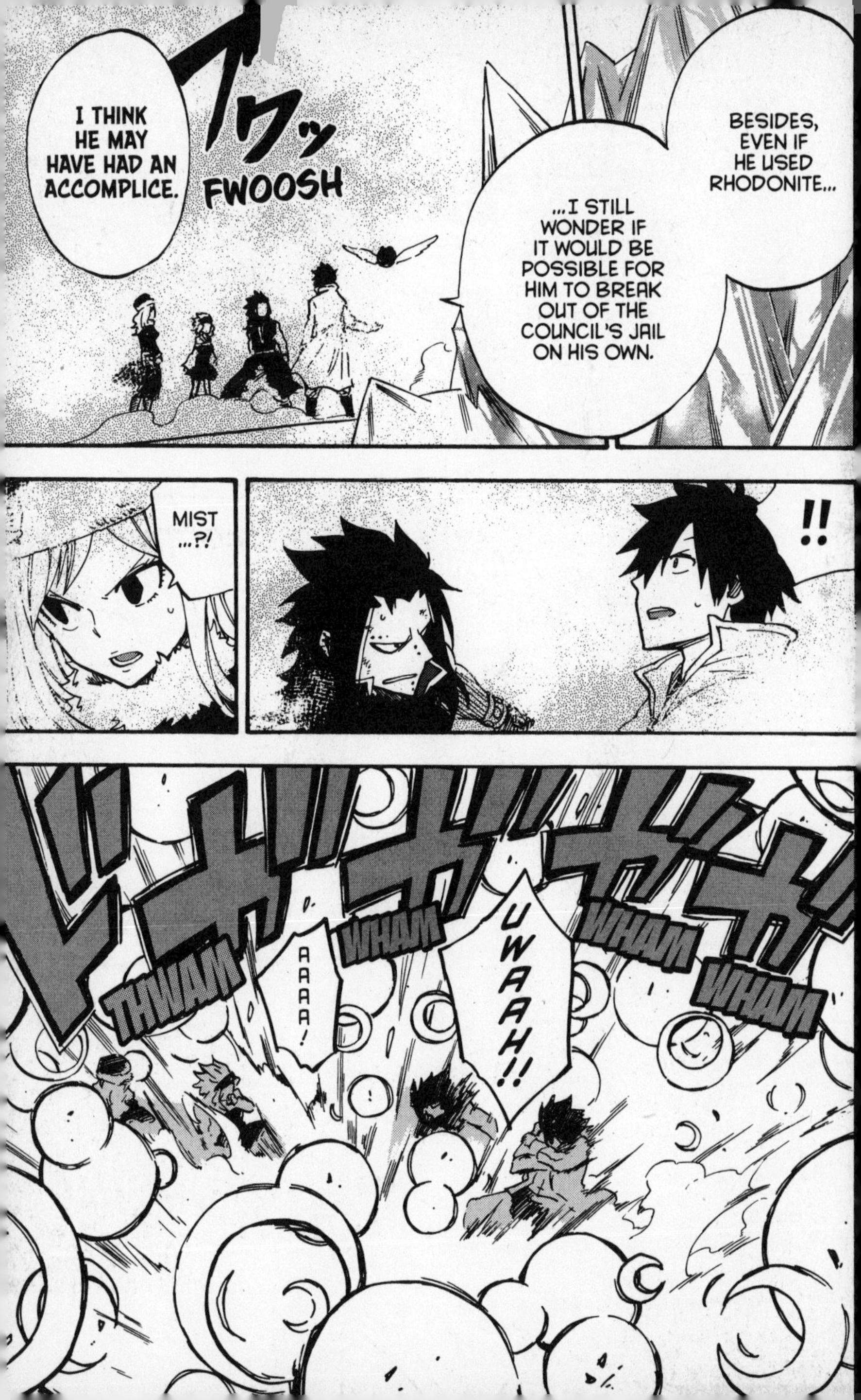
BESIDES, EVEN IF HE USED RHODONITE...
...I STILL WONDER IF IT WOULD BE POSSIBLE FOR HIM TO BREAK OUT OF THE COUNCIL'S JAIL ON HIS OWN.
FWOOSH
I THINK HE MAY HAVE HAD AN ACCOMPLICE.
!!
MIST ...?!
WHAM
WHAM
UWAAAH!!
WHAM
AAAAA!
THWAM

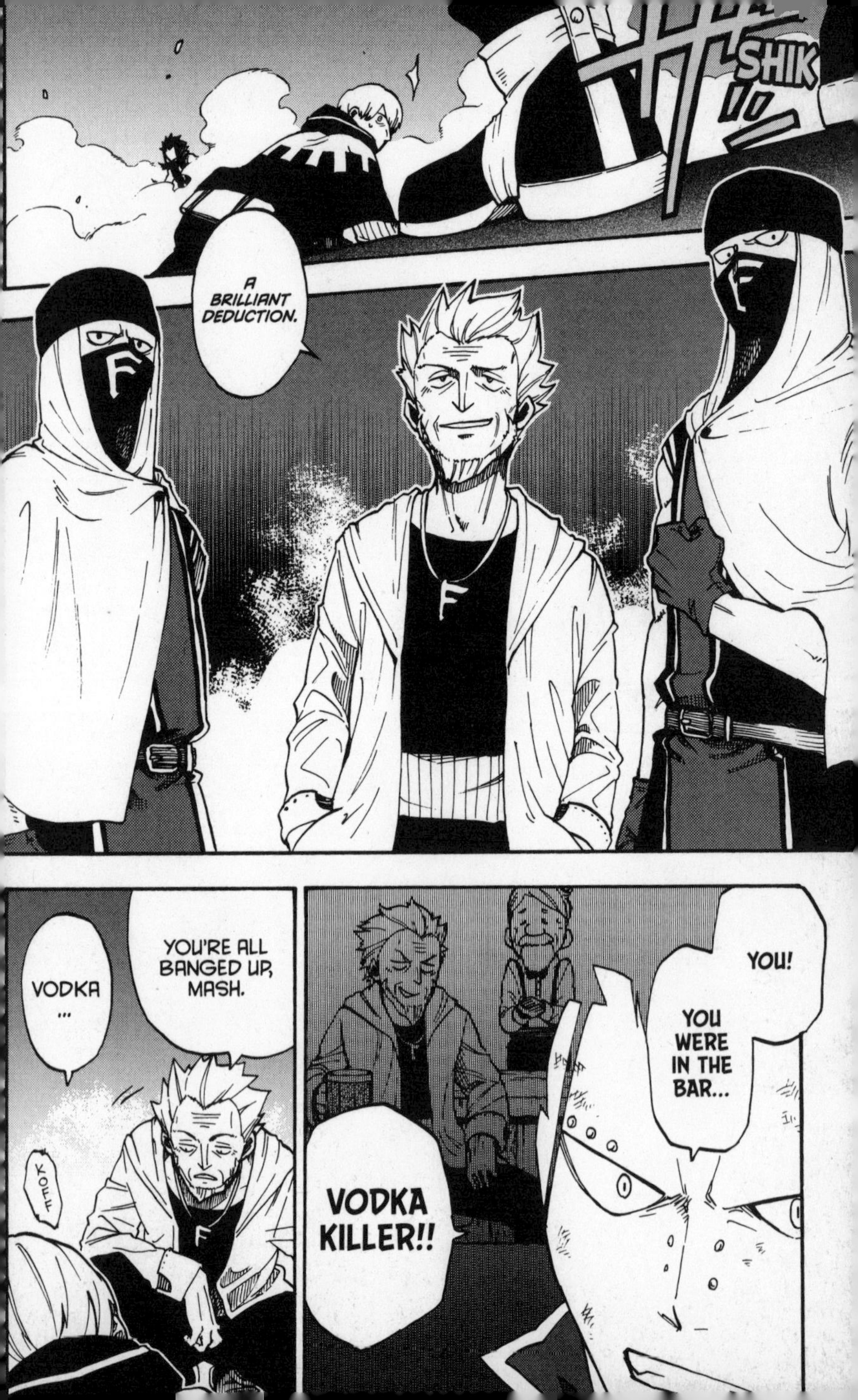
SHIK
A BRILLIANT DEDUCTION.
YOU!
YOU WERE IN THE BAR...
VODKA KILLER!!
YOU'RE ALL BANGED UP, MASH.
VODKA ...
KOFF

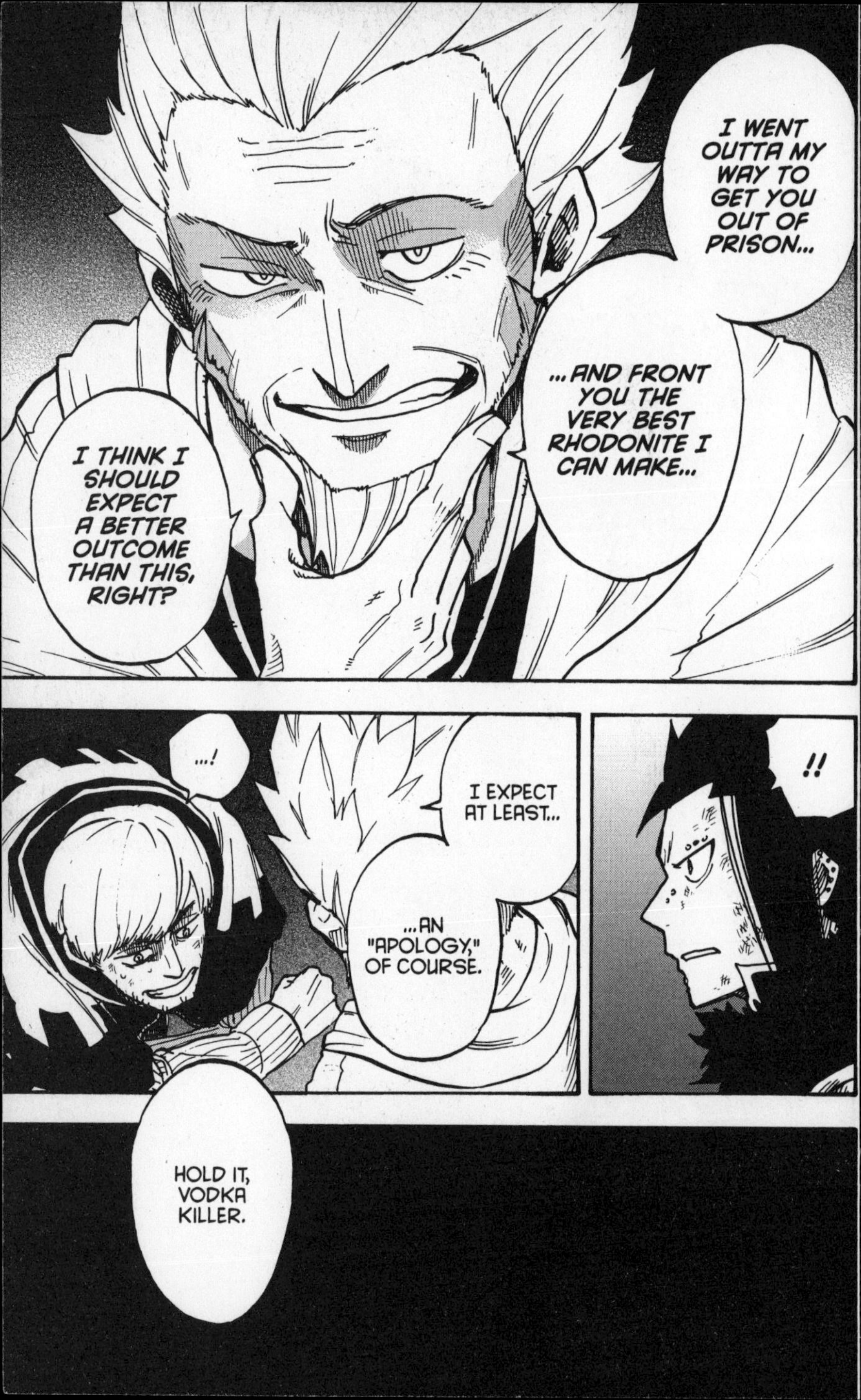
I WENT OUTTA MY WAY TO GET YOU OUT OF PRISON...
...AND FRONT YOU THE VERY BEST RHODONITE I CAN MAKE...
I THINK I SHOULD EXPECT A BETTER OUTCOME THAN THIS, RIGHT?
!!
I EXPECT AT LEAST...
...AN "APOLOGY," OF COURSE.
...!
HOLD IT, VODKA KILLER.

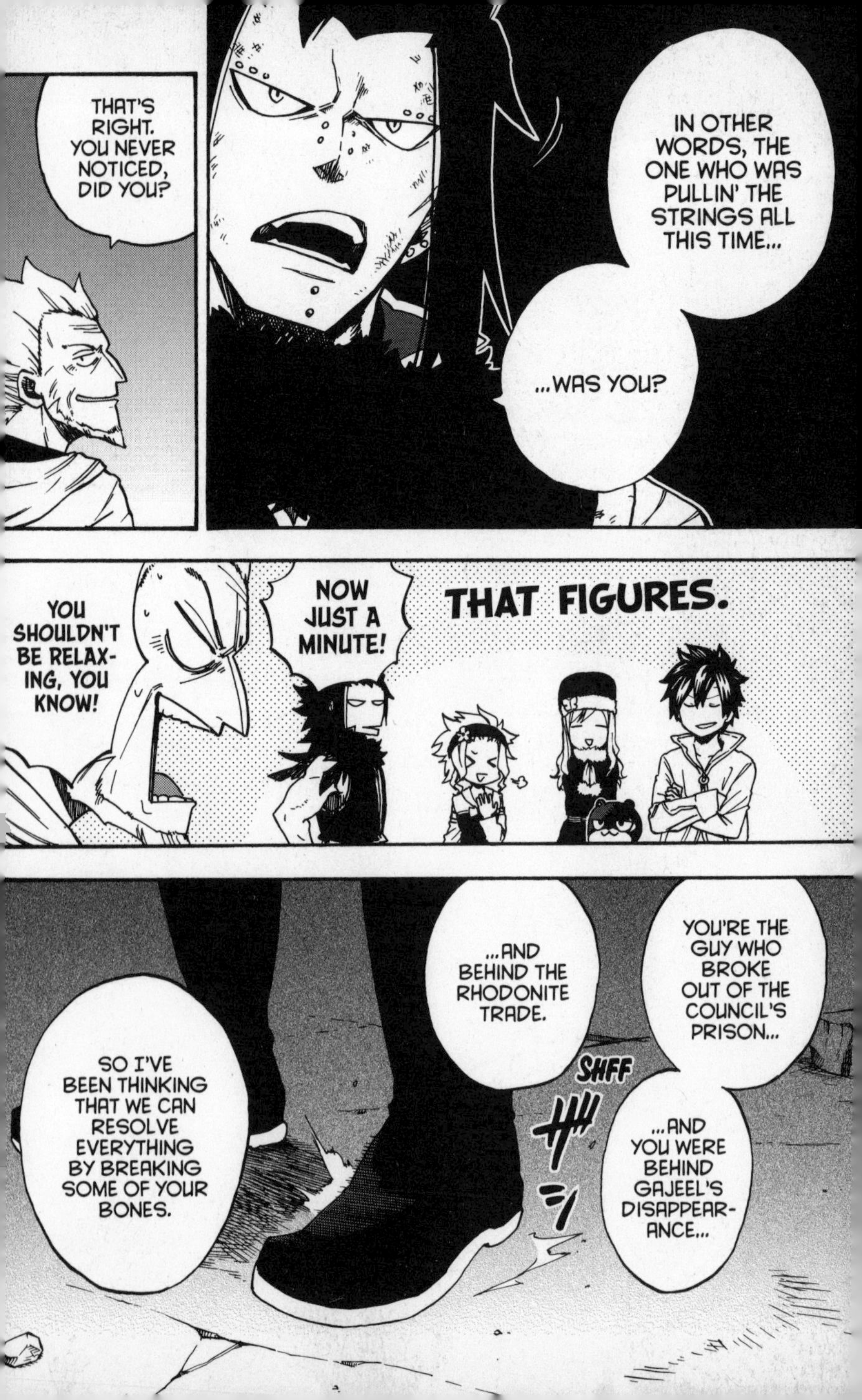
IN OTHER WORDS, THE ONE WHO WAS PULLIN' THE STRINGS ALL THIS TIME...
...WAS YOU?
THAT'S RIGHT. YOU NEVER NOTICED, DID YOU?
THAT FIGURES.
NOW JUST A MINUTE!
YOU SHOULDN'T BE RELAX-ING, YOU KNOW!
YOU'RE THE GUY WHO BROKE OUT OF THE COUNCIL'S PRISON...
...AND BEHIND THE RHODONITE TRADE.
SHFF
...AND YOU WERE BEHIND GAJEEL'S DISAPPEAR-ANCE...
SO I'VE BEEN THINKING THAT WE CAN RESOLVE EVERYTHING BY BREAKING SOME OF YOUR BONES.

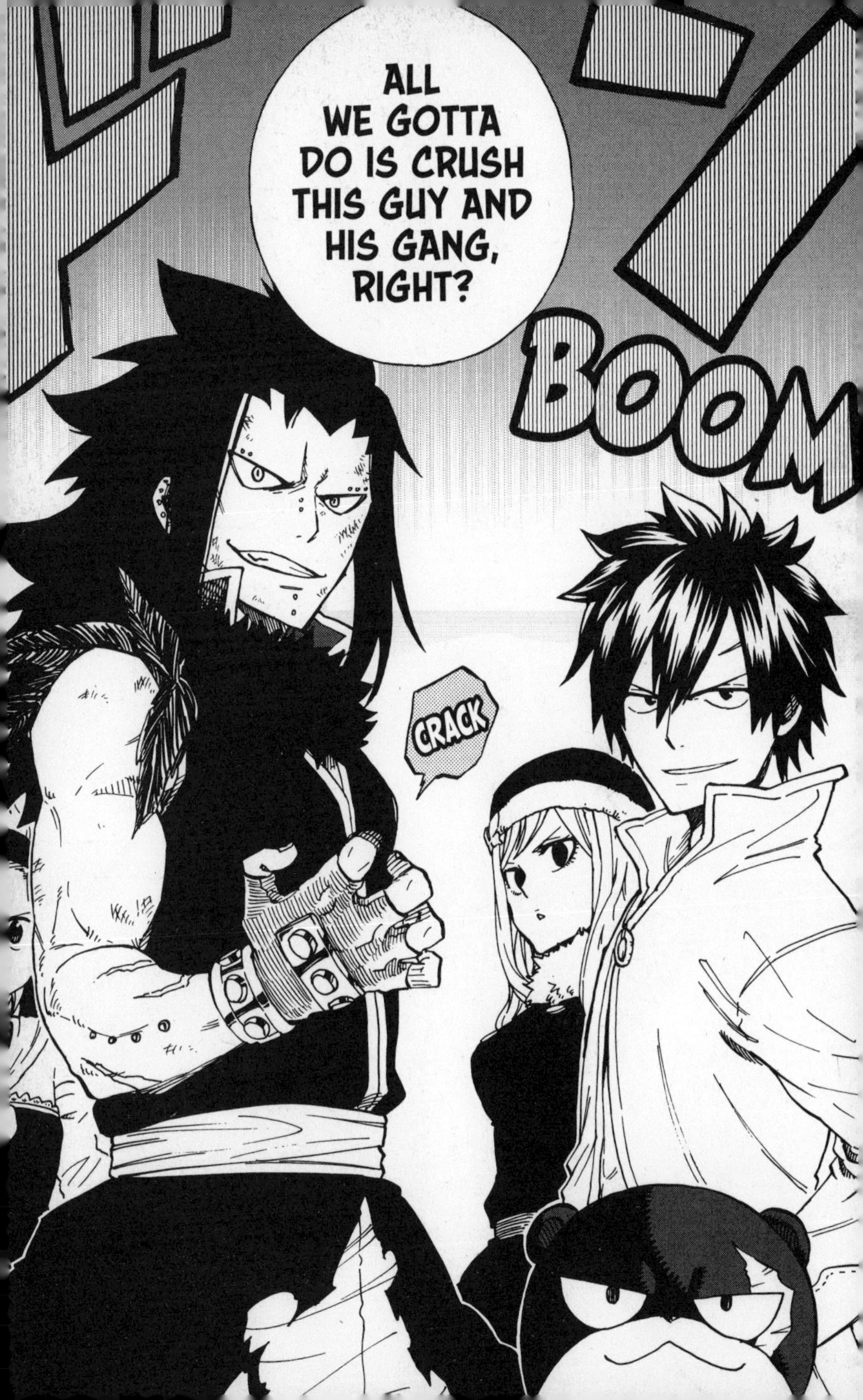
ALL WE GOTTA DO IS CRUSH THIS GUY AND HIS GANG, RIGHT?
BOOM
CRACK

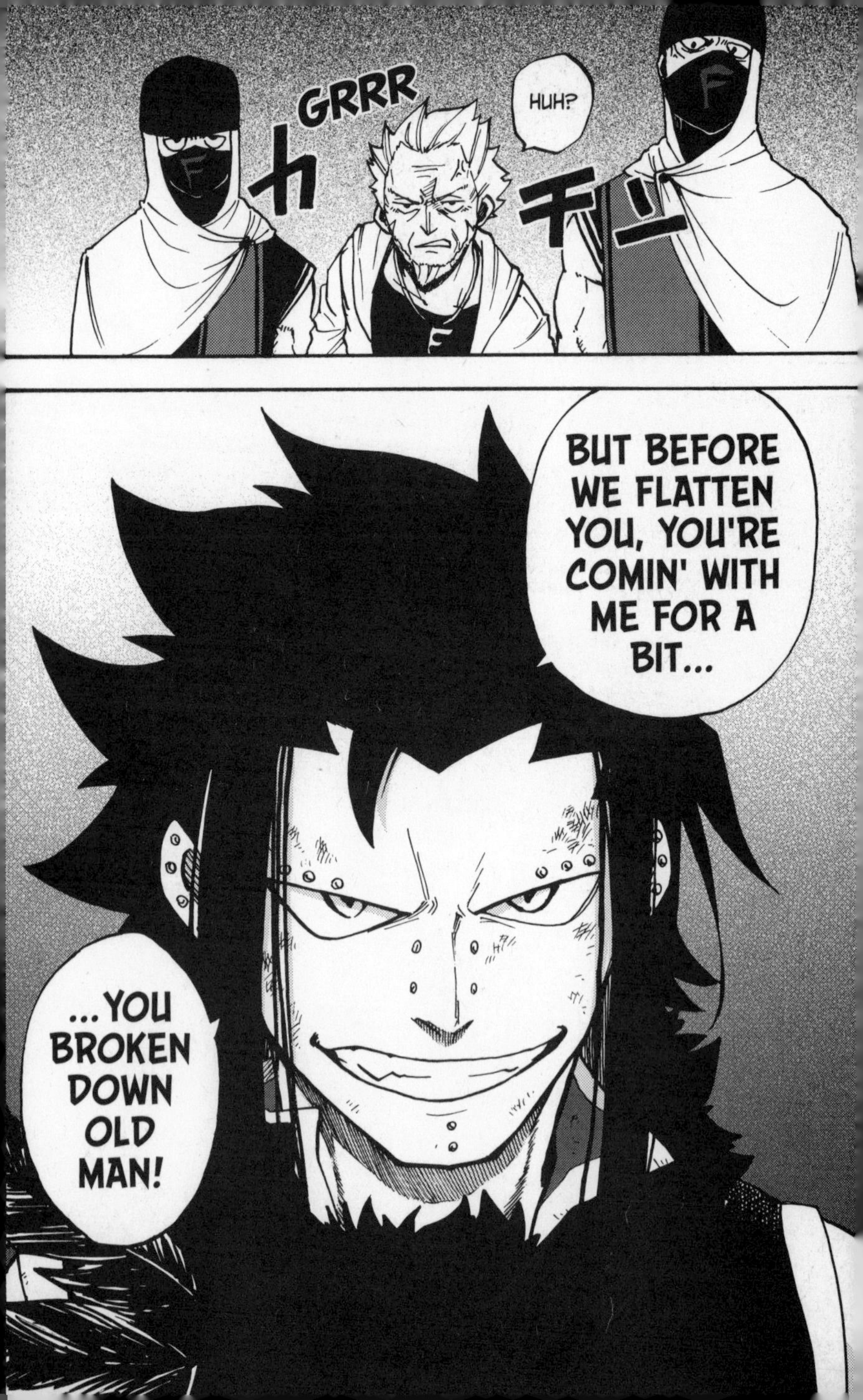
HUH?
GRRR
カ チー
BUT BEFORE WE FLATTEN YOU, YOU'RE COMIN' WITH ME FOR A BIT...
...YOU BROKEN DOWN OLD MAN!

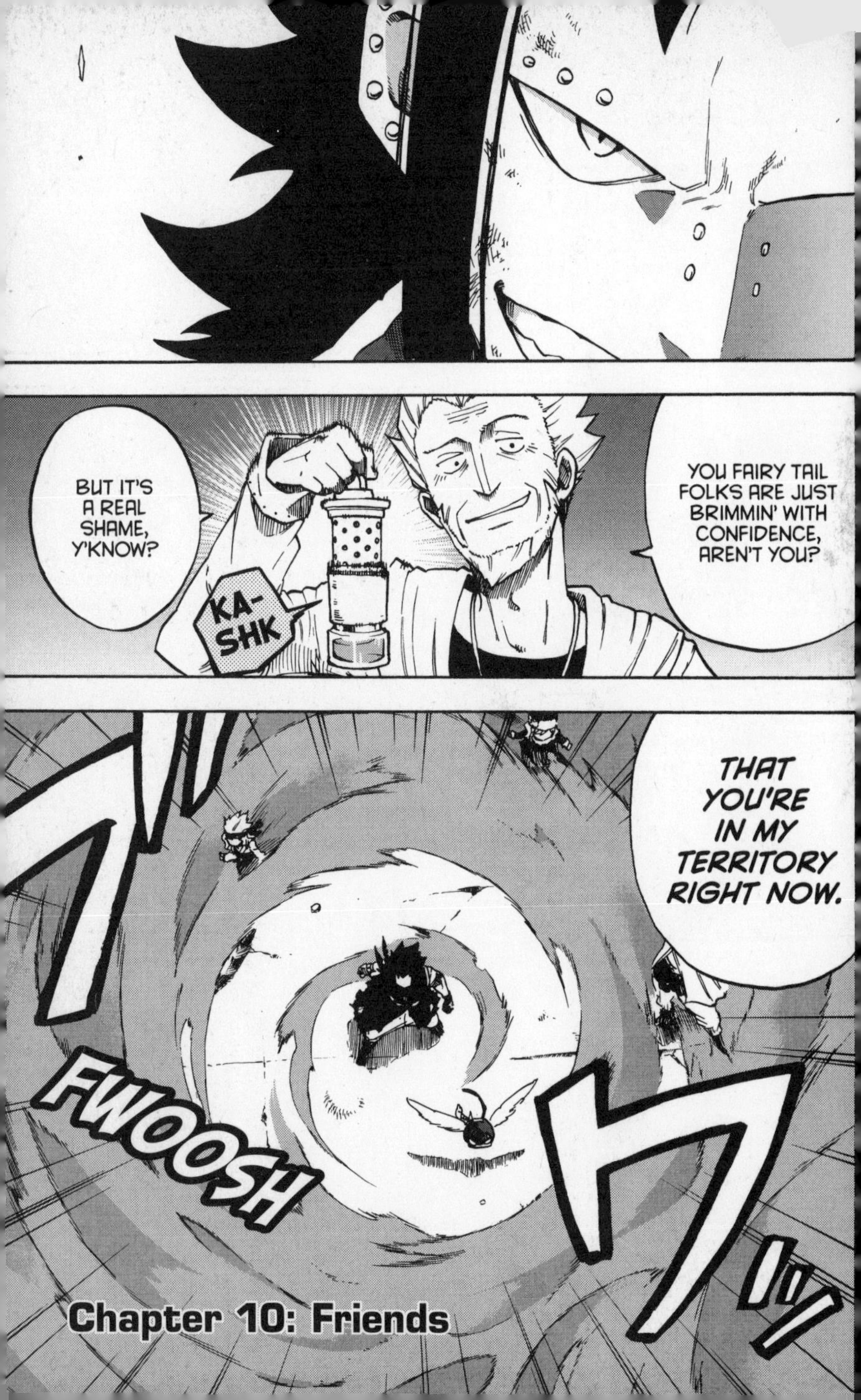
YOU FAIRY TAIL FOLKS ARE JUST BRIMMIN' WITH CONFIDENCE, AREN'T YOU?
BUT IT'S A REAL SHAME, Y'KNOW?
KA-SHK
THAT YOU'RE IN MY TERRITORY RIGHT NOW.
FWOOSH

Chapter 10: Friends

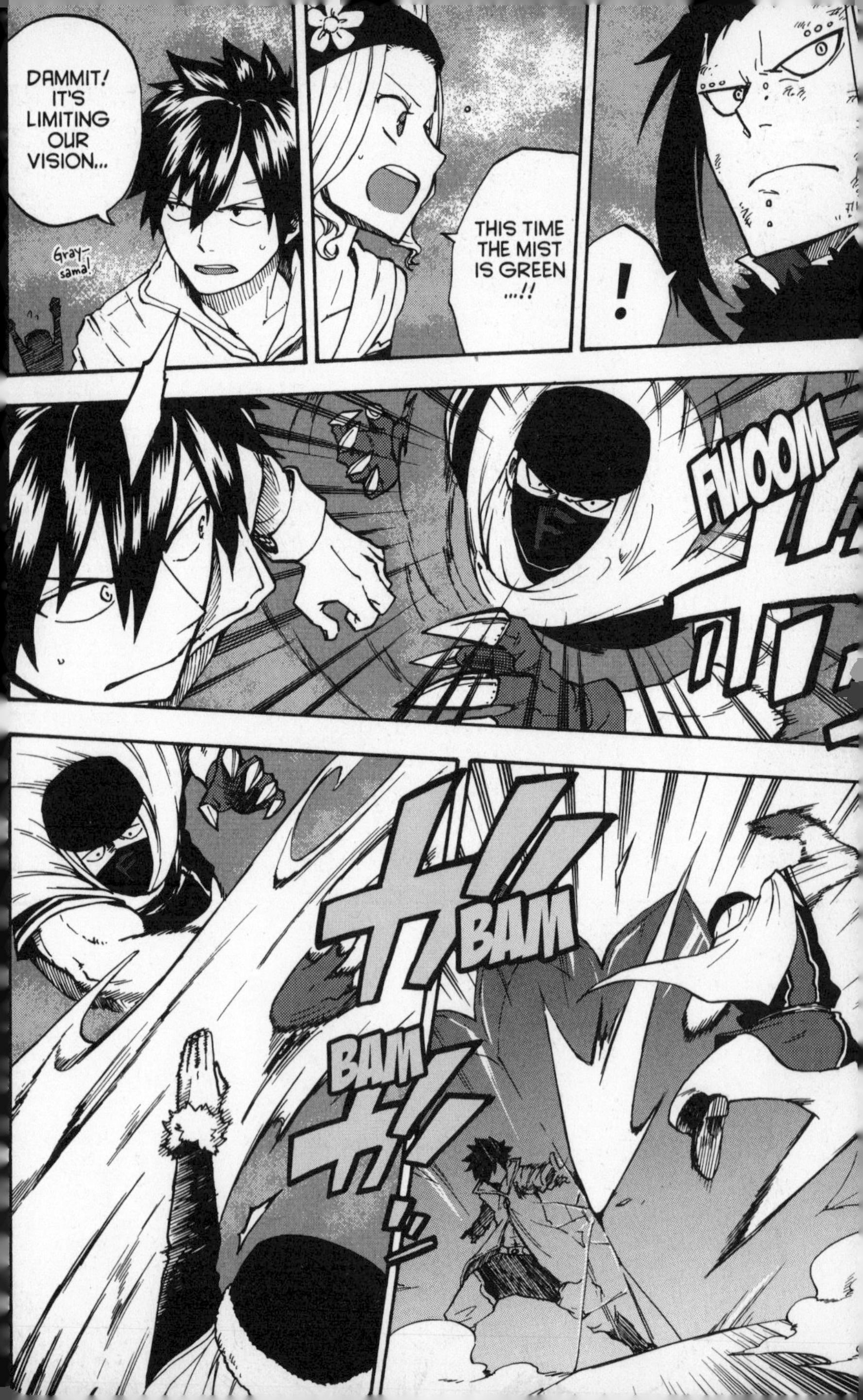
!
THIS TIME THE MIST IS GREEN ...!!
DAMMIT! IT'S LIMITING OUR VISION...
Gray-sama!
FWOOM
BAM
BAM

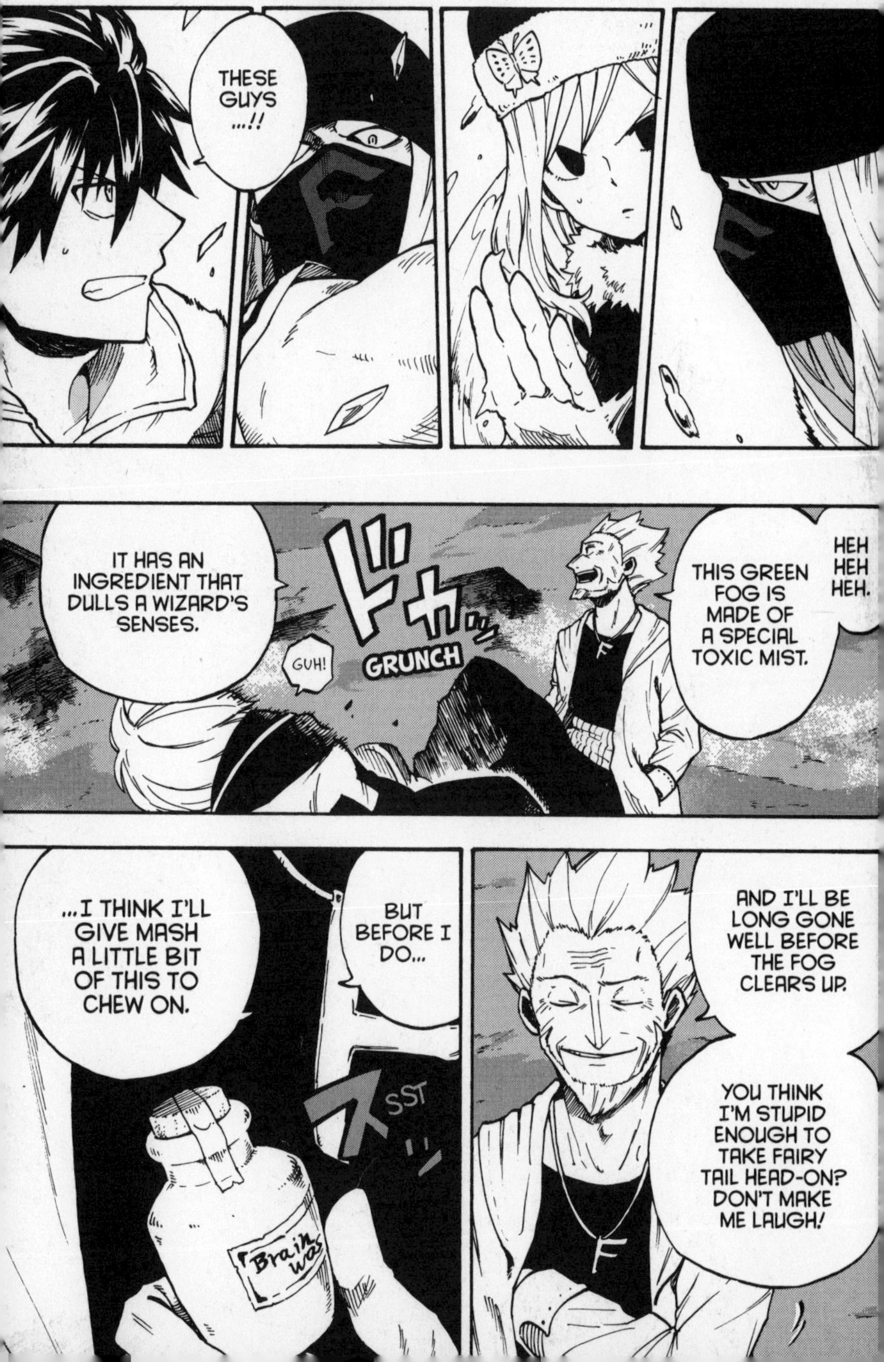
THESE GUYS ...!!
HEH HEH HEH.
THIS GREEN FOG IS MADE OF A SPECIAL TOXIC MIST.
ドカッ
GRUNCH
GUH!
IT HAS AN INGREDIENT THAT DULLS A WIZARD'S SENSES.
AND I'LL BE LONG GONE WELL BEFORE THE FOG CLEARS UP.
YOU THINK I'M STUPID ENOUGH TO TAKE FAIRY TAIL HEAD-ON? DON'T MAKE ME LAUGH!
BUT BEFORE I DO...
...I THINK I'LL GIVE MASH A LITTLE BIT OF THIS TO CHEW ON.
SST
Brain was

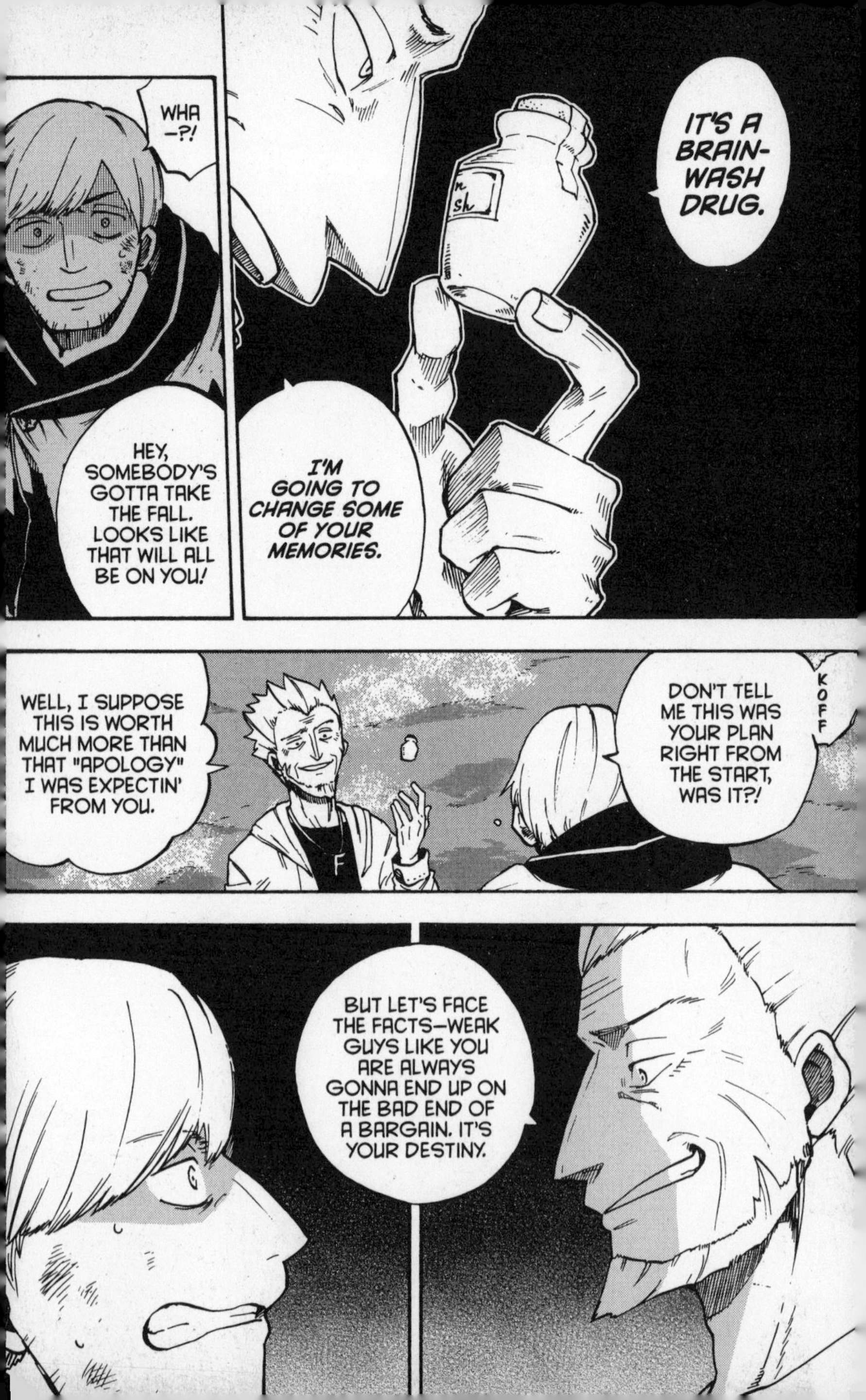
IT'S A BRAIN-WASH DRUG.
I'M GOING TO CHANGE SOME OF YOUR MEMORIES.
WHA—?!
HEY, SOMEBODY'S GOTTA TAKE THE FALL. LOOKS LIKE THAT WILL ALL BE ON YOU!
KOFF
DON'T TELL ME THIS WAS YOUR PLAN RIGHT FROM THE START, WAS IT?!
WELL, I SUPPOSE THIS IS WORTH MUCH MORE THAN THAT "APOLOGY" I WAS EXPECTIN' FROM YOU.
BUT LET'S FACE THE FACTS—WEAK GUYS LIKE YOU ARE ALWAYS GONNA END UP ON THE BAD END OF A BARGAIN. IT'S YOUR DESTINY.

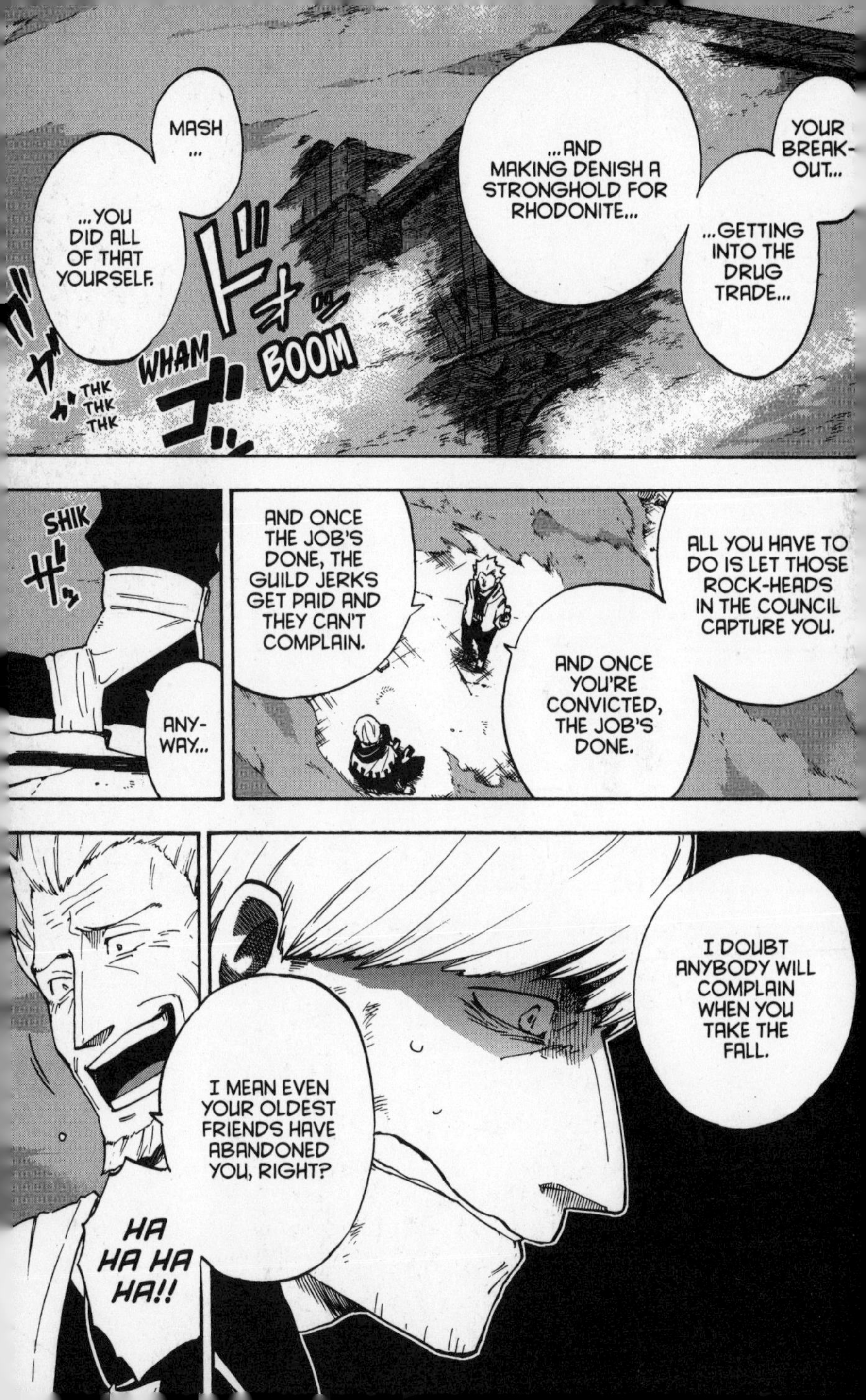
YOUR BREAK-OUT...
...GETTING INTO THE DRUG TRADE...
...AND MAKING DENISH A STRONGHOLD FOR RHODONITE...
MASH ...
...YOU DID ALL OF THAT YOURSELF.
BOOM
WHAM
THK THK THK
ALL YOU HAVE TO DO IS LET THOSE ROCK-HEADS IN THE COUNCIL CAPTURE YOU.
AND ONCE YOU'RE CONVICTED, THE JOB'S DONE.
AND ONCE THE JOB'S DONE, THE GUILD JERKS GET PAID AND THEY CAN'T COMPLAIN.
SHIK
ANY-WAY...
I DOUBT ANYBODY WILL COMPLAIN WHEN YOU TAKE THE FALL.
I MEAN EVEN YOUR OLDEST FRIENDS HAVE ABANDONED YOU, RIGHT?
HA HA HA HA!!

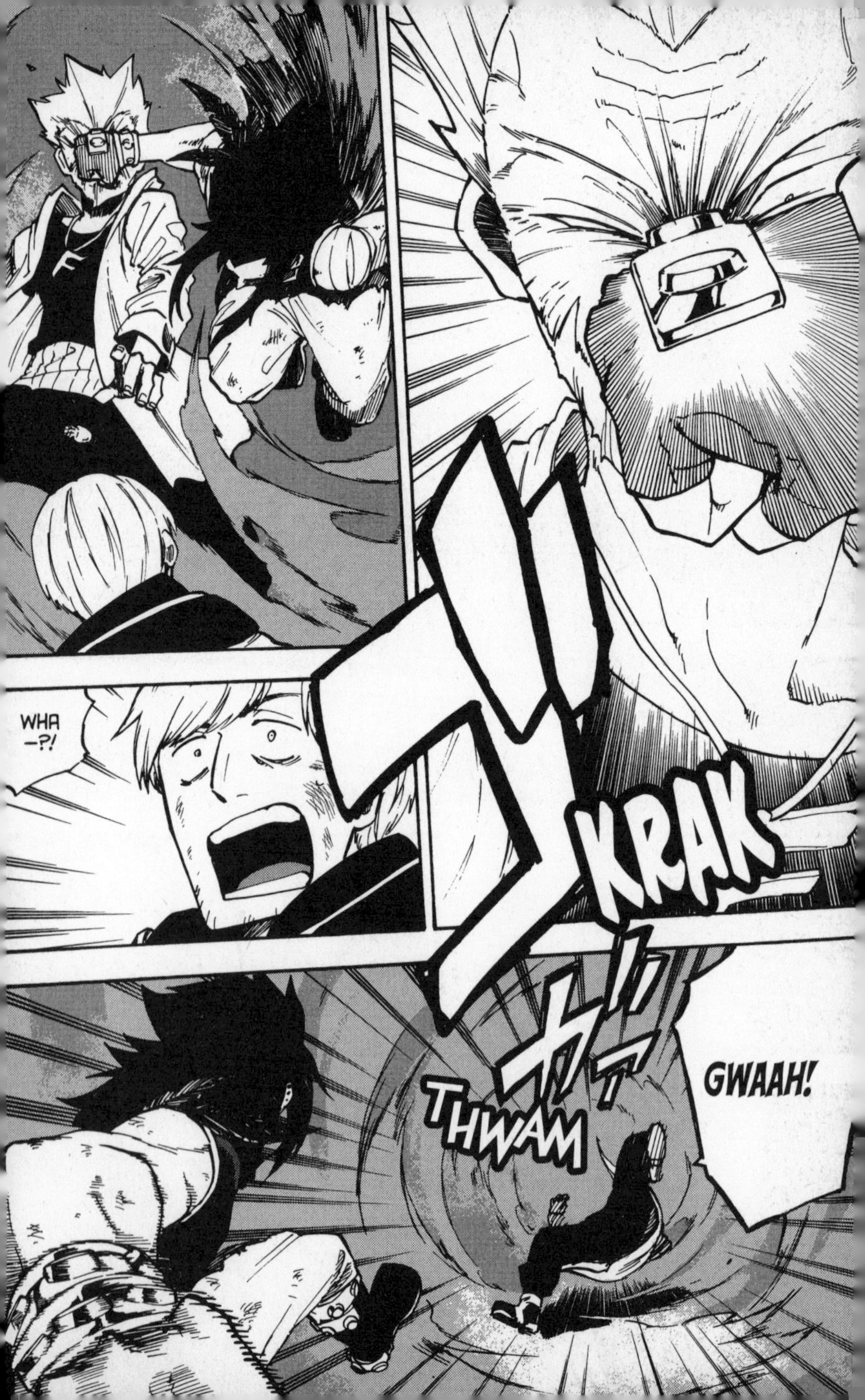
KRAK
WHA—?!
GWAAH!
THWAM

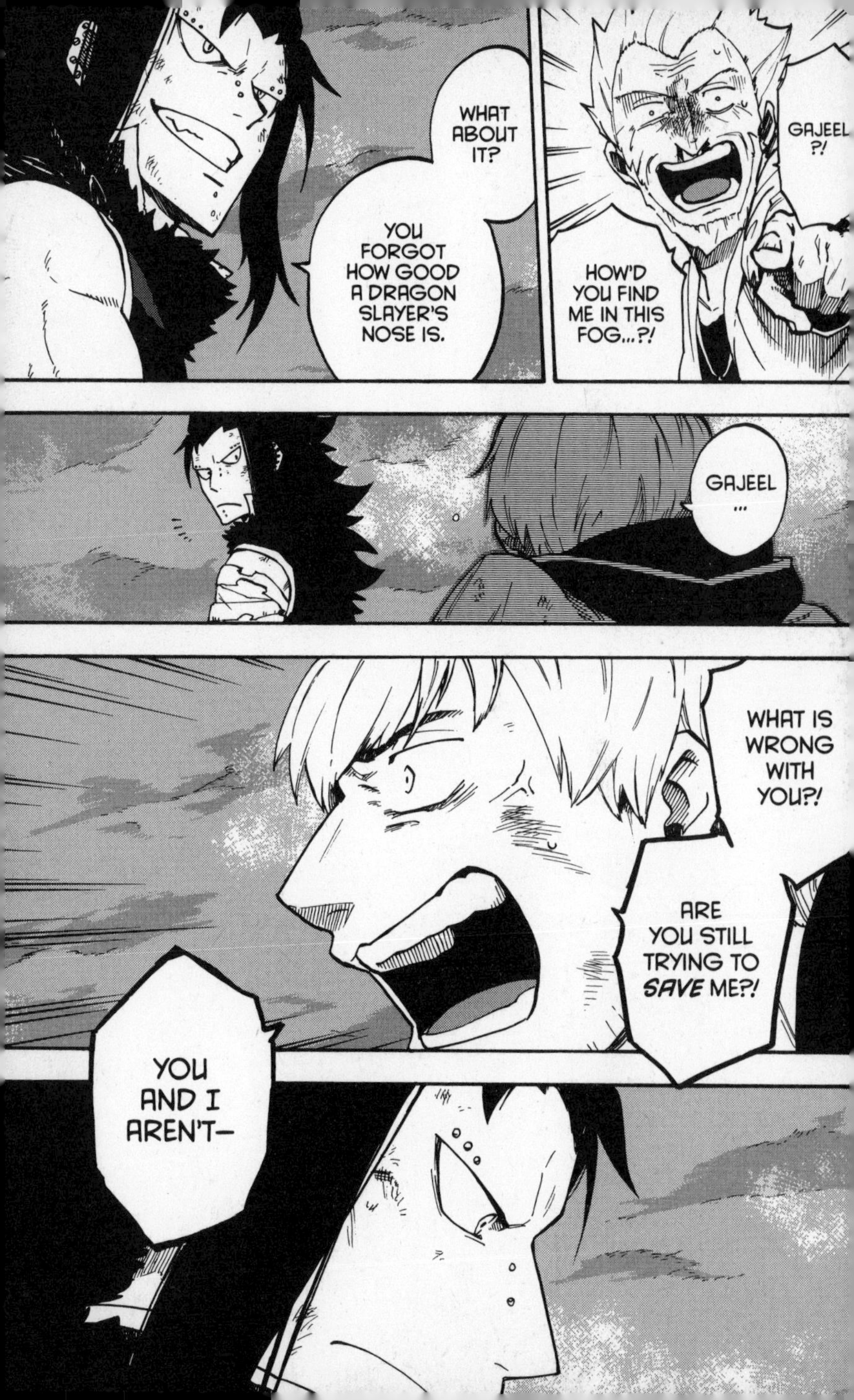
GAJEEL ?!
HOW'D YOU FIND ME IN THIS FOG...?!
WHAT ABOUT IT?
YOU FORGOT HOW GOOD A DRAGON SLAYER'S NOSE IS.
GAJEEL ...
WHAT IS WRONG WITH YOU?!
ARE YOU STILL TRYING TO *SAVE* ME?!
YOU AND I AREN'T—

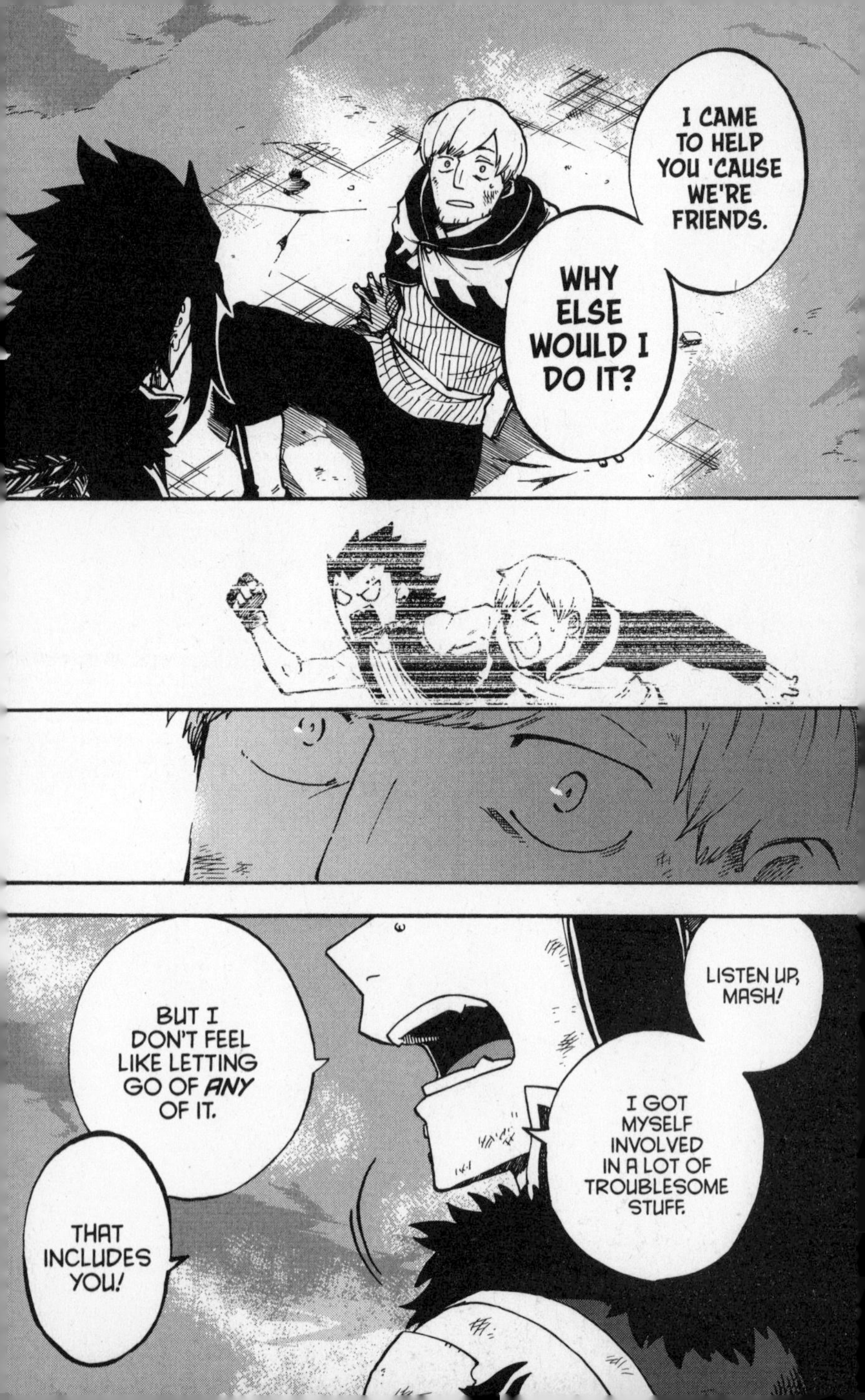
I CAME TO HELP YOU 'CAUSE WE'RE FRIENDS.
WHY ELSE WOULD I DO IT?
LISTEN UP, MASH!
I GOT MYSELF INVOLVED IN A LOT OF TROUBLESOME STUFF.
BUT I DON'T FEEL LIKE LETTING GO OF ANY OF IT.
THAT INCLUDES YOU!

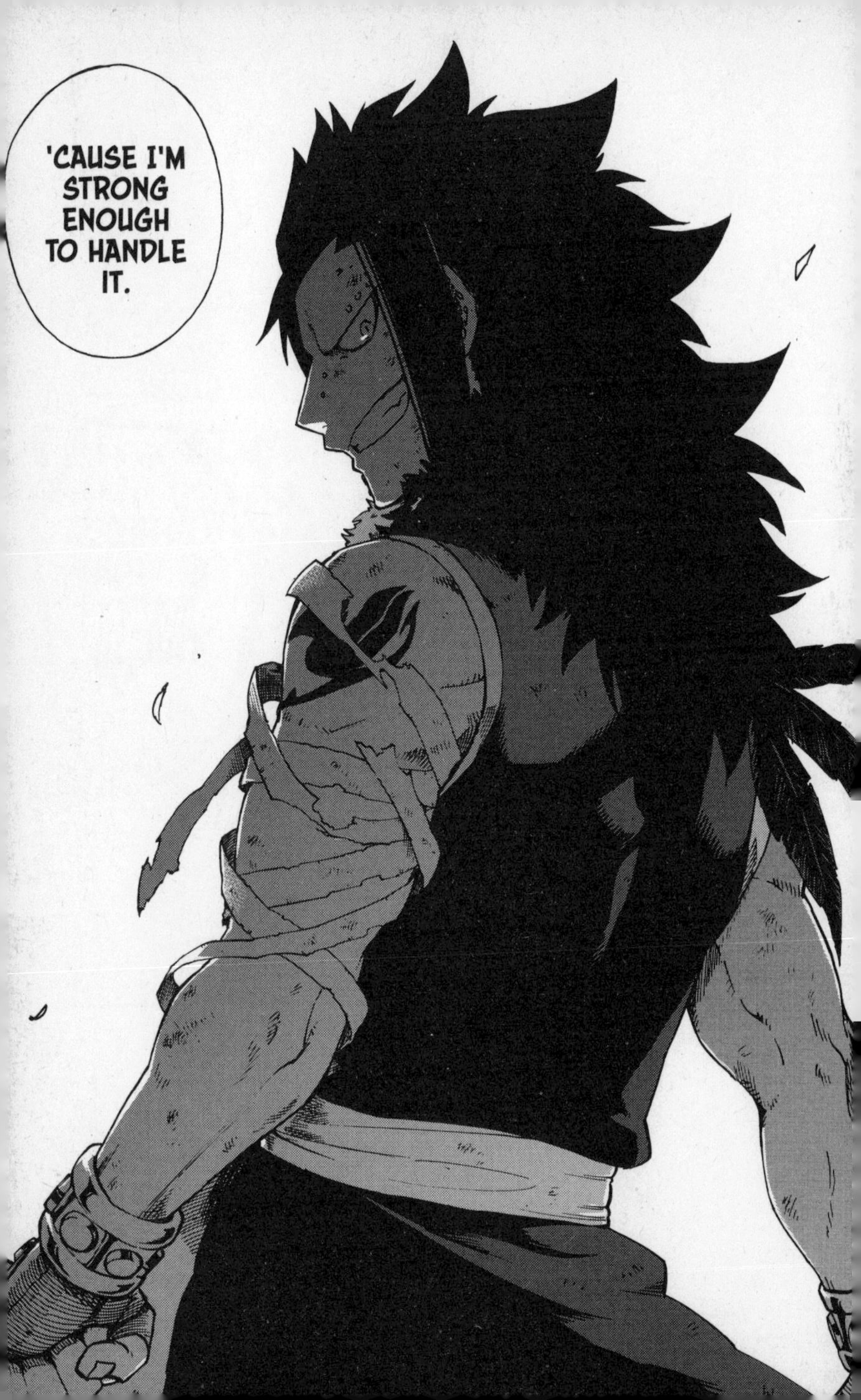
'CAUSE I'M STRONG ENOUGH TO HANDLE IT.

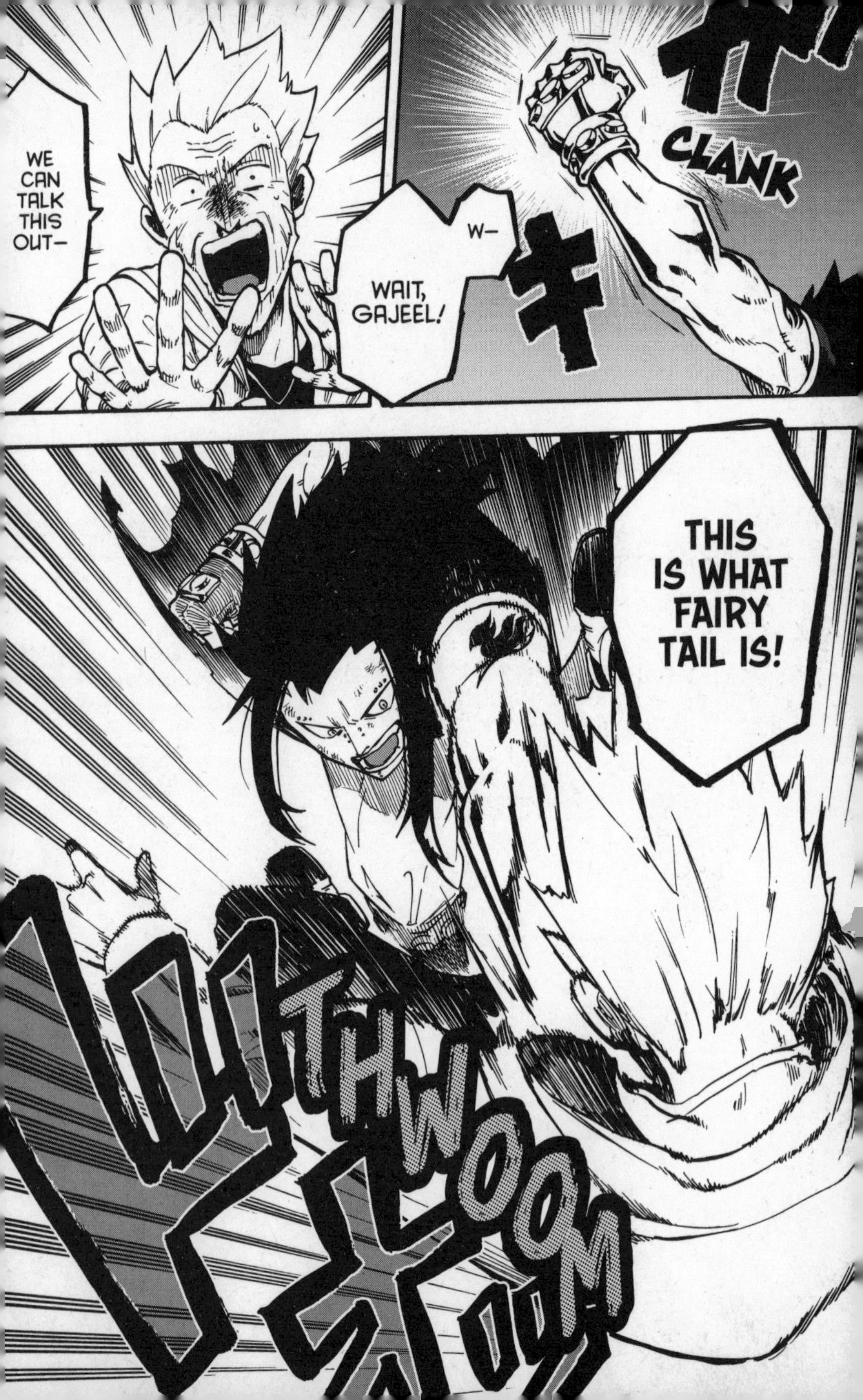
CLANK
W— WAIT, GAJEEL!
WE CAN TALK THIS OUT—
THIS IS WHAT FAIRY TAIL IS!
THWOOM

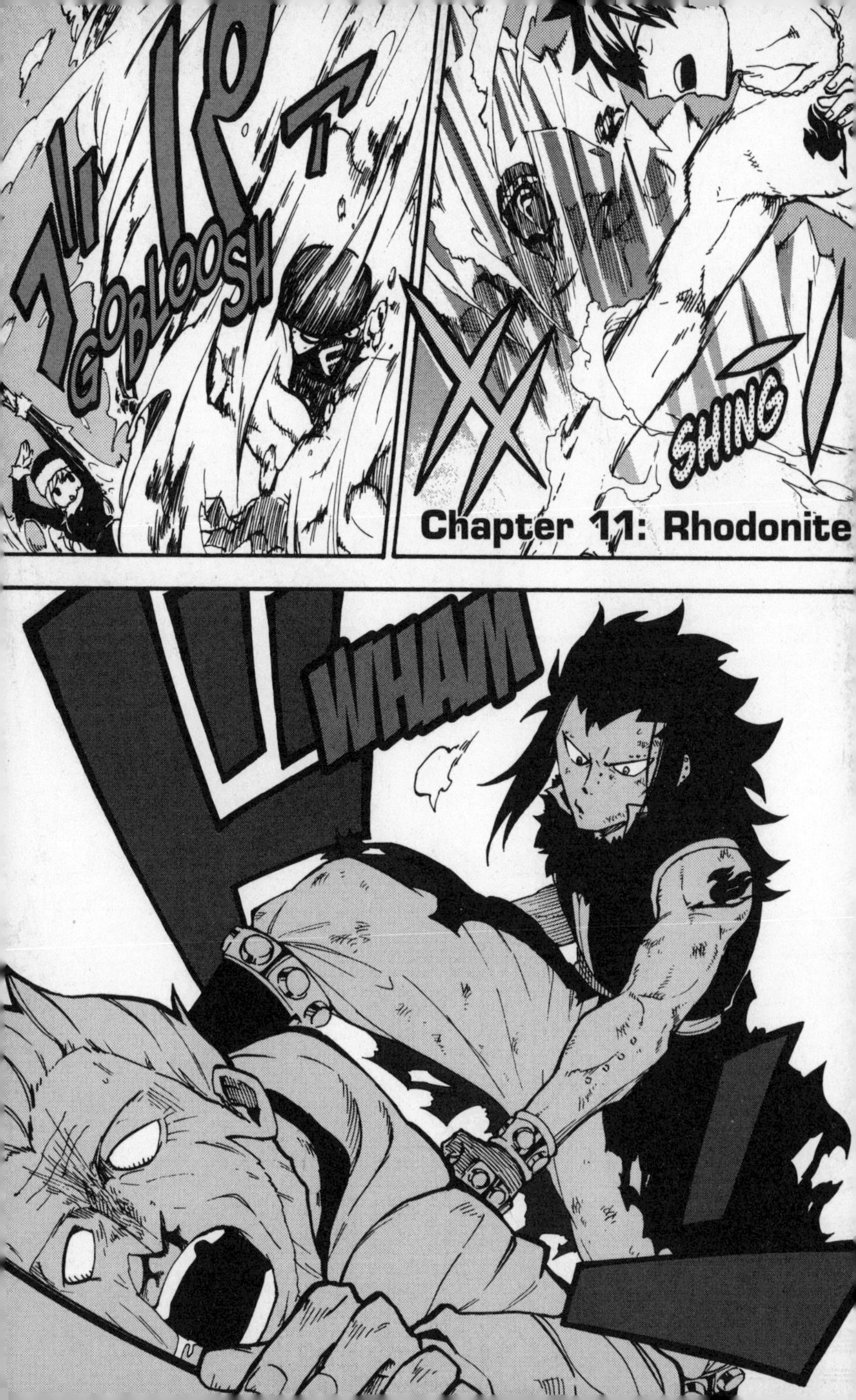
SHING
Chapter 11: Rhodonite
GOBLOOSH
WHAM

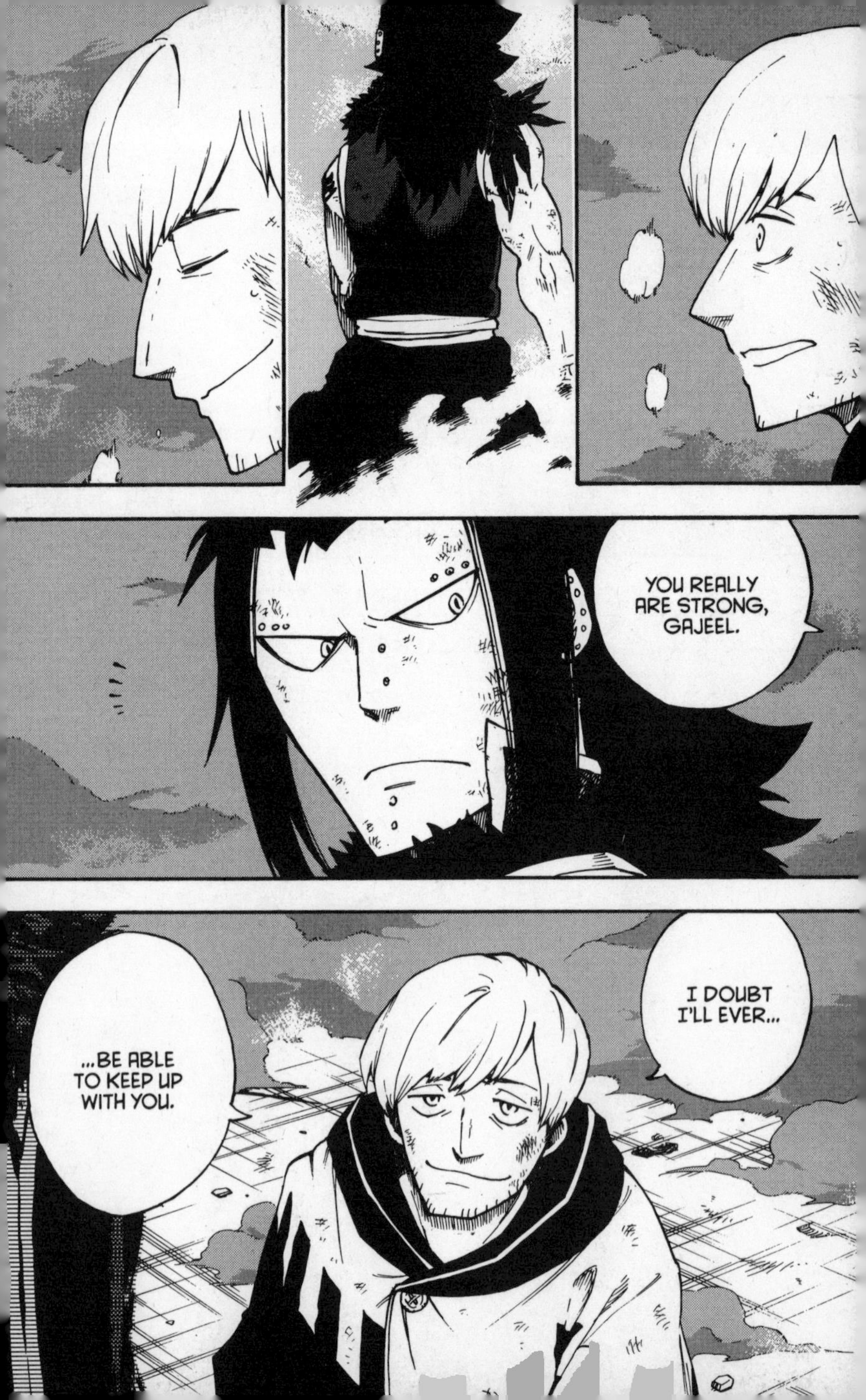
YOU REALLY ARE STRONG, GAJEEL.
I DOUBT I'LL EVER...
...BE ABLE TO KEEP UP WITH YOU.

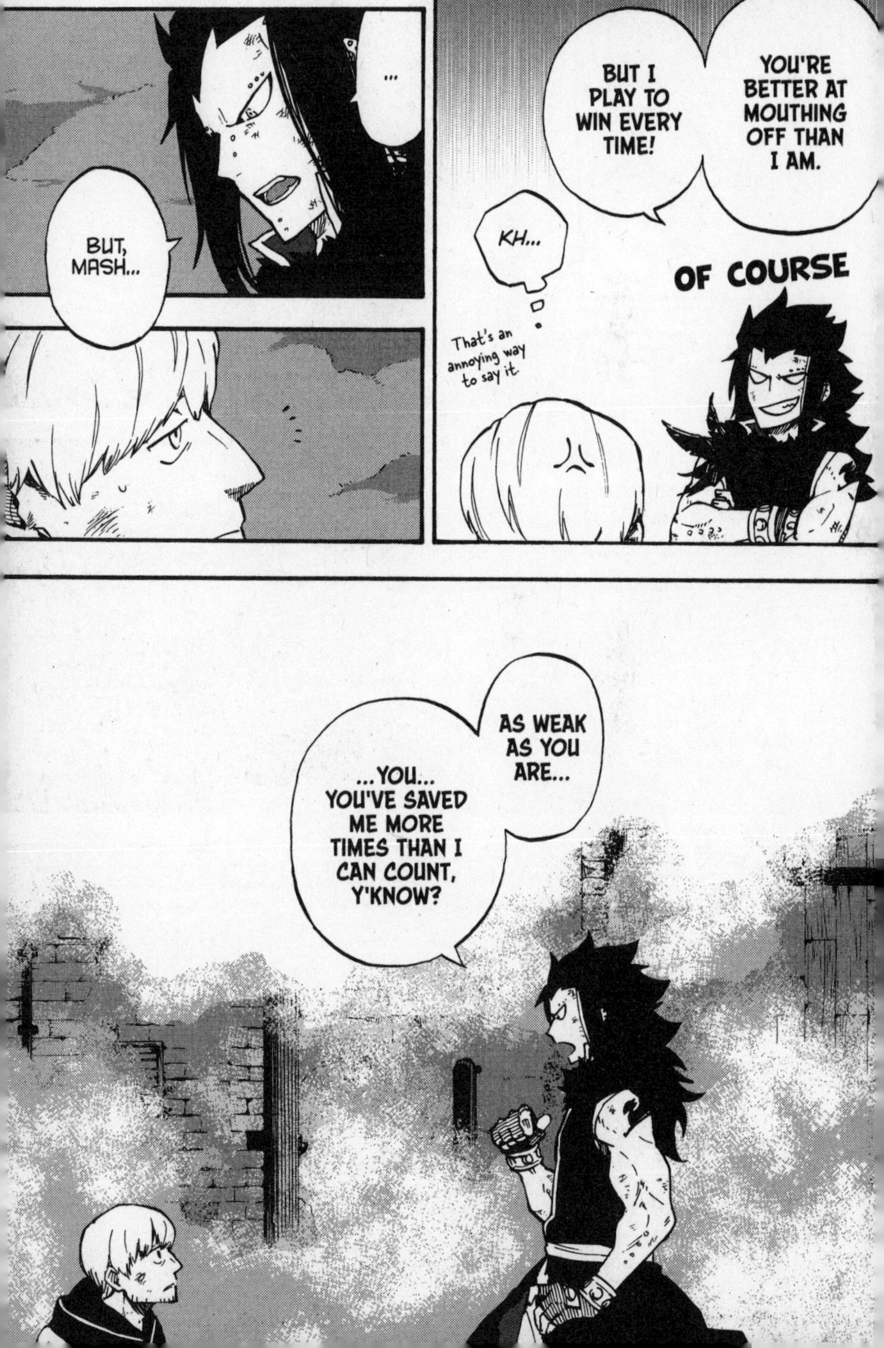
YOU'RE BETTER AT MOUTHING OFF THAN I AM.
BUT I PLAY TO WIN EVERY TIME!
OF COURSE
KH...
That's an annoying way to say it.
...
BUT, MASH...
AS WEAK AS YOU ARE...
...YOU... YOU'VE SAVED ME MORE TIMES THAN I CAN COUNT, Y'KNOW?

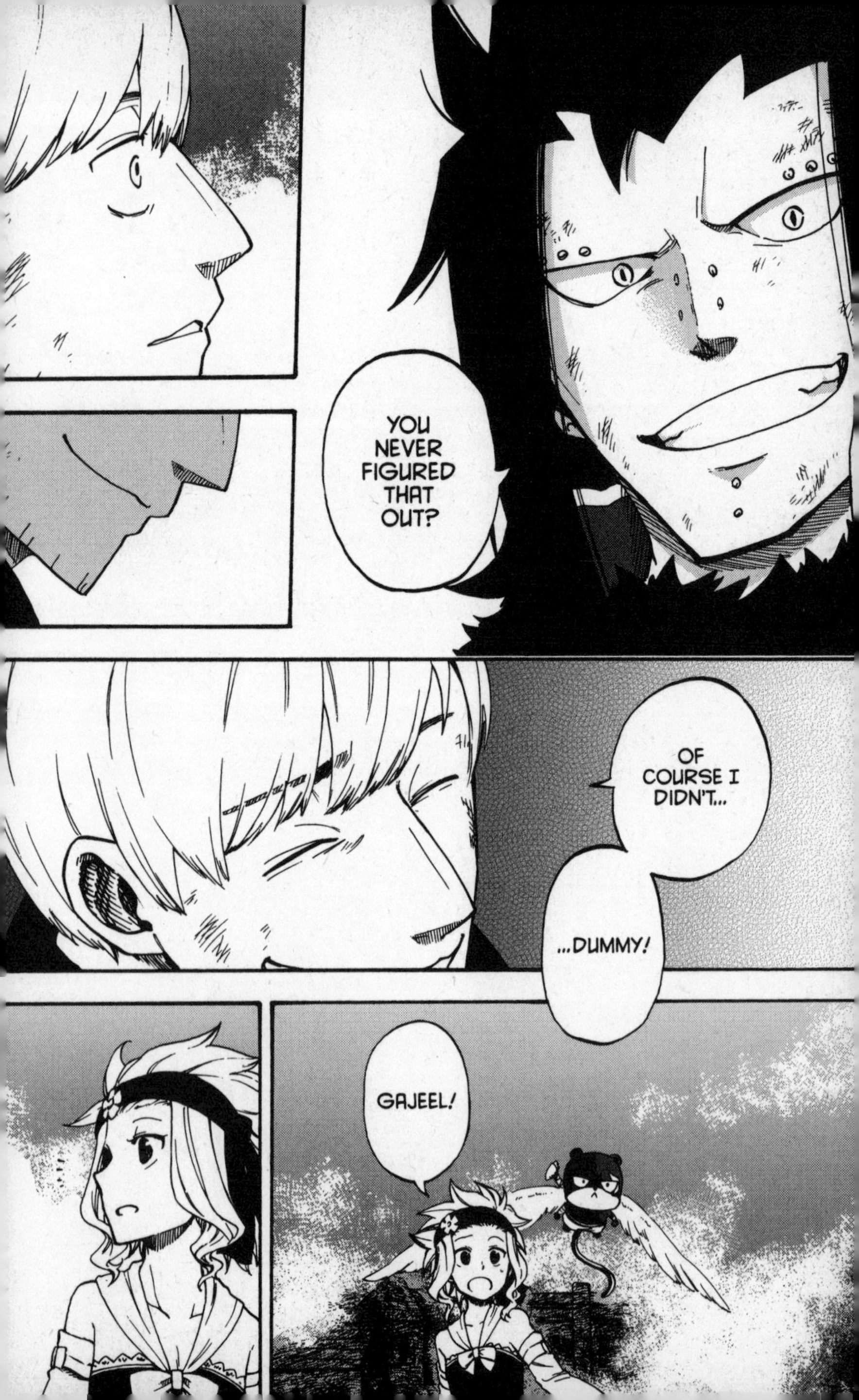
YOU NEVER FIGURED THAT OUT?
OF COURSE I DIDN'T...
...DUMMY!
GAJEEL!

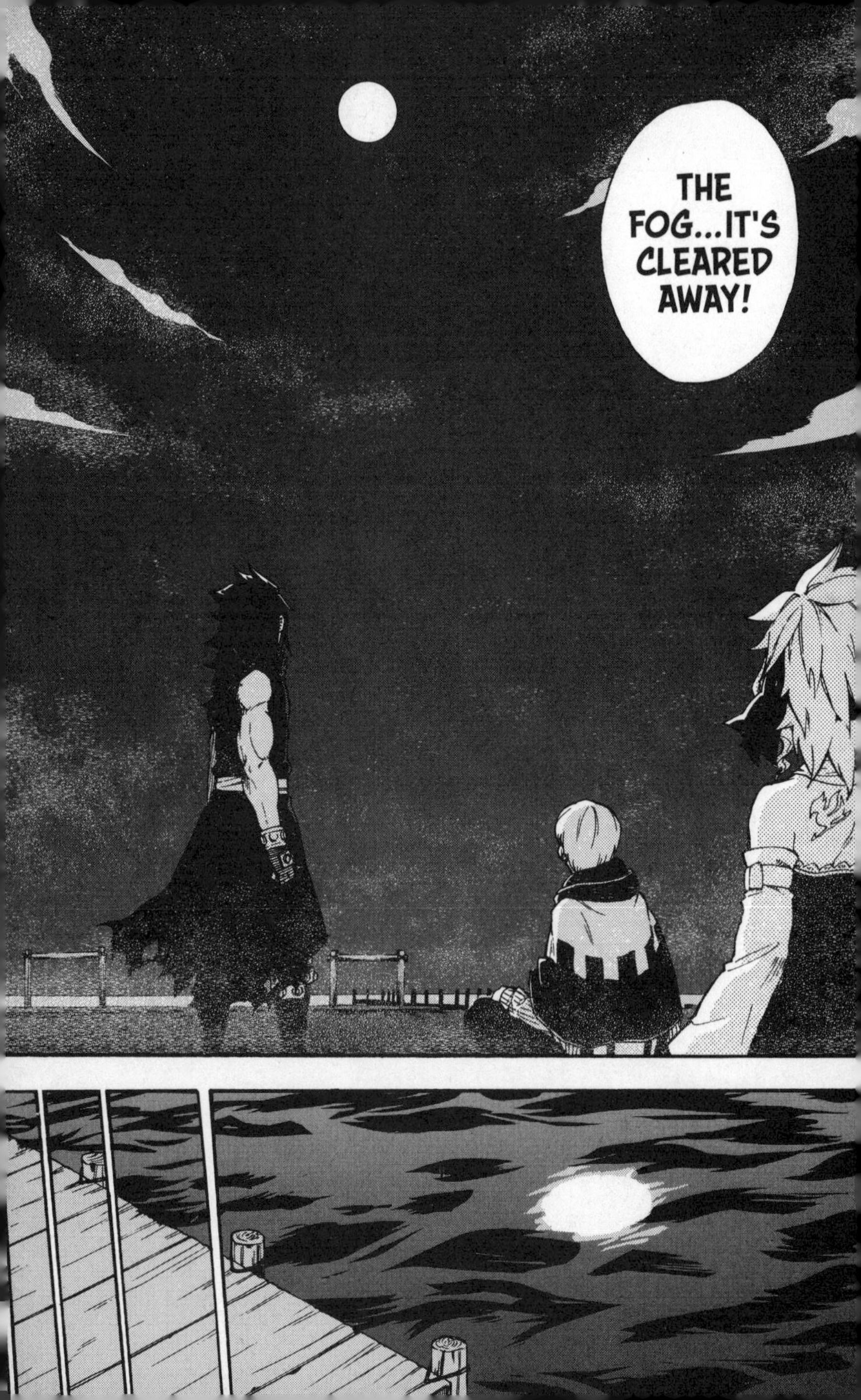
THE FOG...IT'S CLEARED AWAY!

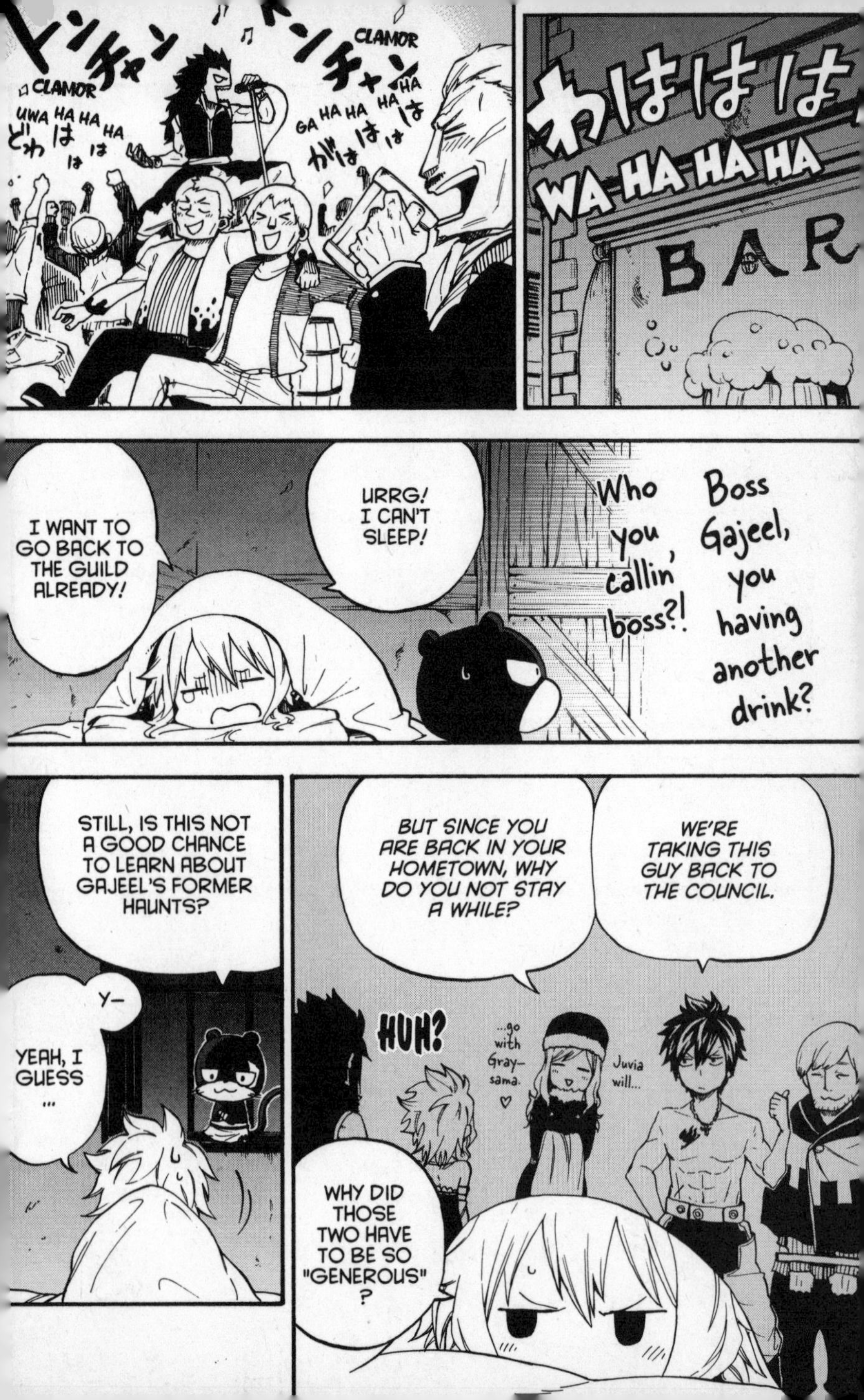

BAR
わははは
WA HA HA HA
トンチャン
CLAMOR
トンチャン
CLAMOR
がははは
GA HA HA HA HA
どわははは
UWA HA HA HA
Boss Gajeel, you having another drink?
Who you callin' boss?!
URRG! I CAN'T SLEEP!
I WANT TO GO BACK TO THE GUILD ALREADY!
WE'RE TAKING THIS GUY BACK TO THE COUNCIL.
BUT SINCE YOU ARE BACK IN YOUR HOMETOWN, WHY DO YOU NOT STAY A WHILE?
Juvia will...
...go with Gray-sama.
HUH?
WHY DID THOSE TWO HAVE TO BE SO "GENEROUS"?
STILL, IS THIS NOT A GOOD CHANCE TO LEARN ABOUT GAJEEL'S FORMER HAUNTS?
Y—
YEAH, I GUESS...

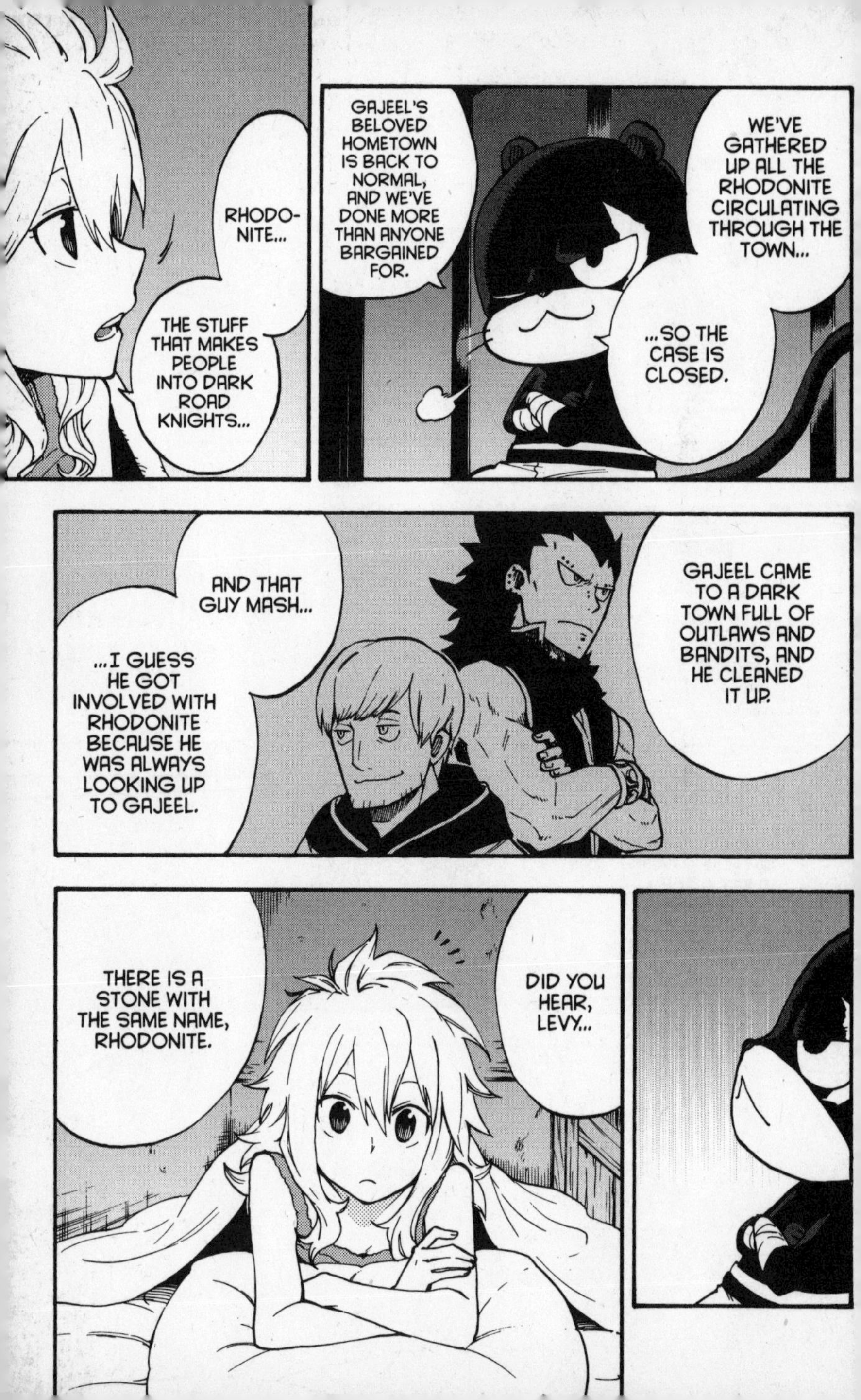
WE'VE GATHERED UP ALL THE RHODONITE CIRCULATING THROUGH THE TOWN...
...SO THE CASE IS CLOSED.
GAJEEL'S BELOVED HOMETOWN IS BACK TO NORMAL, AND WE'VE DONE MORE THAN ANYONE BARGAINED FOR.
RHODO-NITE...
THE STUFF THAT MAKES PEOPLE INTO DARK ROAD KNIGHTS...
GAJEEL CAME TO A DARK TOWN FULL OF OUTLAWS AND BANDITS, AND HE CLEANED IT UP.
AND THAT GUY MASH...
...I GUESS HE GOT INVOLVED WITH RHODONITE BECAUSE HE WAS ALWAYS LOOKING UP TO GAJEEL.
DID YOU HEAR, LEVY...
THERE IS A STONE WITH THE SAME NAME, RHODONITE.

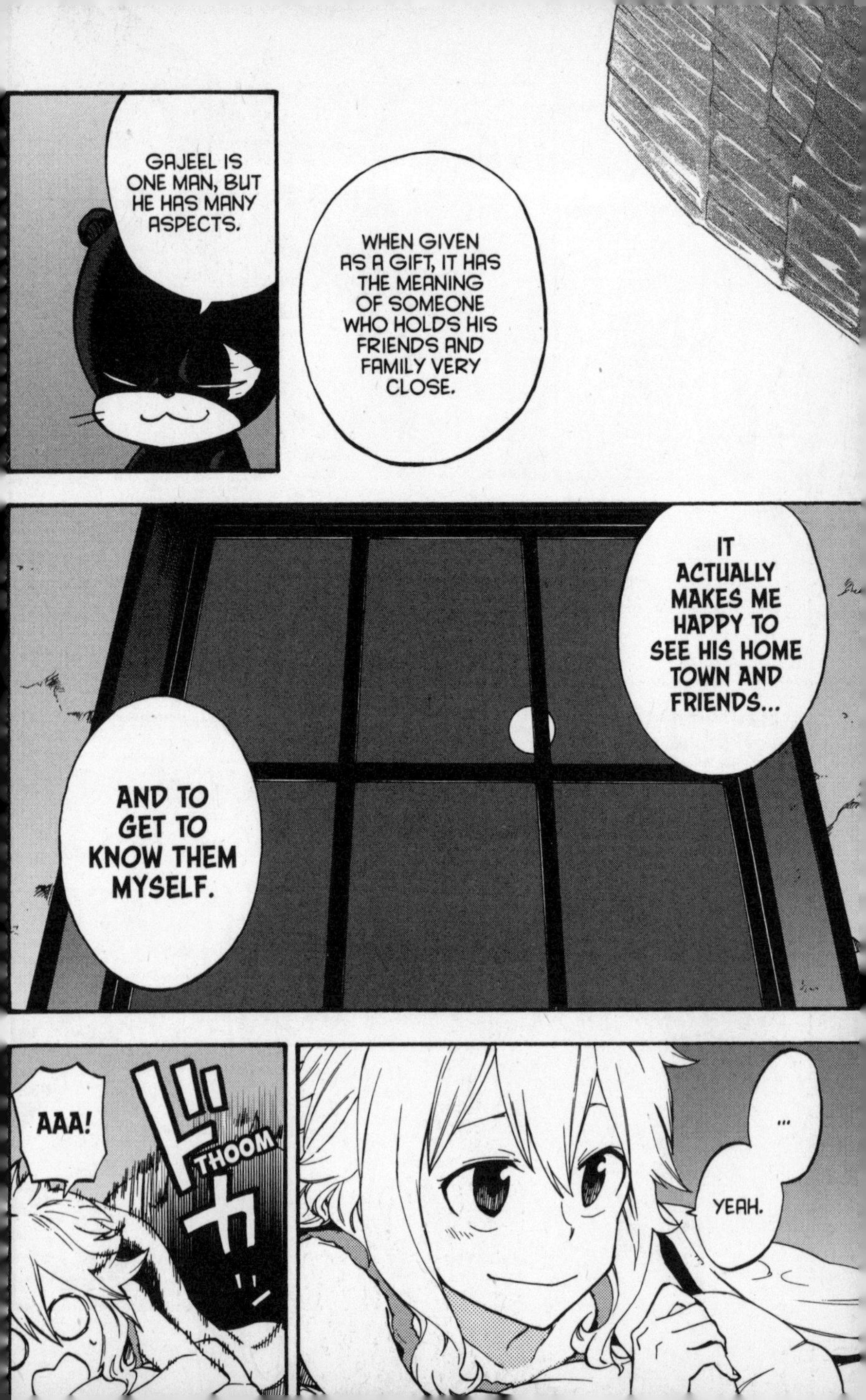
WHEN GIVEN AS A GIFT, IT HAS THE MEANING OF SOMEONE WHO HOLDS HIS FRIENDS AND FAMILY VERY CLOSE.
GAJEEL IS ONE MAN, BUT HE HAS MANY ASPECTS.
IT ACTUALLY MAKES ME HAPPY TO SEE HIS HOME TOWN AND FRIENDS...
AND TO GET TO KNOW THEM MYSELF.
...
YEAH.
AAA!
THOOM

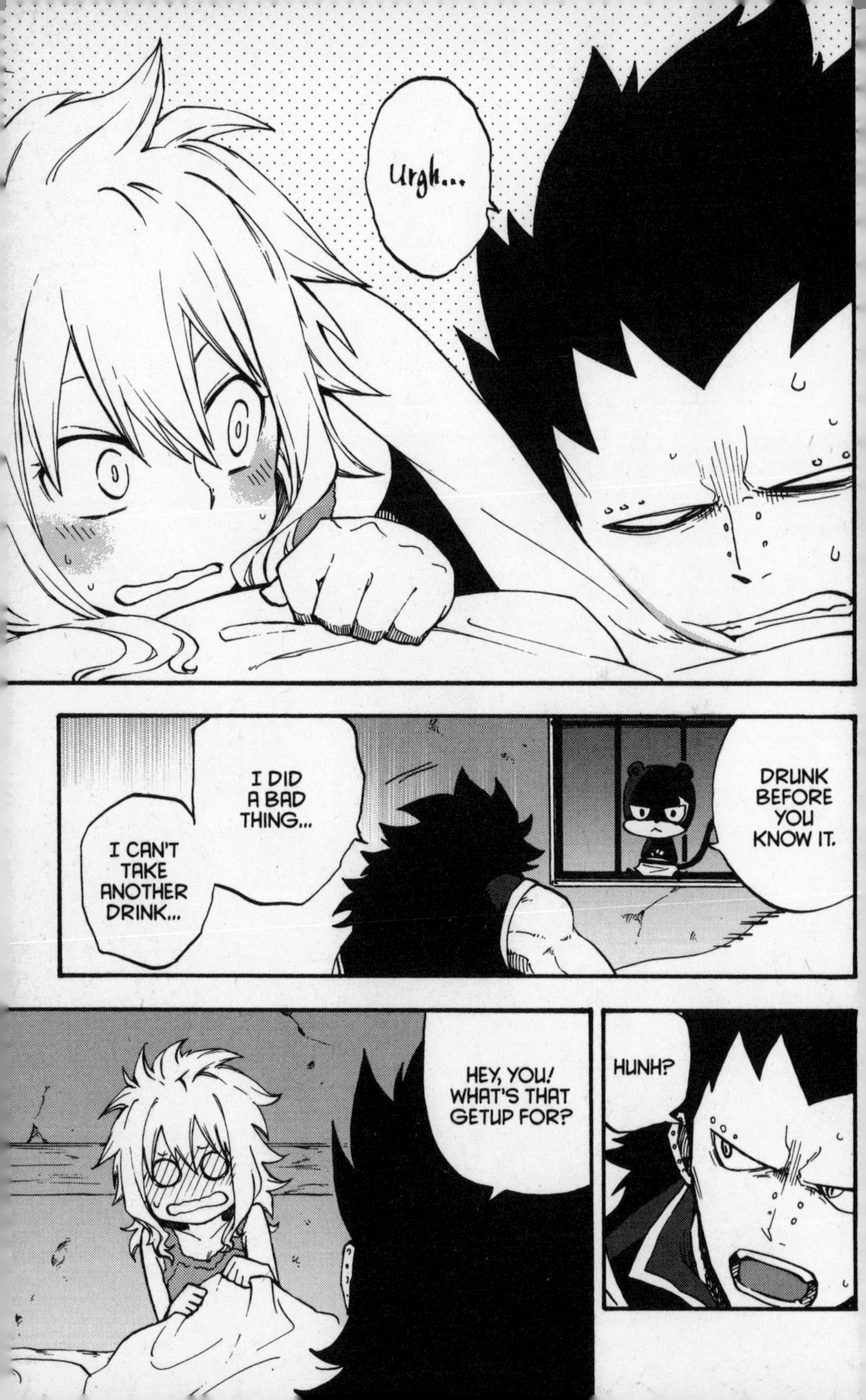
Urgh...
DRUNK BEFORE YOU KNOW IT.
I DID A BAD THING...
I CAN'T TAKE ANOTHER DRINK...
HUNH?
HEY, YOU! WHAT'S THAT GETUP FOR?

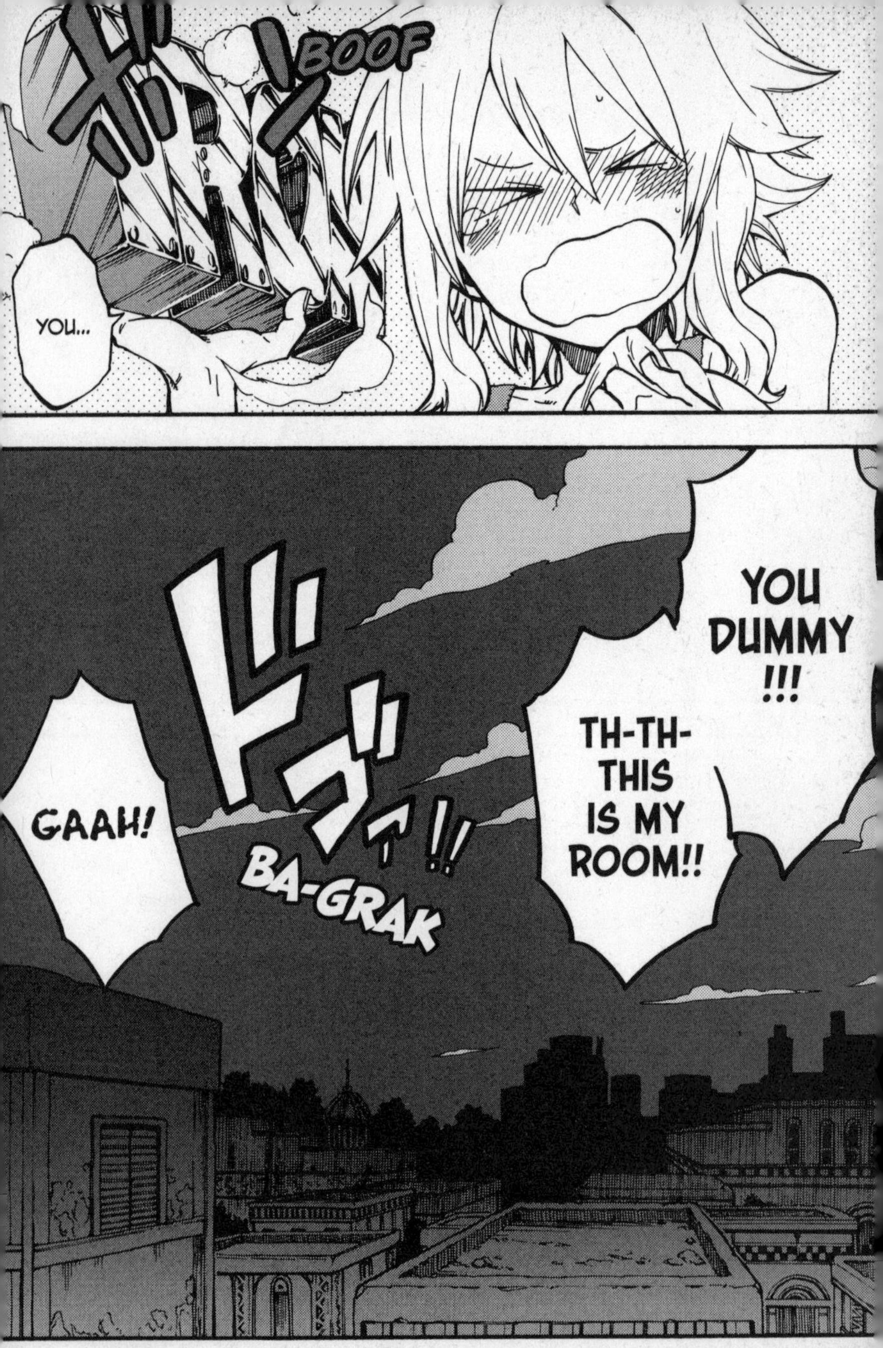
BOOF
YOU...
YOU DUMMY!!!
TH-TH-THIS IS MY ROOM!!
BA-GRAK
GAAH!

FAIRY TAIL: RHODONITE

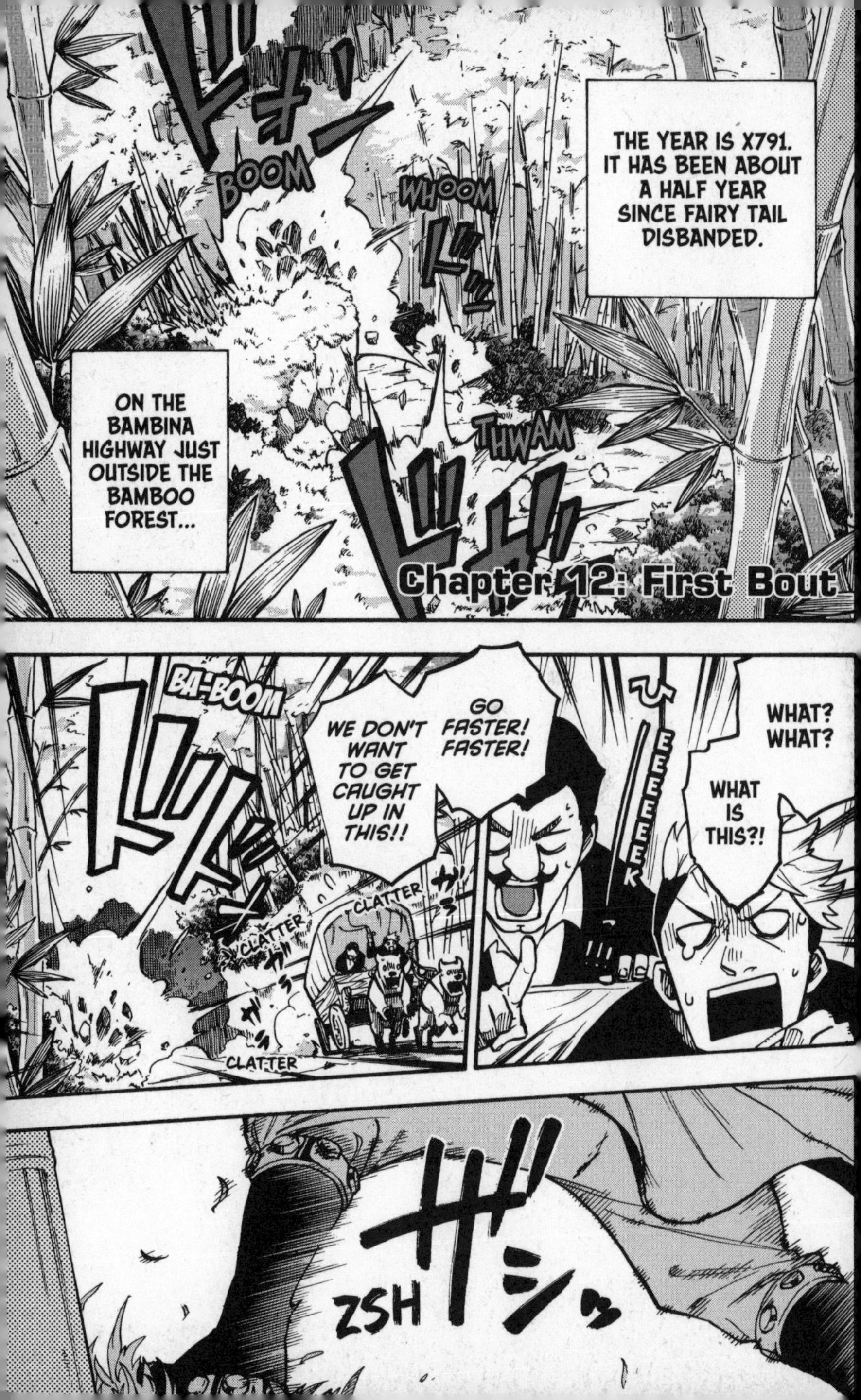
THE YEAR IS X791. IT HAS BEEN ABOUT A HALF YEAR SINCE FAIRY TAIL DISBANDED.
BOOM
WHOOM
ON THE BAMBINA HIGHWAY JUST OUTSIDE THE BAMBOO FOREST...
THWAM
Chapter 12: First Bout
WHAT? WHAT?
WHAT IS THIS?!
EEEEEEEK
GO FASTER! FASTER!
WE DON'T WANT TO GET CAUGHT UP IN THIS!!
BA-BOOM
CLATTER
CLATTER
CLATTER
ZSH

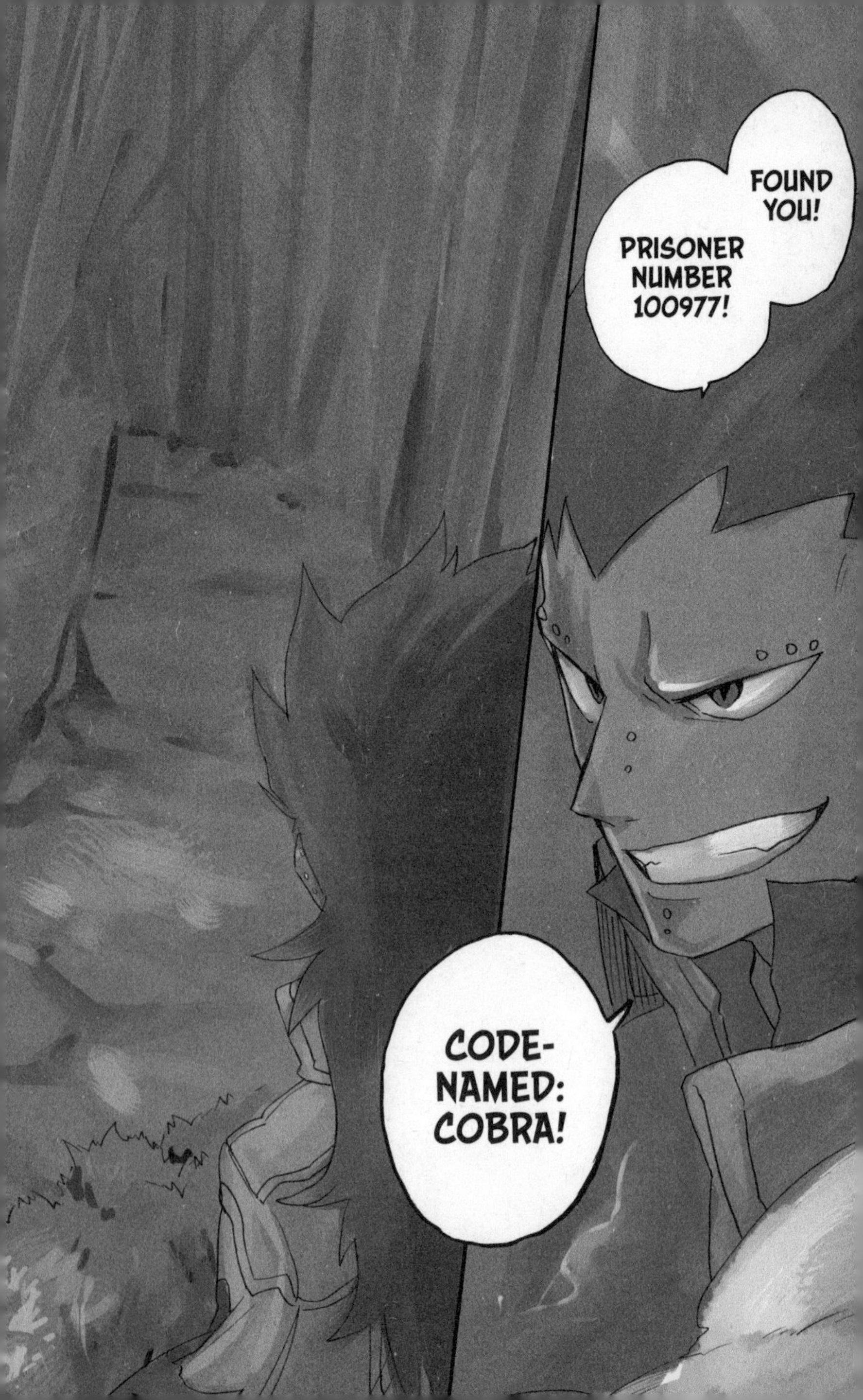
FOUND YOU!
PRISONER NUMBER 100977!
CODE-NAMED: COBRA!

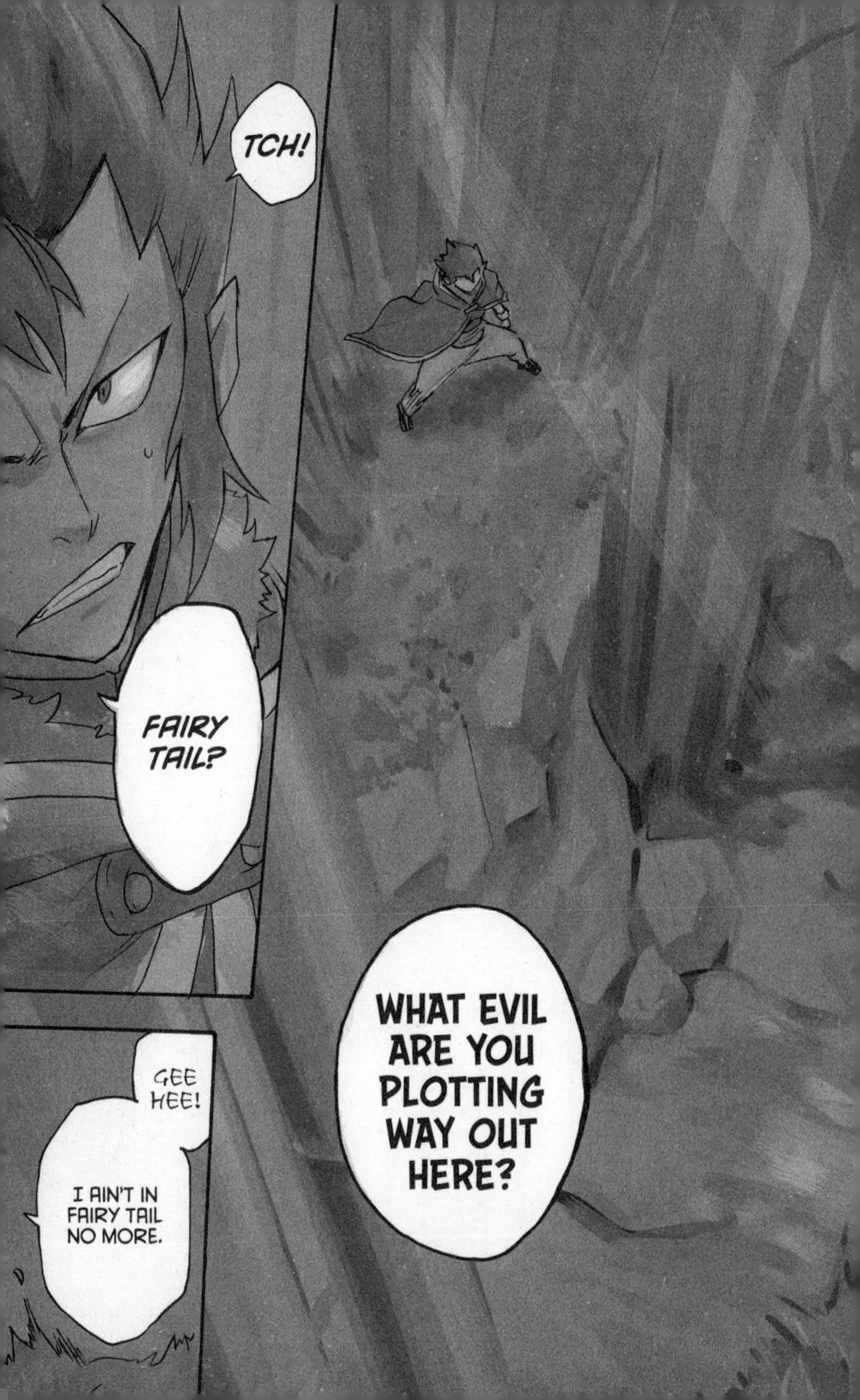
WHAT EVIL ARE YOU PLOTTING WAY OUT HERE?
TCH!
FAIRY TAIL?
GEE HEE!
I AIN'T IN FAIRY TAIL NO MORE.

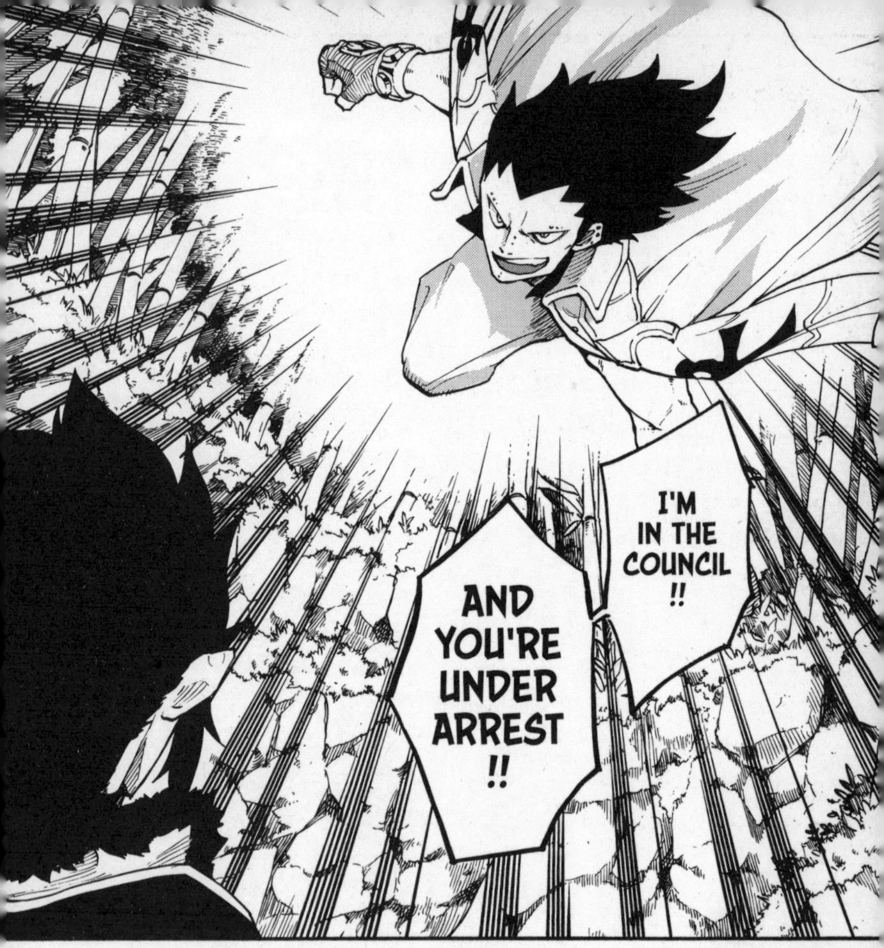
I'M IN THE COUNCIL !!
AND YOU'RE UNDER ARREST !!

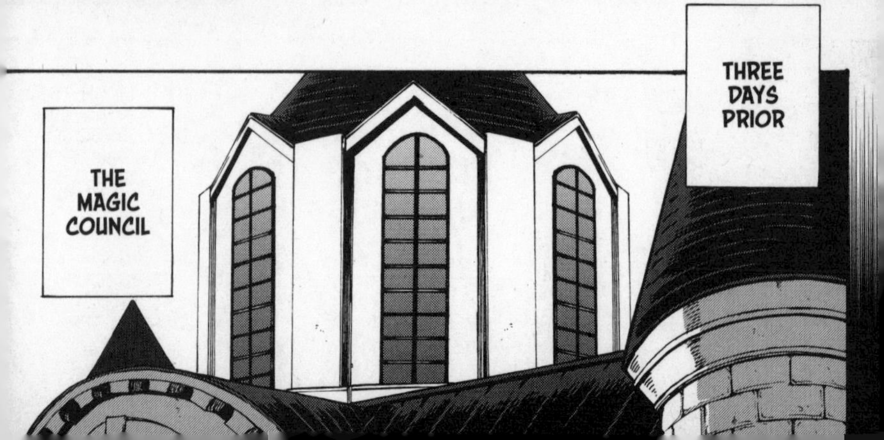
THREE DAYS PRIOR
THE MAGIC COUNCIL

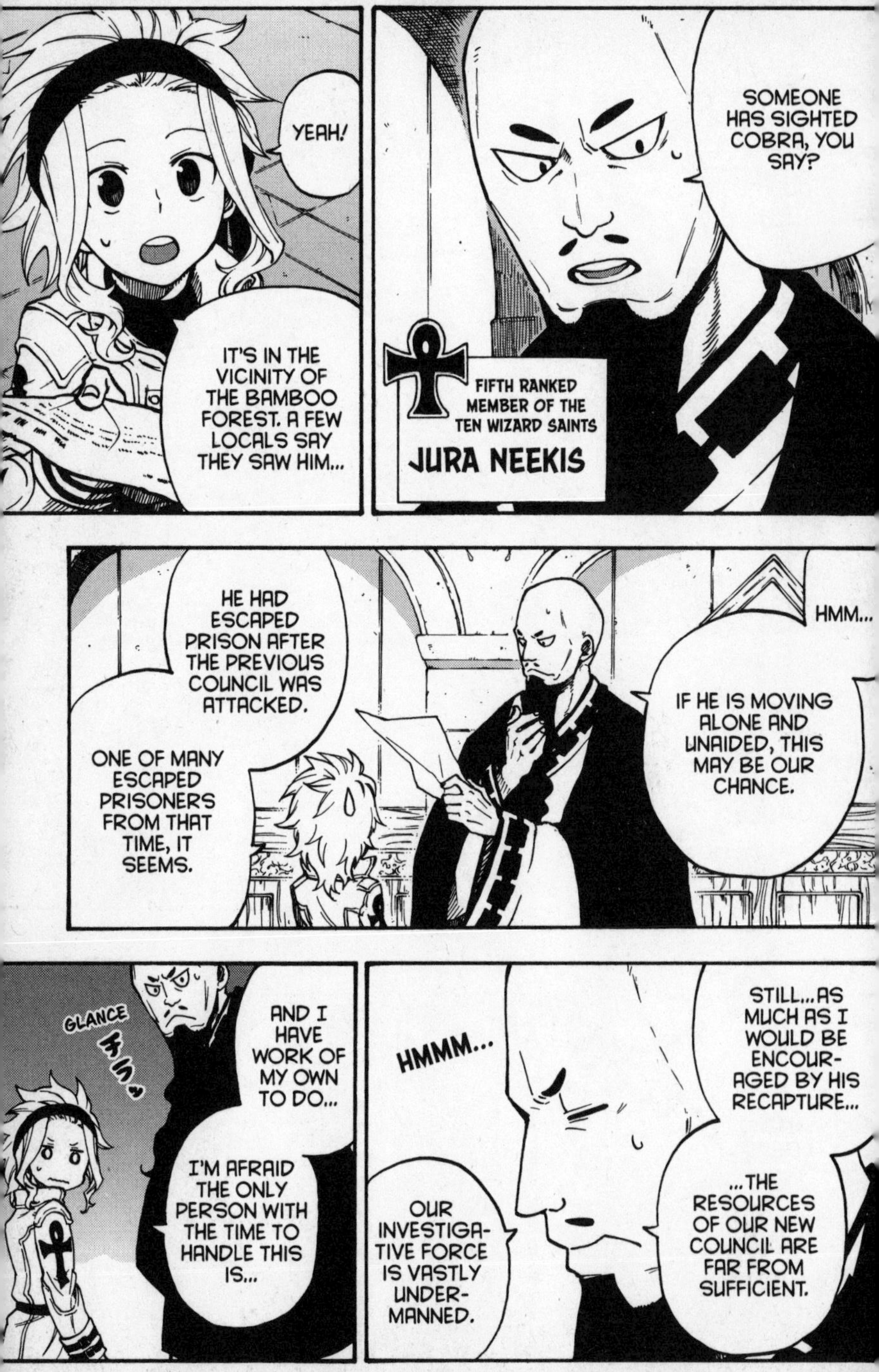
SOMEONE HAS SIGHTED COBRA, YOU SAY?
FIFTH RANKED MEMBER OF THE TEN WIZARD SAINTS
JURA NEEKIS
YEAH!
IT'S IN THE VICINITY OF THE BAMBOO FOREST. A FEW LOCALS SAY THEY SAW HIM...
HMM...
IF HE IS MOVING ALONE AND UNAIDED, THIS MAY BE OUR CHANCE.
HE HAD ESCAPED PRISON AFTER THE PREVIOUS COUNCIL WAS ATTACKED.
ONE OF MANY ESCAPED PRISONERS FROM THAT TIME, IT SEEMS.
STILL...AS MUCH AS I WOULD BE ENCOURAGED BY HIS RECAPTURE...
HMMM...
...THE RESOURCES OF OUR NEW COUNCIL ARE FAR FROM SUFFICIENT.
OUR INVESTIGATIVE FORCE IS VASTLY UNDERMANNED.
AND I HAVE WORK OF MY OWN TO DO...
GLANCE
チラッ
I'M AFRAID THE ONLY PERSON WITH THE TIME TO HANDLE THIS IS...

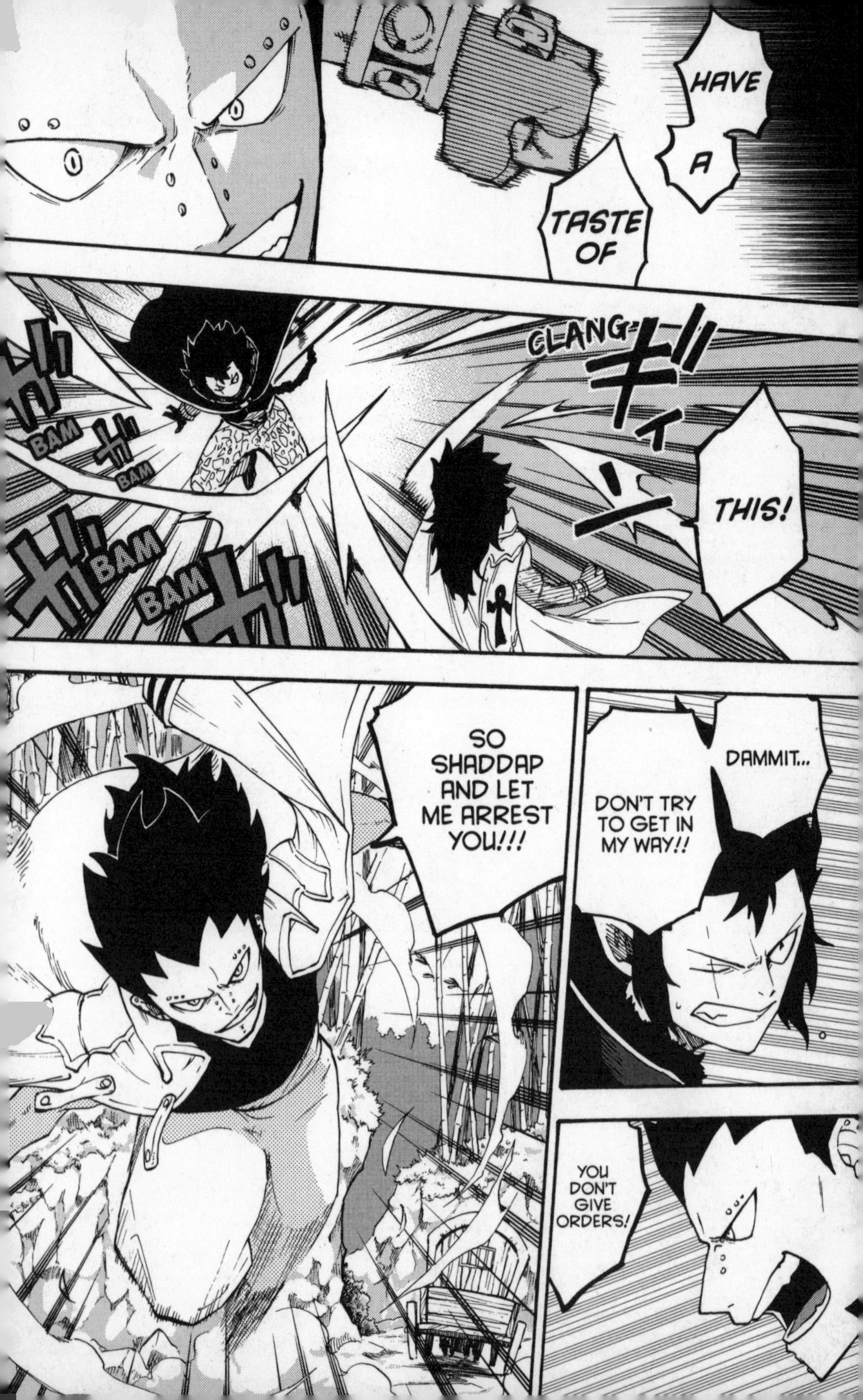
HAVE A
TASTE OF
CLANG
THIS!
BAM
BAM
BAM
BAM
DAMMIT...
DON'T TRY TO GET IN MY WAY!!
YOU DON'T GIVE ORDERS!
SO SHADDAP AND LET ME ARREST YOU!!!

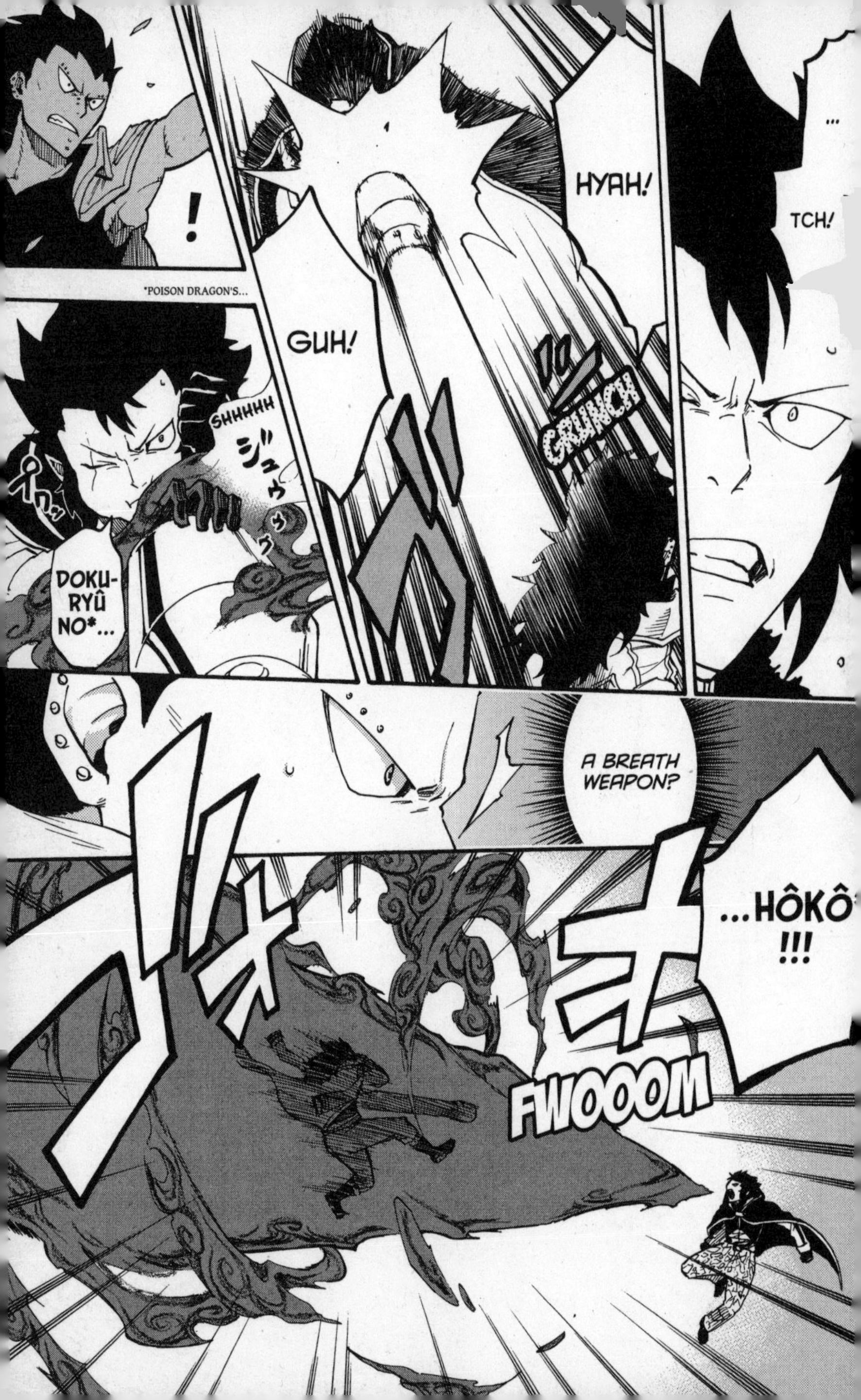
...
TCH!
HYAH!
GUH!
CRUNCH
!
SHHHHH
DOKU-RYÛ NO*...
A BREATH WEAPON?
...HÔKÔ!!!
FWOOOM
*POISON DRAGON'S...

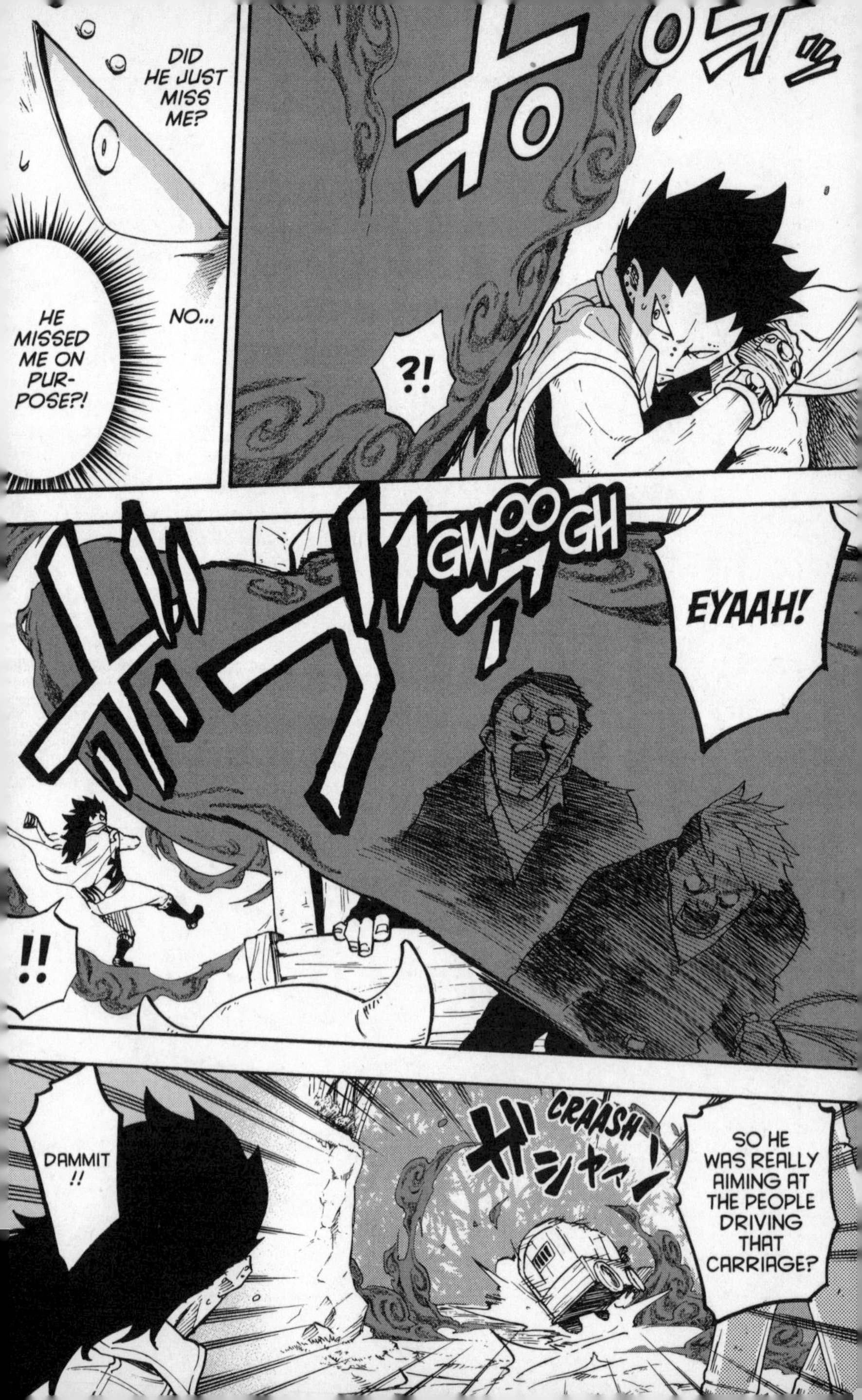
?!
DID HE JUST MISS ME?
NO...
HE MISSED ME ON PUR-POSE?!
GWOOGH
EYAAH!
!!
SO HE WAS REALLY AIMING AT THE PEOPLE DRIVING THAT CARRIAGE?
CRAASH
DAMMIT!!

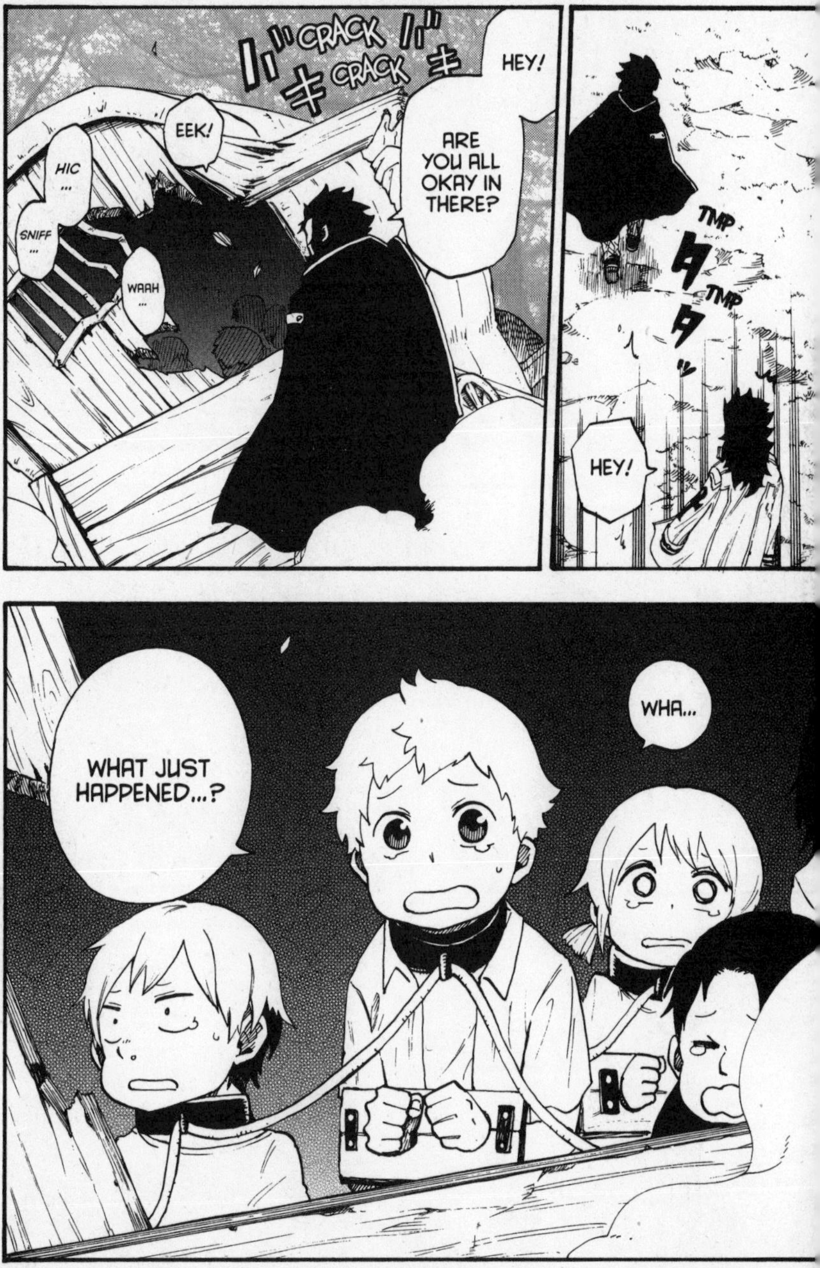

TMP
TMP
タタッ
HEY!
バキ CRACK
バキ CRACK
HEY!
ARE YOU ALL OKAY IN THERE?
EEK!
HIC...
SNIFF...
WAAH...
WHA...
WHAT JUST HAPPENED...?

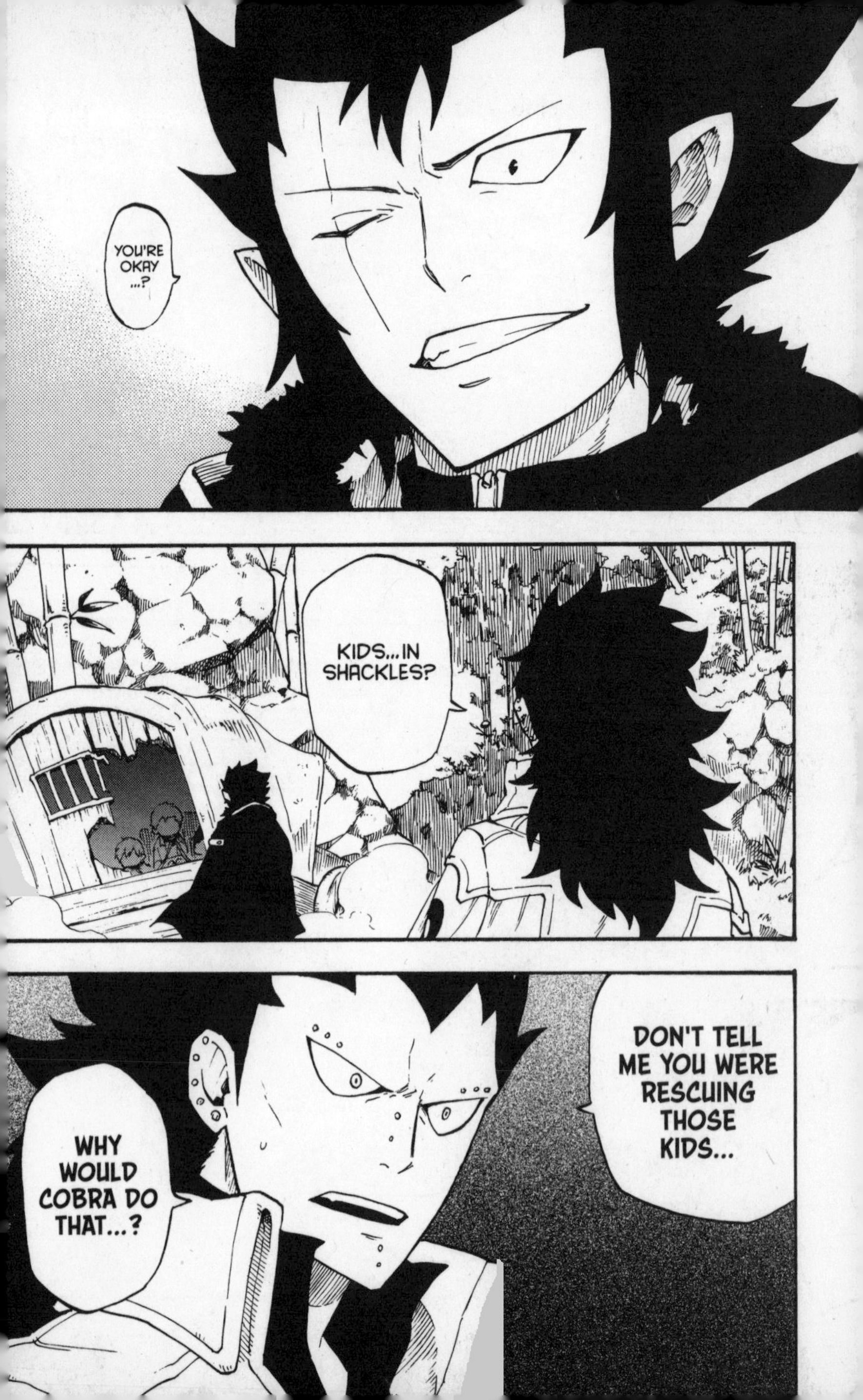
YOU'RE OKAY ...?
KIDS... IN SHACKLES?
DON'T TELL ME YOU WERE RESCUING THOSE KIDS...
WHY WOULD COBRA DO THAT...?

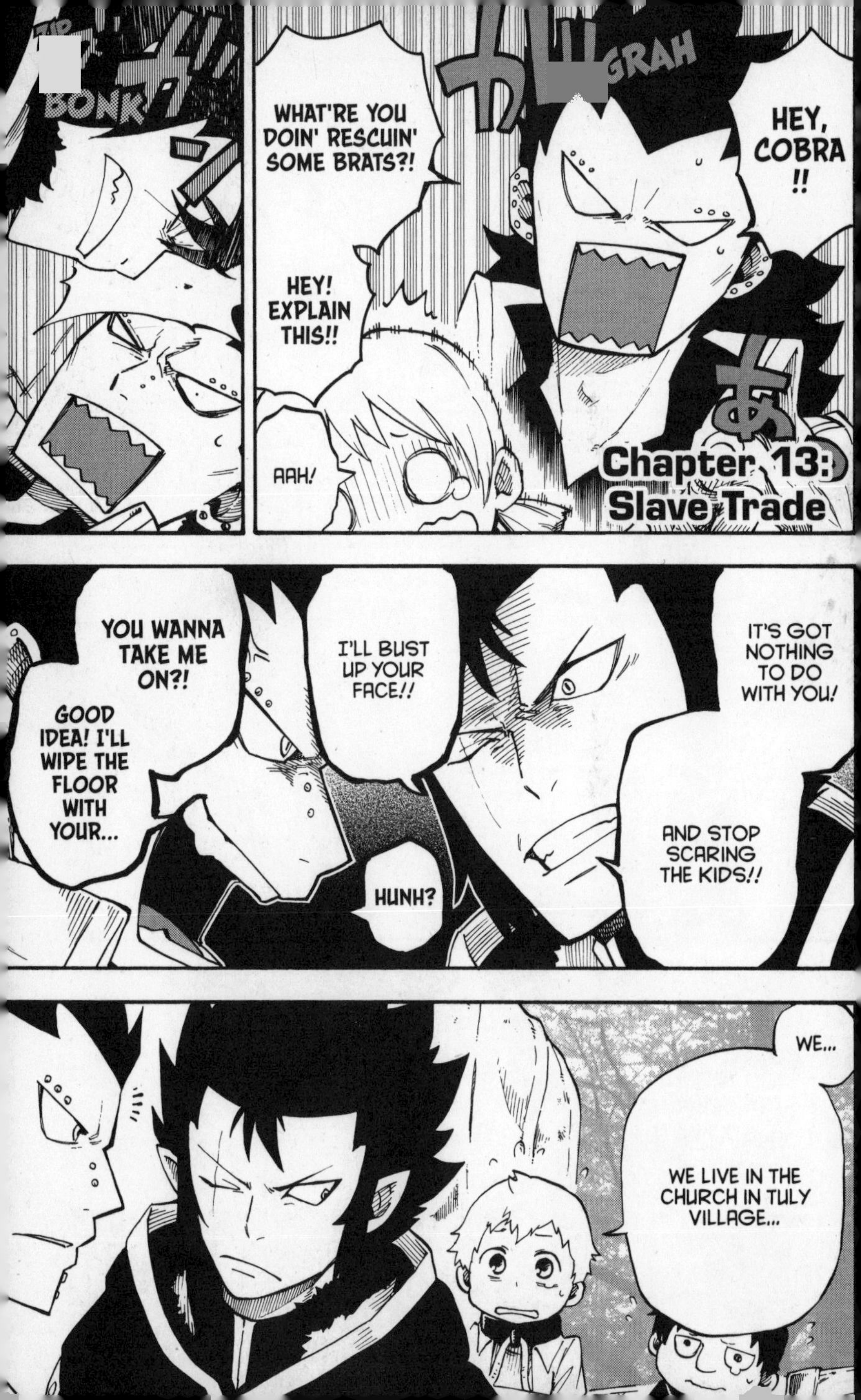
GRAH
HEY, COBRA!!
WHAT'RE YOU DOIN' RESCUIN' SOME BRATS?!
HEY! EXPLAIN THIS!!
AAH!
Chapter 13: Slave Trade
BONK
IT'S GOT NOTHING TO DO WITH YOU!
AND STOP SCARING THE KIDS!!
HUNH?
I'LL BUST UP YOUR FACE!!
YOU WANNA TAKE ME ON?!
GOOD IDEA! I'LL WIPE THE FLOOR WITH YOUR...
WE...
WE LIVE IN THE CHURCH IN TULY VILLAGE...

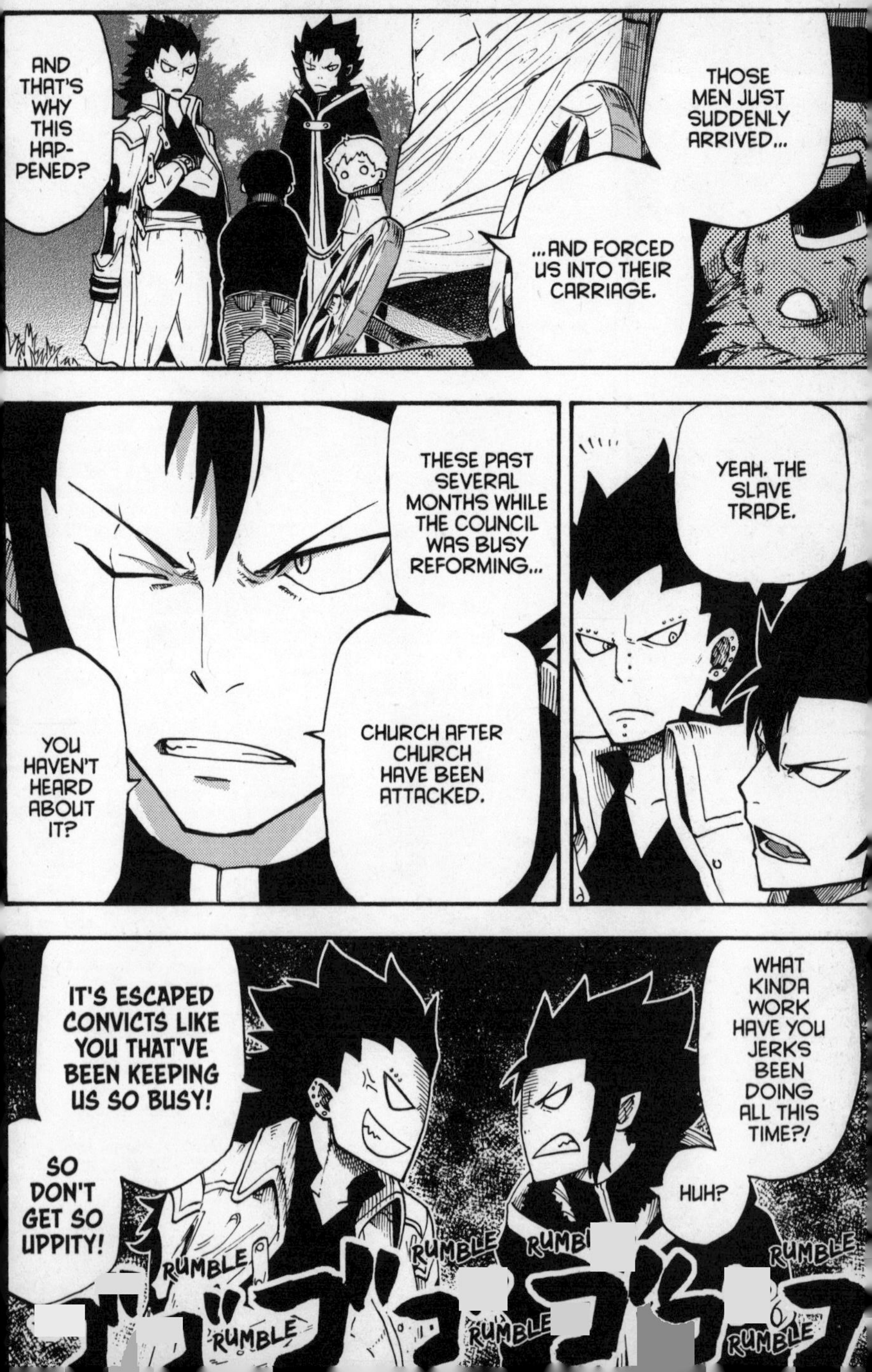
THOSE MEN JUST SUDDENLY ARRIVED...
...AND FORCED US INTO THEIR CARRIAGE.
AND THAT'S WHY THIS HAP-PENED?
YEAH. THE SLAVE TRADE.
THESE PAST SEVERAL MONTHS WHILE THE COUNCIL WAS BUSY REFORMING...
CHURCH AFTER CHURCH HAVE BEEN ATTACKED.
YOU HAVEN'T HEARD ABOUT IT?
WHAT KINDA WORK HAVE YOU JERKS BEEN DOING ALL THIS TIME?!
HUH?
IT'S ESCAPED CONVICTS LIKE YOU THAT'VE BEEN KEEPING US SO BUSY!
SO DON'T GET SO UPPITY!
RUMBLE RUMBLE RUMBLE RUMBLE RUMBLE RUMBLE RUMBLE RUMBLE

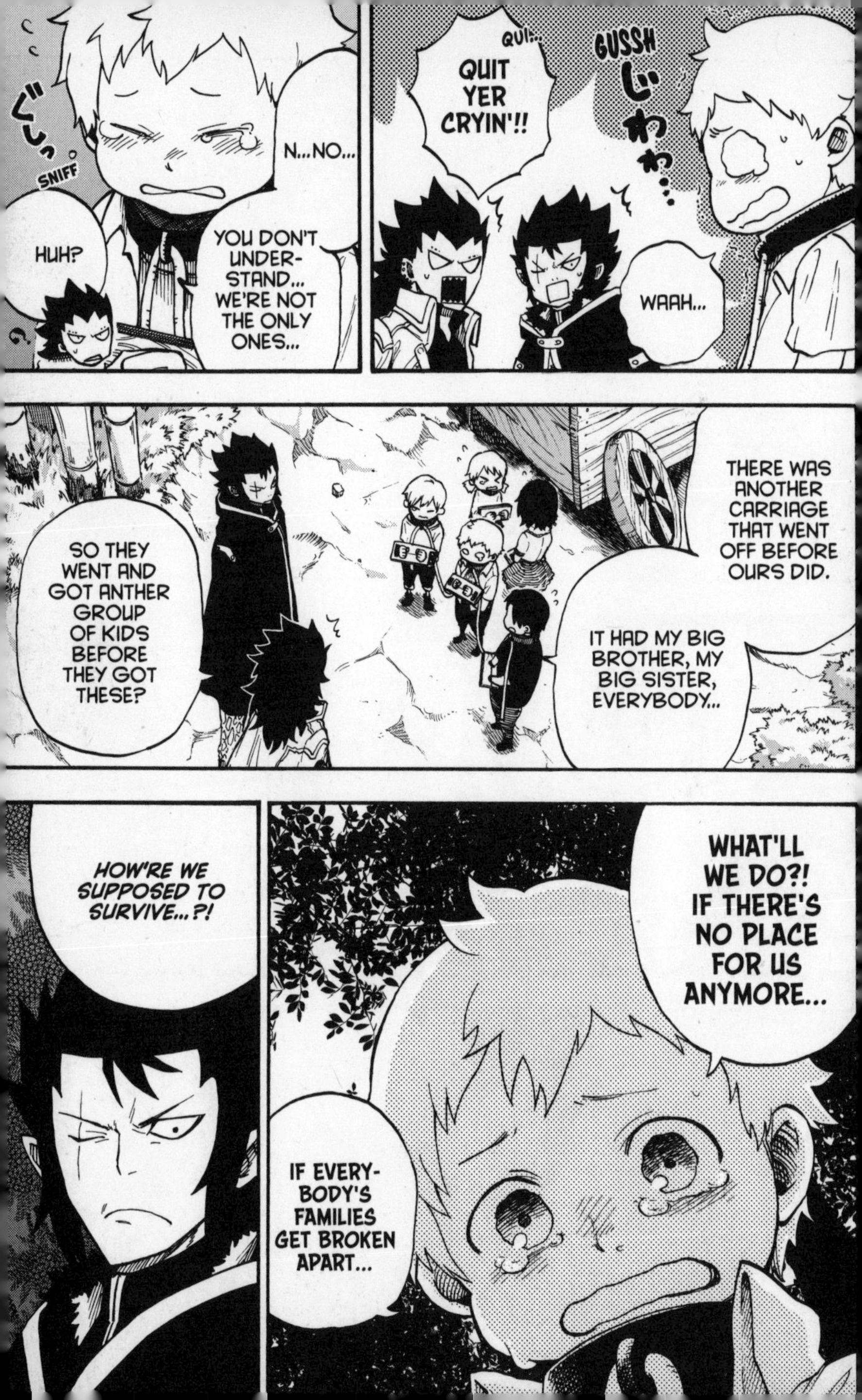
QUI...
QUIT YER CRYIN'!!
GUSSH
じわわ…
WAAH...
N...NO...
YOU DON'T UNDER-STAND... WE'RE NOT THE ONLY ONES...
ぐしっ
SNIFF
HUH?
THERE WAS ANOTHER CARRIAGE THAT WENT OFF BEFORE OURS DID.
IT HAD MY BIG BROTHER, MY BIG SISTER, EVERYBODY...
SO THEY WENT AND GOT ANTHER GROUP OF KIDS BEFORE THEY GOT THESE?
WHAT'LL WE DO?! IF THERE'S NO PLACE FOR US ANYMORE...
IF EVERY-BODY'S FAMILIES GET BROKEN APART...
HOW'RE WE SUPPOSED TO SURVIVE...?!

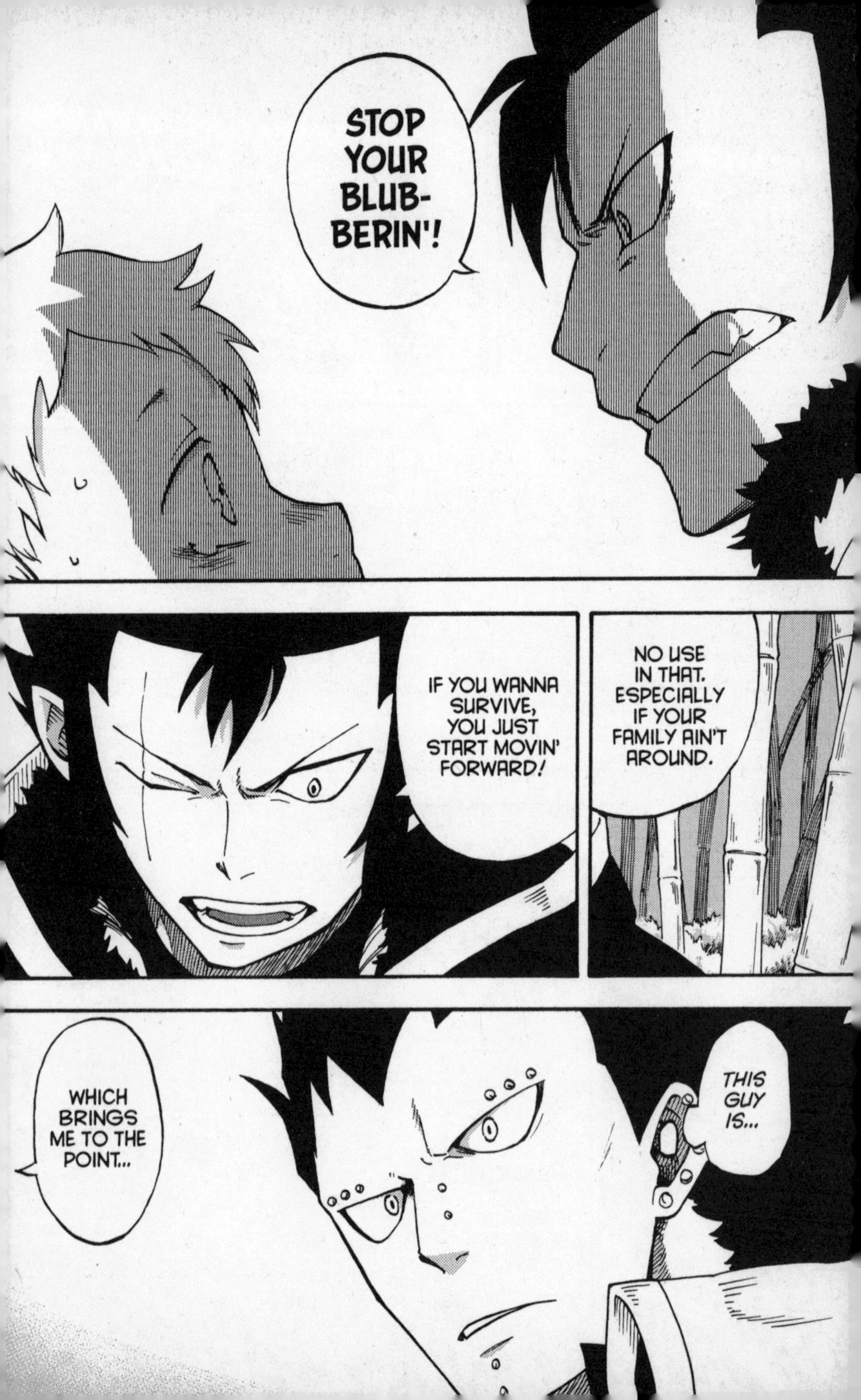
STOP YOUR BLUB-BERIN'!
NO USE IN THAT. ESPECIALLY IF YOUR FAMILY AIN'T AROUND.
IF YOU WANNA SURVIVE, YOU JUST START MOVIN' FORWARD!
THIS GUY IS...
WHICH BRINGS ME TO THE POINT...

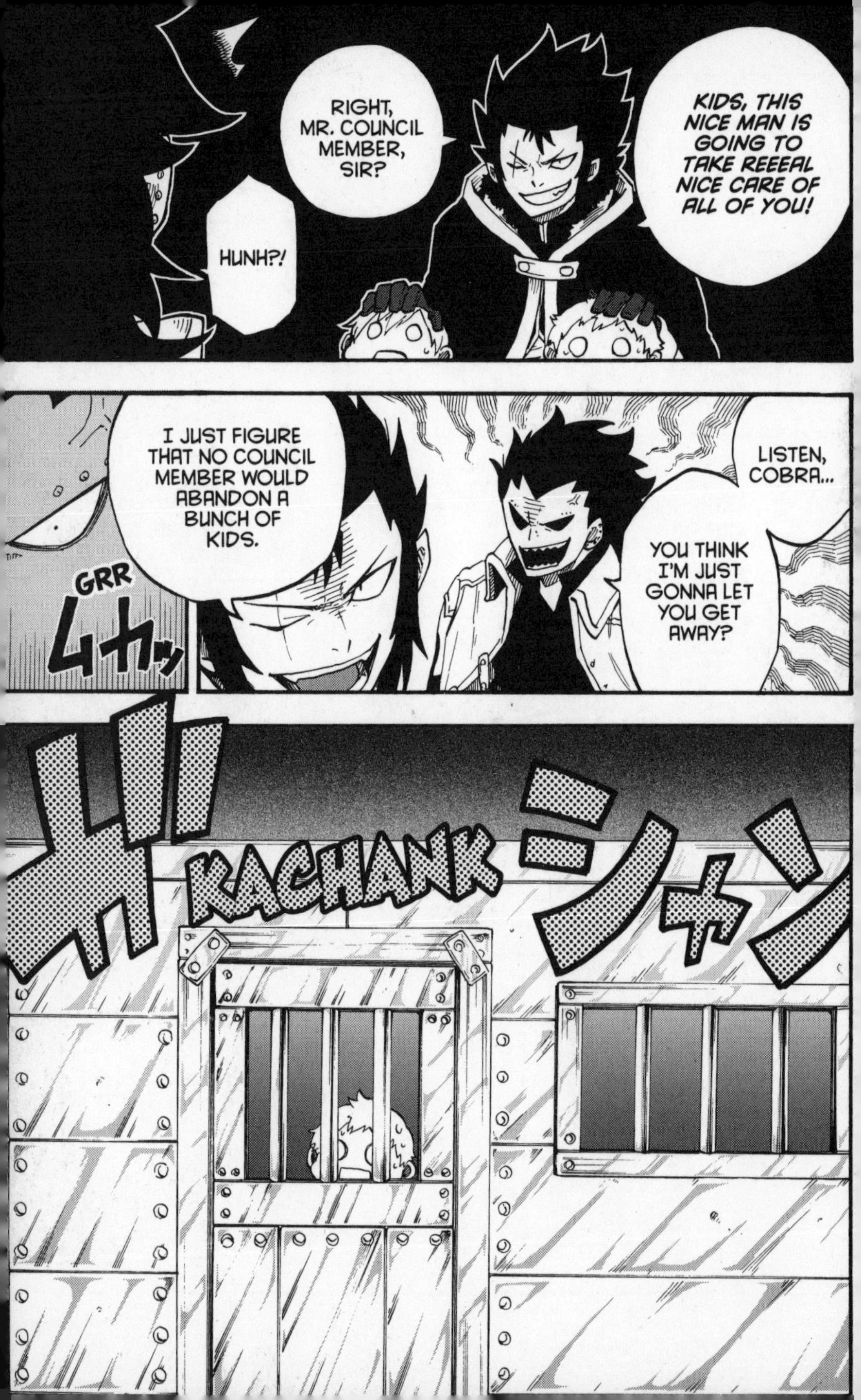
KIDS, THIS NICE MAN IS GOING TO TAKE REEEAL NICE CARE OF ALL OF YOU!
RIGHT, MR. COUNCIL MEMBER, SIR?
HUNH?!
LISTEN, COBRA...
YOU THINK I'M JUST GONNA LET YOU GET AWAY?
I JUST FIGURE THAT NO COUNCIL MEMBER WOULD ABANDON A BUNCH OF KIDS.
GRR
ムカッ
ガシャン
KACHANK

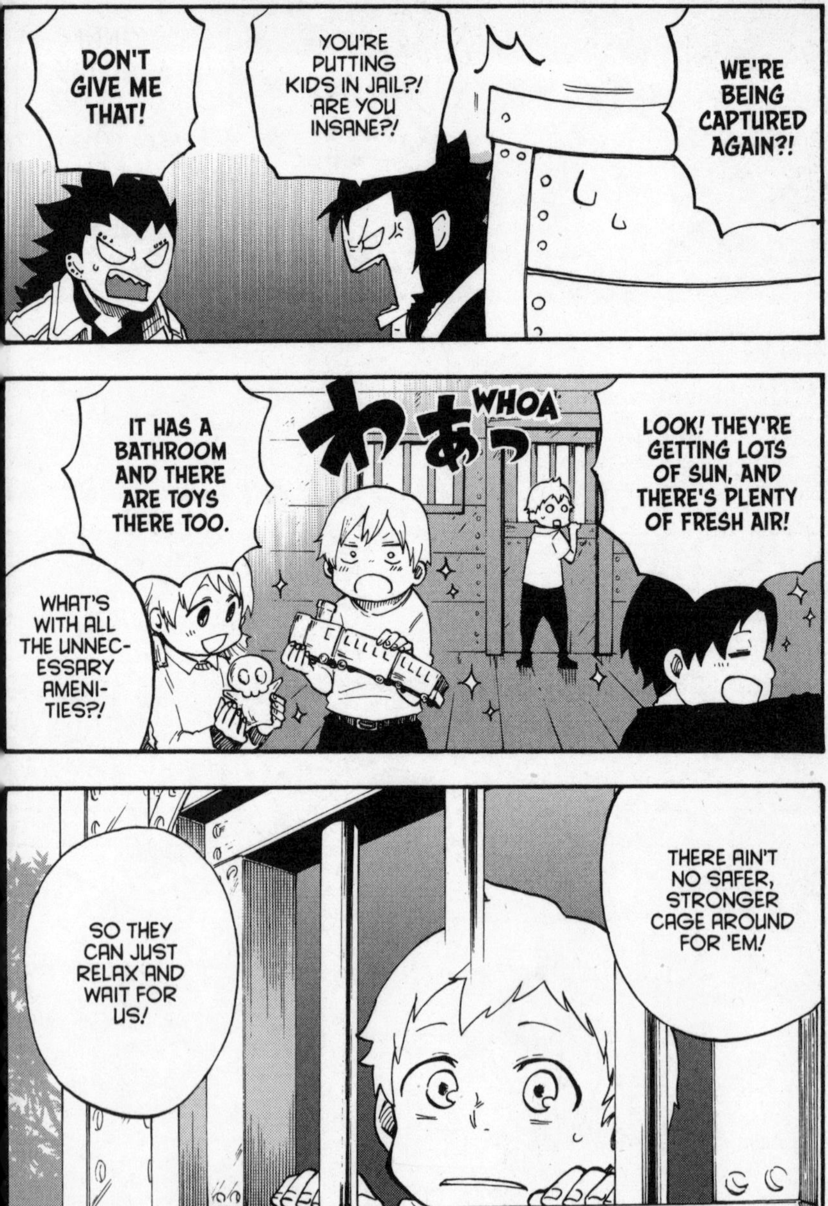
WE'RE BEING CAPTURED AGAIN?!
YOU'RE PUTTING KIDS IN JAIL?! ARE YOU INSANE?!
DON'T GIVE ME THAT!
LOOK! THEY'RE GETTING LOTS OF SUN, AND THERE'S PLENTY OF FRESH AIR!
わあっ WHOA
IT HAS A BATHROOM AND THERE ARE TOYS THERE TOO.
WHAT'S WITH ALL THE UNNEC-ESSARY AMENI-TIES?!
THERE AIN'T NO SAFER, STRONGER CAGE AROUND FOR 'EM!
SO THEY CAN JUST RELAX AND WAIT FOR US!

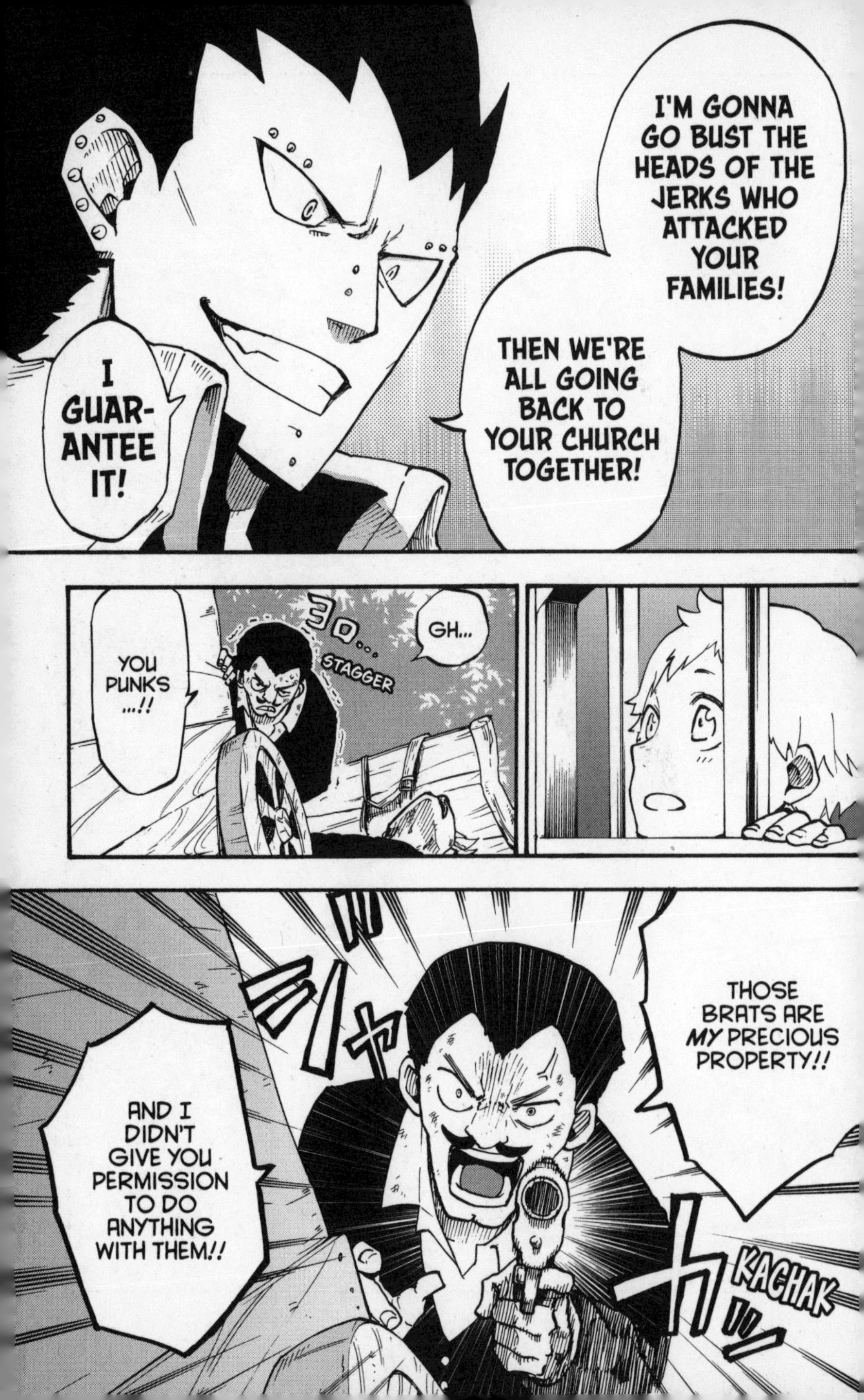

I'M GONNA GO BUST THE HEADS OF THE JERKS WHO ATTACKED YOUR FAMILIES!
THEN WE'RE ALL GOING BACK TO YOUR CHURCH TOGETHER!
I GUARANTEE IT!
GH...
STAGGER
YOU PUNKS ...!!
THOSE BRATS ARE *MY* PRECIOUS PROPERTY!!
AND I DIDN'T GIVE YOU PERMISSION TO DO ANYTHING WITH THEM!!
KACHAK

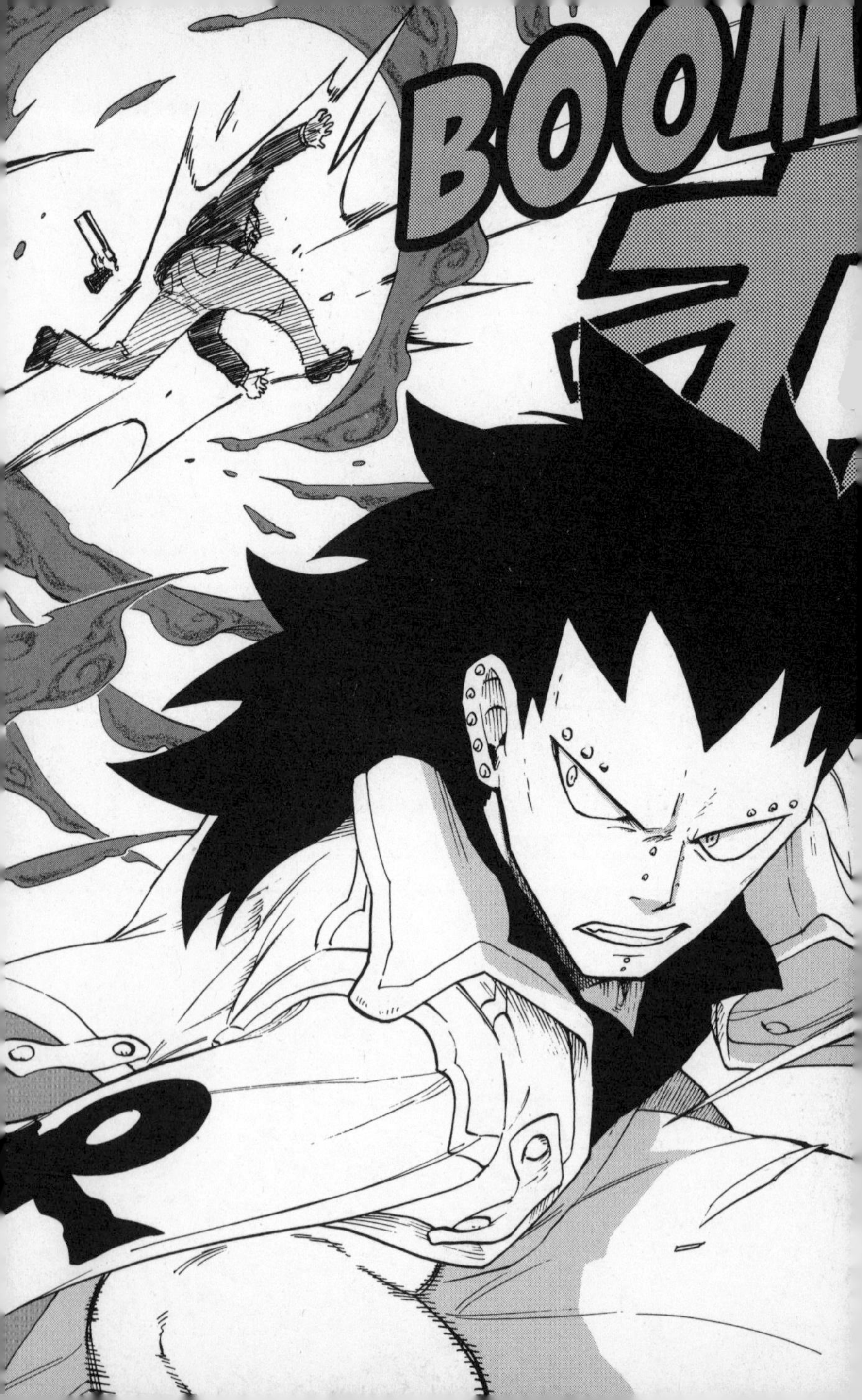
BOOM

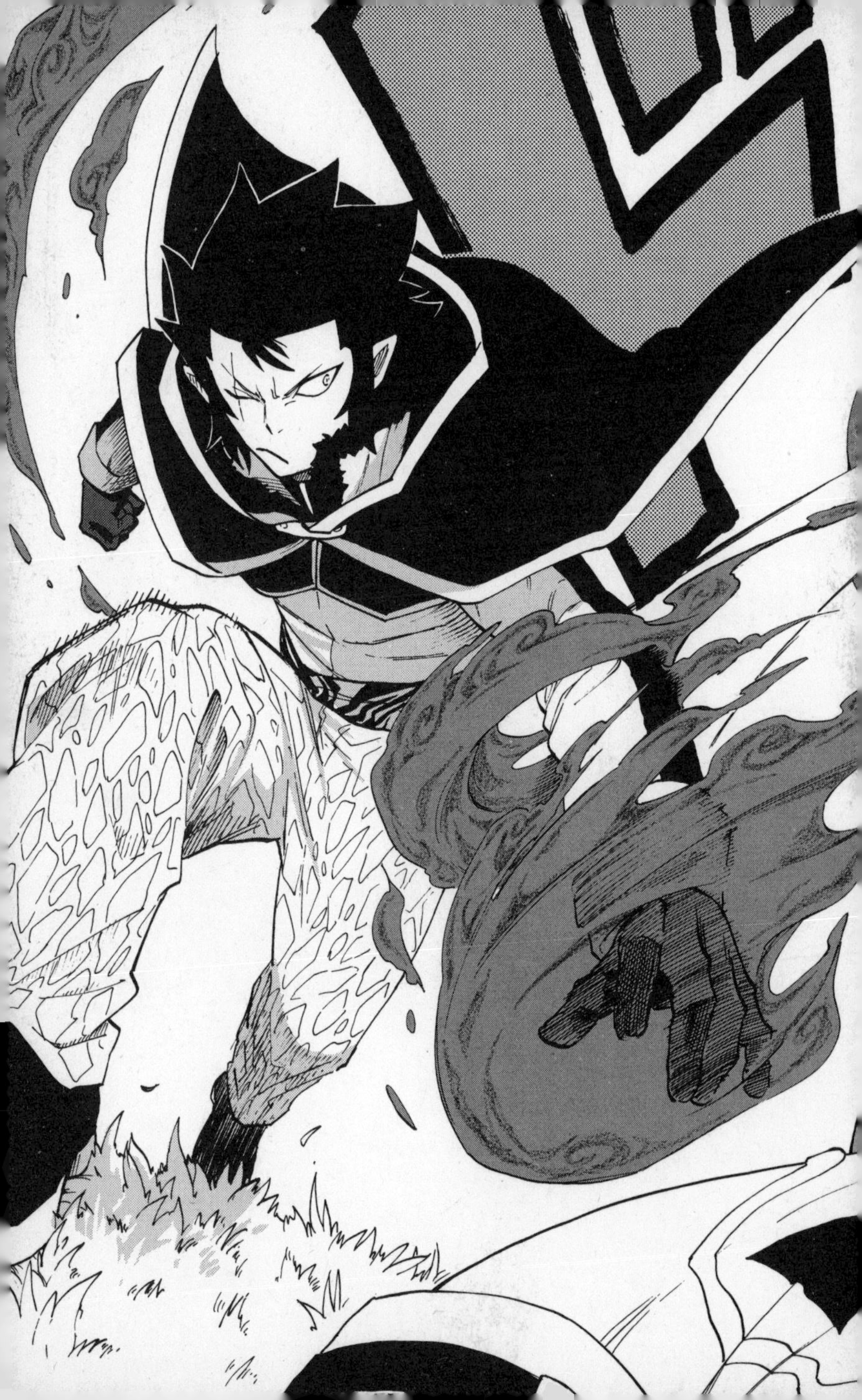

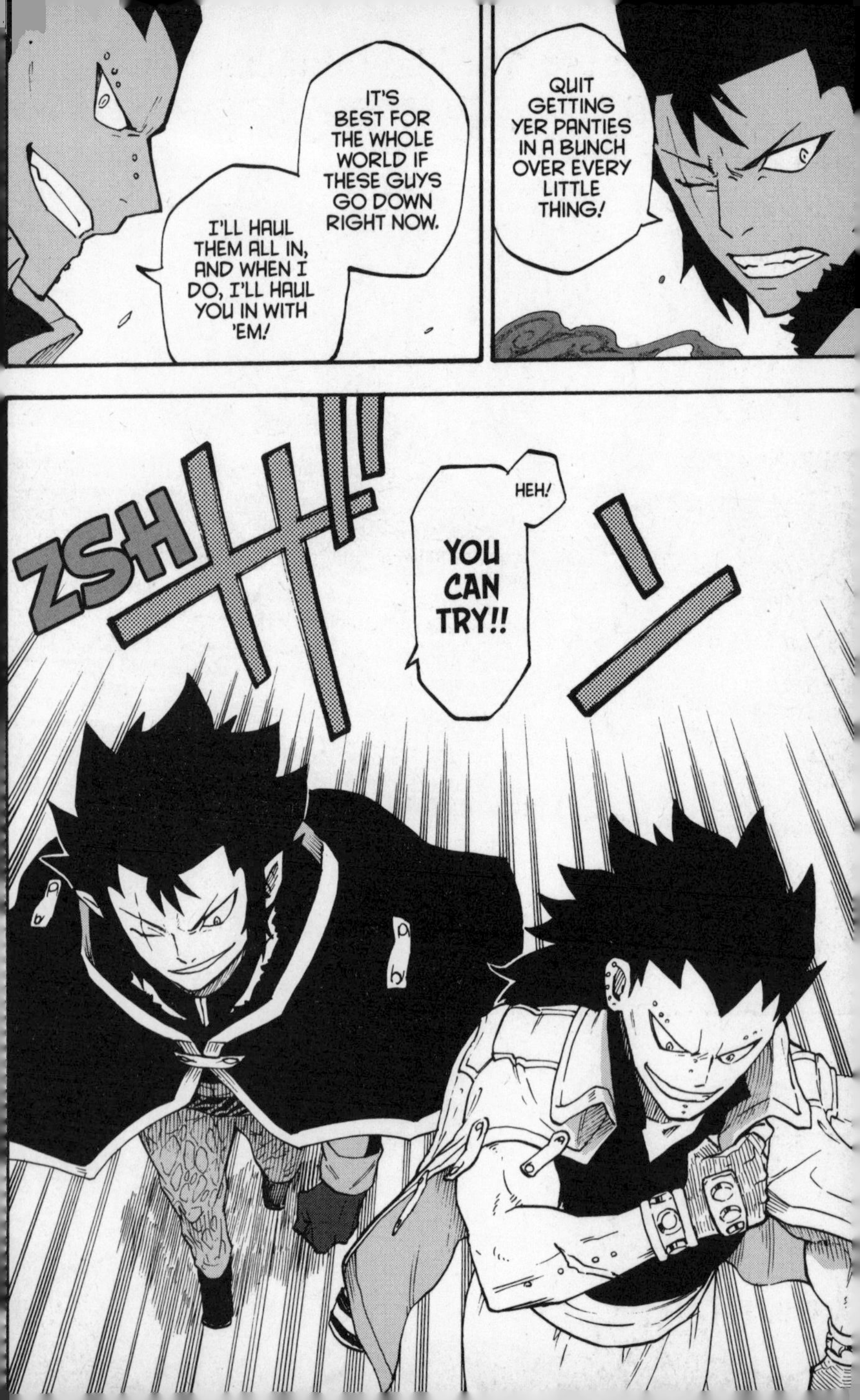
QUIT GETTING YER PANTIES IN A BUNCH OVER EVERY LITTLE THING!
IT'S BEST FOR THE WHOLE WORLD IF THESE GUYS GO DOWN RIGHT NOW.
I'LL HAUL THEM ALL IN, AND WHEN I DO, I'LL HAUL YOU IN WITH 'EM!
HEH!
YOU CAN TRY!!
ZSH

Chapter 14: The Infallible Plan

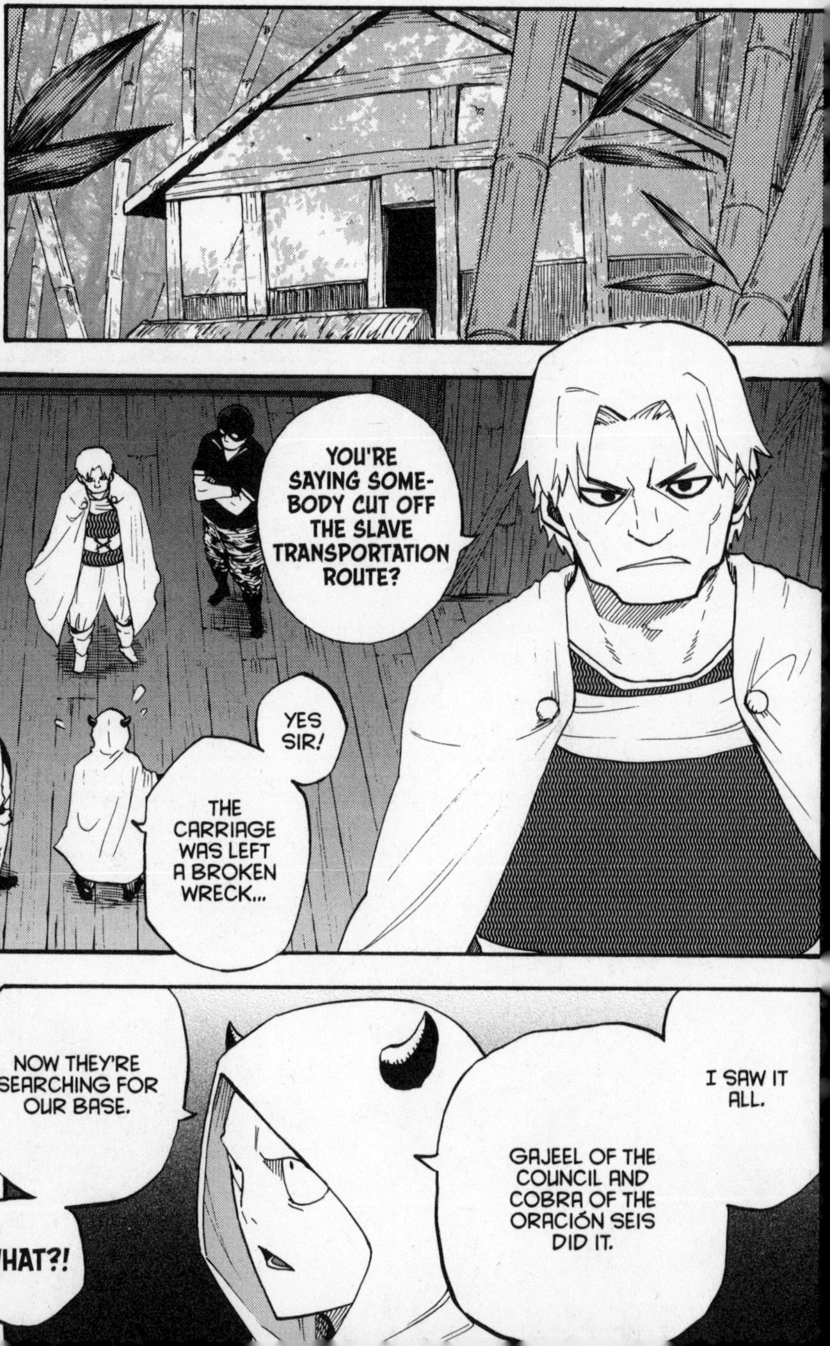
YOU'RE SAYING SOMEBODY CUT OFF THE SLAVE TRANSPORTATION ROUTE?
YES SIR!
THE CARRIAGE WAS LEFT A BROKEN WRECK...
I SAW IT ALL.
GAJEEL OF THE COUNCIL AND COBRA OF THE ORACIÓN SEIS DID IT.
NOW THEY'RE SEARCHING FOR OUR BASE.
WHAT?!

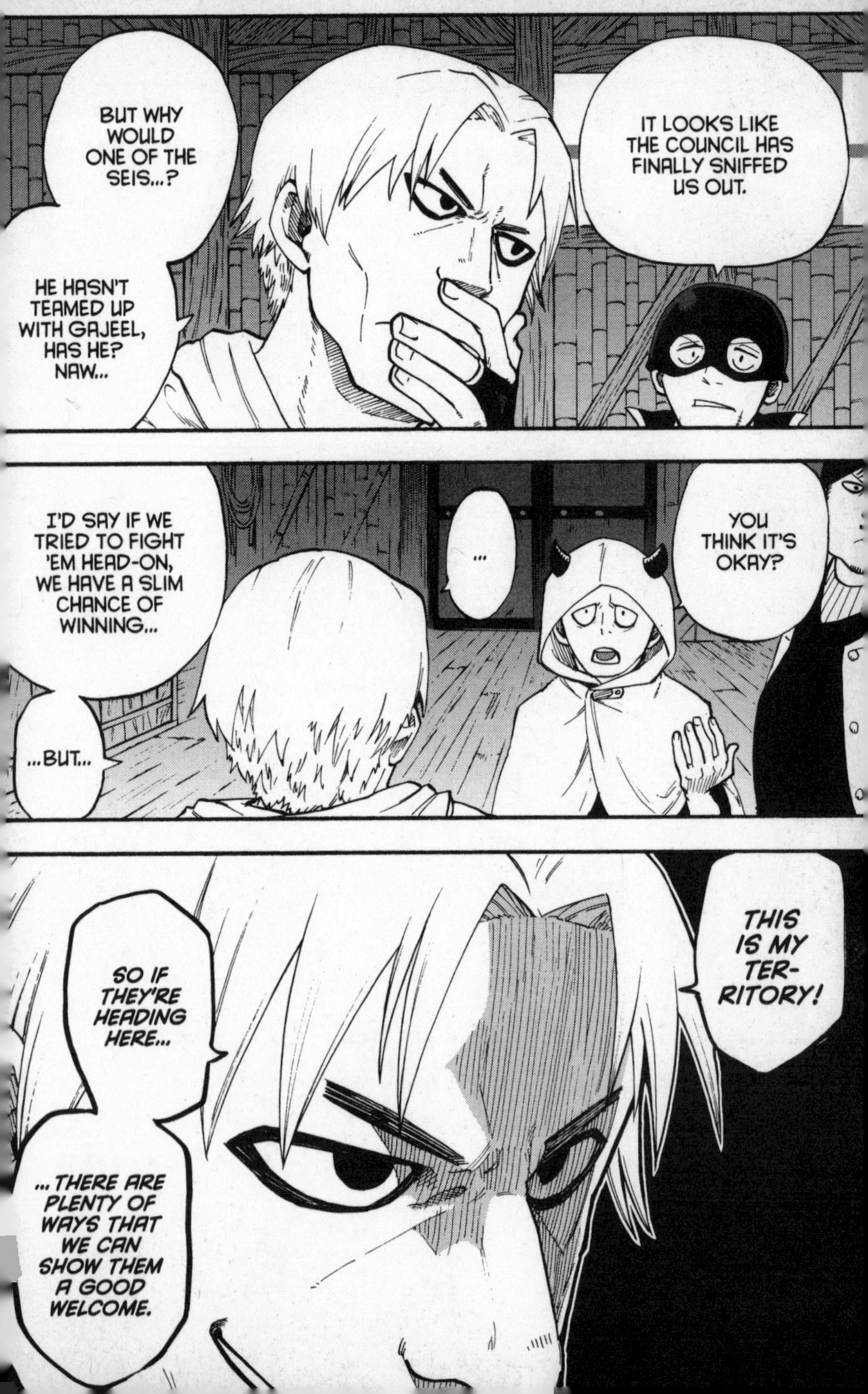
IT LOOKS LIKE THE COUNCIL HAS FINALLY SNIFFED US OUT.
BUT WHY WOULD ONE OF THE SEIS...?
HE HASN'T TEAMED UP WITH GAJEEL, HAS HE? NAW...
YOU THINK IT'S OKAY?
...
I'D SAY IF WE TRIED TO FIGHT 'EM HEAD-ON, WE HAVE A SLIM CHANCE OF WINNING...
...BUT...
THIS IS MY TER-RITORY!
SO IF THEY'RE HEADING HERE...
...THERE ARE PLENTY OF WAYS THAT WE CAN SHOW THEM A GOOD WELCOME.

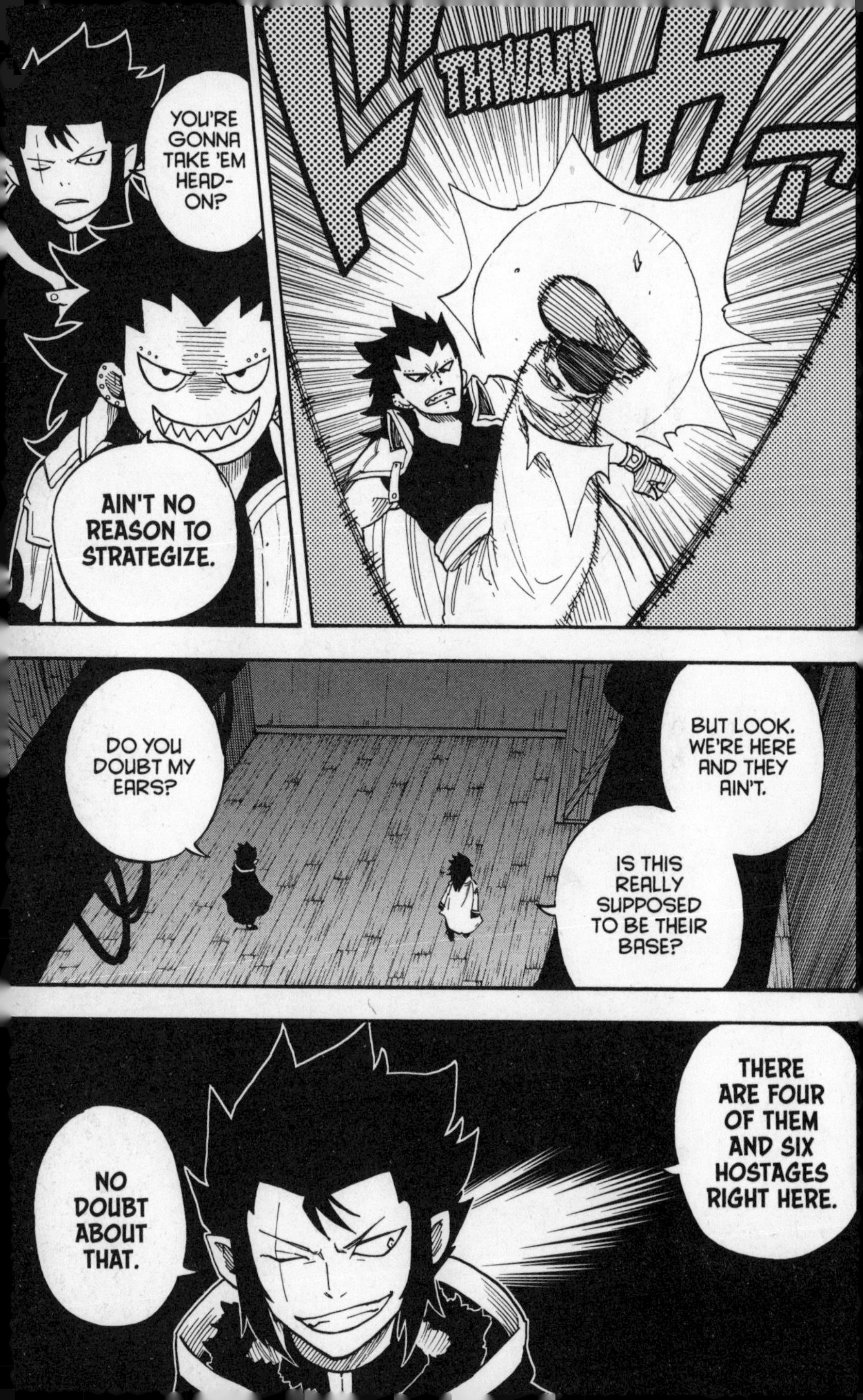
THWAM
YOU'RE GONNA TAKE 'EM HEAD-ON?
AIN'T NO REASON TO STRATEGIZE.
BUT LOOK. WE'RE HERE AND THEY AIN'T.
IS THIS REALLY SUPPOSED TO BE THEIR BASE?
DO YOU DOUBT MY EARS?
THERE ARE FOUR OF THEM AND SIX HOSTAGES RIGHT HERE.
NO DOUBT ABOUT THAT.

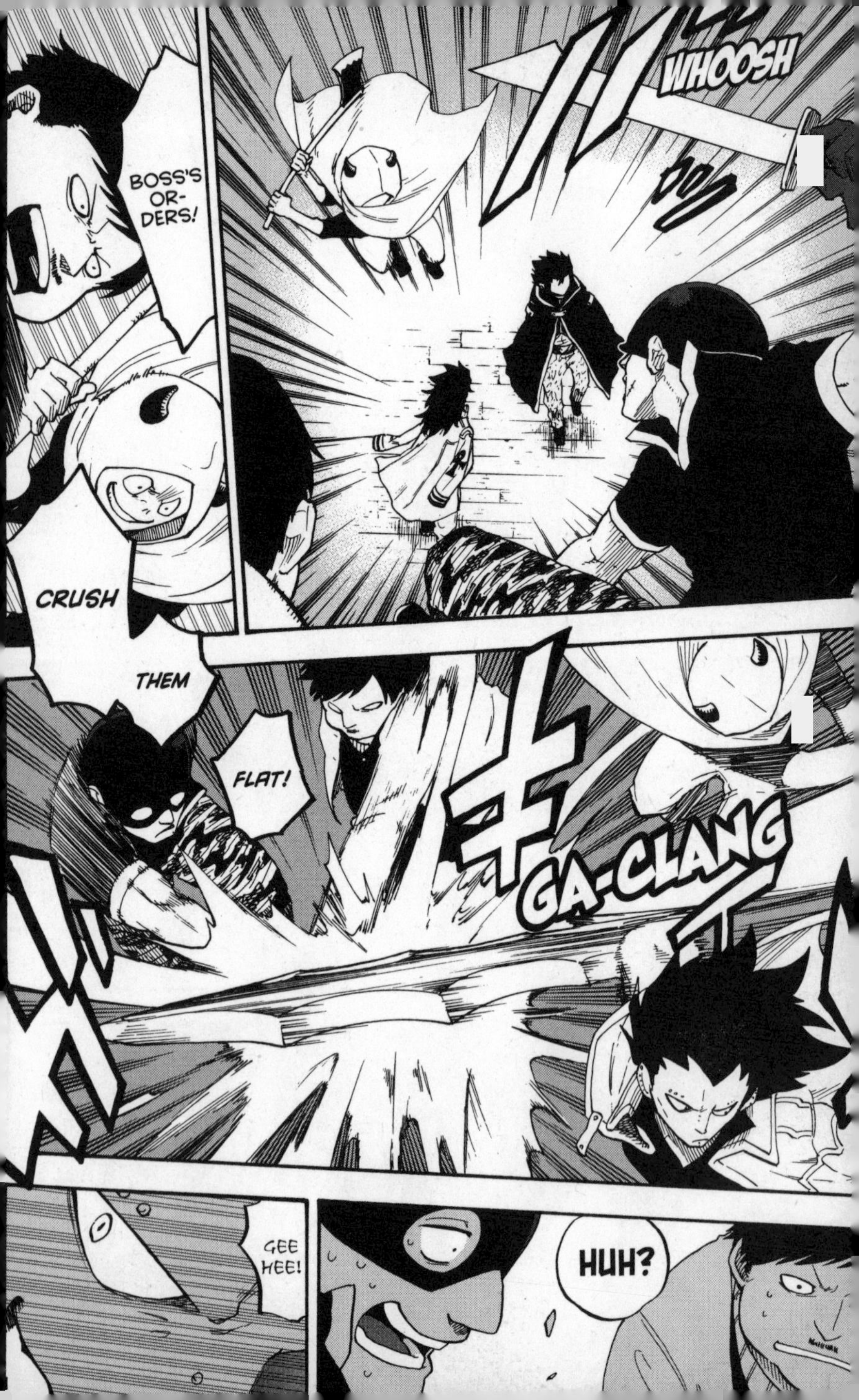
WHOOSH
BOSS'S ORDERS!
CRUSH
THEM
FLAT!
GA-CLANG
HUH?
GEE HEE!

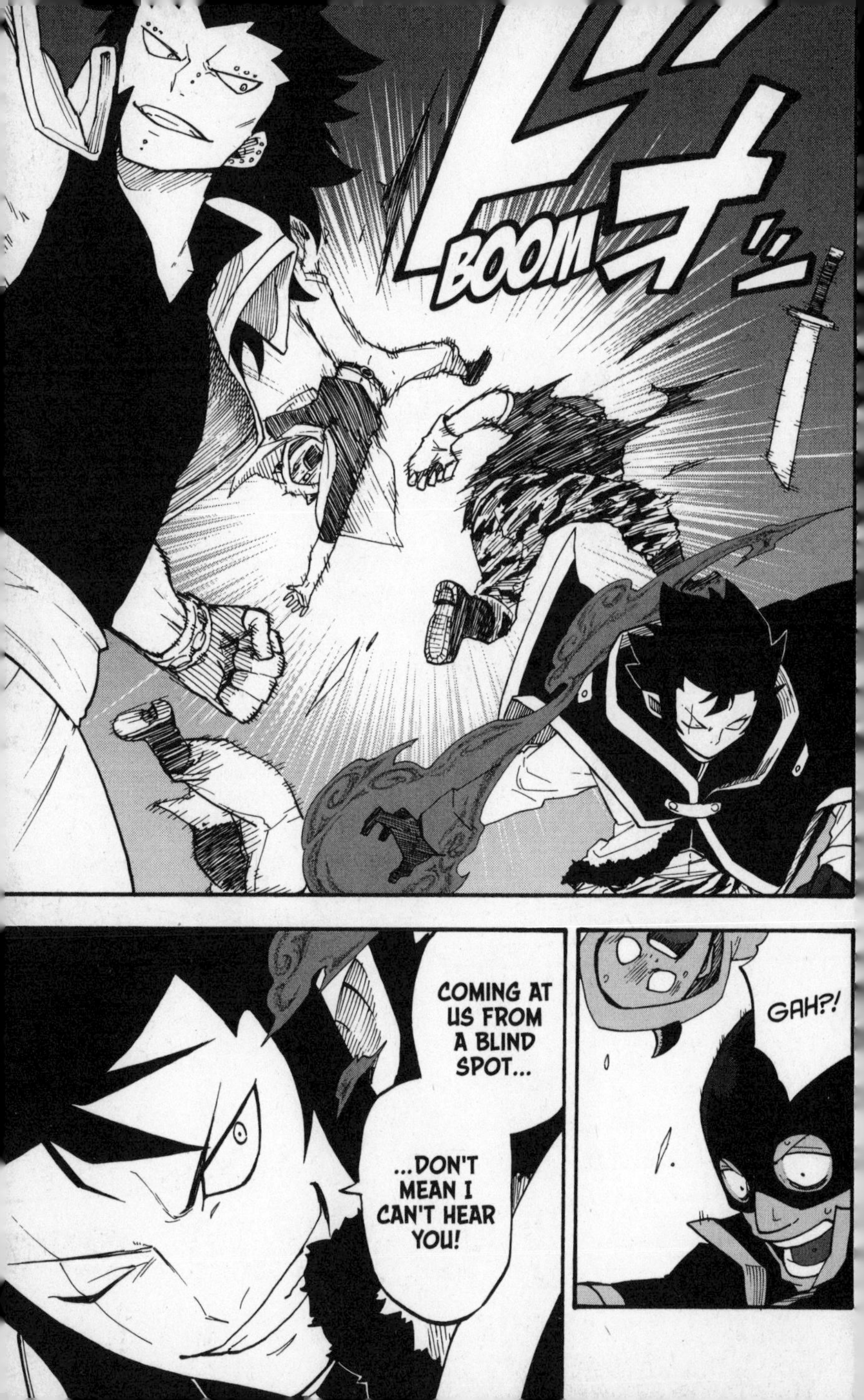
BOOM
GAH?!
COMING AT US FROM A BLIND SPOT...
...DON'T MEAN I CAN'T HEAR YOU!

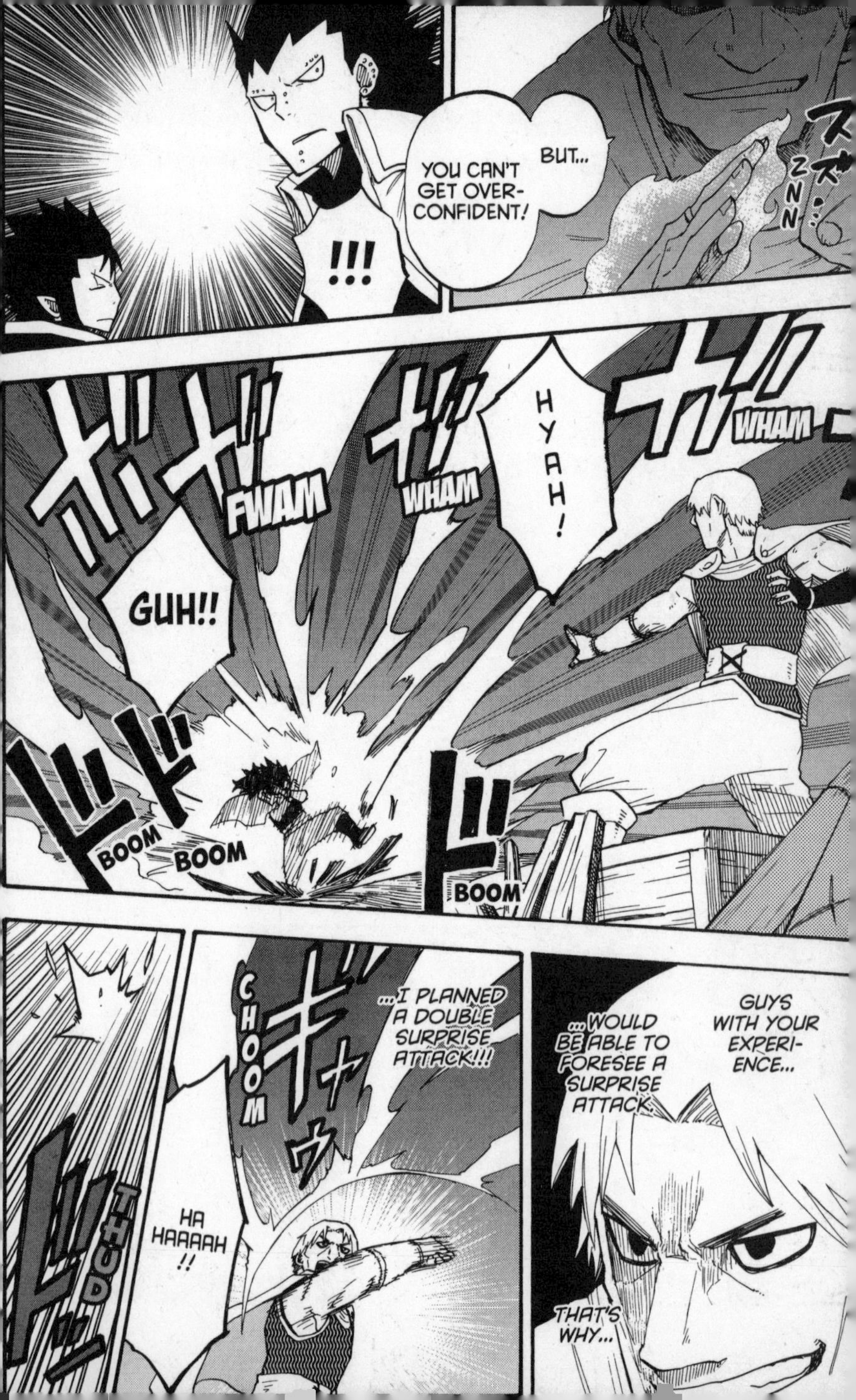
ZNN
BUT...
YOU CAN'T GET OVER-CONFIDENT!
!!!
WHAM
HYAH!
WHAM
FWAM
GUH!!
BOOM
BOOM BOOM
GUYS WITH YOUR EXPERIENCE...
...WOULD BE ABLE TO FORESEE A SURPRISE ATTACK.
THAT'S WHY...
...I PLANNED A DOUBLE SURPRISE ATTACK!!!
CHOOOM
HA HAAAAAH!!
THUD

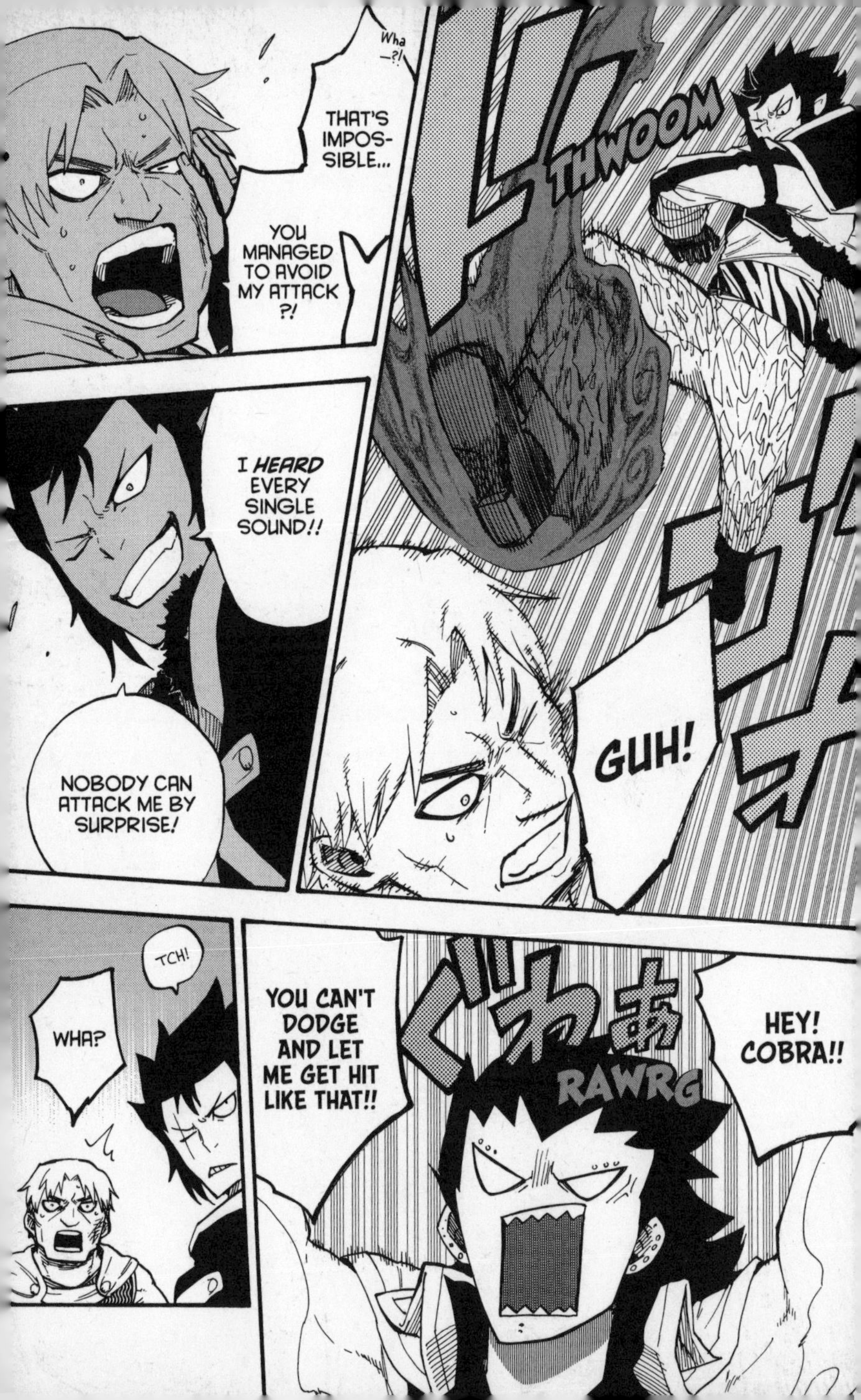
THWOOM
GUH!
Wha—?!
THAT'S IMPOS-SIBLE...
YOU MANAGED TO AVOID MY ATTACK?!
I HEARD EVERY SINGLE SOUND!!
NOBODY CAN ATTACK ME BY SURPRISE!
HEY! COBRA!!
くわぁ
RAWRG
YOU CAN'T DODGE AND LET ME GET HIT LIKE THAT!!
TCH!
WHA?

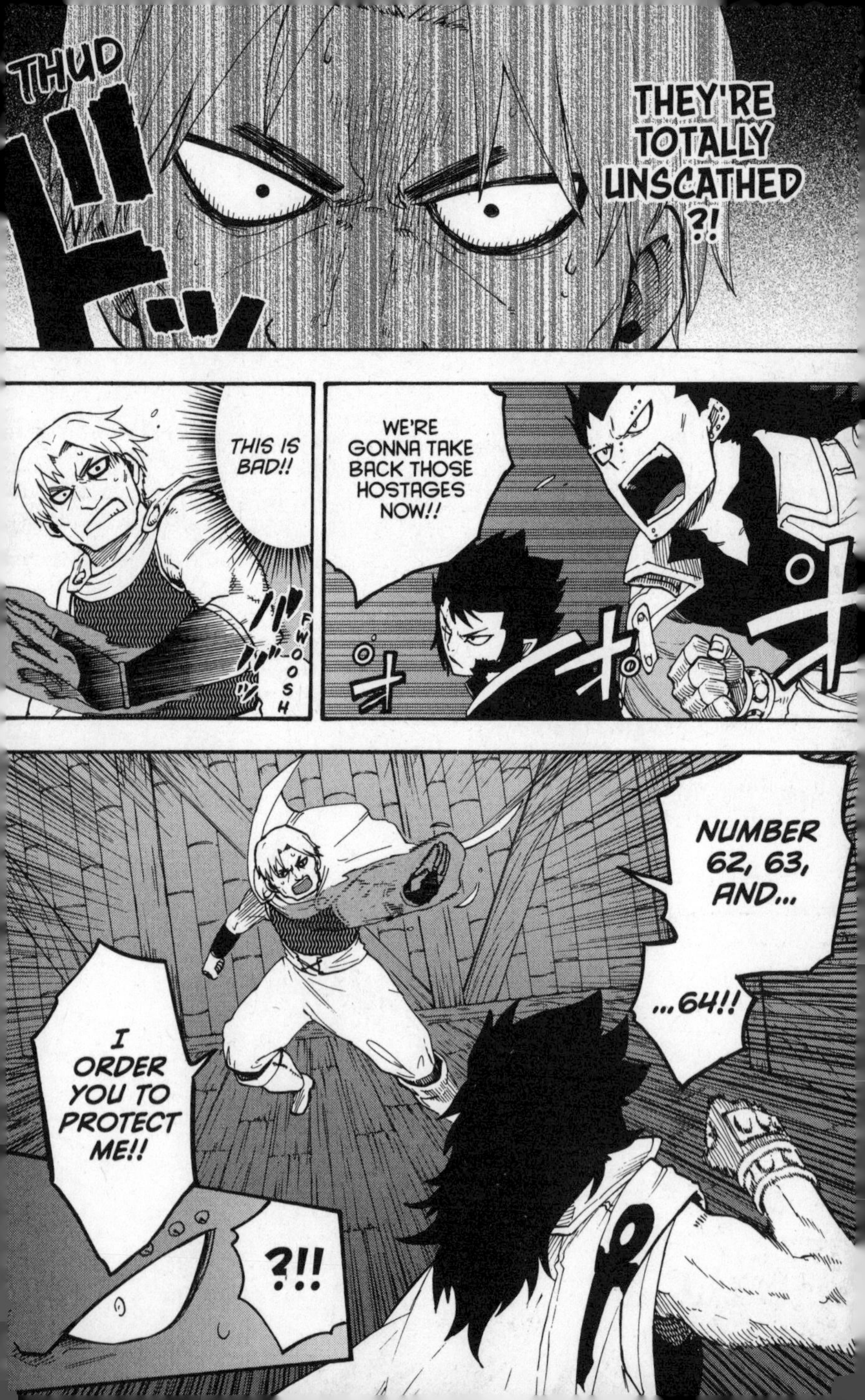
THEY'RE TOTALLY UNSCATHED ?!
THUD
WE'RE GONNA TAKE BACK THOSE HOSTAGES NOW!!
THIS IS BAD!!
FWOOSH
NUMBER 62, 63, AND...
...64!!
I ORDER YOU TO PROTECT ME!!
?!!

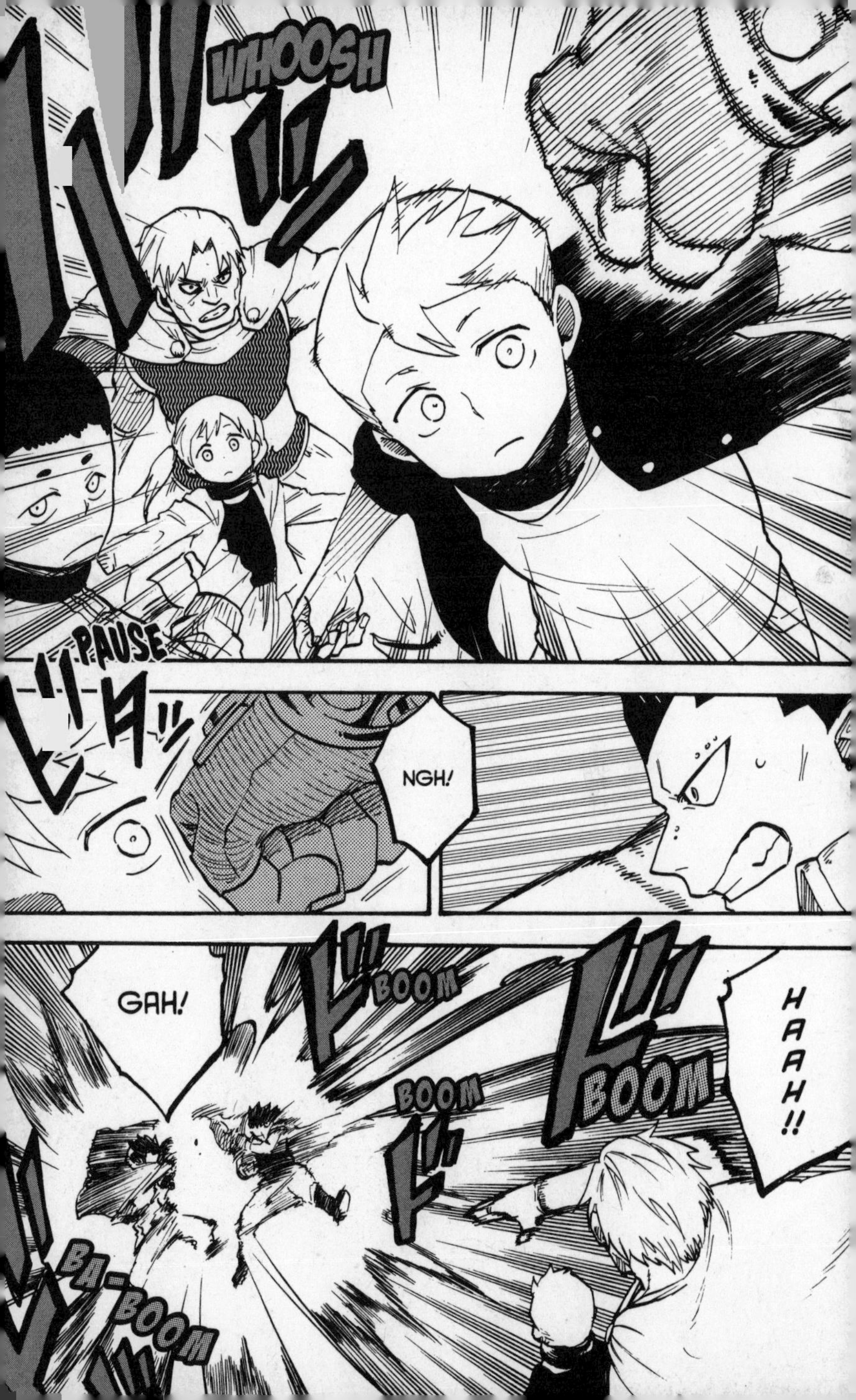
WHOOSH
PAUSE
NGH!
HAAAH!!
BOOM
BOOM
GAH!
BOOM
BA-BOOM

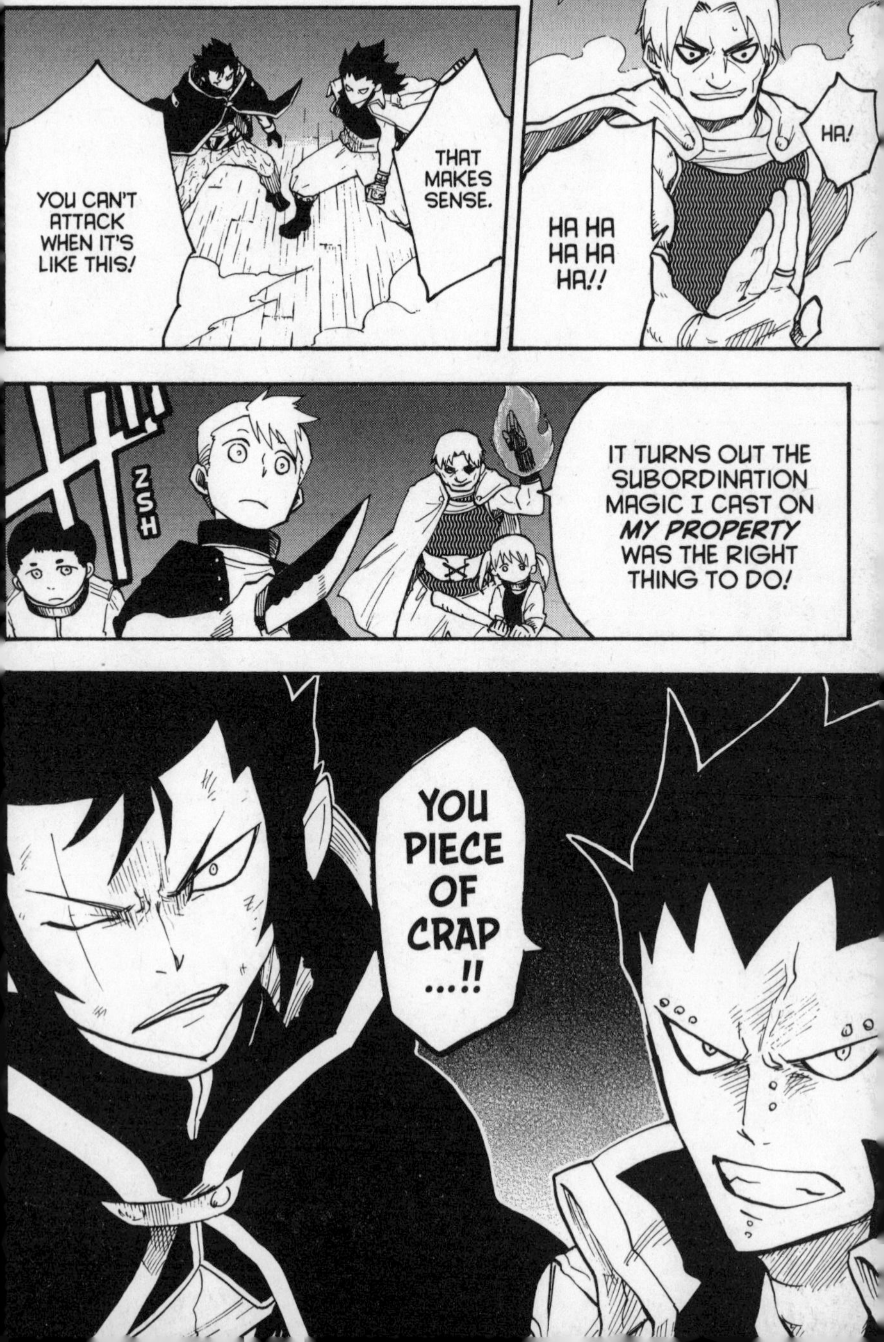
HA!
HA HA HA HA HA!!
THAT MAKES SENSE.
YOU CAN'T ATTACK WHEN IT'S LIKE THIS!
IT TURNS OUT THE SUBORDINATION MAGIC I CAST ON *MY PROPERTY* WAS THE RIGHT THING TO DO!
ZSH
YOU PIECE OF CRAP ...!!

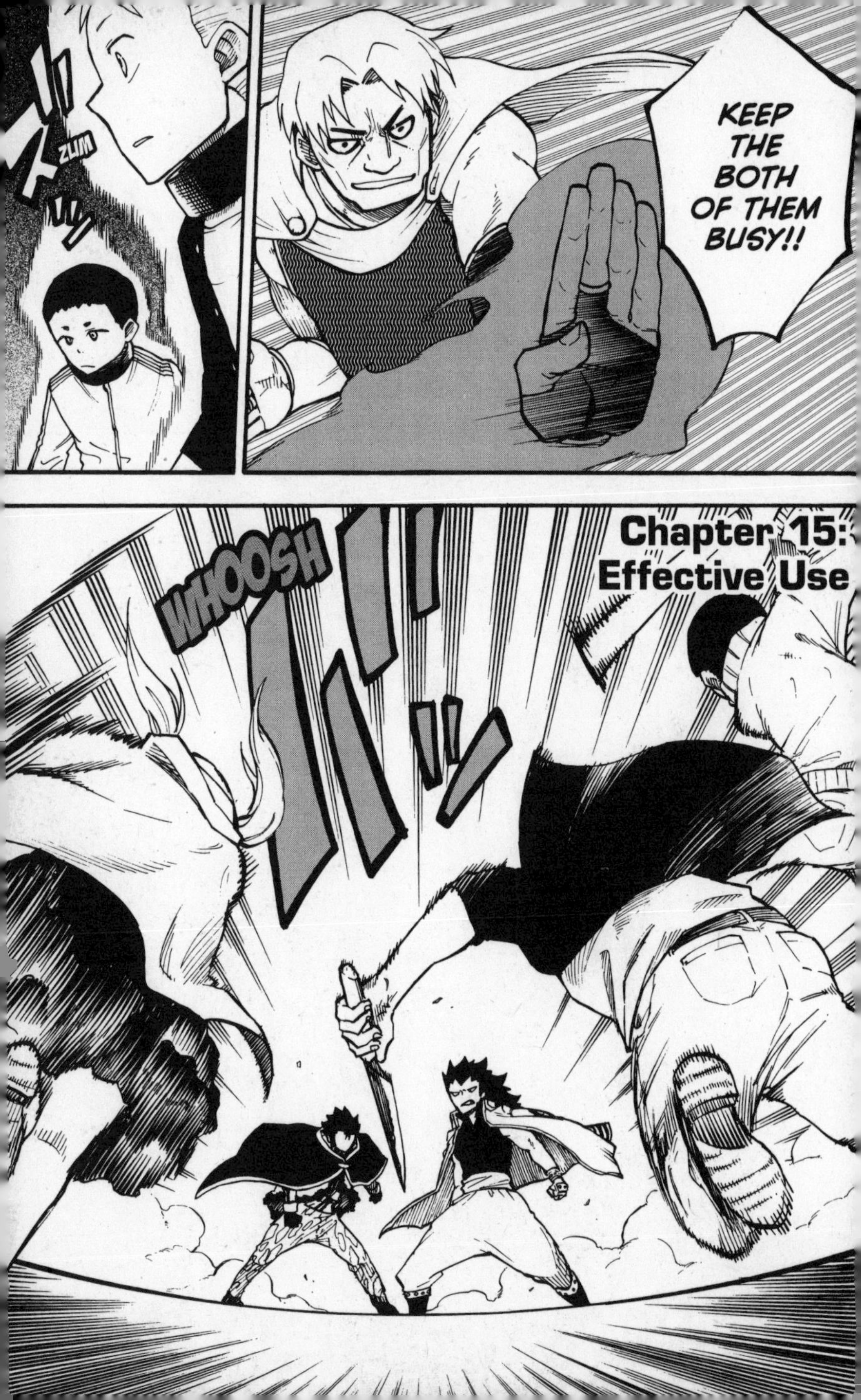
KEEP THE BOTH OF THEM BUSY!!
ZUM
Chapter 15: Effective Use
WHOOSH

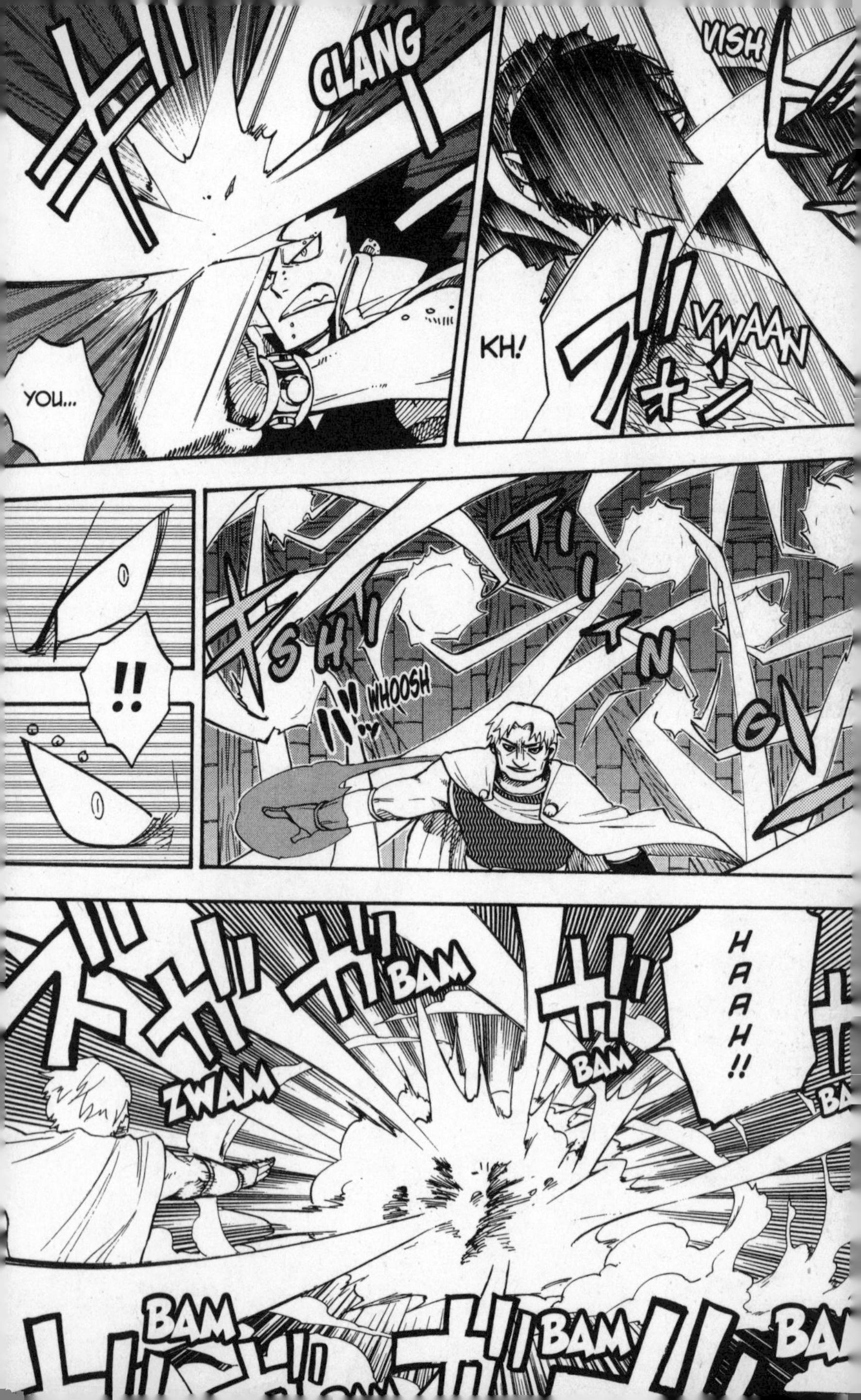
VISH
KH!
VWAAN
CLANG
YOU...
T I N G
S H I
WHOOSH
!!
BA
HAAAH!!
BAM
BAM
ZWAM
BA
BAM
BAM

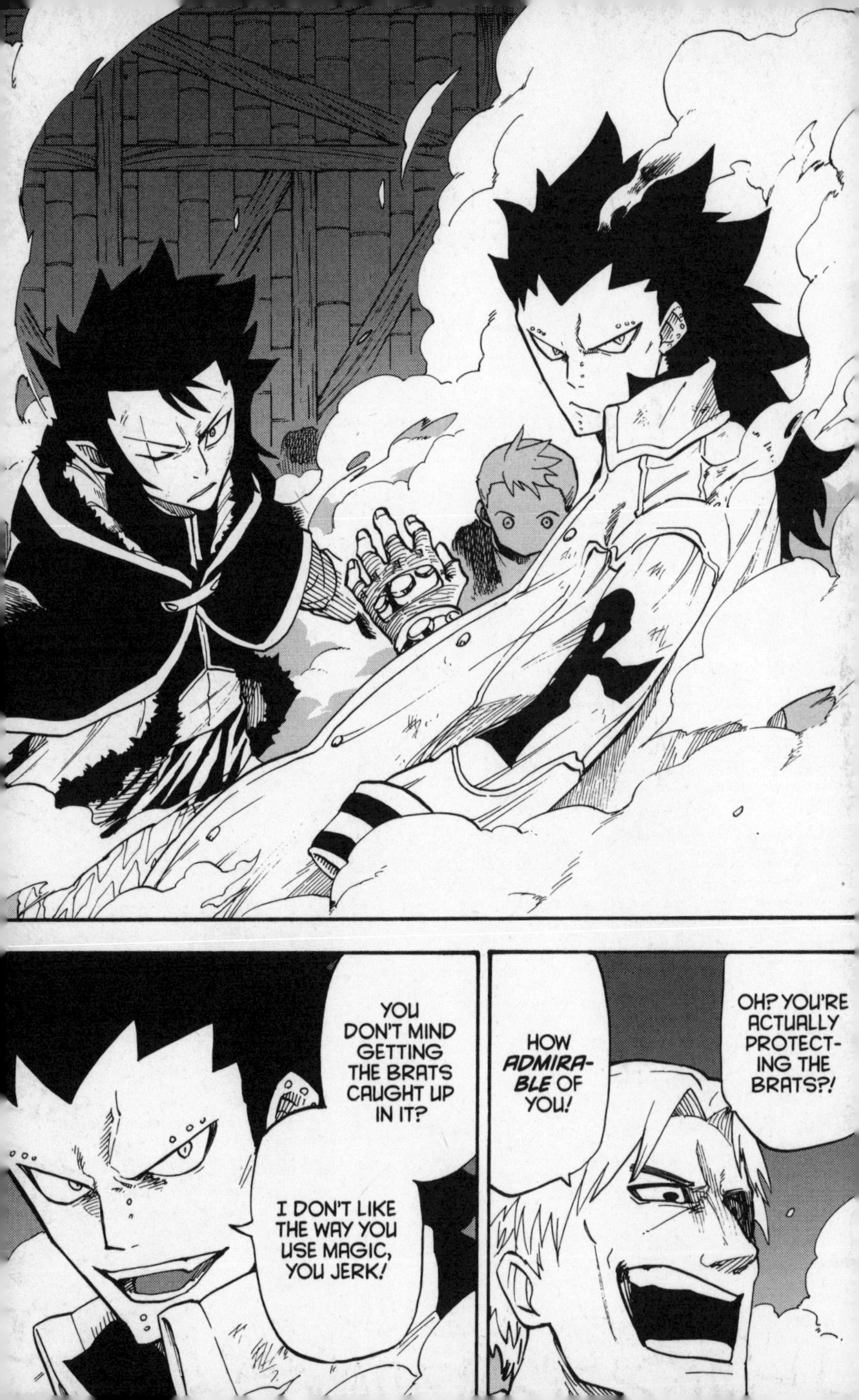
OH? YOU'RE ACTUALLY PROTECTING THE BRATS?!
HOW *ADMIRABLE* OF YOU!
YOU DON'T MIND GETTING THE BRATS CAUGHT UP IN IT?
I DON'T LIKE THE WAY YOU USE MAGIC, YOU JERK!

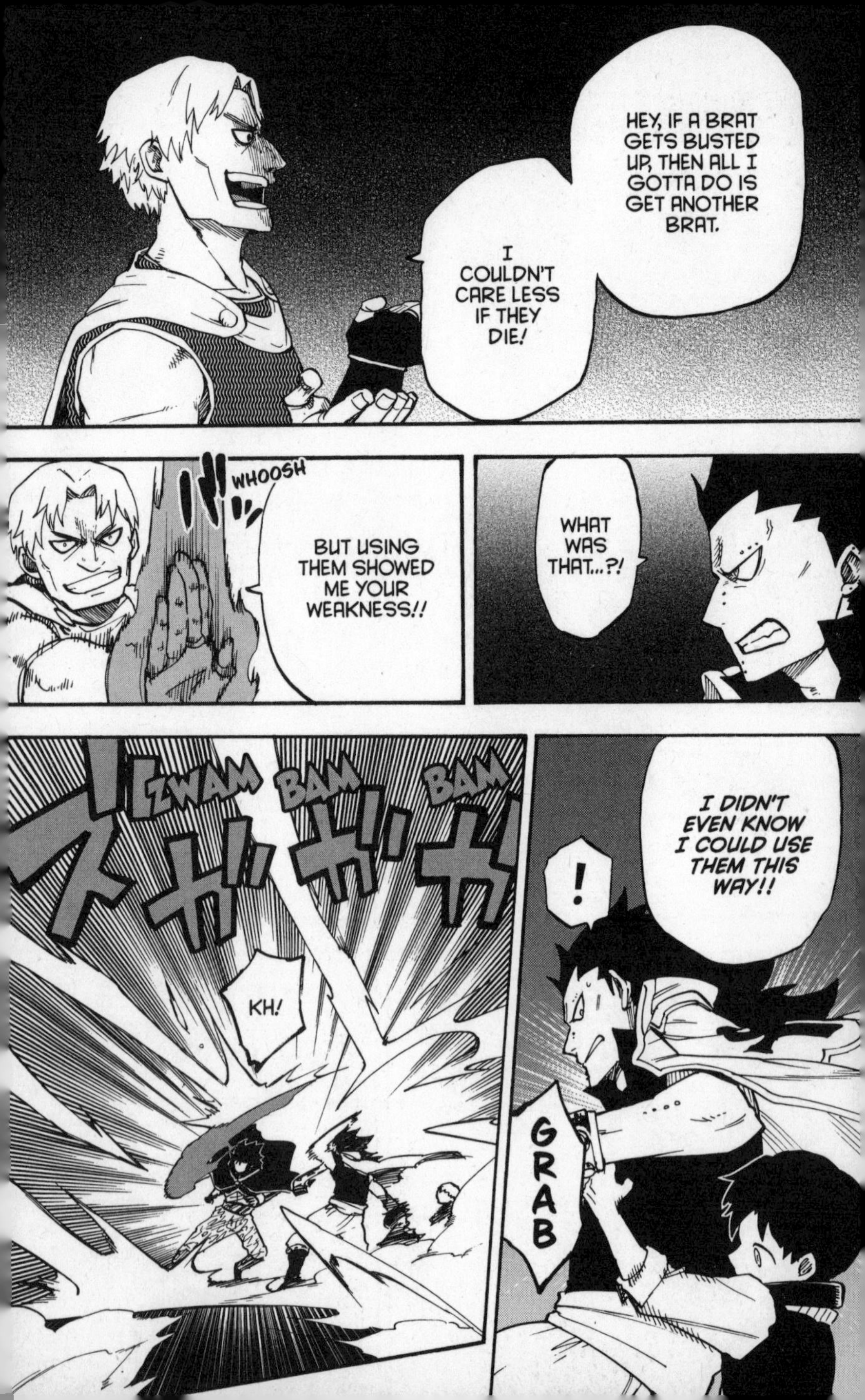
HEY, IF A BRAT GETS BUSTED UP, THEN ALL I GOTTA DO IS GET ANOTHER BRAT.
I COULDN'T CARE LESS IF THEY DIE!
WHAT WAS THAT...?!
WHOOSH
BUT USING THEM SHOWED ME YOUR WEAKNESS!!
I DIDN'T EVEN KNOW I COULD USE THEM THIS WAY!!
!
GRAB
ZWAM BAM BAM
KH!

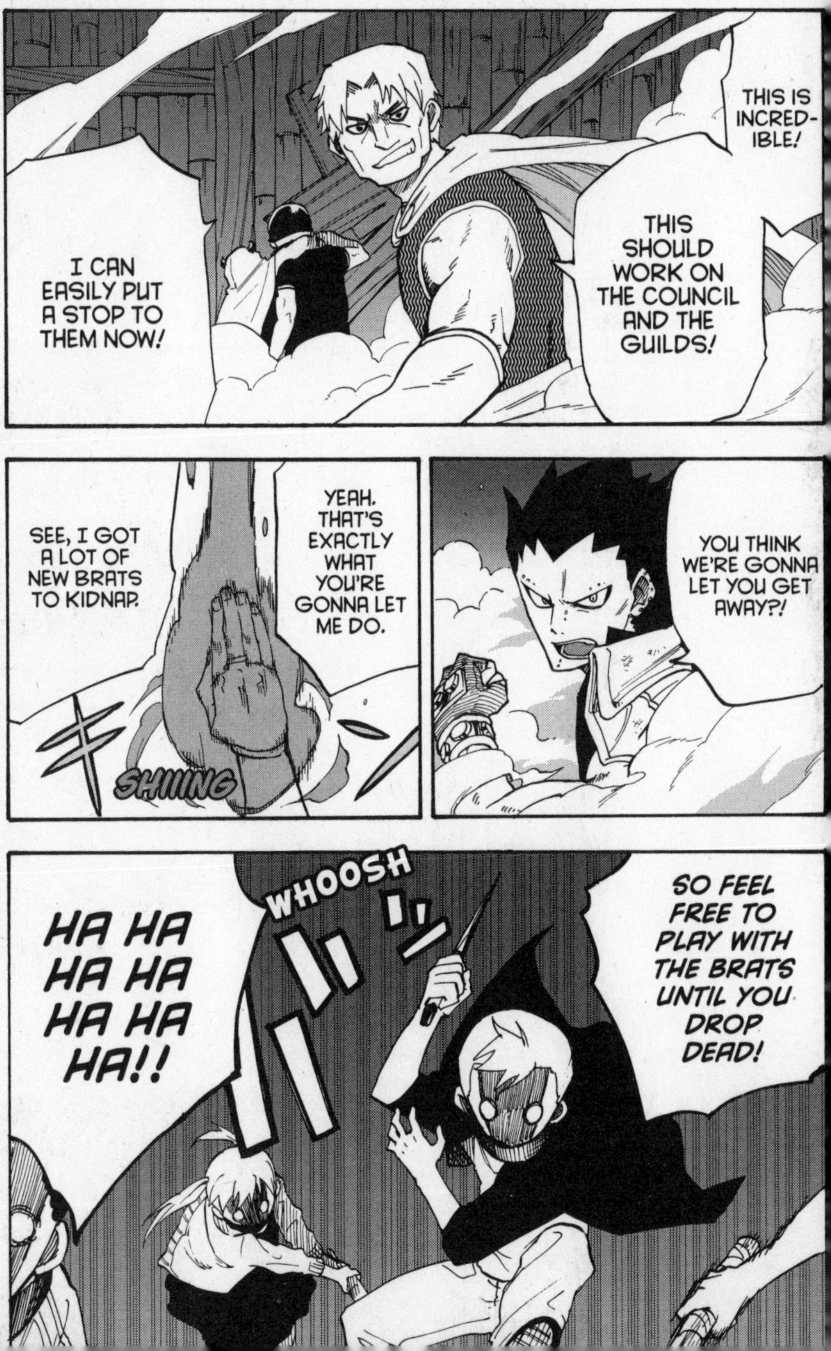
THIS IS INCREDIBLE!
THIS SHOULD WORK ON THE COUNCIL AND THE GUILDS!
I CAN EASILY PUT A STOP TO THEM NOW!
YOU THINK WE'RE GONNA LET YOU GET AWAY?!
YEAH. THAT'S EXACTLY WHAT YOU'RE GONNA LET ME DO.
SEE, I GOT A LOT OF NEW BRATS TO KIDNAP.
SHIIING
SO FEEL FREE TO PLAY WITH THE BRATS UNTIL YOU DROP DEAD!
WHOOSH
HA HA HA HA HA HA HA!!

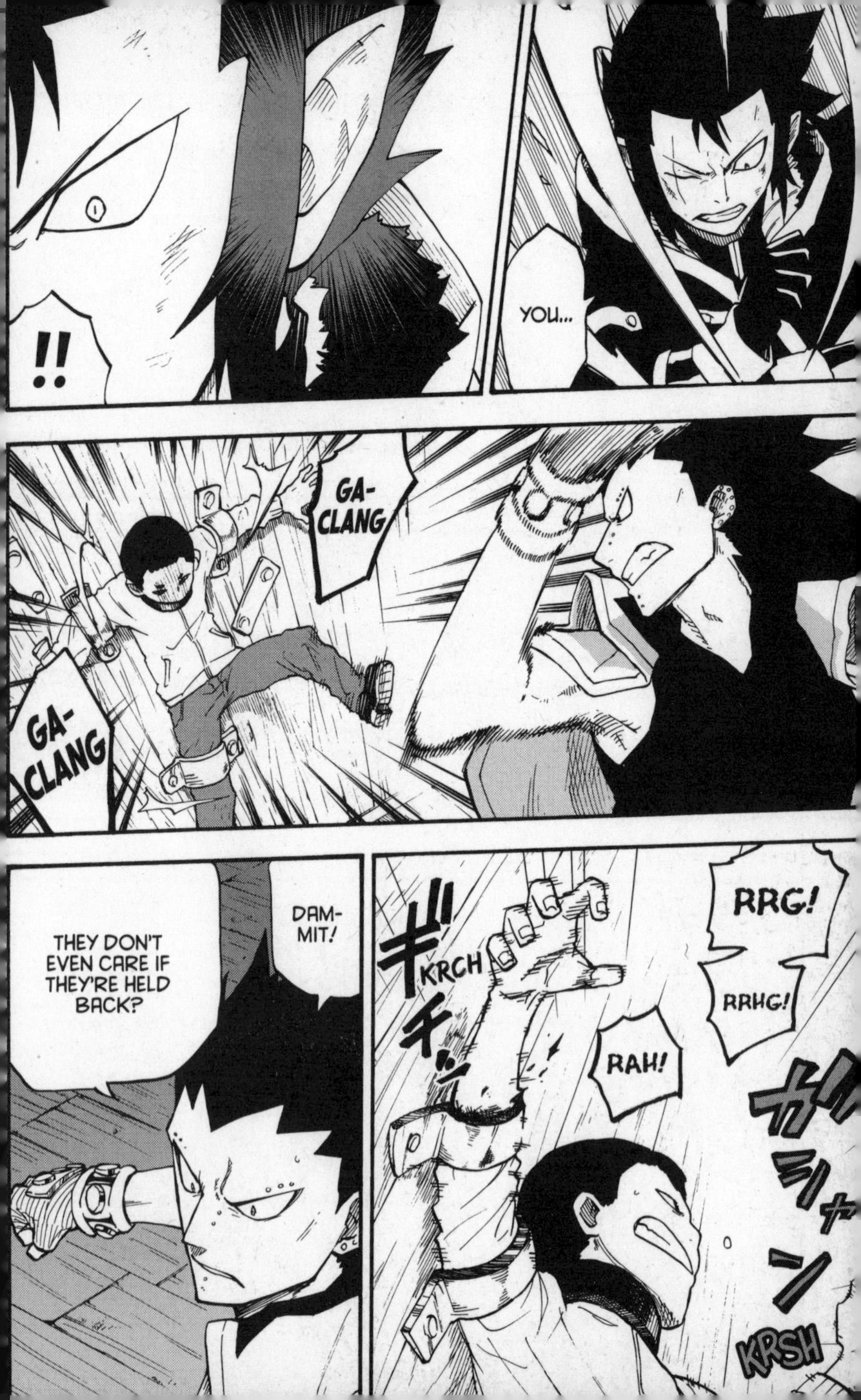
YOU...
!!
GA-CLANG
GA-CLANG
RRG!
RRHG!
RAH!
KRCH
KRSH
DAM-MIT!
THEY DON'T EVEN CARE IF THEY'RE HELD BACK?

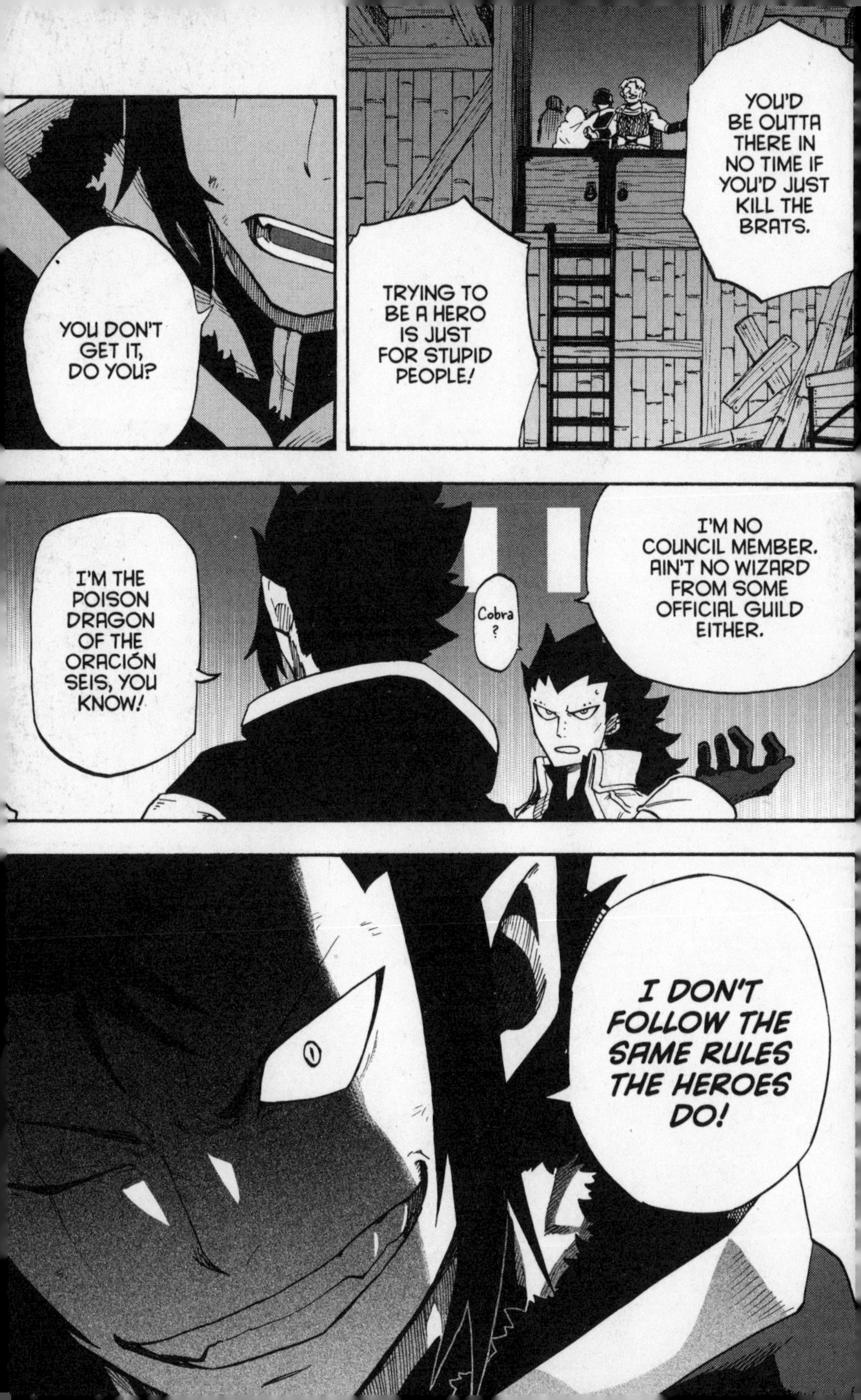
YOU'D BE OUTTA THERE IN NO TIME IF YOU'D JUST KILL THE BRATS.
TRYING TO BE A HERO IS JUST FOR STUPID PEOPLE!
YOU DON'T GET IT, DO YOU?
I'M NO COUNCIL MEMBER. AIN'T NO WIZARD FROM SOME OFFICIAL GUILD EITHER.
Cobra?
I'M THE POISON DRAGON OF THE ORACIÓN SEIS, YOU KNOW!
I DON'T FOLLOW THE SAME RULES THE HEROES DO!

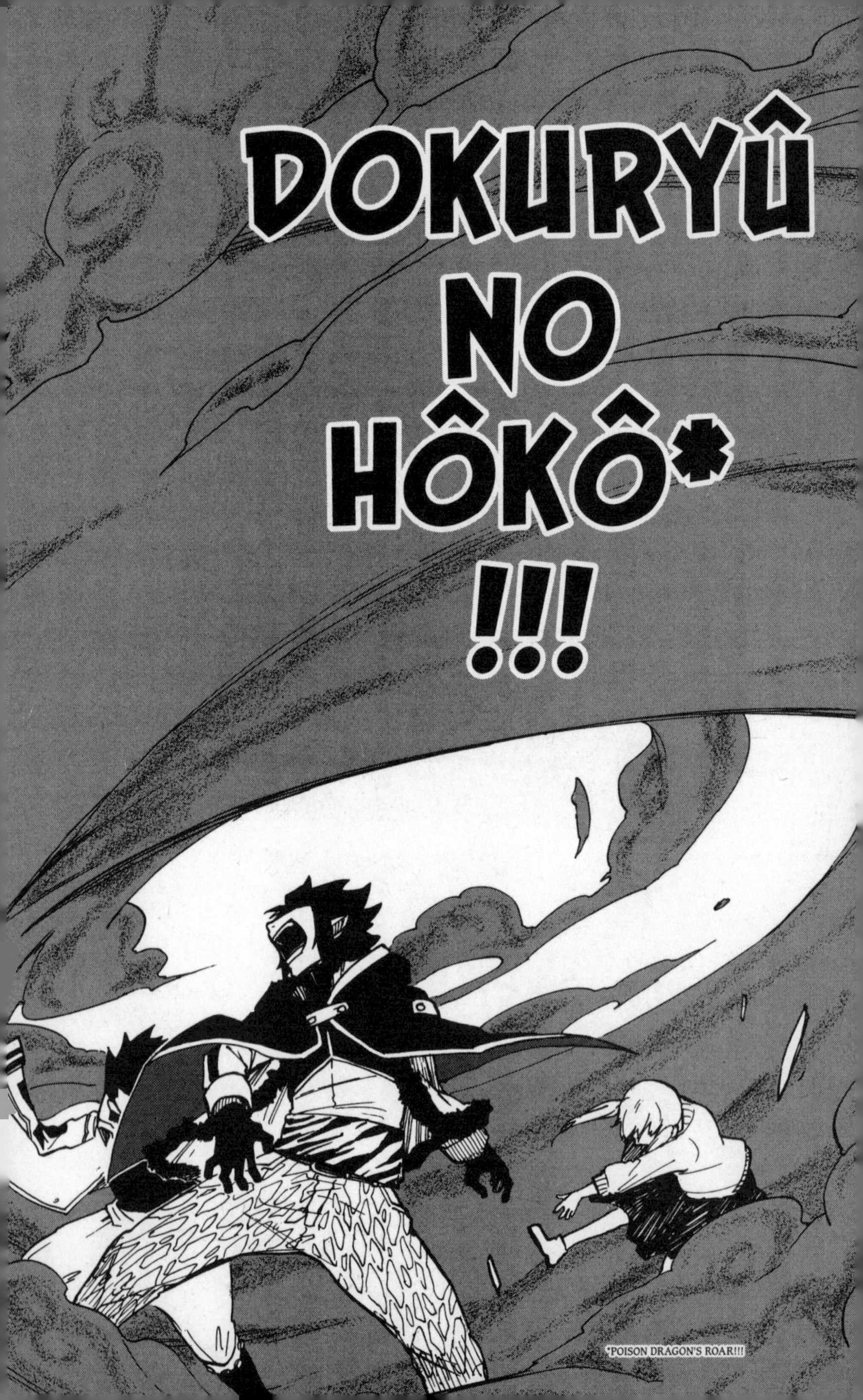
DOKURYÛ NO HÔKÔ* !!!
*POISON DRAGON'S ROAR!!!

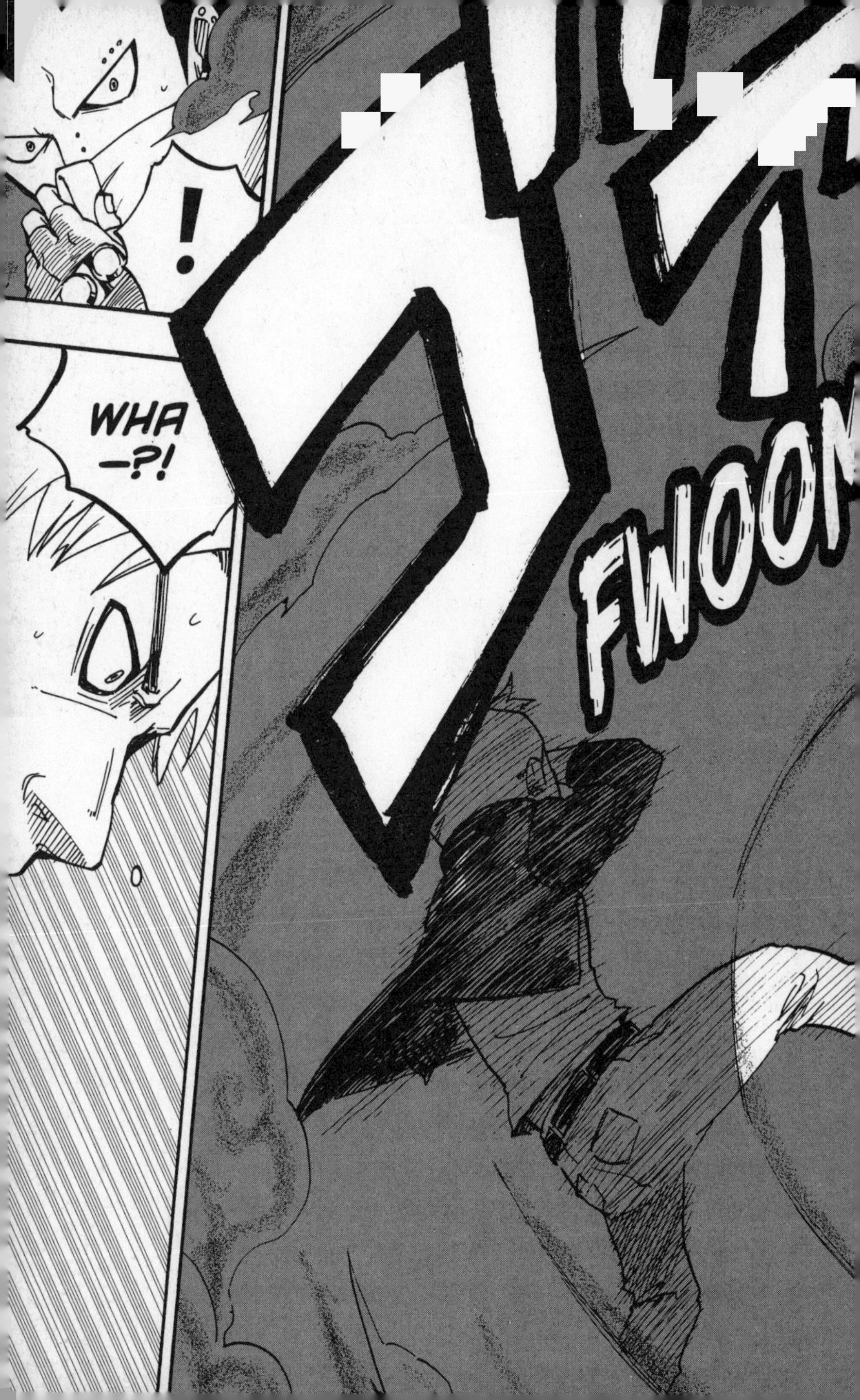
FWOOM
!
WHA—?!

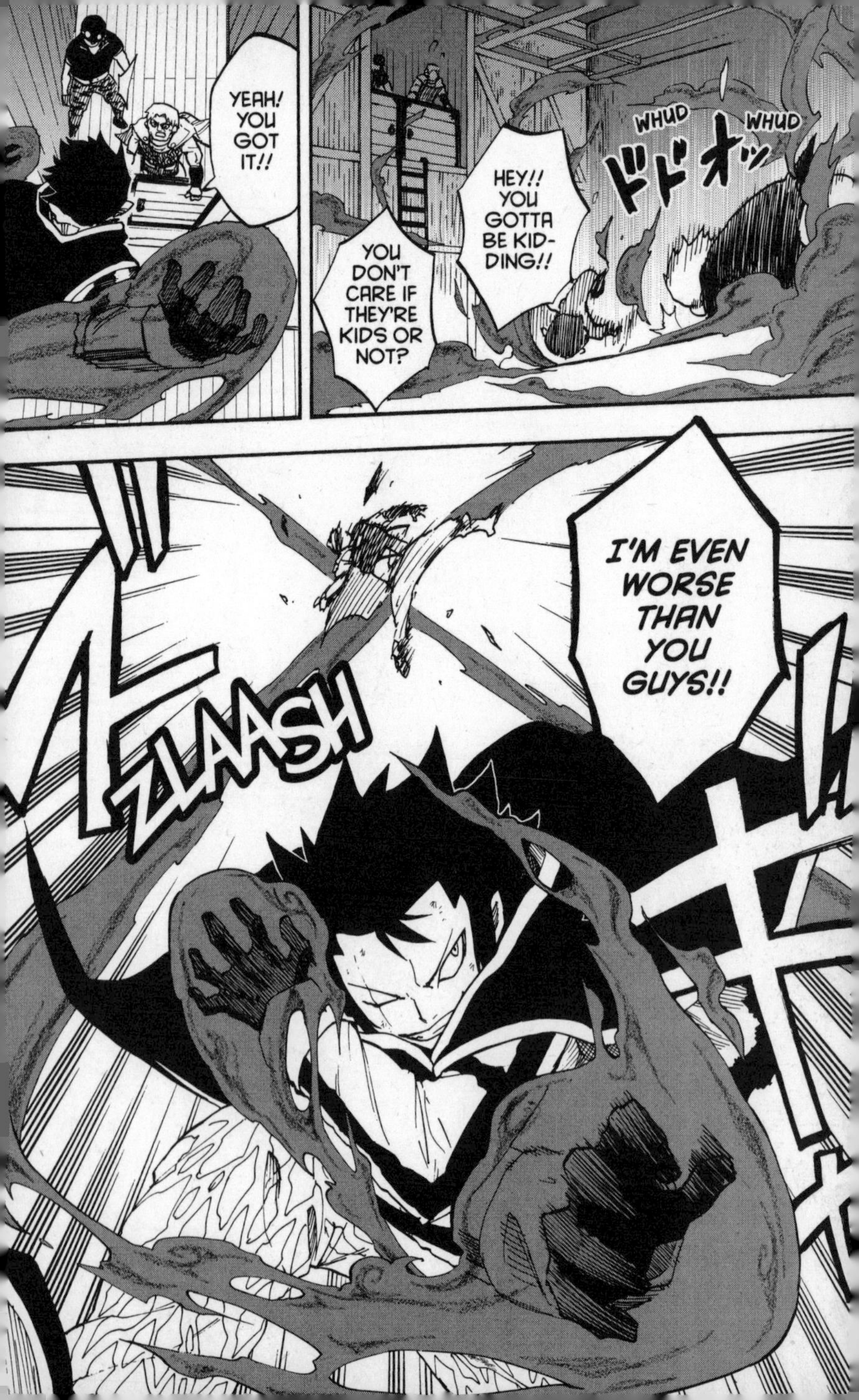
WHUD WHUD
ドドオッ
HEY!! YOU GOTTA BE KID-DING!!
YOU DON'T CARE IF THEY'RE KIDS OR NOT?
YEAH! YOU GOT IT!!
I'M EVEN WORSE THAN YOU GUYS!!
ZLAASH

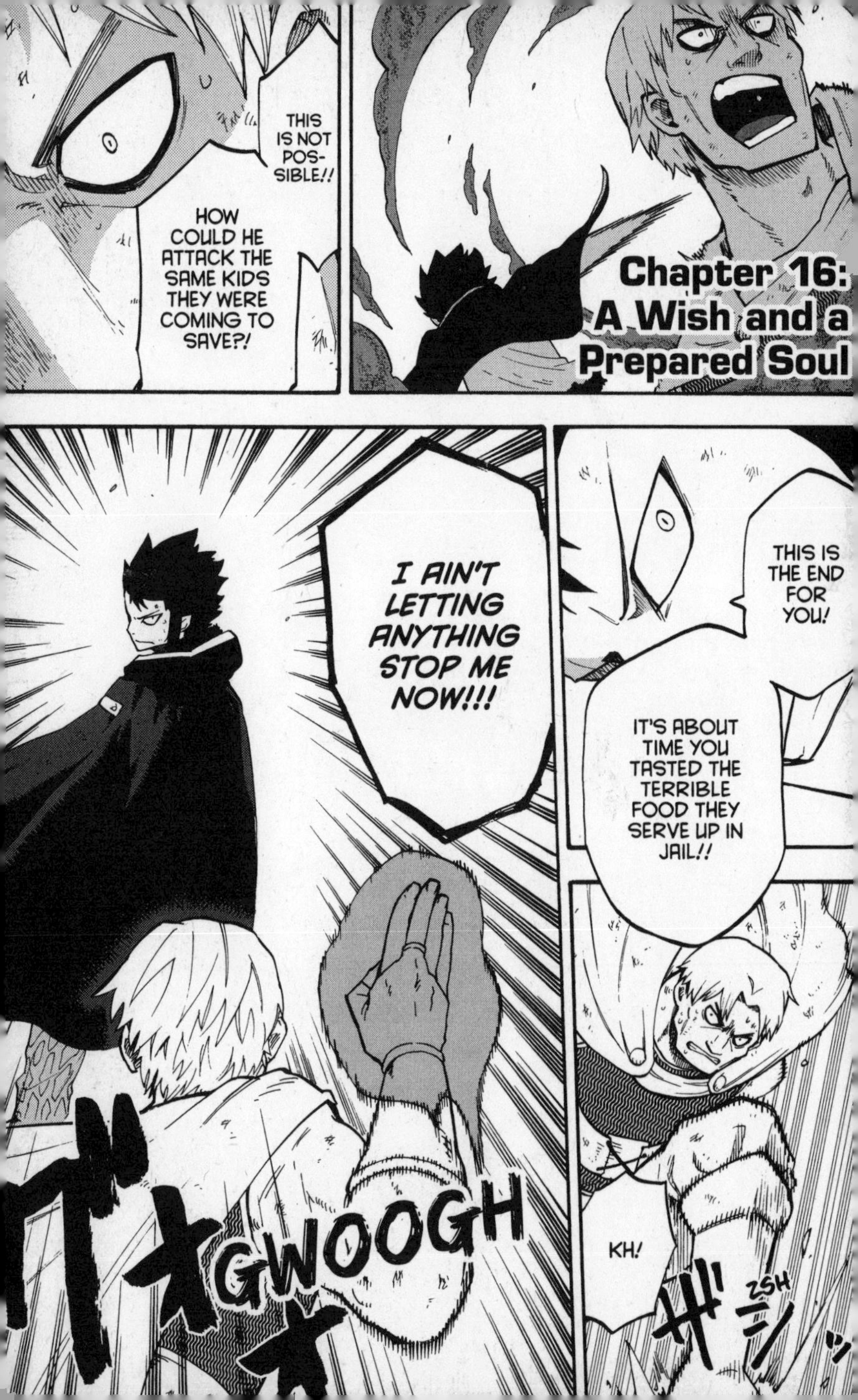
Chapter 16: A Wish and a Prepared Soul
THIS IS NOT POSSIBLE!!
HOW COULD HE ATTACK THE SAME KIDS THEY WERE COMING TO SAVE?!
THIS IS THE END FOR YOU!
IT'S ABOUT TIME YOU TASTED THE TERRIBLE FOOD THEY SERVE UP IN JAIL!!
KH!
ZSH
I AIN'T LETTING ANYTHING STOP ME NOW!!!
GWOOGH

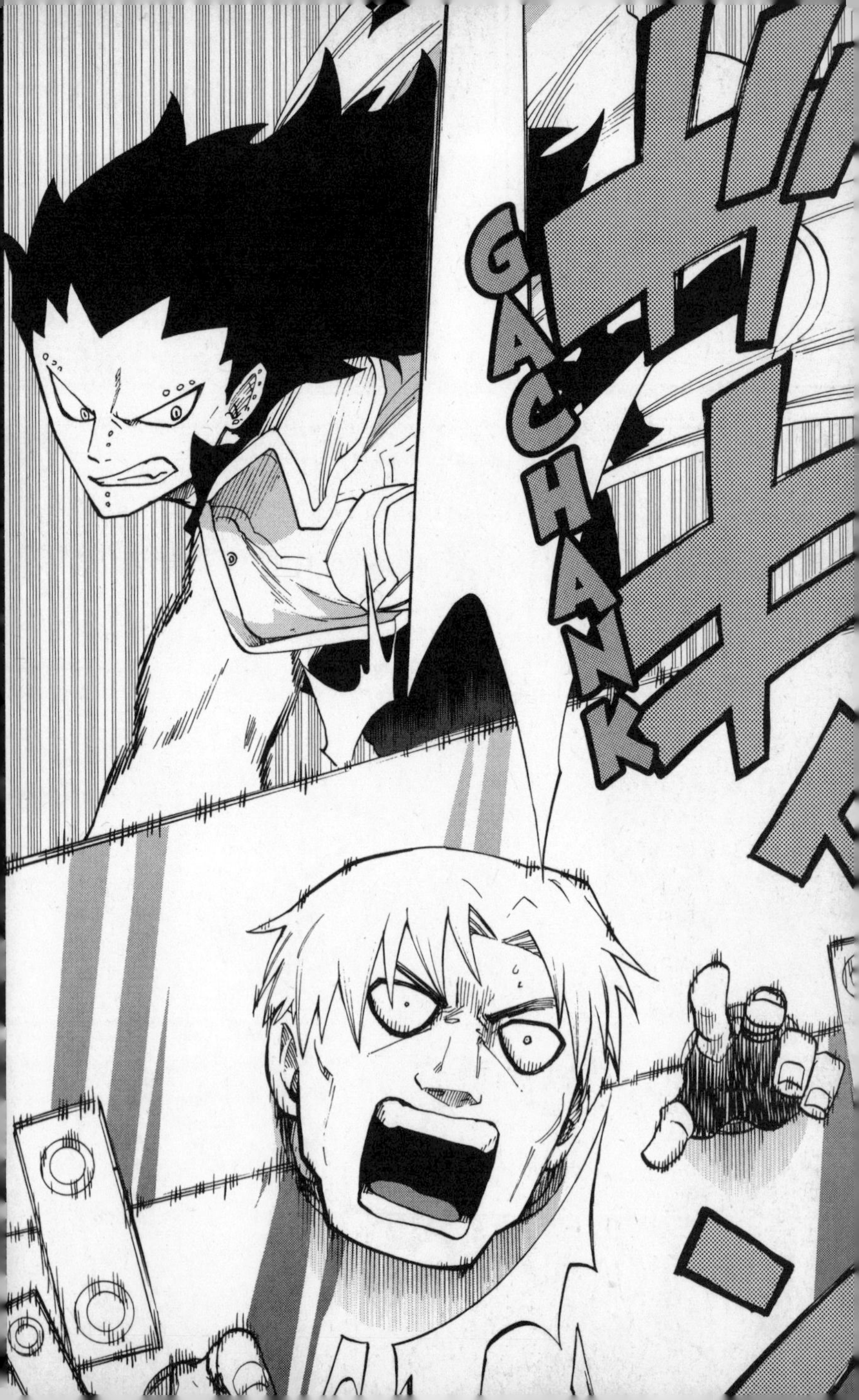
GACHANK

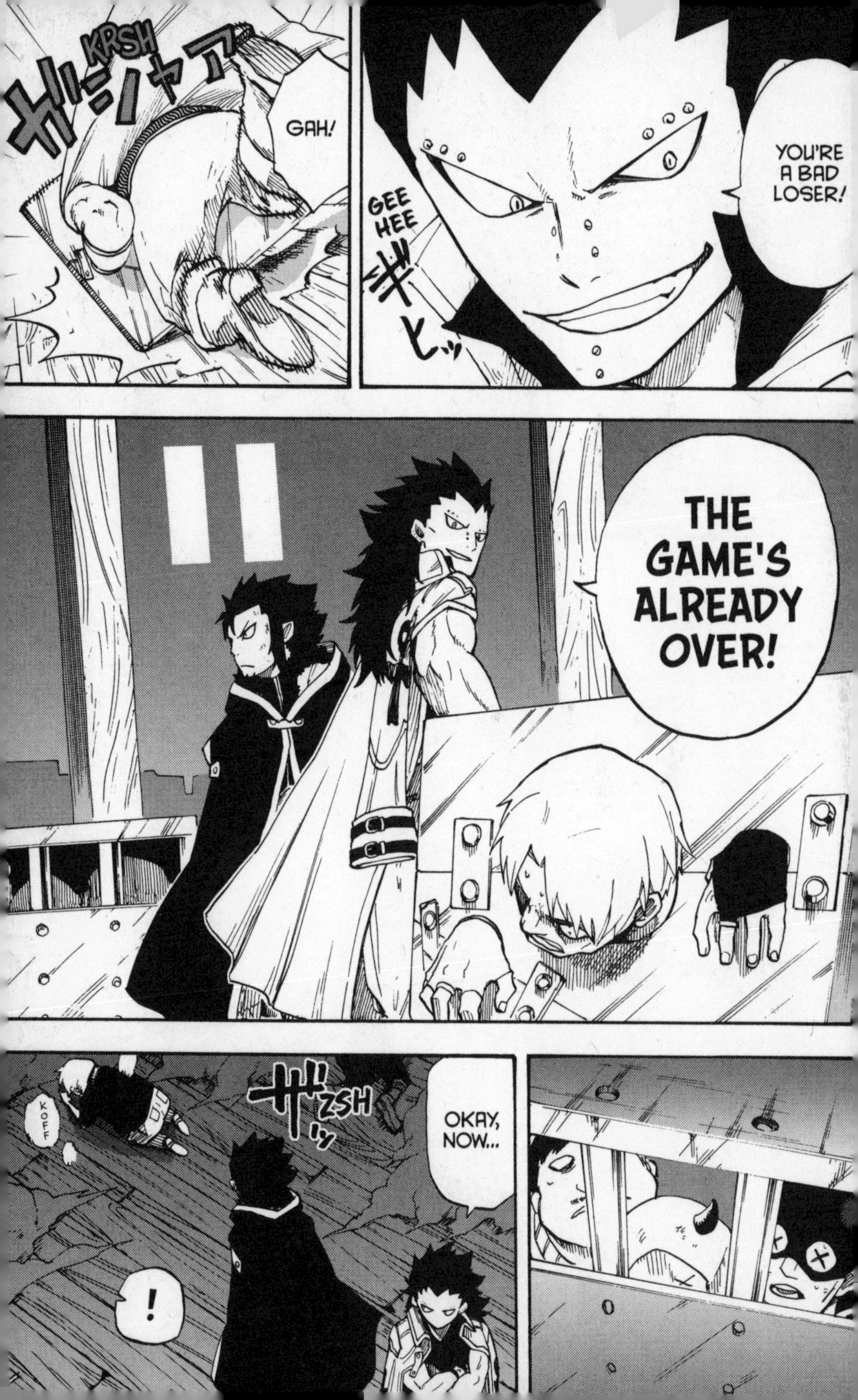
YOU'RE A BAD LOSER!
GEE HEE
KRSH
GAH!
THE GAME'S ALREADY OVER!
OKAY, NOW...
ZSH
KOFF
!

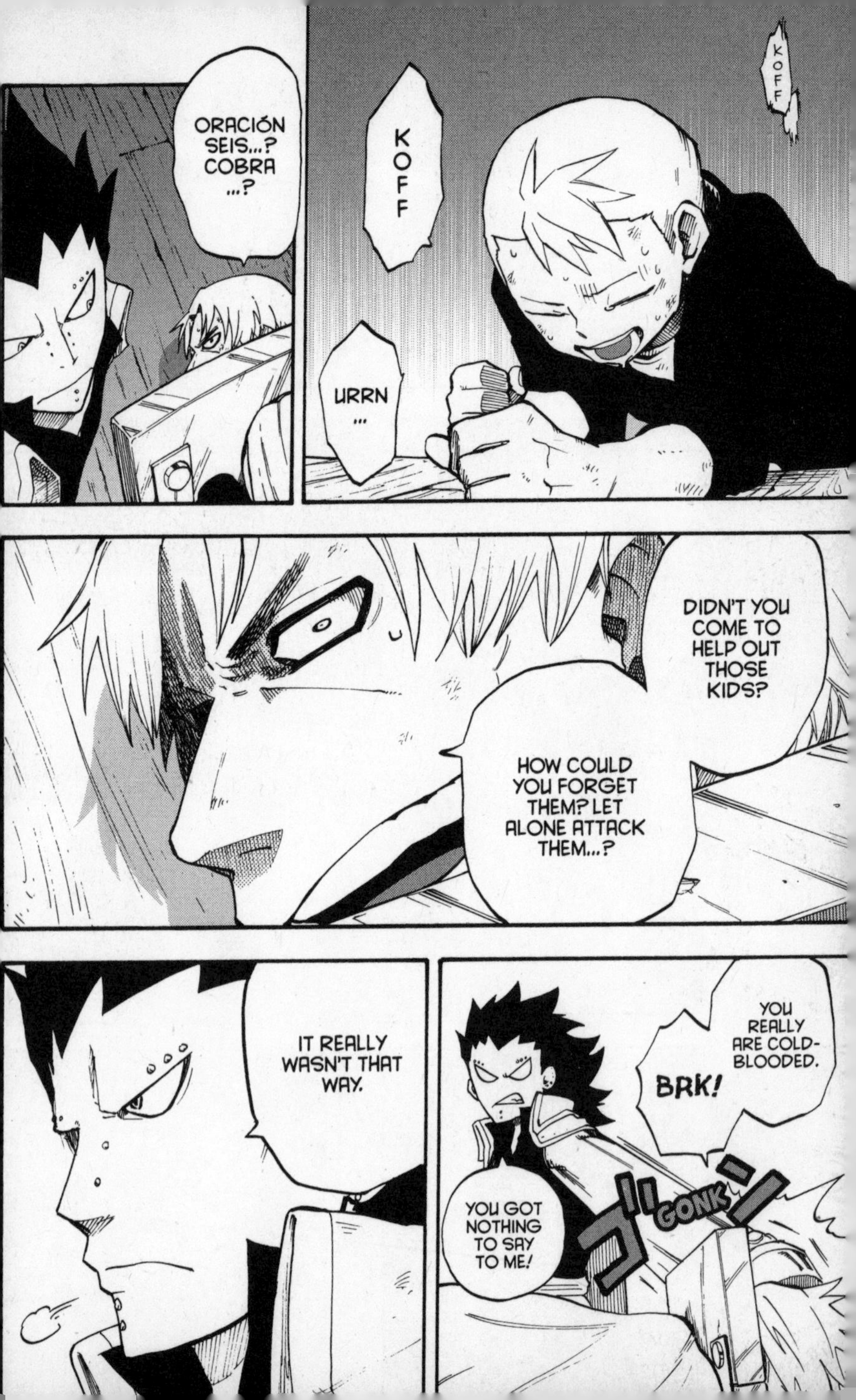
KOFF
KOFF
URRN ...
ORACIÓN SEIS...? COBRA ...?
DIDN'T YOU COME TO HELP OUT THOSE KIDS?
HOW COULD YOU FORGET THEM? LET ALONE ATTACK THEM...?
YOU REALLY ARE COLD-BLOODED.
BRK!
GONK
YOU GOT NOTHING TO SAY TO ME!
IT REALLY WASN'T THAT WAY.

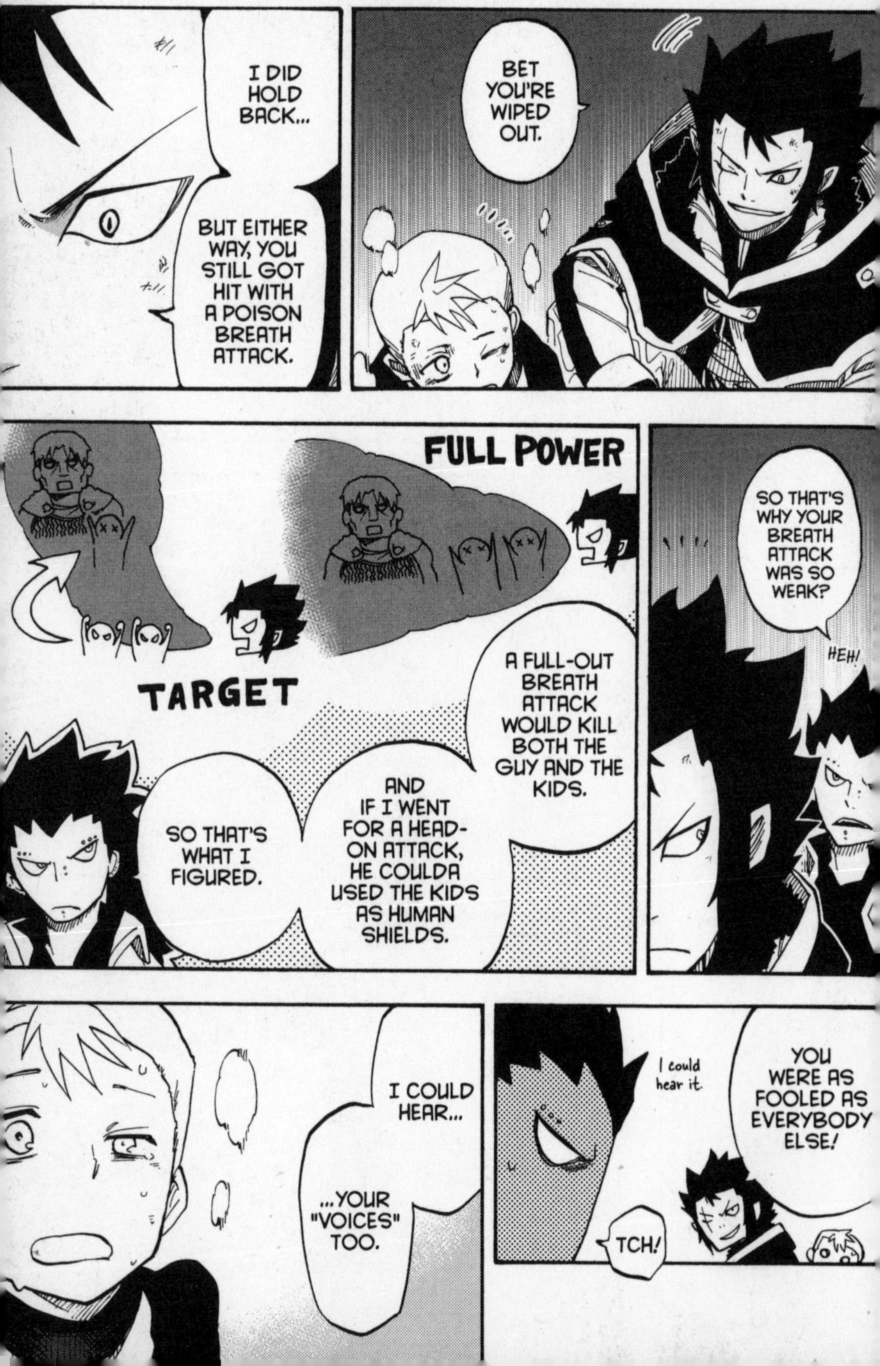
BET YOU'RE WIPED OUT.
I DID HOLD BACK...
BUT EITHER WAY, YOU STILL GOT HIT WITH A POISON BREATH ATTACK.
SO THAT'S WHY YOUR BREATH ATTACK WAS SO WEAK?
HEH!
FULL POWER
TARGET
A FULL-OUT BREATH ATTACK WOULD KILL BOTH THE GUY AND THE KIDS.
AND IF I WENT FOR A HEAD-ON ATTACK, HE COULDA USED THE KIDS AS HUMAN SHIELDS.
SO THAT'S WHAT I FIGURED.
YOU WERE AS FOOLED AS EVERYBODY ELSE!
I could hear it.
TCH!
I COULD HEAR...
...YOUR "VOICES" TOO.

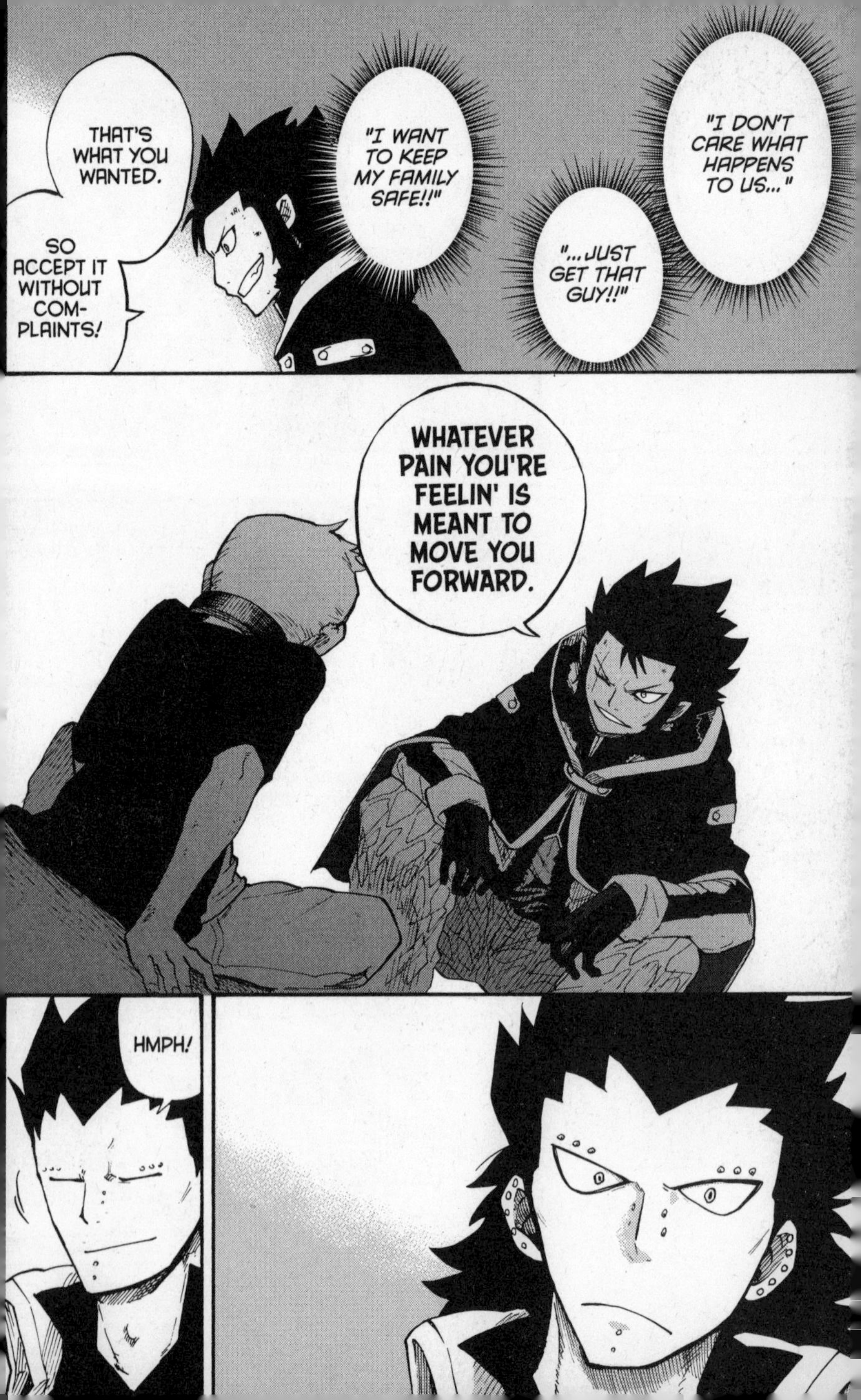
"I DON'T CARE WHAT HAPPENS TO US..."
"...JUST GET THAT GUY!!"
"I WANT TO KEEP MY FAMILY SAFE!!"
THAT'S WHAT YOU WANTED.
SO ACCEPT IT WITHOUT COM-PLAINTS!
WHATEVER PAIN YOU'RE FEELIN' IS MEANT TO MOVE YOU FORWARD.
HMPH!

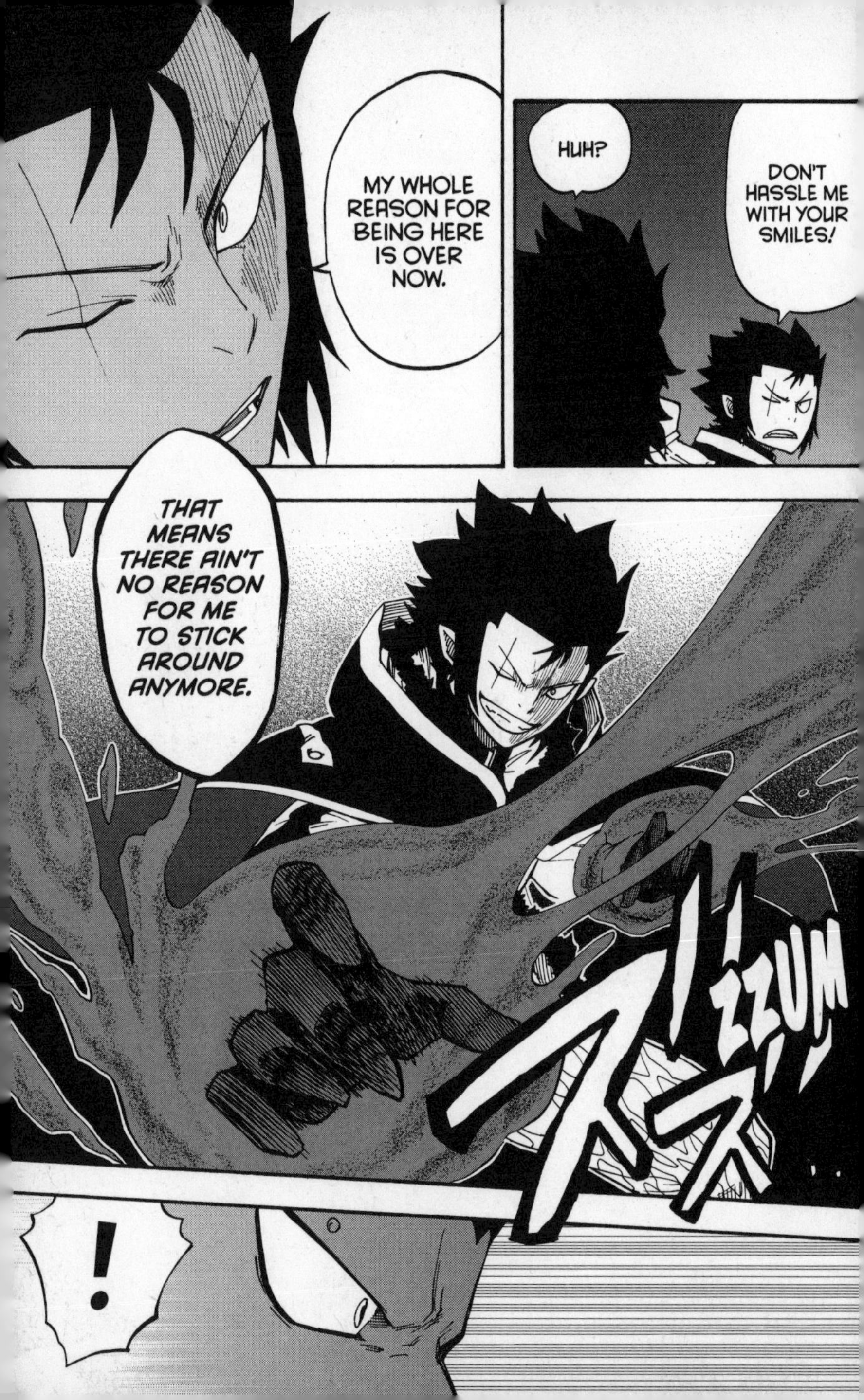

DON'T HASSLE ME WITH YOUR SMILES!
HUH?
MY WHOLE REASON FOR BEING HERE IS OVER NOW.
THAT MEANS THERE AIN'T NO REASON FOR ME TO STICK AROUND ANYMORE.
ZZUM
!

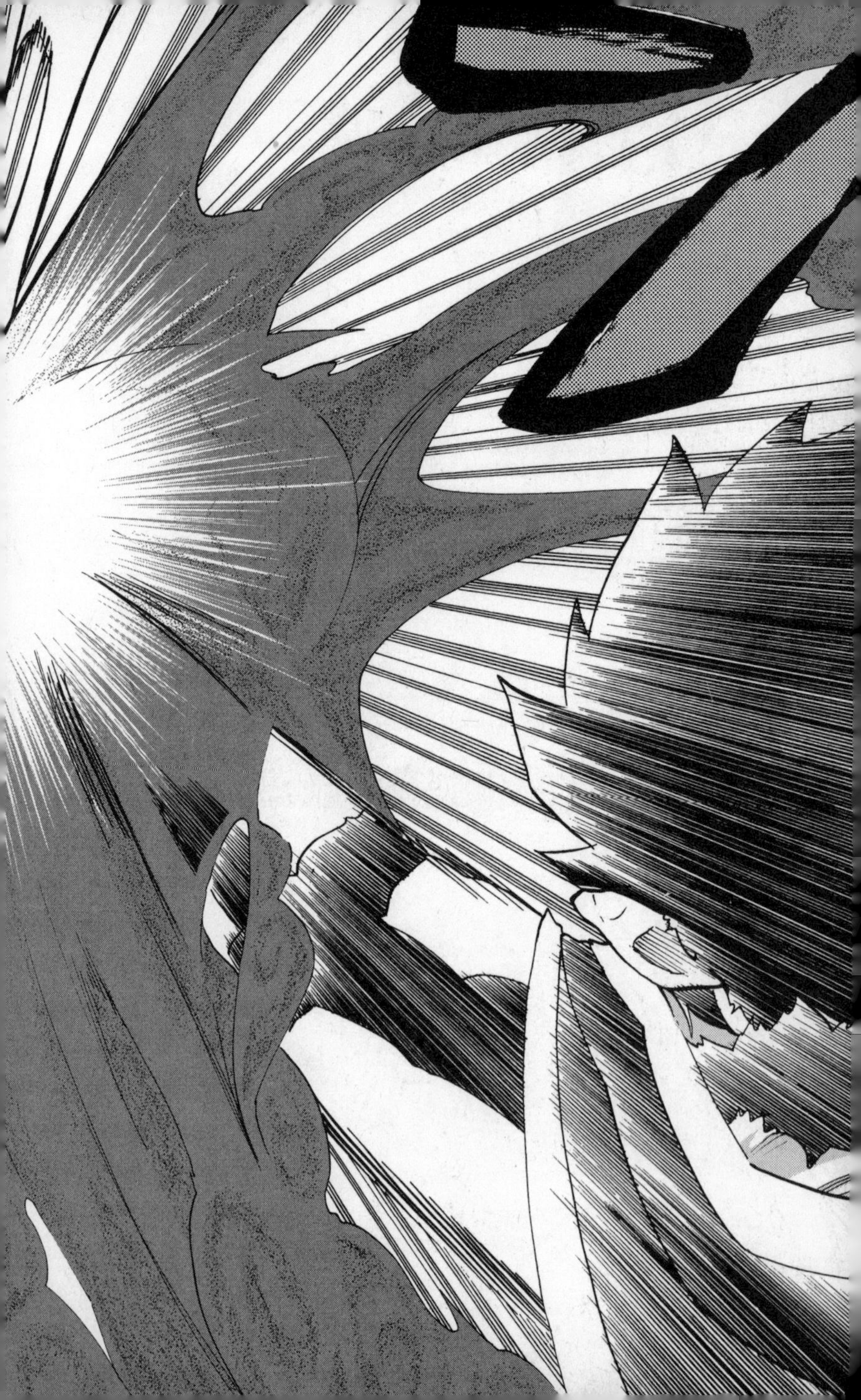

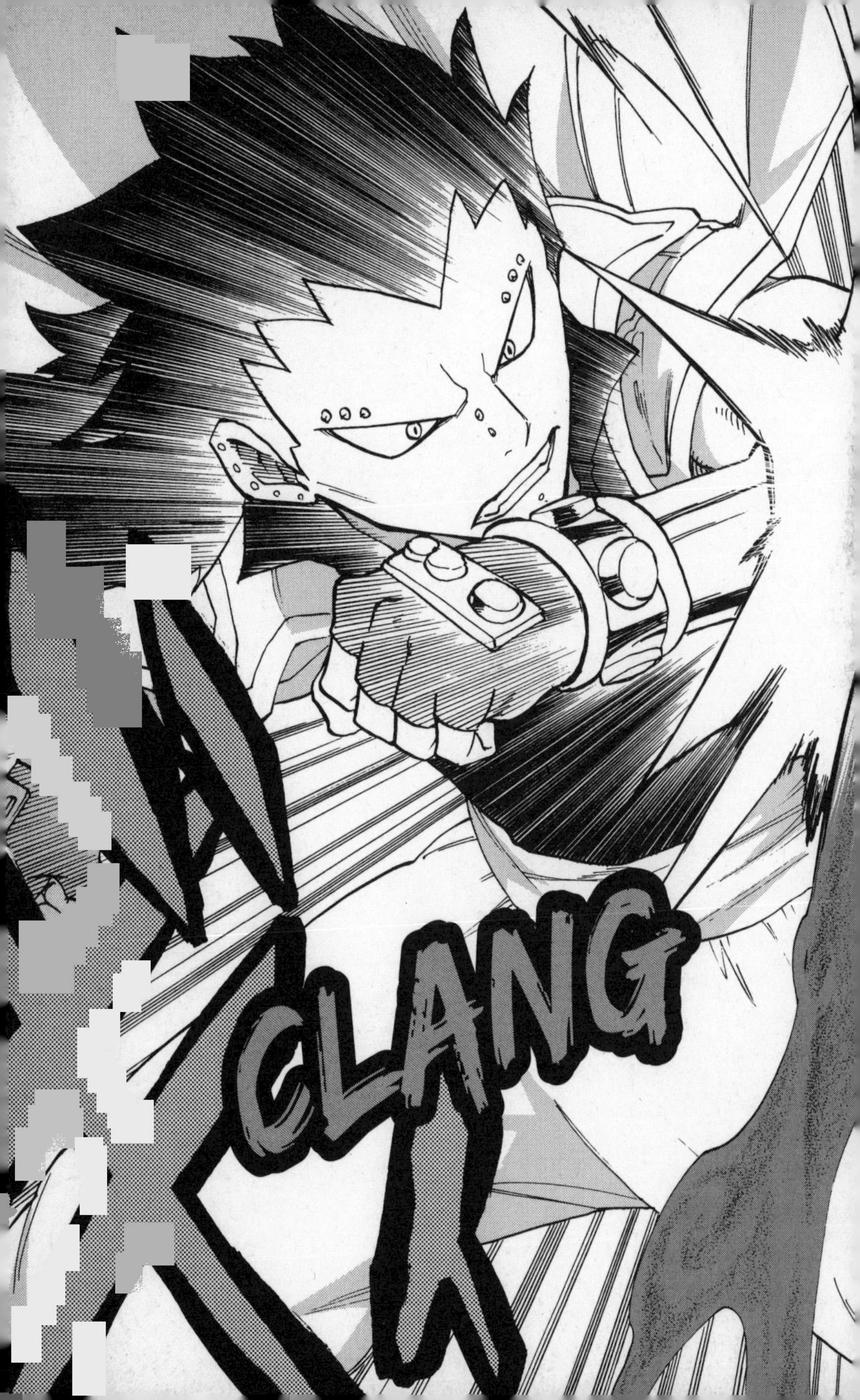
CLANG

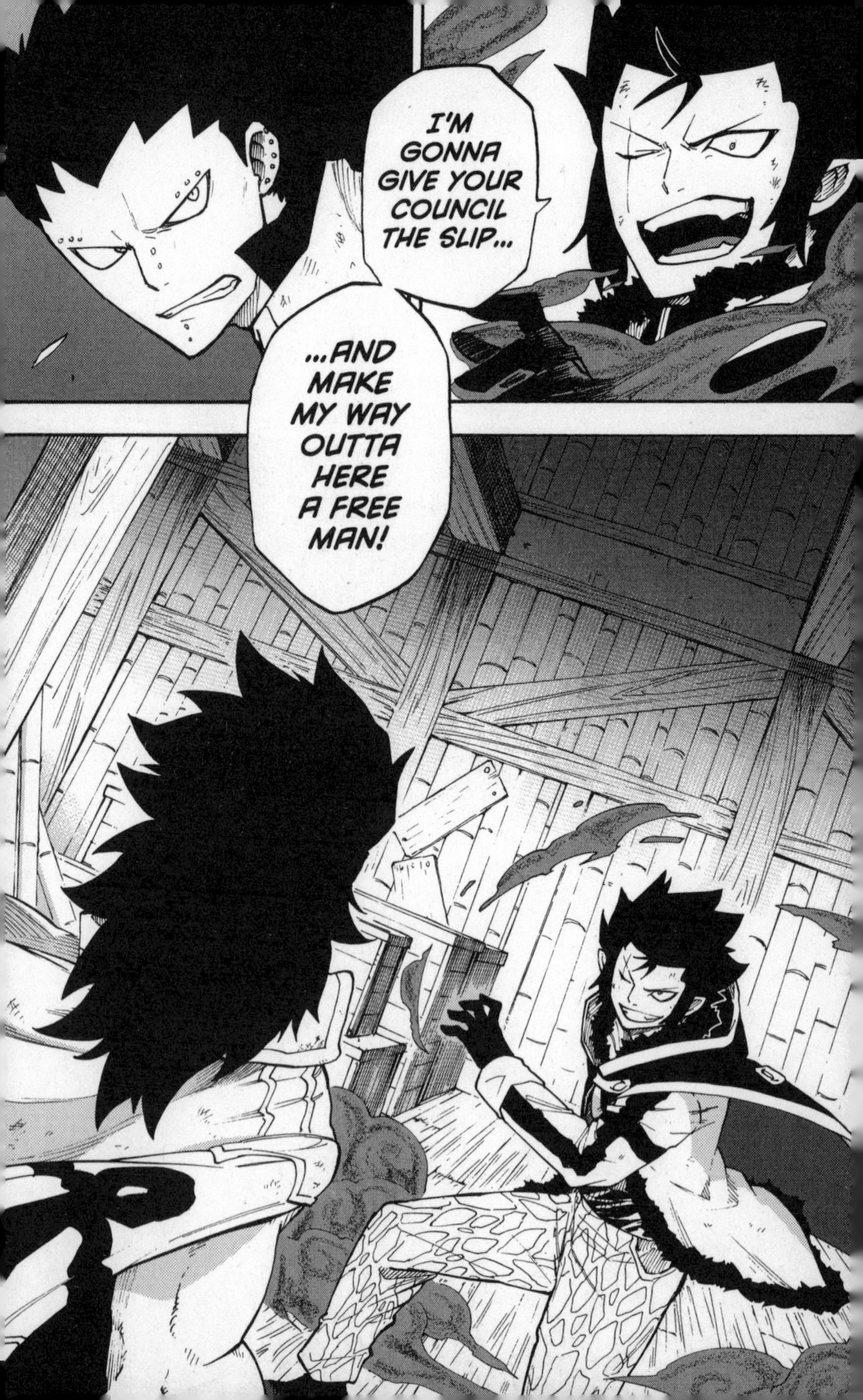
I'M GONNA GIVE YOUR COUNCIL THE SLIP...
...AND MAKE MY WAY OUTTA HERE A FREE MAN!

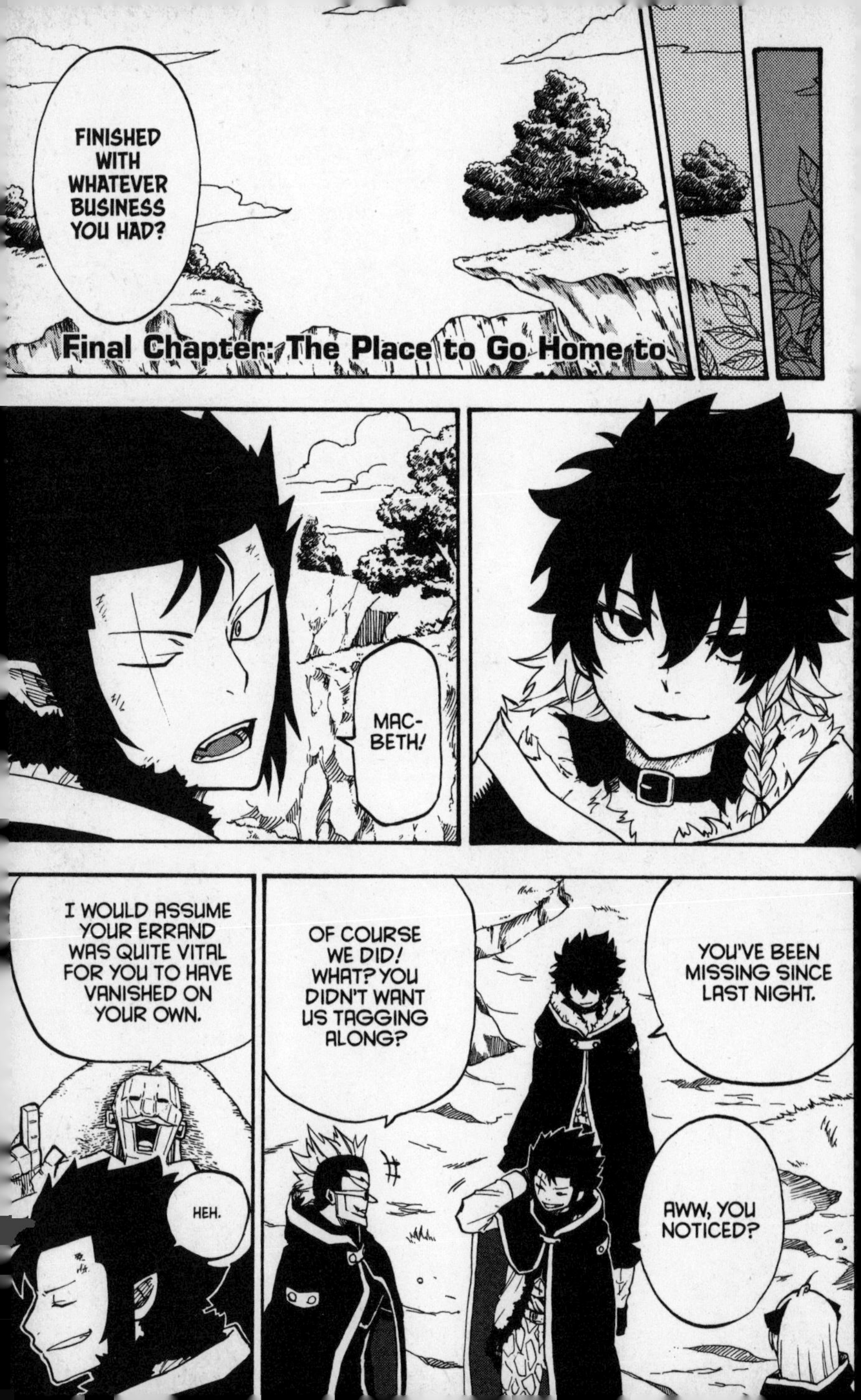
FINISHED WITH WHATEVER BUSINESS YOU HAD?
Final Chapter: The Place to Go Home to
MAC-BETH!
YOU'VE BEEN MISSING SINCE LAST NIGHT.
AWW, YOU NOTICED?
OF COURSE WE DID! WHAT? YOU DIDN'T WANT US TAGGING ALONG?
I WOULD ASSUME YOUR ERRAND WAS QUITE VITAL FOR YOU TO HAVE VANISHED ON YOUR OWN.
HEH.

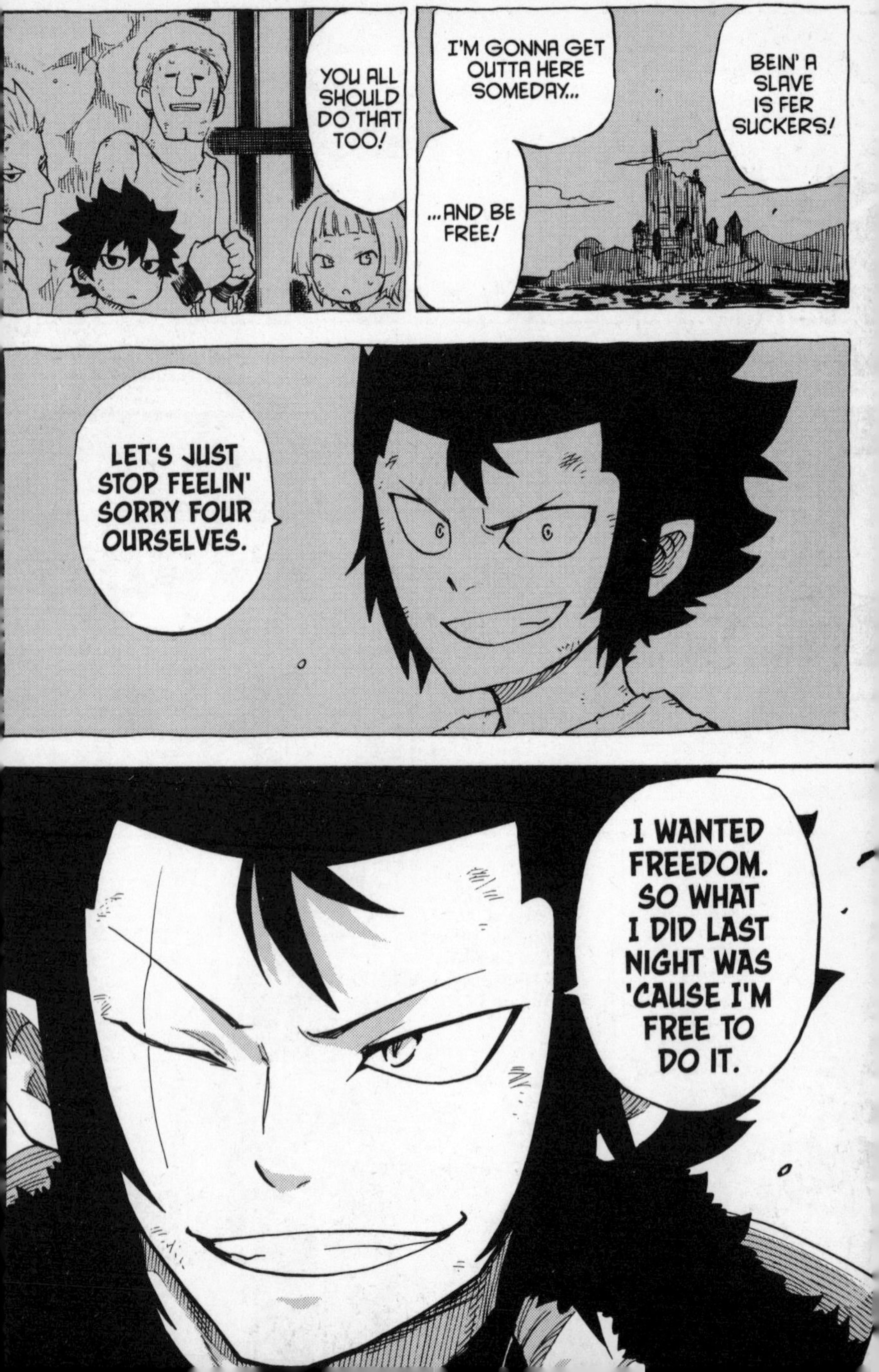
BEIN' A SLAVE IS FER SUCKERS!
I'M GONNA GET OUTTA HERE SOMEDAY...
...AND BE FREE!
YOU ALL SHOULD DO THAT TOO!
LET'S JUST STOP FEELIN' SORRY FOUR OURSELVES.
I WANTED FREEDOM. SO WHAT I DID LAST NIGHT WAS 'CAUSE I'M FREE TO DO IT.

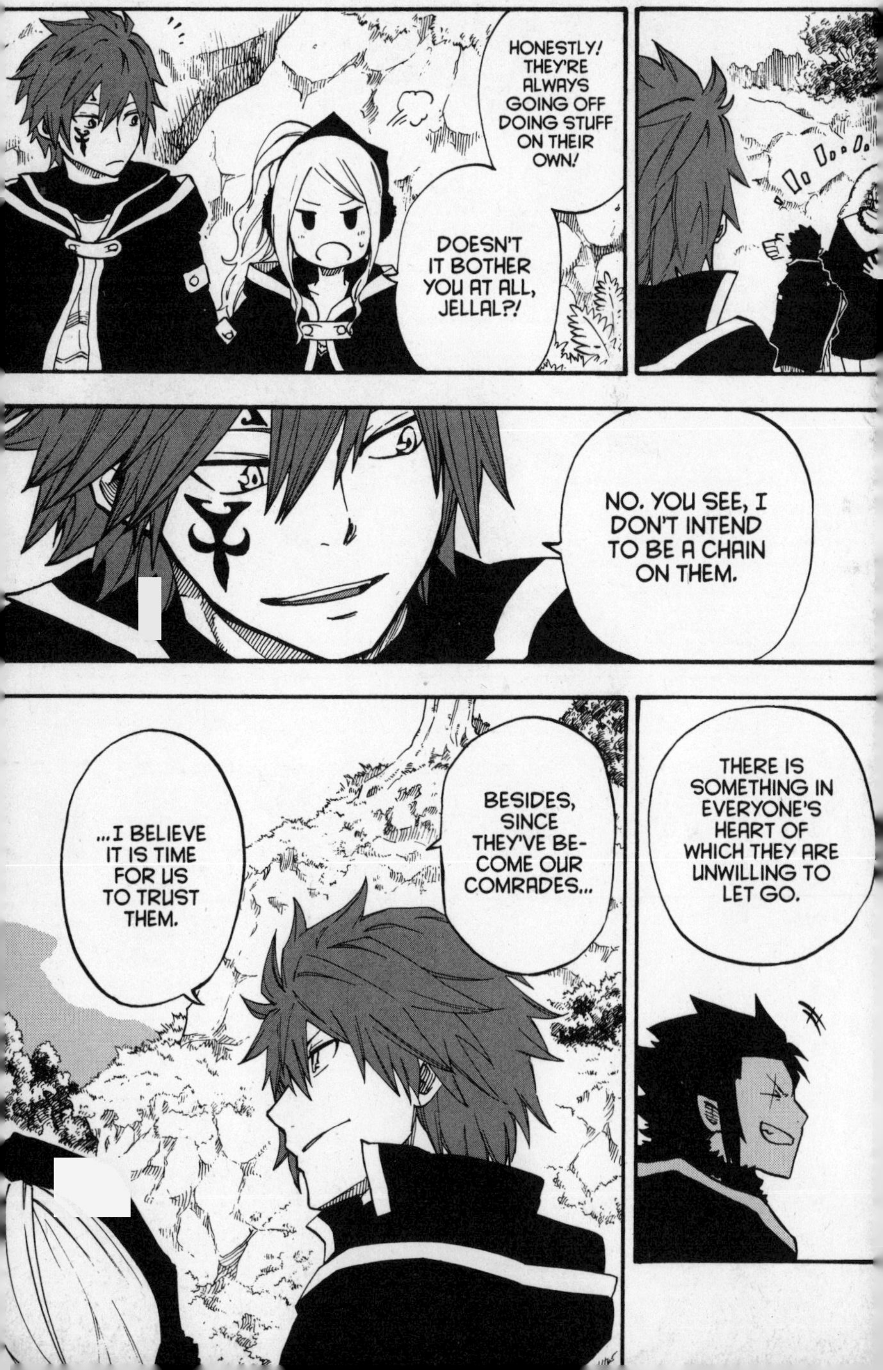
HONESTLY! THEY'RE ALWAYS GOING OFF DOING STUFF ON THEIR OWN!
DOESN'T IT BOTHER YOU AT ALL, JELLAL?!
NO. YOU SEE, I DON'T INTEND TO BE A CHAIN ON THEM.
THERE IS SOMETHING IN EVERYONE'S HEART OF WHICH THEY ARE UNWILLING TO LET GO.
BESIDES, SINCE THEY'VE BE-COME OUR COMRADES...
...I BELIEVE IT IS TIME FOR US TO TRUST THEM.

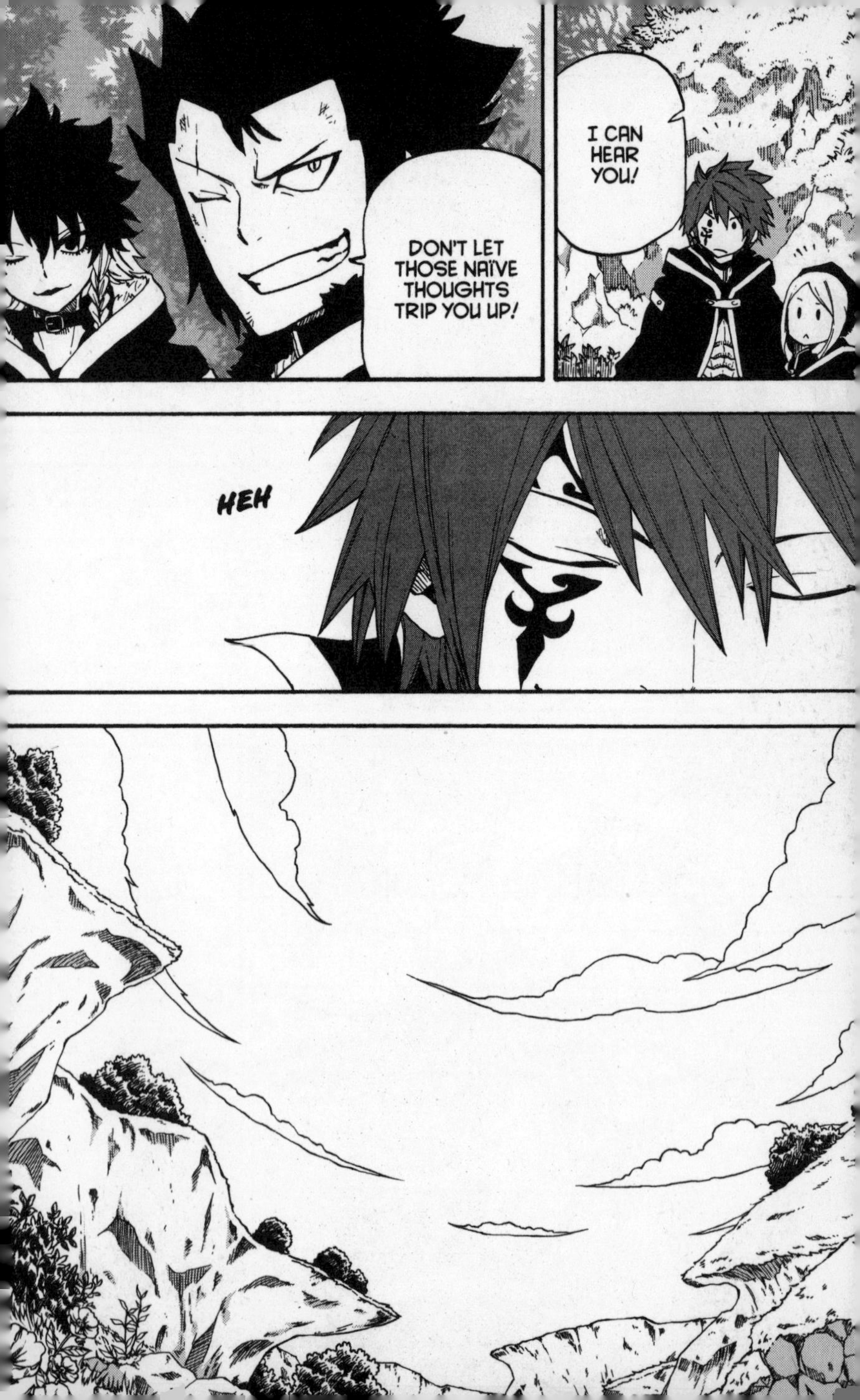
I CAN HEAR YOU!
DON'T LET THOSE NAÏVE THOUGHTS TRIP YOU UP!
HEH

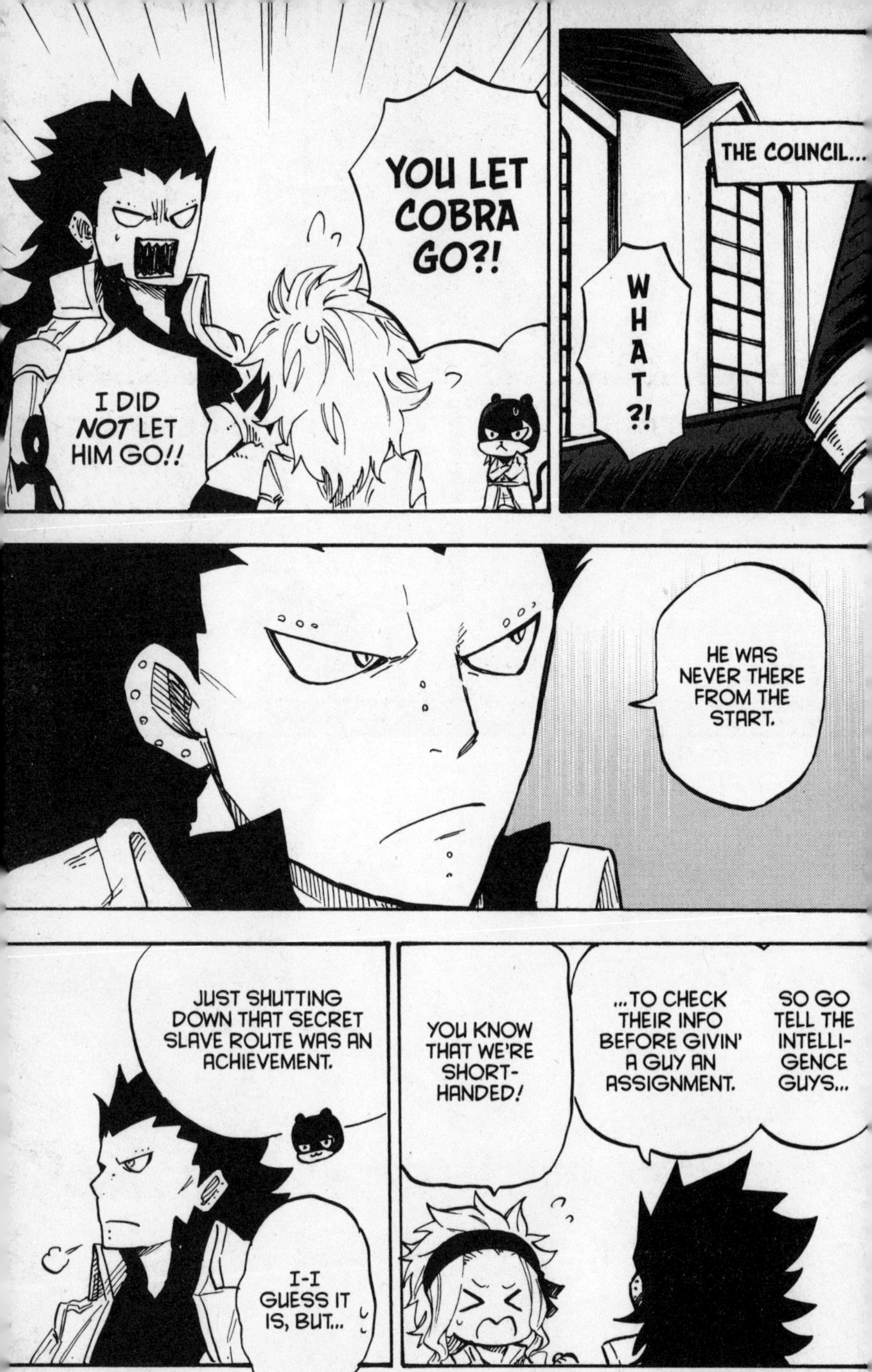
THE COUNCIL...
WHAT?!
YOU LET COBRA GO?!
I DID *NOT* LET HIM GO!!
HE WAS NEVER THERE FROM THE START.
SO GO TELL THE INTELLI-GENCE GUYS...
...TO CHECK THEIR INFO BEFORE GIVIN' A GUY AN ASSIGNMENT.
YOU KNOW THAT WE'RE SHORT-HANDED!
JUST SHUTTING DOWN THAT SECRET SLAVE ROUTE WAS AN ACHIEVEMENT.
I-I GUESS IT IS, BUT...

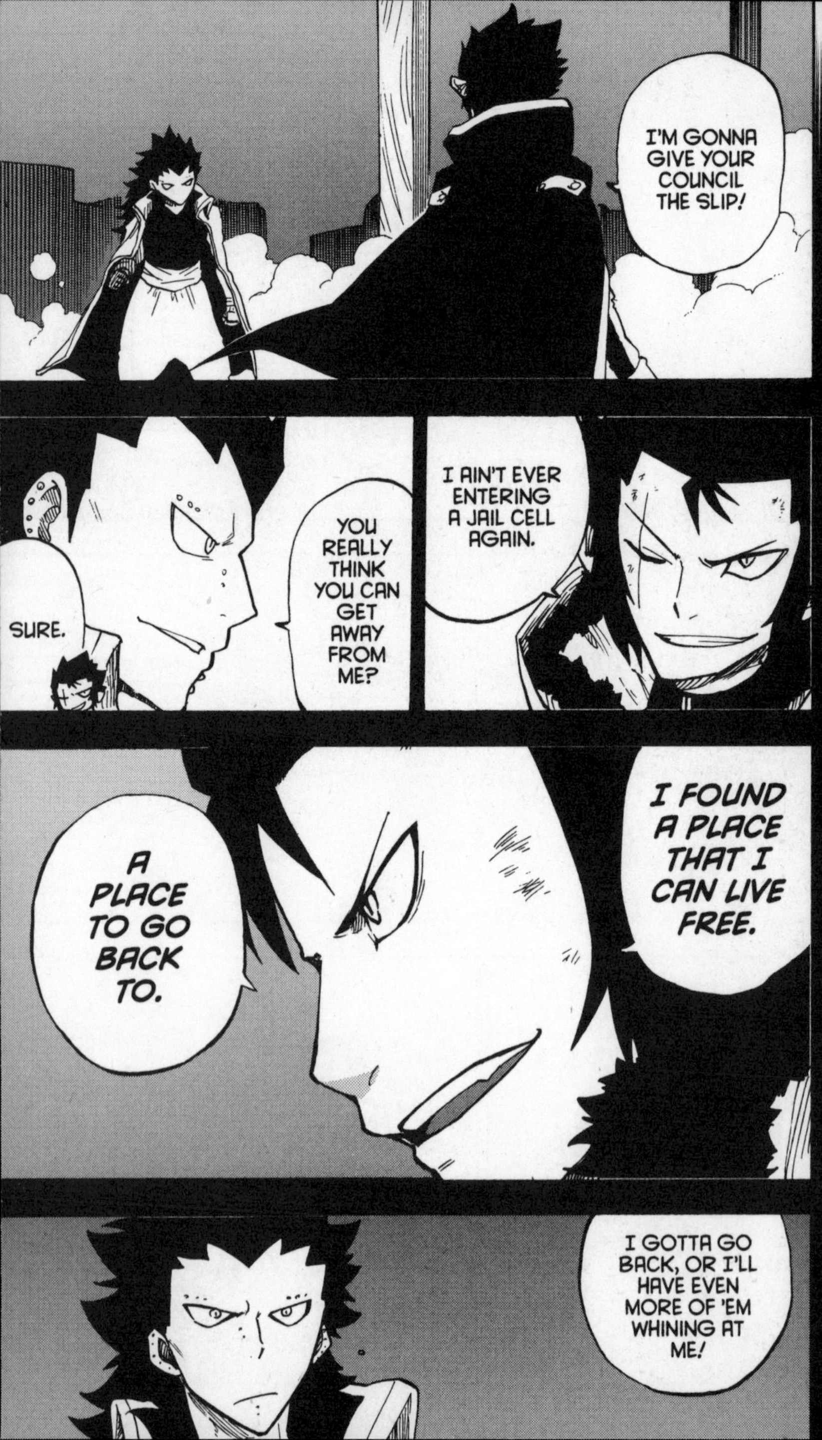
I'M GONNA GIVE YOUR COUNCIL THE SLIP!
I AIN'T EVER ENTERING A JAIL CELL AGAIN.
YOU REALLY THINK YOU CAN GET AWAY FROM ME?
SURE.
I FOUND A PLACE THAT I CAN LIVE FREE.
A PLACE TO GO BACK TO.
I GOTTA GO BACK, OR I'LL HAVE EVEN MORE OF 'EM WHINING AT ME!

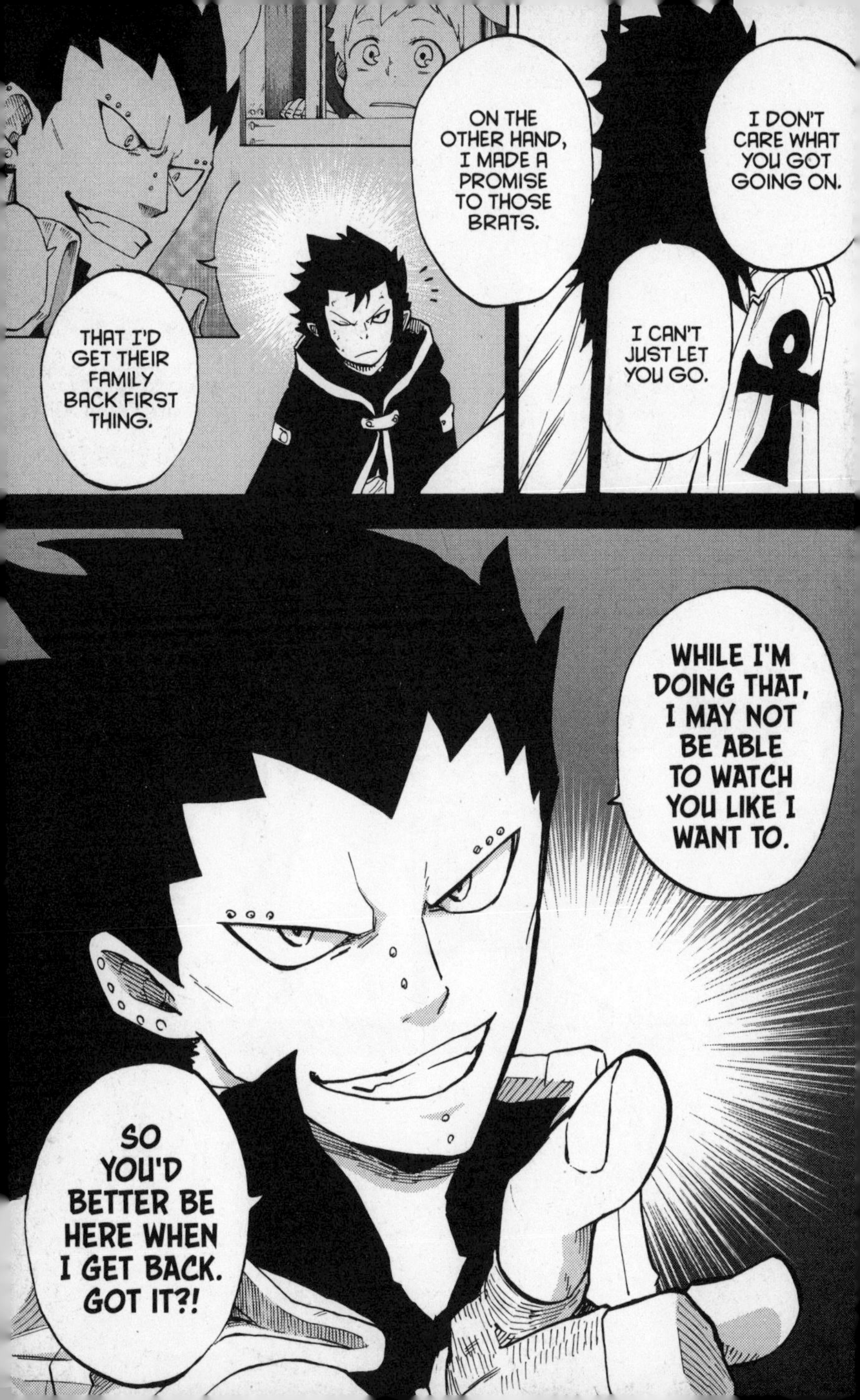
I DON'T CARE WHAT YOU GOT GOING ON.
I CAN'T JUST LET YOU GO.
ON THE OTHER HAND, I MADE A PROMISE TO THOSE BRATS.
THAT I'D GET THEIR FAMILY BACK FIRST THING.
WHILE I'M DOING THAT, I MAY NOT BE ABLE TO WATCH YOU LIKE I WANT TO.
SO YOU'D BETTER BE HERE WHEN I GET BACK. GOT IT?!

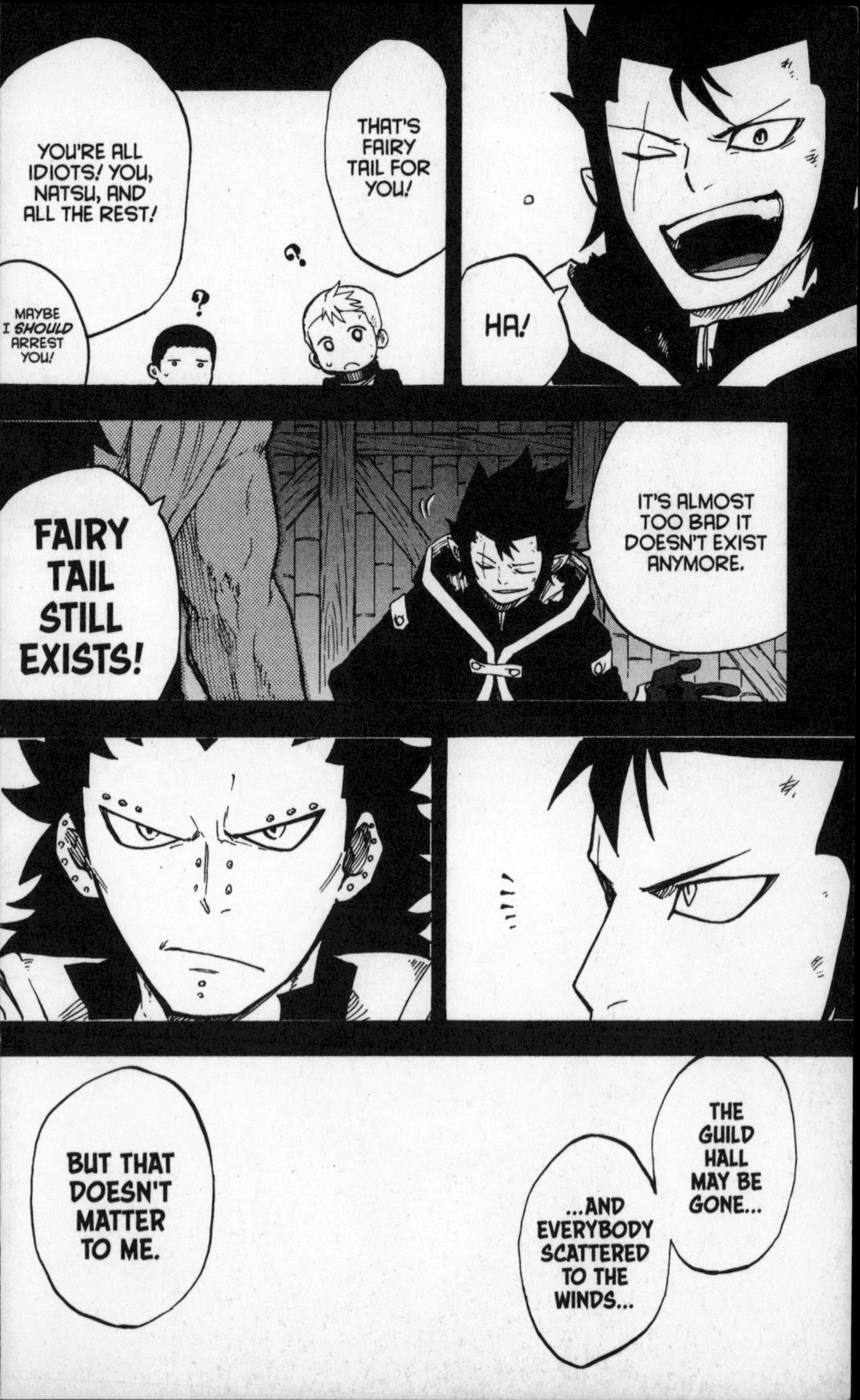
HA!
THAT'S FAIRY TAIL FOR YOU!
YOU'RE ALL IDIOTS! YOU, NATSU, AND ALL THE REST!
MAYBE I SHOULD ARREST YOU!
IT'S ALMOST TOO BAD IT DOESN'T EXIST ANYMORE.
FAIRY TAIL STILL EXISTS!
THE GUILD HALL MAY BE GONE...
...AND EVERYBODY SCATTERED TO THE WINDS...
BUT THAT DOESN'T MATTER TO ME.

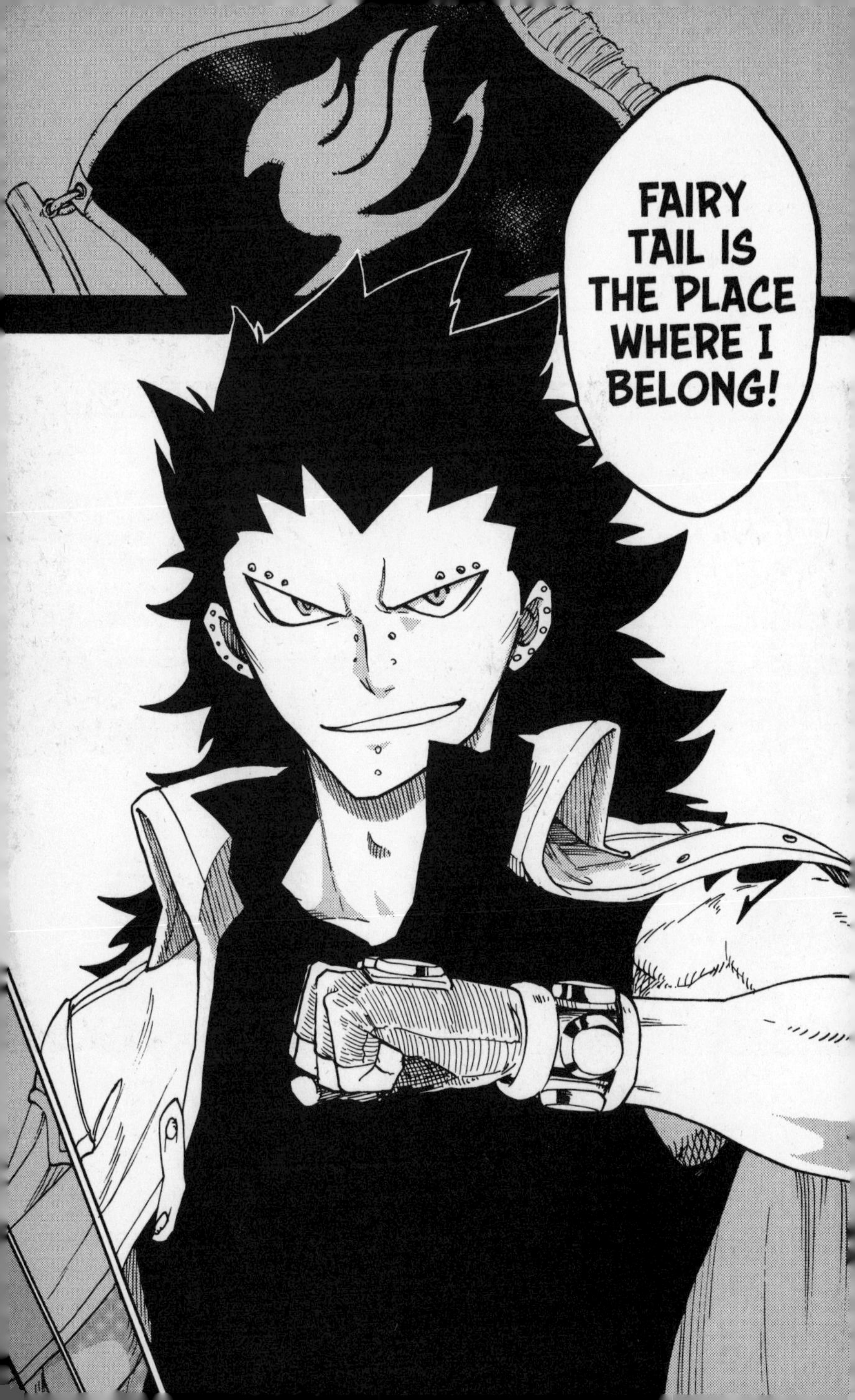
FAIRY TAIL IS THE PLACE WHERE I BELONG!

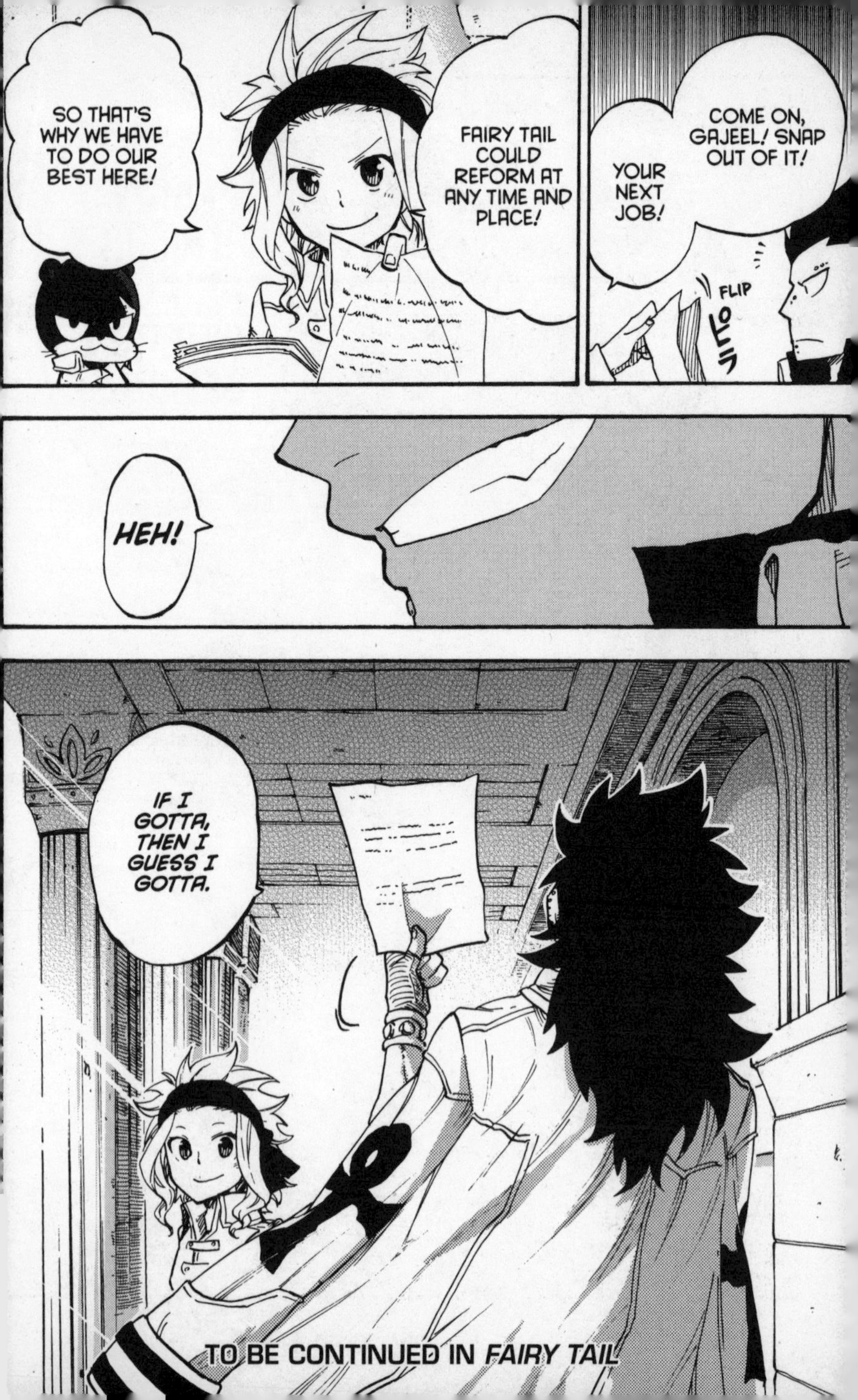
COME ON, GAJEEL! SNAP OUT OF IT!
YOUR NEXT JOB!
FLIP
FAIRY TAIL COULD REFORM AT ANY TIME AND PLACE!
SO THAT'S WHY WE HAVE TO DO OUR BEST HERE!
HEH!
IF I GOTTA, THEN I GUESS I GOTTA.
TO BE CONTINUED IN *FAIRY TAIL*

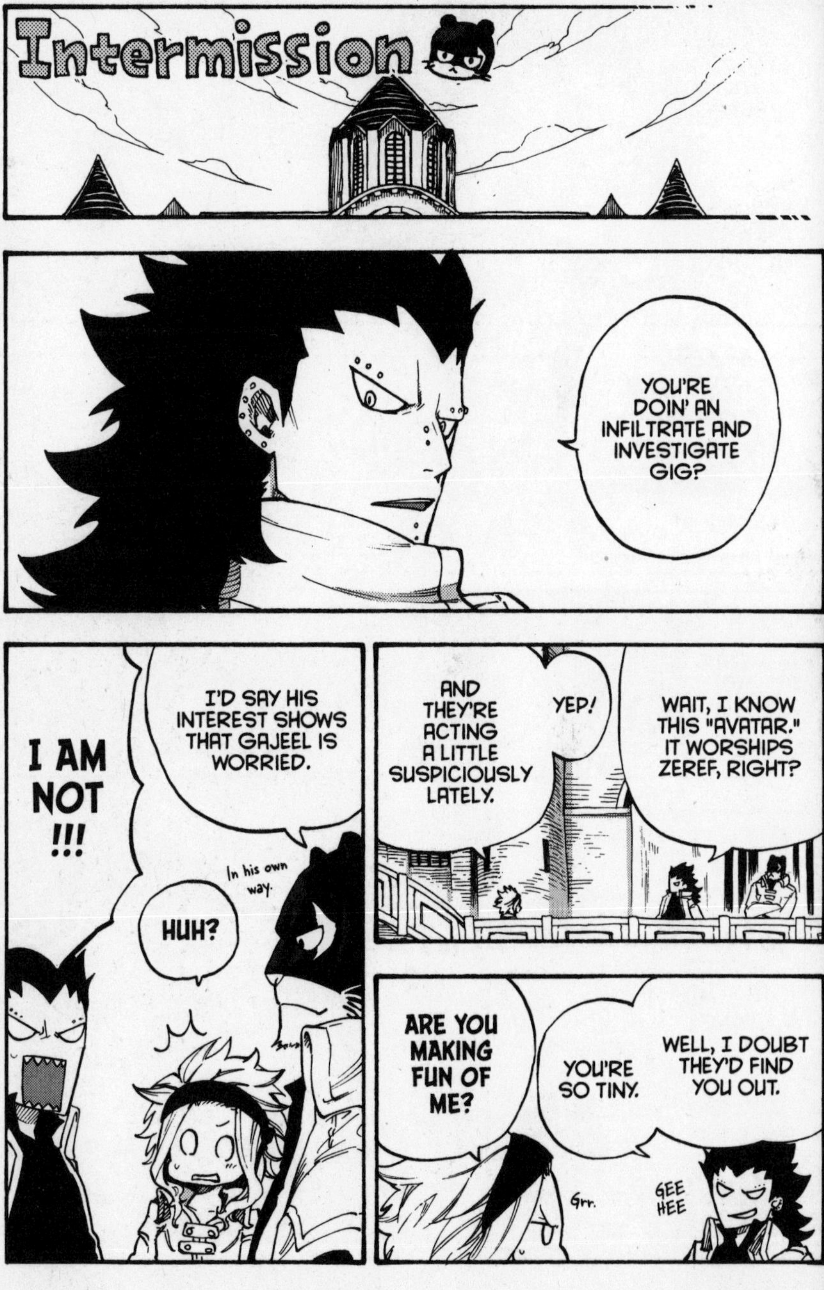
Intermission
YOU'RE DOIN' AN INFILTRATE AND INVESTIGATE GIG?
WAIT, I KNOW THIS "AVATAR." IT WORSHIPS ZEREF, RIGHT?
YEP!
AND THEY'RE ACTING A LITTLE SUSPICIOUSLY LATELY.
WELL, I DOUBT THEY'D FIND YOU OUT.
YOU'RE SO TINY.
ARE YOU MAKING FUN OF ME?
GEE HEE
Grr.
I'D SAY HIS INTEREST SHOWS THAT GAJEEL IS WORRIED.
In his own way.
HUH?
I AM NOT !!!

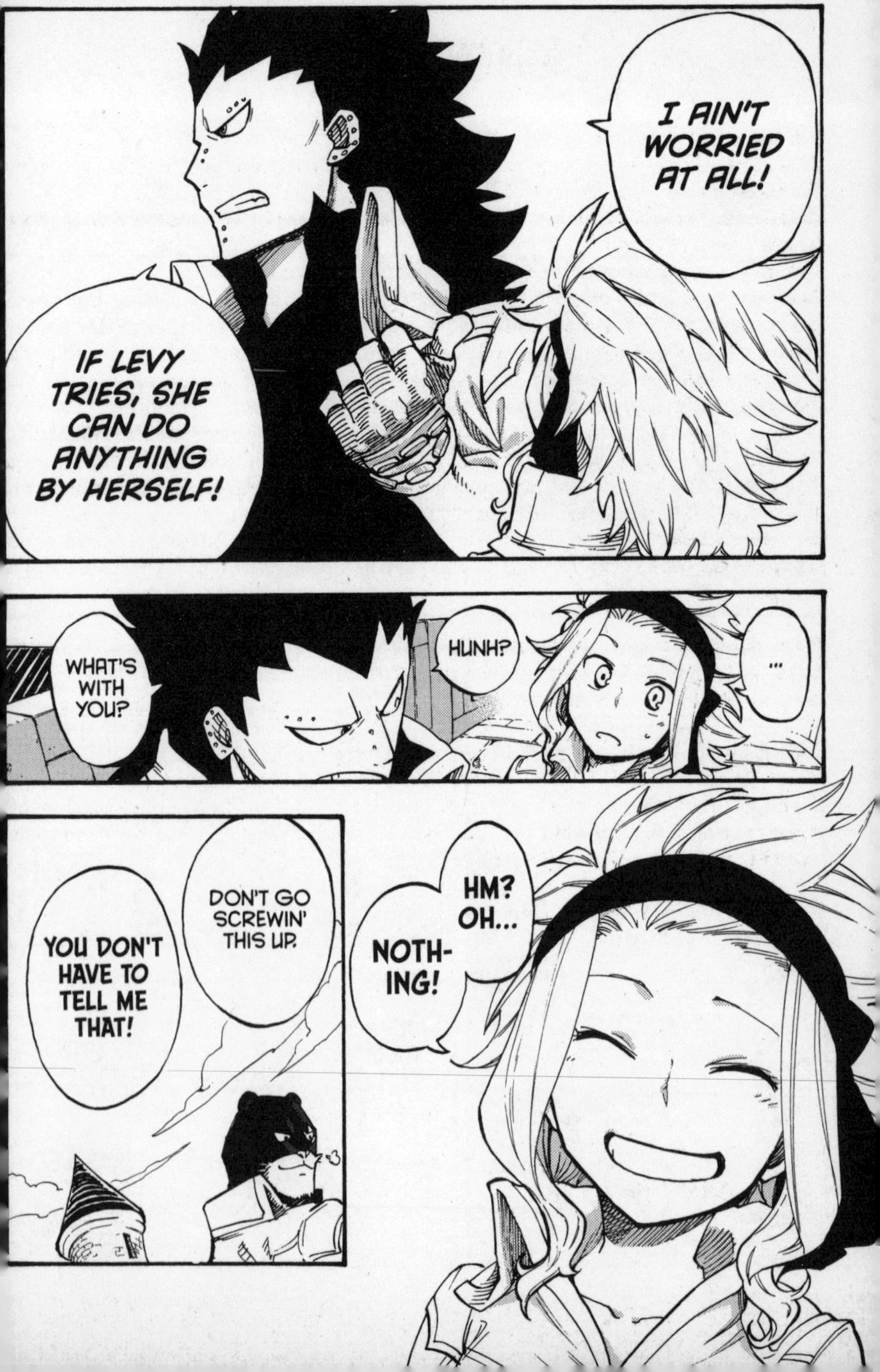
I AIN'T WORRIED AT ALL!
IF LEVY TRIES, SHE CAN DO ANYTHING BY HERSELF!
...
HUNH?
WHAT'S WITH YOU?
HM? OH...
NOTH-ING!
DON'T GO SCREWIN' THIS UP.
YOU DON'T HAVE TO TELL ME THAT!

AFTERWORD

It's the second volume of Fairy Tail Gaiden!
This time, Gajeel is the main character, and to tell the truth, Gajeel is a Fairy Tail wizard that I particularly like.
And since this story touches on parts of Gajeel's past, it introduces a character by the name of Mash.
Actually, I really worried about whether or not to include Mash.
But even so...and I mentioned this in the last volume's Afterword, but I'm a personal fan of Fairy Tail, and I really like the Fairy Tail worldview. On top of that, I get to work with a wizard I like and get into his past, so I wondered if it's okay to stuff in a character that I created? I mean, really, is that okay...? As manga creator Shibano, this makes me happier than anything, but Fairy Tail-fan Shibano screamed at me for wanting to add an original character, and I couldn't get past that.
And that's why I worry. I mean if it's an enemy character, the hero can hit them, and BOOM, it's over. You don't worry too much about that...
So when I talked to my editor about it he said, "If your enemy character is compelling, doesn't that make the hero (Gajeel) who defeats him even more compelling?"
Hey, that's true!!!!!
If I'm going to draw a really cool Gajeel, I can't have him go up against a half-baked antagonist! And that's how Mash gradually became the character that he is. And I have to say that I'm really liking Mash now.

And although it was a bit of a short story, I had Gajeel do a tag-team with Cobra. Since Gajeel's with the council, and Cobra broke out of the council's jail cell, I thought this might be the perfect chance to team them up. Since neither of them ever actually say what they're really thinking or feeling, I think it gave their dialog a bit of a unique atmosphere.

Anyway, let's meet again in the next volume!

KYOUTA SHIBANO

STAFF: ATSUO UEDA, MINAMI YASAKA, MERIO YUKINA
SPECIAL THANKS: KIMI-C

Translation Notes:

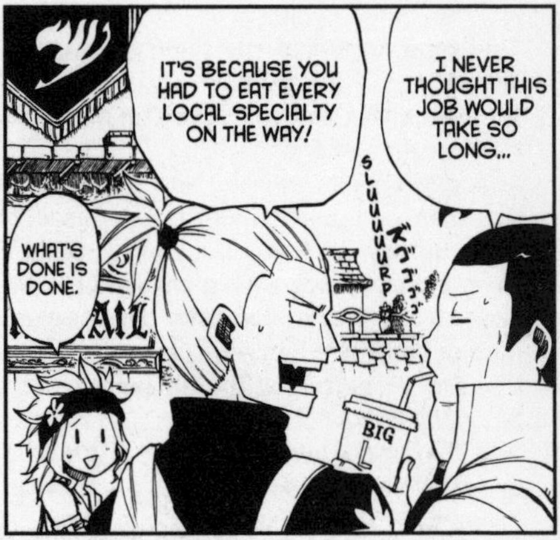
I NEVER THOUGHT THIS JOB WOULD TAKE SO LONG...
IT'S BECAUSE YOU HAD TO EAT EVERY LOCAL SPECIALTY ON THE WAY!
SLUUUUURP
WHAT'S DONE IS DONE.
BIG

Page 5, Local Specialty

There's a tradition in Japan that when traveling, every region has a dish or two that is considered their signature dish. Sometimes it's related to the crops grown or animals available in the region and other times related to certain ways of preparing food. The smart traveler researches these before he takes off on his journey, and there are some who simply memorize all the local specialties all over Japan. Some examples include Okonomiyaki (a meat & veggie pancake-like dish) for places like Hiroshima and Osaka, fried prawns for Nagoya, or Champon (a Chinese noodle dish) for Nagasaki.

Page 23, Don of the Pepper Gang

As the readers probably figured, Sanro Pepper is not named Donald. The Japanese also uses the word "Don," and, of course, it's the same word as we know in the phrase "mafia don." Just for those who don't know, it's originally an Italian word *donno* which

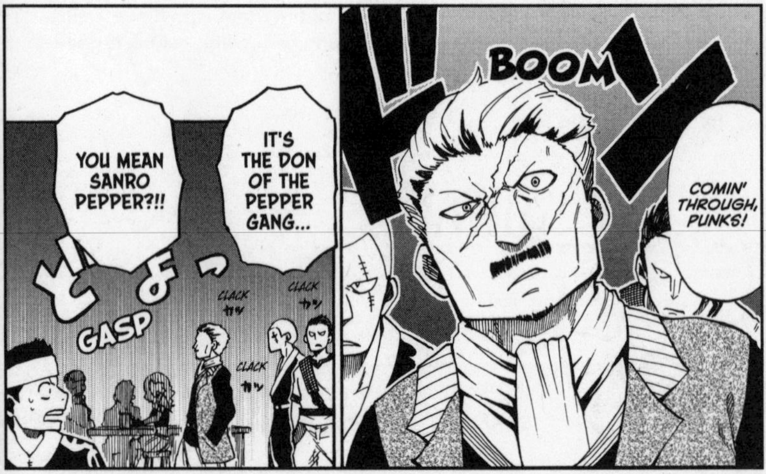
BOOM
COMIN' THROUGH, PUNKS!
IT'S THE DON OF THE PEPPER GANG...
YOU MEAN SANRO PEPPER?!!
CLACK
CLACK
CLACK
GASP

is a word of respect, although it was originally a word for "lord" (it comes from the Latin, *dominus*).

Page 61, Road Knight

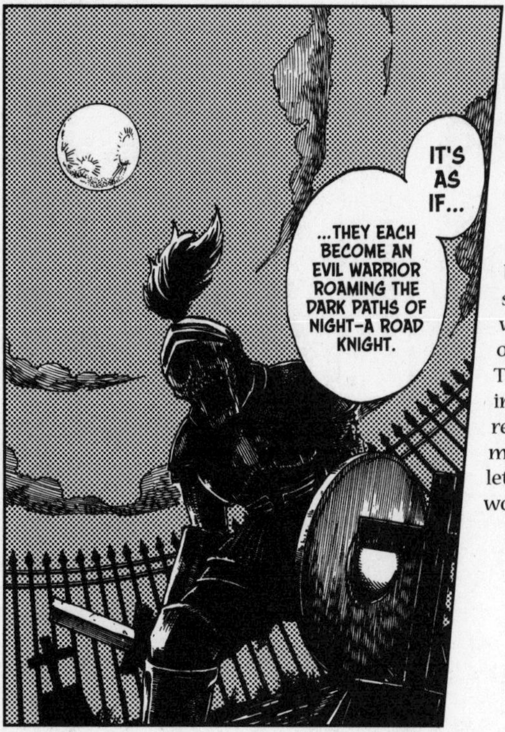
IT'S AS IF...
...THEY EACH BECOME AN EVIL WARRIOR ROAMING THE DARK PATHS OF NIGHT—A ROAD KNIGHT.

There are unique aspects of the Japanese language that make the way the Japanese spell Rhodonite exactly the same as the way the Japanese would spell the English words, Road Knight. But in this case, the "road" is referring to a dark, scary road, and the "knight" would be more like a warrior or swordsman. And you wouldn't want to meet a swordsman on a dark road, would you? That's the nuance that is being imparted to the Japanese reader when they read the meaning (in small Japanese letters next to the English words).

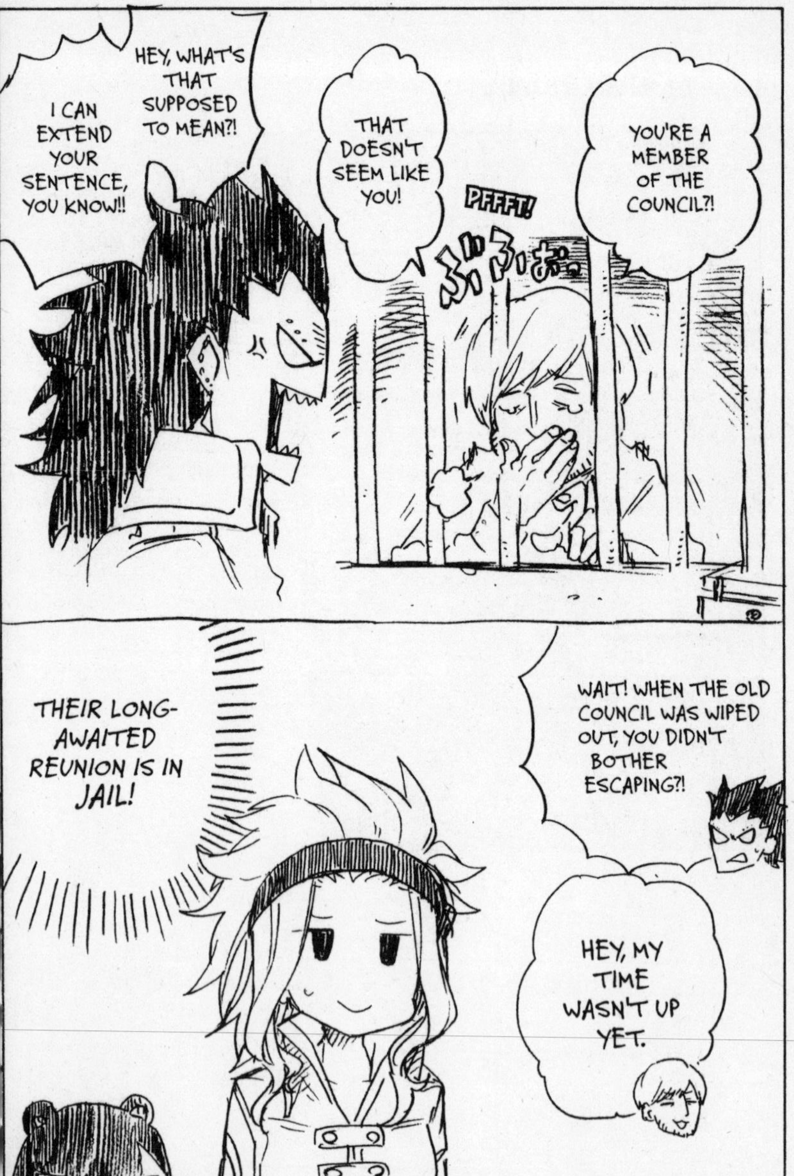
YOU'RE A MEMBER OF THE COUNCIL?!
PFFFT!
THAT DOESN'T SEEM LIKE YOU!
HEY, WHAT'S THAT SUPPOSED TO MEAN?!
I CAN EXTEND YOUR SENTENCE, YOU KNOW!!
WAIT! WHEN THE OLD COUNCIL WAS WIPED OUT, YOU DIDN'T BOTHER ESCAPING?!
HEY, MY TIME WASN'T UP YET.
THEIR LONG-AWAITED REUNION IS IN JAIL!

MASH

He wasn't a wizard himself, but he was able to use his easy-going conversation style to become a seller of magic items (although it seems an easy-going personality can't successfully sell all items). He also learned swordsmanship for self-defense.

The council became aware of him after he sold defective magic items in a fraud case, and he was jailed. But one thing he kept a secret was that he claimed responsibility for all the actions of his accomplices, allowing them to go free.

He always seemed to rely on Gajeel's overwhelming strength, and because he could never match Gajeel's strength, he started getting jealous. After they talked things over, he returned to jail, and awaited the end of his now-extended sentence.

FAIRY TAIL | RHODONITE

MANGA
KYOUTA
SHIBANO

ORIGINAL WORK:
HIRO
MASHIMA

FAIRY TAIL
BLUE MISTRAL

Wendy's Very Own Fairy Tail!

The new adventures of everyone's favorite Sky Dragon Slayer, Wendy Marvell, and her faithful friend Carla!

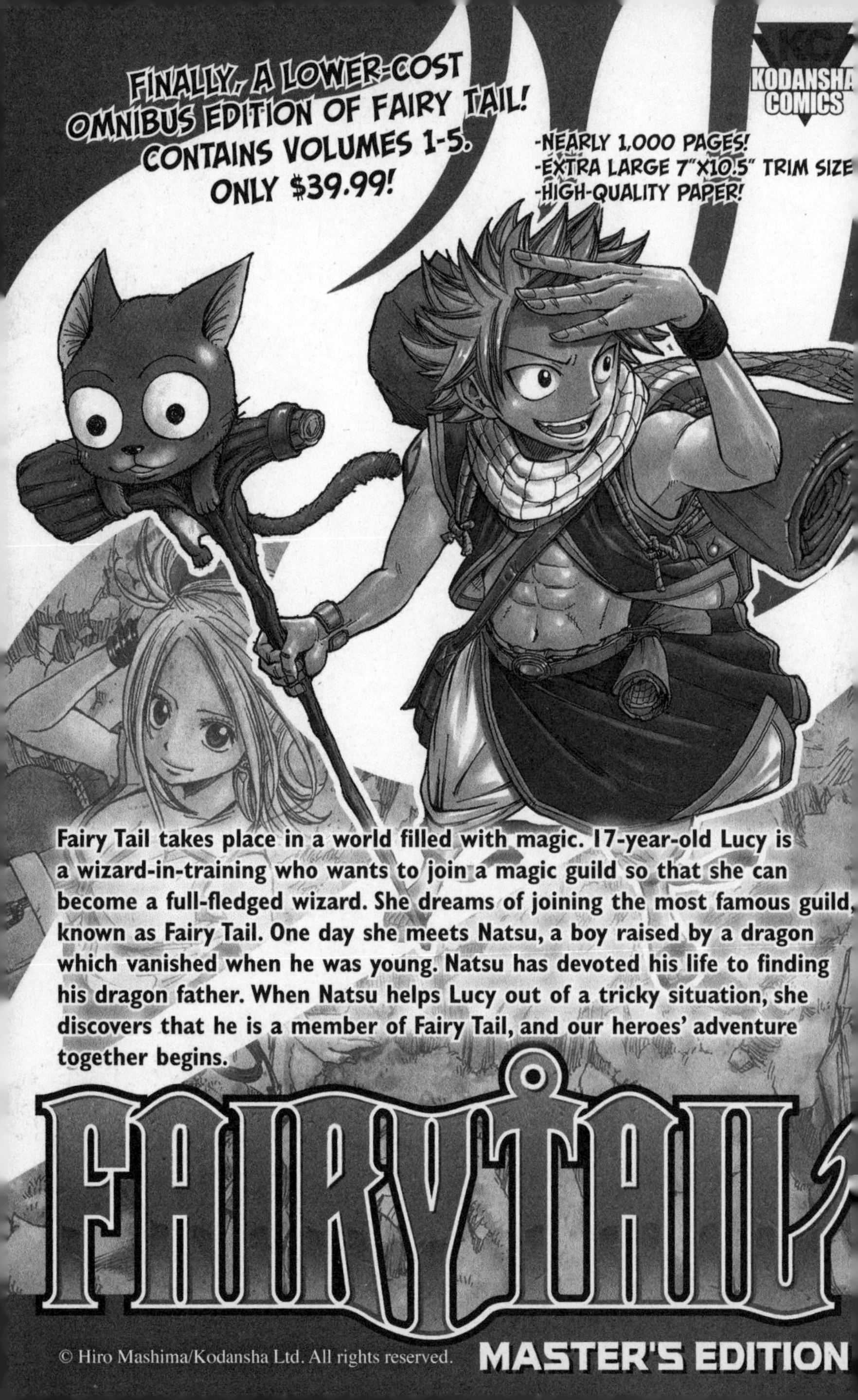

FINALLY, A LOWER-COST OMNIBUS EDITION OF FAIRY TAIL! CONTAINS VOLUMES 1-5. ONLY $39.99!

KC
KODANSHA
COMICS

- NEARLY 1,000 PAGES!
- EXTRA LARGE 7"x10.5" TRIM SIZE
- HIGH-QUALITY PAPER!

Fairy Tail takes place in a world filled with magic. 17-year-old Lucy is a wizard-in-training who wants to join a magic guild so that she can become a full-fledged wizard. She dreams of joining the most famous guild, known as Fairy Tail. One day she meets Natsu, a boy raised by a dragon which vanished when he was young. Natsu has devoted his life to finding his dragon father. When Natsu helps Lucy out of a tricky situation, she discovers that he is a member of Fairy Tail, and our heroes' adventure together begins.

FAIRY TAIL

MASTER'S EDITION

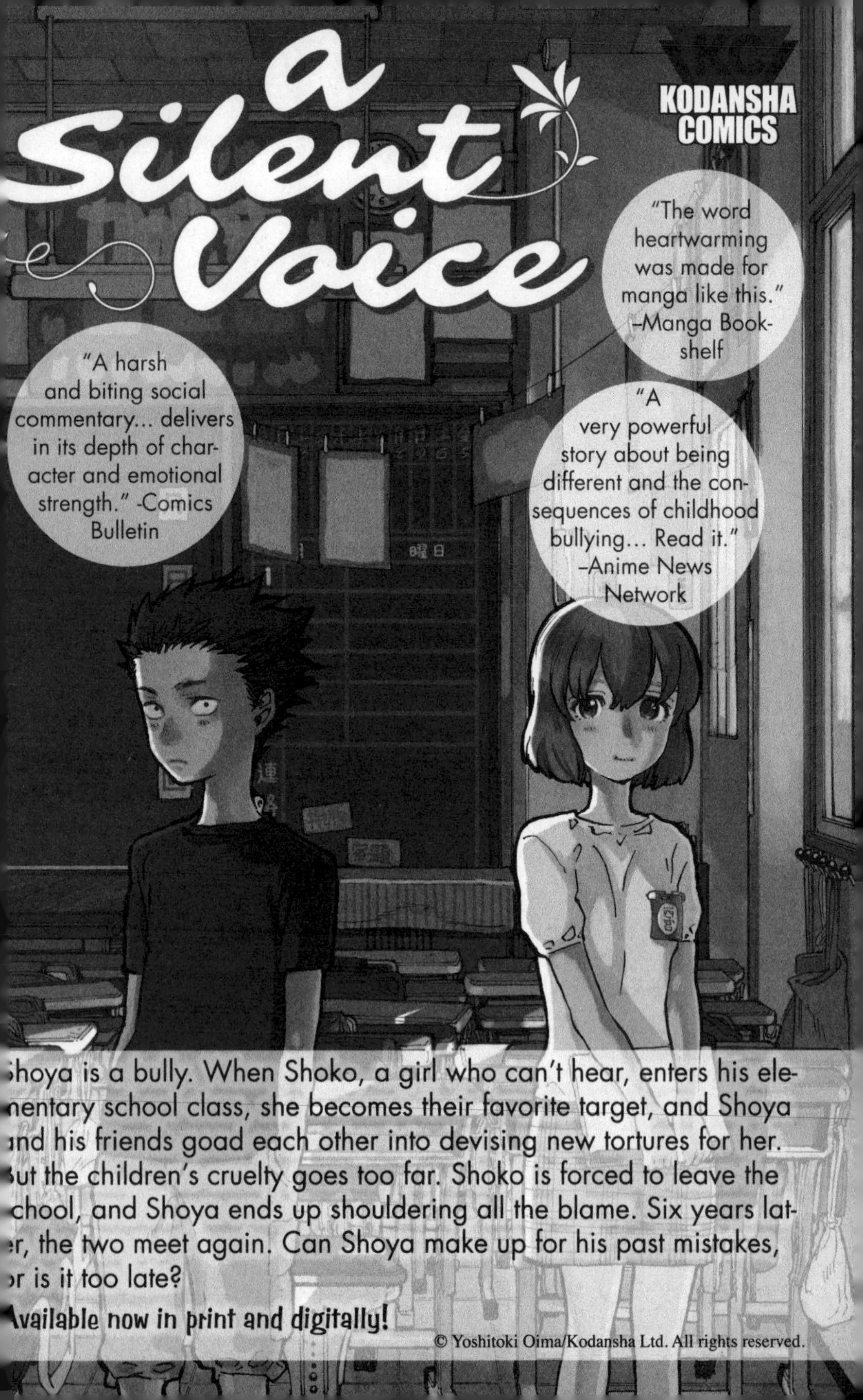
a Silent Voice
KODANSHA COMICS
"The word heartwarming was made for manga like this." –Manga Bookshelf
"A harsh and biting social commentary... delivers in its depth of character and emotional strength." -Comics Bulletin
"A very powerful story about being different and the consequences of childhood bullying... Read it." –Anime News Network
hoya is a bully. When Shoko, a girl who can't hear, enters his ele-
nentary school class, she becomes their favorite target, and Shoya
ind his friends goad each other into devising new tortures for her.
ut the children's cruelty goes too far. Shoko is forced to leave the
chool, and Shoya ends up shouldering all the blame. Six years lat-
r, the two meet again. Can Shoya make up for his past mistakes,
r is it too late?
vailable now in print and digitally!
© Yoshitoki Oima/Kodansha Ltd. All rights reserved.

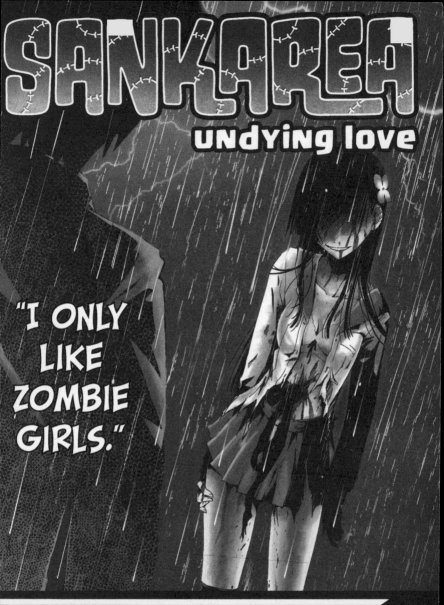

SANKAREA
undying love

"I ONLY LIKE ZOMBIE GIRLS."

Chihiro has an unusual connection to zombie movies. He doesn't feel bad for the survivors – he wants to comfort the undead girls they slaughter! When his pet passes away, he brews a resurrection potion. He's discovered by local heiress Sanka Rea, and she serves as his first test subject!

KODANSHA COMICS

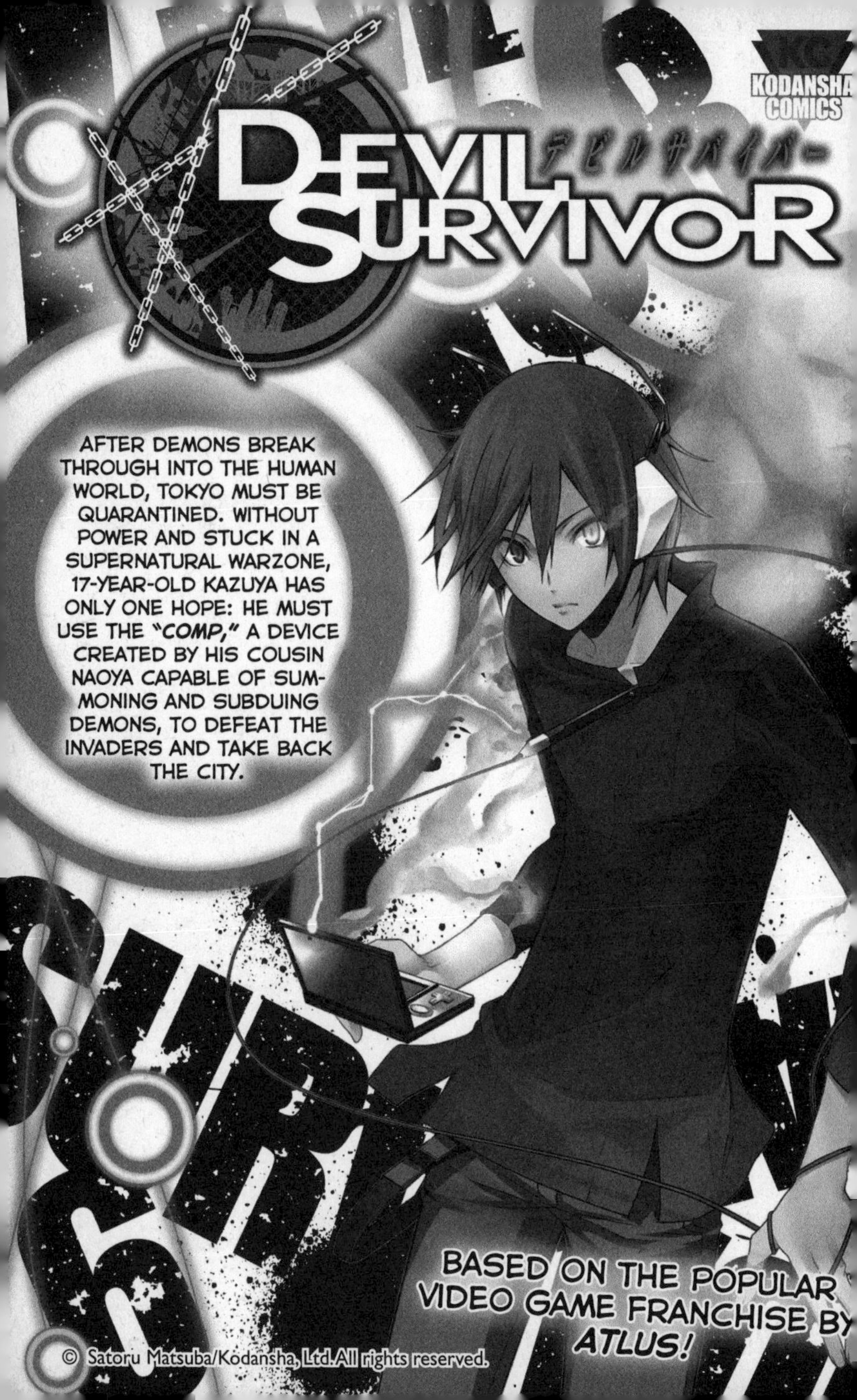
KODANSHA COMICS
DEVIL SURVIVOR
デビルサバイバー
AFTER DEMONS BREAK THROUGH INTO THE HUMAN WORLD, TOKYO MUST BE QUARANTINED. WITHOUT POWER AND STUCK IN A SUPERNATURAL WARZONE, 17-YEAR-OLD KAZUYA HAS ONLY ONE HOPE: HE MUST USE THE "COMP," A DEVICE CREATED BY HIS COUSIN NAOYA CAPABLE OF SUMMONING AND SUBDUING DEMONS, TO DEFEAT THE INVADERS AND TAKE BACK THE CITY.
BASED ON THE POPULAR VIDEO GAME FRANCHISE BY ATLUS!
© Satoru Matsuba/Kodansha, Ltd. All rights reserved.

INUYASHIKI

A superhero like none you've ever seen, from the creator of "Gantz"!

ICHIRO INUYASHIKI IS DOWN ON HIS LUCK. HE LOOKS MUCH OLDER THAN HIS 58 YEARS, HIS CHILDREN DESPISE HIM, AND HIS WIFE THINKS HE'S A USELESS COWARD. SO WHEN HE'S DIAGNOSED WITH STOMACH CANCER AND GIVEN THREE MONTHS TO LIVE, IT SEEMS THE ONLY ONE WHO'LL MISS HIM IS HIS DOG.

THEN A BLINDING LIGHT FILLS THE SKY, AND THE OLD MAN IS KILLED... ONLY TO WAKE UP LATER IN A BODY HE ALMOST RECOGNIZES AS HIS OWN. CAN IT BE THAT ICHIRO INUYASHIKI IS NO LONGER HUMAN?

COMES IN EXTRA-LARGE EDITIONS WITH COLOR PAGES!

Maria
THE VIRGIN WITCH

PURITY AND POWER

As a war to determine the rightful ruler of medieval France ravages the land, the witch Maria decides she will not stand idly by as men kill each other in the name of God and glory. Using her powerful magic, she summons various beasts and demons —even going as far as using a succubus to seduce soldiers into submission under the veil of night— all to stop the needless slaughter. However, after the Archangel Michael puts an end to her meddling, he curses her to lose her powers if she ever gives up her virginity. Will she forgo the forbidden fruit of adulthood in order to bring an end to the merciless machine of war?
Available now in print and digitally!

My Little Monster

OPPOSITES ATTRACT...MAYBE?

Haru Yoshida is feared as an unstable and violent "monster." Mizutani Shizuku is a grade-obsessed student with no friends. Fate brings these two together to form the most unlikely pair. Haru firmly believes he's in love with Mizutani and she firmly believes he's insane.

KC
KODANSHA
COMICS

NO.6

A PERFECT LIFE IN A PERFECT CITY

r Shion, an elite student in the technologically sophisticated
ty No. 6, life is carefully choreographed. One fateful day, he
kes a misstep, sheltering a fugitive his age from a typhoon.
lping this boy throws Shion's life down a path to discovering
e appalling secrets behind the "perfection" of No. 6.

KC/
KODANSHA
COMICS

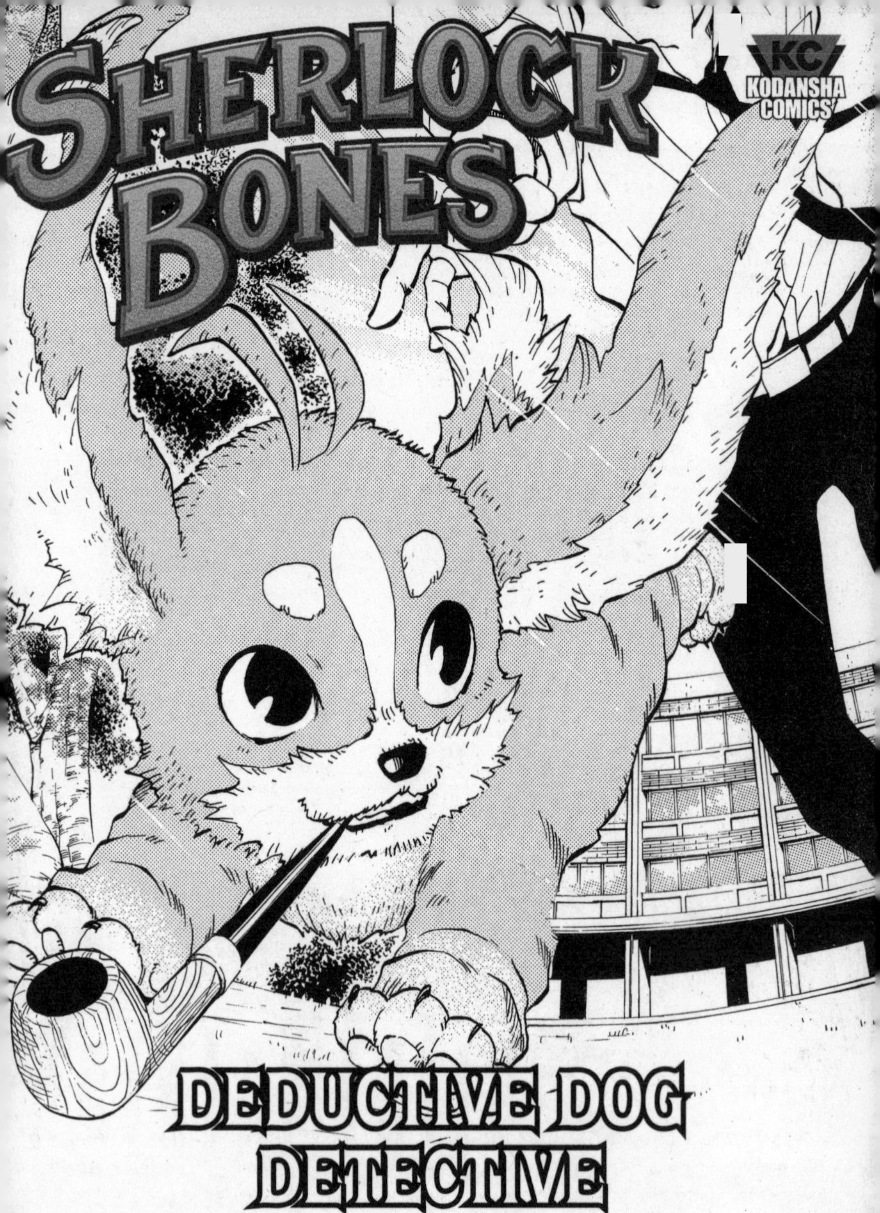
SHERLOCK BONES
KC
KODANSHA COMICS

DEDUCTIVE DOG DETECTIVE

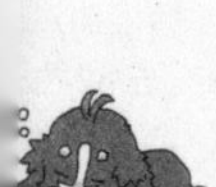

When Takeru adopts a new pet, he's in for a surprise—the dog is none other than the reincarnation of Sherlock Holmes. With no one else able to communicate with Holmes, Takeru is roped into becoming Sherdog's assistant, John Watson. Using his sleuthing skills, Holmes uncovers clues to solve the trickiest crimes.

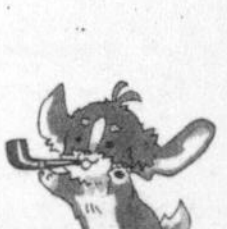